T0323555

Tourism Dynamics in Everyday Places

This title offers a dynamic understanding of tourism, usually defined in terms of clearly circumscribed places and temporalities, to grasp its changing spatial patterns.

The first part looks at the "befores" – everyday places such as daily markets, flea markets, urban neighbourhoods, that have captured the tourists' interest and have progressively experienced new development in their ordinary patterns. The second part investigates the "afters" – former tourist spaces moving beyond the tourism sphere and becoming places of everyday life, study, or work. Chapters explore what this means for local societies and examine this contemporary phenomenon of former tourist attractions becoming ordinary and everyday, and of ordinary places beginning to take on a tourist dimension. The hybridisation of tourist practices and ordinary practices is also explored through a range of international case studies and examples written by highly regarded and interdisciplinary academics.

This edited volume will be of great interest to upper-level students, academics, and researchers in tourism, urban studies, and land use planning.

Aurélie Condevaux holds a PhD in anthropology from the Université of Aix-Marseille 1 and the Center for Research and Documentation on Oceania (Marseille). She is currently Associate Professor at Paris 1 Panthéon-Sorbonne University and Institute for Research and Higher Studies in Tourism.

Maria Gravari-Barbas is an architect and a geographer and Professor of Geography at Paris 1 Panthéon-Sorbonne University (France) and Institute for Research and Higher Studies in Tourism (France). She is the UNESCO Chair of Culture, Tourism, Development. Her research interests focus on the intersection between heritage and tourism, mainly in urban areas.

Sandra Guinand is an urban planner and urban geographer. She teaches in the Department of Geography and Regional Research at the University of Vienna (Austria) and is Associate Researcher of EIREST Paris 1 Panthéon-Sorbonne (France). Her research interests focus on urban regeneration projects and socio-economic transformations of urban landscape, with a specific focus on heritage processes, public-private partnerships and tourism.

Contemporary Geographies of Leisure, Tourism and Mobility

Series Editor: C. Michael Hall, *Professor at the Department of Management, College of Business and Economics, University of Canterbury, Christchurch, New Zealand*

The aim of this series is to explore and communicate the intersections and relationships between leisure, tourism and human mobility within the social sciences.

It will incorporate both traditional and new perspectives on leisure and tourism from contemporary geography, e.g. notions of identity, representation and culture, while also providing for perspectives from cognate areas such as anthropology, cultural studies, gastronomy and food studies, marketing, policy studies and political economy, regional and urban planning, and sociology, within the development of an integrated field of leisure and tourism studies.

Also, increasingly, tourism and leisure are regarded as steps in a continuum of human mobility. Inclusion of mobility in the series offers the prospect to examine the relationship between tourism and migration, the sojourner, educational travel, and second home and retirement travel phenomena.

The series comprises two strands:

Contemporary Geographies of Leisure, Tourism and Mobility aims to address the needs of students and academics, and the titles will be published simultaneously in hardback and paperback.

Routledge Studies in Contemporary Geographies of Leisure, Tourism and Mobility is a forum for innovative new research intended for research students and academics, and the titles will initially be available in hardback only. Titles include:

Socialising Tourism
Rethinking Tourism for Social and Ecological Justice
Edited by Freya Higgins-Desbiolles, Adam Doering and Bobbie Chew Bigby

Tourism Dynamics in Everyday Places
Before and After Tourism
Edited by Aurélie Condevaux, Maria Gravari-Barbas and Sandra Guinand

For more information about this series, please visit: www.routledge.com/ Contemporary-Geographies-of-Leisure-Tourism-and-Mobility/book-series/ SE0522

Tourism Dynamics in Everyday Places

Before and After Tourism

Edited by Aurélie Condevaux, Maria Gravari-Barbas and Sandra Guinand

LONDON AND NEW YORK

First published 2022
by Routledge
2 Park Square, Milton Park, Abingdon, Oxon OX14 4RN

and by Routledge
605 Third Avenue, New York, NY 10158

Routledge is an imprint of the Taylor & Francis Group, an informa business

British Library Cataloguing-in-Publication Data
A catalogue record for this book is available from the British Library

Library of Congress Cataloging-in-Publication Data
A catalog record for this book has been requested

ISBN: 978-0-367-68681-9 (hbk)
ISBN: 978-0-367-68682-6 (pbk)
ISBN: 978-1-003-13860-0 (ebk)

DOI: 10.4324/9781003138600

Typeset in Bembo
by Apex CoVantage, LLC

Contents

Figures

Tables

Contributors

Thiago Allis is Assistant Professor of Leisure and Tourism at the School of Arts, Sciences and Humanities at the University of São Paulo (Brazil). He holds a PhD in urban and regional planning, with research and teaching backgrounds in urban tourism and mobilities.

Salvador Anton Clavé is Distinguished Full Professor of Regional Geographical Analysis and Principal Investigator of the Research Group on Territorial Analysis and Tourism Studies at the University Rovira i Virgili (Spain), Department of Geography. He is Director of Research of the Department of Tourism Innovation at Eurecat-Technology Centre of Catalonia.

Elizabeth Auclair holds a PhD in geography. She is a senior lecturer in planning in the Geography Department at CY Cergy Paris University (France). In charge of the master's degree programme "Cultural Development and Heritage Valorisation" for 20 years, she has been since 2019 the head of the geography research centre MRTE. The general theme underlying her work concerns the articulation between artistic, cultural and heritage projects and alternative approaches for sustainable cities and territories.

Jonathan Ayebakuro Orama is a doctoral student in the Faculty of Tourism and Geography at the University Rovira i Virgili (Spain) under the supervision of Prof. Antonio Moreno and Dr. Joan Borràs and a research trainee at the Department of Tourism Innovation, Eurecat-Technology Centre of Catalonia.

Philippe Bachimon is a professor of geography at the University of Avignon (France) and a member of UMR Espace-Dev (IRD). His research focuses on experiential tourism and more particularly on wastelands as a memorial temporality participating in the cultural heritage of touristic places.

Joan Borràs Nogués is ICT & Tourism Project Manager at the Department of Tourism Innovation, Eurecat-Technology Centre of Catalonia and a part-time lecturer at the Faculty of Tourism and Geography of the University Rovira i Virgili (Spain). He received his PhD in computer science in 2015.

Philippe Bourdeau is a professor at the Institute of Urban Planning and Alpine Geography, (Grenoble-Alpes University, France) and a member of

PACTE-CNRS social sciences research centre. His research and teaching focuses on tourism and mountain sports in the Alps.

Myriam Casamayor, an urban planner and an associate researcher at the PASSAGES laboratory in Bordeaux (France), defended her thesis in 2019 about how the heritage of a tourism development policy (MIACA) can serve as a support for reflection on a vision of elected representatives.

Sophie Chevalier is Professor of Anthropology at the University of Picardie (France) and the head of the research centre Habiter le Monde. Her main interests are in urban anthropology and economic life. She is the author (with E. Lallement and S. Corbillé) of *Paris, résidence secondaire* (2013).

Aurélie Condevaux holds a PhD in anthropology from the Université of Aix-Marseille 1 and the Center for Research and Documentation on Oceania (Marseille). She is currently Associate Professor at Paris 1 Panthéon-Sorbonne University (France) and Institute for Research and Higher Studies in Tourism (France).

Tim Freytag is Professor of Human Geography at the Institute of Environmental Social Sciences and Geography, University of Freiburg (Germany). His research interests are in urban studies, social and cultural geography, and tourism and mobility studies with a particular focus on tourist practices and transformations in European urban tourism.

Alain Girard is Senior Lecturer in Sociology at the University of Perpignan (France). He is a member of the CRESEM (Center of Studies and Research on Mediterranean Environments) at the same university. His main area of research focuses on tourism practices. He proposes to contribute to a socio-anthropology of tourism that combines pragmatic and critical sociology approaches.

Maria Gravari-Barbas is an architect and a geographer and Professor of Geography at Paris 1 Panthéon-Sorbonne University (France) and Institute for Research and Higher Studies in Tourism (France). She is the director of the UNESCO Chair "Culture, Tourism, Development. Her research interests focus on the intersection between heritage and tourism, mainly in urban areas.

Mariachiara Guerra is an architect, fellow and freelance cultural project manager. She has a PhD in history and valorisation of architectural, town-planning and environmental heritage (2010, Politecnico di Torino).

Sandra Guinand is urban planner and urban geographer. She teaches in the Department of Geography and Regional Research at the University of Vienna (Austria) and is Associate Researcher of EIREST Paris 1 Panthéon-Sorbonne (France). Her research interests focus on urban regeneration projects and socio-economic transformations of urban landscape, with a specific focus on heritage processes, public-private partnerships and tourism.

Emeline Hatt is Associate Professor in Development and Urban Planning at Aix-Marseille University (France) and Researcher at Environment and Town Planning Interdisciplinary Laboratory (LIEU; France). She works on regional tourist planning. She particularly analyses the development trajectories of mountain and coastal destinations and within this context, the place attributed to the development of public spaces and preservation of natural spaces.

Anne Hertzog is an assistant professor in geography at CY Cergy Paris University (France) and the coordinator of the master's degree programme "Cultural Development and Heritage Valorisation". She studies how war memory shapes tourism policies, planning and tourism practices, as well as war heritage, war museums and how politics of the past impact urban or territorial development. She also studies memorial practices in minorities living in France, more specifically Chinese or Indian diasporas from a post-colonial and comparative perspective.

Merryl Joly is a PhD student in geography at the EIREST laboratory (inter-disciplinary research team on tourism) of the University Paris 1 Panthéon-Sorbonne (France). Her thesis aims to question North-South relations through European tourism entrepreneurs in the medina of Fez and Essaouira in Morocco.

Cornelia Korff is a post-doctoral researcher and lecturer at the Institute of Environmental Social Sciences and Geography at the University of Freiburg (Germany). Her research interests are in rural studies with a focus on tourism, endogenous rural development and structural changes of agriculture and old industries. Furthermore, she explores cultural landscapes from a historical geographical perspective.

Emmanuelle Lallement is Professor of Urban Ethnography at Paris 8 University's Institute for European Studies and Researcher with the CNRS-funded Architecture City, Urbanism research unit. She coordinates a programme on Re-thinking the Contemporary City at Maison des Sciences de l'Homme Paris-Nord (France). Her ethnographic work focuses on Paris, festive events, commercial relations and global mobilities.

Marine Loisy is an anthropologist and researcher at the *Conservatoire national des arts et métiers* (CNAM), Paris, France, where she teaches sociology of tourism. She is a PhD student in social and cultural anthropology at the *Ecole des Hautes Etudes en Sciences Sociales* (EHESS), Paris, and a research associate at the Paris City Hall. Her research aims to analyse and understand the cultural and social issues involved in the relationship between inhabitants and visitors in Paris.

Ana Carolina Padua Machado holds a Bachelor in Tourism from the University of São Carlos and a Master in Tourism from the University of São Paulo. She is Professor of the Bachelor of Tourism at the University of São

Paulo and of the Tourism Management Course at the Federal Institute of Education, Science and Technology of São Paulo.

Milos Nicic holds a research position at the Center for Cultural Studies, Faculty of Political Sciences, University of Belgrade (Serbia). His main interests are in heritage, tourism and urban studies, with particular focus on creativity and post-socialist transformation.

Marie-Laure Poulot is a lecturer in social and cultural geography at University Paul-Valéry Montpellier III (France) and UMR 5281 ART-Dev. Her current research interests are urban heritage and production of urban spaces in metropolises through the study of narratives, practices and representations.

Bernard Schéou holds a PhD in economics and is a lecturer at the University of Perpignan Via Domitia (France). He is the author of publications about the relationship between ethics and tourism and also has been involved as a volunteer for 20 years in fair trade tourism operators.

Maria Trinitat Rovira Soto is a post-doctoral researcher at the Research Group on Territorial Analysis and Tourism Studies and part-time lecturer in the Geography and Planning bachelor programme at the University Rovira i Virgili (Spain), Department of Geography. Her research interests are the spatial development of tourism destinations and GIS.

Nora Winsky is a PhD candidate and a research associate at the Institute of Environmental Social Sciences and Geography at the University of Freiburg (Germany). Her research interests are in the field of tourism geography and mediatisation. Her current work focuses on tourist practices and related social media representations in Freiburg and the Black Forest.

New urban tourists

In search of the life more ordinary

Robert Maitland

When I began researching tourism in cities in the 1980s, tourism scholars and urbanists, like the travel industry and many visitors, drew sharp distinctions – between tourist destinations and ordinary places, between visitors and locals, between touristic and non-touristic behaviour. My home city of Bradford, a former industrial city in the north of England, had launched a pioneering campaign to attract tourists with the slogan 'Bradford – a surprising place'. Aptly, the slogan encompassed both the possibility of visitors being pleasantly surprised by what they found, and that it was surprising that they visited at all. The marketing campaign was suitably self-deprecating. In a competition, the first prize was a weekend in Bradford; the second prize, two weekends. The possibility that tourism could help revive the economies of declining cities was novel, and the research I was engaged in did not show cities celebrating their everyday life (Beioley et al. 1990). Far from it. They were generally using their tangible heritage assets to create what came to be known as "tourist bubbles" (Judd 1998) in which attractions for tourists were sharply differentiated from the rest of the city with its images of decline and decay. For a while, tourist bubbles became the default approach to tourism development in cities, but even then, the idea that the true attraction of cities stemmed from their everyday life was starting to emerge (Maitland 2000). Over 30 years, sharp distinctions have been eroded and smoothed out, as attitudes have evolved and visitor demands, understandings and practices have changed. It is increasingly implausible – at least in western metropolises – to distinguish the tourist and non-tourist city; to separate visitors and locals, and touristic and non-touristic behaviours; to differentiate attractions and the life of the city. In many ways, for many visitors, the everyday life of the city is the attraction.

How has this change come about? Three interrelated dynamics stand out: the changing nature of visitors and residents, the experiences that they seek, and the way in which tourism is interwoven with the city and its economy. A brief consideration of them inevitably simplifies a very complicated process, and equally inevitably not everything has changed. Many of today's first-time visitors to world tourism cities such as London and Paris (Maitland and Newman 2009) behave much as they would have done 30 years ago – visiting the Eiffel Tower, watching the Changing of the Guard, going to well-known

DOI: 10.4324/9781003138600-1

galleries and museums. But the tendency has been for tourism in the city to become a more complex process, and for practices and behaviours to be more mixed.

Decades of globalisation and uninterrupted growth in tourism (before the COVID-19 pandemic) meant travellers became increasingly experienced and that "tourism" was one of a suite of mobilities (Hannam 2009). Understanding the implications for city tourism has lagged, in part because official statistics define tourism in terms of distance travelled, and time spent, rather than demand, behaviour and practices. In a metropolis such as London, this fails to capture the reality. Conventional distinctions between leisure, business and visiting friends and relations (VFR) are breaking down in multi-purpose visits and indeed, many of those classed as tourists do not see themselves in that way. There are more "connected tourists" (Maitland 2010, 2014) who know the city well since they previously lived, worked or studied there, or are frequent visitors for VFR or business. They do not think of themselves as tourists: "Many . . . people have two homelands: their own and London" (Kuper 2021, 5). Their practices in the city reflect this familiarity and sense of belonging. At the same time many "residents" behave "as if" they were tourists (Clark 2003). Some are temporary residents – students, professionals on assignment, temporary migrants seeing the world and improving their language skills – who want to explore the city. For more permanent residents, their own experience of travel to other cities has influenced their tastes and practices and their demands overlap with those of visitors. Resident members of global elites value at least some visitors, whose shared tastes and consumption patterns can make for convivial relationships in gentrified neighbourhoods. And for the highly mobile, the very idea of the city is blurred. Easy and rapid rail connections create a "Londonsphere" including Manchester, Paris, Rotterdam; a "Parisphere" extending to London, Lyon, Brussels, Amsterdam. Visitors from these connected cities may seem themselves as internal tourists, if they think of themselves as tourists at all.

In these circumstances many "tourists" and "residents" become "urban explorers" who want to "get off the beaten track" and away from "the sights" if only for part of their visit (Maitland and Newman 2009). This creates a "soft tourism", as visitors attempt to temporarily embed themselves in the city, occupying and experiencing the same spaces as their hosts and sharing their practices (Maitland 2019; Jenkins and Oliver 2001). Urban explorers, or new urban tourists, seek "the real city" – places that do not seem to have been commodified for tourists. Such places do not have the carefully choreographed arrangements of land uses characteristic of monumental or commercialised environments, in which visitor experiences have been carefully programmed. Rather they are characterised by intricate street patterns, a rich mix of land uses and activities and a human scale that invites exploration, and lets visitors feel they are creating their own experience rather than consuming one designed for them. Perhaps most importantly, these are places in which visitors can encounter locals (i.e. city residents) whose presence is a key marker that this is the "real city" (Maitland 2007, 2008, 2010). Places that have not been planned for tourist consumption but have arisen organically through micro-interactions of the market with user demands are seen as authentic so that being there bestows cultural capital. The sense that they are off the beaten track imbues them with coolness, a sense they are known only to insiders; the presence of visitors and residents who seem cool is mutually satisfying (Pappalepore et al. 2014). Here, everyday life and quotidian activities are not mundane but valued evidence of authenticity. Shopping, eating, drinking and wandering around have always been fundamental to the tourist experience, but they are revalorised off the beaten track as they become part of the life of the city rather than a service provided for tourists. Smaller independent shops, studios and restaurants fit particularly well with tourist imaginaries of the city. Visitors may almost feel they are discovering the remains of an earlier less commodified city, and a more authentic time. This is a kind of urban archaeology rather than simply exploration. Of course, most visitors understand that this is indulging a fantasy of an idealised city, but they are aware it is one shared with at least some of the city residents. So the city can be both unreal − a pleasant fantasy − and real − because it is shared with local people, who are the markers of the real. In this account we can see that notions of "tourists" and "residents" have limited analytical value, and it may be more helpful to include them within an overlapping hybrid − the "city user" (Martinotti 1999).

So the new tourism areas that meet changing tourism demands have been created by large metropolises, world tourism cities, not in a planned way, but more organically, through market interactions. This is unlike the deliberately planned, often publicly funded, tourist bubbles and urban entertainment districts that characterised earlier phases of city tourism development. It is wider processes of urban change that determine the nature and location of these new areas. Rapid economic change, real estate development and speculation and gentrification and urban preferences shared amongst the global middle class − whether residents, workers or visitors − have combined with rising visitor numbers to revalorise rundown areas off the beaten track as desirable places. However in inner area of London (and other cities), the rapidity of change is making the creation of such places more difficult. Substantial population increase, property speculation driven significantly by foreign investment and a desire to enjoy fashionable city life has meant that few areas are "undiscovered" − and therefore cheap. There is no longer a clear development process in which cheap and partly derelict areas can be colonised by artists and creatives, and then developed synergistically with pioneer gentrifiers and exploring visitors and residents (Zukin 2005). Much of inner London has become "a vast gated community of the world's richest people" (Kuper 2015, 5), and we can see similar processes at work on other metropolises. It is possible that the systemic shock of the COVID-19 pandemic − in London's case combined with the impact of Brexit − will disrupt these long-standing processes, but that would require substantial change in economic and urban preferences.

This does not mean that urban exploration is at an end in inner areas. Many gentrified areas remain off the main tourist tracks and retain their appeal with a pleasant built environment, interesting consumption opportunities and the chance to mingle with the like minded. However it is becoming harder to see these as everyday places unless everyday life has become the preserve of the middle class. Their distinctiveness has also been eroded by the growth of what we might call "hipster standardisation" around the world – exemplified by cafés with exposed brick walls where single estate coffee is brewed by bearded baristas for customers sitting on mismatched chairs, which can now be found everywhere. Those in search of everyday places have to look further afield – perhaps to the suburbs (Maitland 2019).

In one sense this would be simply a continuation of established spatial patterns of development common to many cities as ordinary neighbourhoods further out from the centre become first edgy and bohemian, then "discovered" and then incorporated in the city circuits of visitors and locals alike. In London, the King's Road emerged in the 1960s and 1970s; Notting Hill in the 1980s and 1990s; Shoreditch, Hoxton and then Peckham at the start of this century. Moreover, for those in search of the everyday, suburbs should be the obvious place to go. They are inevitably the scene of everyday life since many or most of the population live there. However there is more to this than the city's spatial organisation or the location of its population. "Everyday life" is inflected with the notion of everyday life *of local people* – which we can understand as referring to people whose main home and long-standing residence is in a particular place. As inner areas become more dominated by mobile and global elites, the everyday life of locals goes on in the suburbs.

Attempts to draw a sharp distinction between suburbs and the city are as unhelpful as sharp distinctions between locals and visitors. Differences exist but are often exaggerated and outweighed by similarities. After all, much of what is now "the city" comprises the suburbs of earlier times. Suburban morphology is varied but includes some or all the features that proved attractive in creating new tourism areas in the inner city. In some areas, human scale and architectural variety derive from early "village" origins; in others, former industrial buildings are repurposed as studios or apartments. Despite popular stereotypes and the arguments of Florida (2005), creative activities and the "creative class" are not confined to the inner city; there are clusters of creative workers in the suburbs (Collis et al. 2013). Indeed, post-pandemic, professional and creative businesses with locational flexibility may be expected to value high amenity suburbs where they can enjoy green spaces and opportunity to work from home whilst still having access to regional professional and business networks. And suburbs are diverse – certainly in London. In 2011, around two thirds of the Asian heritage population and half the black population lived suburban lives, whilst substantial clusters of Somalis, Afghans and Poles and many others can be found in suburban centres (Judah 2016). This diverse population together with lower property prices are enough to attract some visitors, who will be visiting friends and relations, or looking for cheaper accommodation, often though Airbnb or similar platforms that offer lower prices and potential contact with local people. For urban explorers seeking everyday life, suburbs can offer the mix of appealing morphology, the opportunity to take part in quotidian life whilst mingling with and observing local people, encountering creatives and a diverse population with associated consumption opportunities – and the satisfaction of doing something cool and outside the mainstream.

Will suburbs become the next location of the new urban tourism? The obstacles are not the nature of objective material space but the way in which suburban spaces are imagined (Lefebvre 1991; Collis et al. 2010). In academic and professional discourse, in popular and high culture, suburbs and their imagined geography are disdained and dismissed. Suburbs are "maligned . . . connoted an inferior form of city . . . an easy [insulting] epithet . . . shorthand for superficiality" in part because scholars have largely ignored them, which means their image derives from "an odd mix of cliché and dated pop culture" (Kirby and Modarres 2010, 65). Sometimes this dismissal of suburbs – and thus their inhabitants' everyday lives – is also inflected with unease or fear of what may be found there. This negative imagined geography is a formidable barrier but may not be insurmountable. Imagined geographies can change, as they have in now fashionable areas of cities that not so long ago were seen as derelict, unappealing and unsafe. Wynn (2010) suggests that visitors can take the very stuff of everyday life – culture, people, history, place – and transform it into their own imaginaries and narratives of the city. He calls this "urban alchemy", and we can see suburbs as a promising site for this transformation. Visitors who want to experience the everyday life of the city, to fit in rather than stand out, and who are willing to challenge conventional narratives, can find rich material in suburbs from which they can create the extraordinary which, as Till (2009) says, is to be found in the ordinary by those who are prepared to look. If the volume of international travel is permanently reduced in response to pandemics and action to mitigate climate change, then tourism will be less about distance travelled; exploring the everyday and enjoying the ordinary closer to home will become more important. Travelling deeper will be more important than travelling further. Perhaps the new urban tourism will evolve to become the new suburban tourism – in hybrid places where town and country intertwine, the "tourist" and "non-tourist" city merge, where "visitors" and "locals" mingle and everyday life is the attraction.

Lack of attention to the possibilities of suburban tourism reflects a lack of scholarly interest in tourism in everyday places. The focus of this book on "ordinary places" and the people who live and go there is invaluable, as is its concern with tourism as an intrinsic part of urban development processes. Too much of the literature implicitly assumes that places are tourism destinations, or they are not. It is most helpful to recognise that tourism is integral to how cities develop and change – whether that is through "ordinary" places acquiring a stronger tourism dimension, or through cities transforming from places where high amenity attracted visitors to ones that appeal to residents seeking pleasant places to live. This volume both improves our understanding and prompts further research. Perhaps it will also prompt tourism authorities to think more carefully about how tourism in the city is measured, so we can have a sounder statistical basis for discussion. After all, in globalised and increasingly homogenised world, distinctiveness is an increasingly important competitive advantage. It is unlikely that policymakers can themselves create such distinctive places, but they can facilitate their development by aiding understanding of their production.

References

Beioley Steve, Maitland Robert and Vaughan David Roger. 1990. *Tourism and the Inner City: An Evaluation of the Impact of Grant Assisted Projects*. London: HMSO.

Clark, Terry Nichols. 2003. *The City as an Entertainment Machine*. San Diego: Elsevier.

Collis, Christy, Felton Emma and Phil Graham. 2010. "Beyond the Inner City: Real and Imagined Places in Creative Place Policy and Practice." *The Information Society* 26: 104–112.

Collis, Christy, Simon Freebody and Terry Flew. 2013. "Seeing the Outer Suburbs: Addressing the Urban Bias in Creative Place Thinking." *Regional Studies* 47(2): 148–160.

Florida, Richard. 2005. *The Rise of the Creative Class*. New York: Basic Books.

Hannam, Kevin. 2009. "The End of Tourism? Nomadology and the Mobilities Paradigm." In *Philosophical Issues in Tourism*, edited by J. Tribe. Bristol: Channel View, pp. 101–113.

Jenkins, Tim and Tove Oliver. 2001. *Integrated Tourism: A Conceptual Framework*. Deliverable 1, SPRITE Project. Aberystwyth: University of Wales.

Judah, Ben. 2016. *This Is London: Life and Death in the World City*. London: Picador.

Judd, Dennis. 1998. "Constructing the Tourist Bubble." In *The Politics of Urban America: A Reader*, edited by Dennis Judd and Paul Kantor. Needham Heights, MA: Allyn and Bacon, 2nd edition.

Kuper, Simon. 2015. "This Is Freedom? London's Reinvention." In *Soft Power*, edited by Ben Rogers. London Essays, 1. London: Centre for London.

Kuper, Simon. 2021. "The Triple Threats to London's Top Spot." *Financial Times Magazine* 5, 9–10 January.

Kirby, Andrew and Ali Modarres. 2010. "The Suburban Question: An Introduction." *Cities* 27: 65–67.

Lefebvre, Henri. 1991. *The Production of Space*. New York: Wiley.

Maitland Robert. 2000. "The Development of New Tourism Areas in Cities: Why Is Ordinary Interesting?" keynote paper given at Finnish University Network for Tourism Studies Opening Seminar 2000/01: Managing Local and Regional Tourism in the Global Market, Savonlinna, Finland, 18 September.

Maitland, Robert. 2007. "Tourists, the Creative Class, and Distinctive Areas in Major Cities." In *Tourism, Creativity and Development*, edited by G. Richards and J. Wilson. London: Routledge.

Maitland, Robert. 2008. "Conviviality and Everyday Life: The Appeal of New Areas of London for Visitors." *International Journal of Tourism Research* 10(1): 15–25.

Maitland, Robert. 2010. "Everyday Life as a Creative Experience in Cities." *International Journal of Culture, Tourism and Hospitality Research* 4(3): 176–185.

Maitland, Robert. 2014. "Urban Explorers: Looking for the Real (Outer) London?" In *Alternative and Creative Tourism*, edited by G. Richards and Russo Paolo. Arnhem: Atlas.

Maitland, Robert. 2019. "Extending the Frontiers of City Tourism: Suburbs and the Real London." In *Destination London: The Expansion of the Visitor Economy*, edited by Andrew Smith and Anne Grahan. London: University of Westminster Press, 15–33.

Maitland, Robert and Paul Newman. 2009. *World Tourism Cities: Developing Tourism Off the Beaten Track*. Abingdon: Routledge.

Martinotti, Guido. 1999. "A City for Whom? Transients and Public Life in the Second-Generation Metropolis." In *The Urban Moment*, edited by Robert A. Beauregard and Sophie Body-Gendrot. London: Sage, 155–184.

Pappalepore, Ilaria, Robert Maitland and Andrew Smith. 2014. "Prosuming Creative Urban Areas: Evidence from East London." *Annals of Tourism Research* 44: 227–240.

Till, Jeremy. 2009. *Architecture Depends*. Cambridge, MA: MIT Press.

Wynn, Jonathan. 2010. "City Tour Guides: Urban Alchemists at Work." *City and Community* 9(2): 145–163.

Zukin, Sharon. 2005. *Point of Purchase*. New York: Routledge.

1 Before and after tourism

How spaces "enter" and "exit" tourism

Aurélie Condevaux, Maria Gravari-Barbas and Sandra Guinand

Introduction

This edited volume examines the in-between situations of two types of place. On the one hand, former tourist places are currently "exiting" the tourism sphere; these include former seaside resorts evolving into year-round towns (Violier 2002), ski resorts entering into decline and theme parks that are losing their tourist appeal and turning into everyday leisure venues for local customers or even being abandoned and becoming brownfield sites. These "extraordinary" places, initially created as tourist destinations, are undergoing changes transforming them – slowly or suddenly – into "ordinary" places in which people live on a permanent basis, work and perform everyday activities.

On the other hand, everyday places – daily markets, flea markets, urban neighbourhoods, industrial areas and modern architecture – are increasingly attracting the interest of tourists. Without necessarily becoming tourist spots (although this is often the case), they are undergoing a gradual evolution that tends to modify their "ordinary patterns".

This volume examines the development of tourism in these "ordinary" places and its societal implications at a local level. It addresses this dichotomy whereby former tourist locations become "ordinary" everyday places, and ordinary places start to take on a touristic dimension. It also looks at the process of hybridisation of tourism practices and ordinary practices. Hybridisation is a key notion in this book. It involves overcoming and rejecting hierarchies, grand narratives and fixed forms, and highlights the interpenetration of different fields and stakeholders on different scales. It thus avoids traditional dichotomies through the emergence of the trans, the plural and the augmented (Gwiazdzinski 2016).

The chapters explore tourism transformation by looking at tourism as an autonomous field of social practices, and examining its interaction not only with traditional stakeholders, but also with stakeholders in civil society (Pirotte 2007), that is those who do not fall within the institutionalised policy or commercial market fields. While focusing mainly on the extension of tourism to ordinary places and their potential "touristification", these chapters also address

DOI: 10.4324/9781003138600-2

the transformation of specialised tourist places (seaside or ski resorts) into "ordinary" places keen to welcome permanent residents (Violier 2002).

How can we analyse the hybridisation process whereby tourist spots become ordinary places (resorts developing into towns; Sauthier 2011) and, conversely, ordinary places become new tourist spots? What can developments on the fringes of major tourist cities, ranging from industrial zones, production and storage areas to workers' housing, tell us about the dynamics at work?

Tourism must be examined as a process through a diachronic and dynamic lens, considering both before and after tourism. The transition from functional places to tourist places has been well documented in the literature, notably through the study of the tourist imaginaries that usually precede travelling. However, existing research has not placed sufficient emphasis on the impacts of the progressive and dynamic transformation of "ordinary" places into tourist spots and vice versa. There is still much scope to explore the "afters" of tourism, in the form of places, the practices that shape them, and the tourists who "come home" to them.

The idea of an "after" must also be considered from a broader, and sometimes metaphorical, perspective. Even before the COVID-19 crisis, we were investigating and verifying the relevance of analyses that view major transformations in the tourism fields as signs of an "after" tourism, and examining the role played by civil society in these transformations. Even before 2020, the issue had already been raised of whether we were entering a new era of tourism, marked by disruptions rather than continuities, and how it could be defined. What are the main causes and mechanisms of this change? How do different stakeholders (public authorities, tourism entrepreneurs, non-profit associations, individuals, etc.) participate in the contemporary dynamics of tourism? Have we reached the beginning of a new tourism paradigm, defined as post-tourism or hyper-tourism, with the hybridisation of tourist places, practices and stakeholders as one of its key characteristics? These questions are taking on new meaning today, as will be shown in our conclusion, and these insights will allow us to view the tourism crisis associated with COVID-19 as a process of continuity rather than disruption.

Tourism hybridisations

For a long time, tourism has focused on the places created to host it; since the very beginning of the tourism phenomenon over two centuries ago, tourism has operated as a formidable producer of spaces (Gravari-Barbas 2013). Seaside and ski resorts, leisure and theme parks, tourist complexes and enclaves were created in response to a specific demand from tourists for functional, organised places dedicated to tourism in all its guises. In parallel, tourism was rediscovering, and often subverting, historic towns, picturesque villages, sites and monuments and also turning them into tourist spots. Tourism infrastructure (hotels and other forms of accommodation, transport, ski slopes, beaches with facilities) was developed as novel architectural and urban forms to meet the new demand. Tourism development in these specific sites has historically been the preserve of specialised service providers: tour operators who organise "turnkey" trips, hoteliers, professional guides, transport companies, and so forth. The history of tourism is also the history of the invention of a sectoral economy of businesses and services involving a number of local and remote stakeholders.

This specialised tourism system is still the dominant force today and continues to be responsible for a significant share of what is known as "mass" tourism (Deprest 1997). However, there have been significant developments in recent years. On the one hand, tourism infrastructures and their designated functions at a particular point in the history of tourism are struggling because they have not always succeeded in reinventing themselves and keeping pace with changing tourist tastes. On the other hand, seasoned tourists are now expressing a desire to venture beyond the defined (and often all-inclusive) tourist enclaves laid out and designed for them or far away from places which have been subverted by other tourists (Delaplace and Gravari-Barbas 2016a). These two developments, which are related to the digital revolution and the collaborative economy, are closely connected and involve not just tourists but also all stakeholders in the tourism system, both local and remote. These changes disrupt the tourism landscape, often in a radical way (as has notably been the case since the 2010s with the advent of online tourism booking platforms such as Airbnb); they promote hybridisation which introduces new stakeholders, places and practices into the tourism sector (Delaplace and Gravari-Barbas 2016b). As a result, tourism practices appear to be becoming more disintermediated and dedifferentiated from other practices, some of which are increasingly associated with ordinary life, while civil society, although not strictly speaking organised around the tourist economy, is playing an ever greater role.

New forms of continuum are developing between ordinary places and tourism places. They are challenging the distinction between tourists and non-tourists, between tourism practices and ordinary life. Maitland points out that when tourists try to live like the local population, globalised middle-class residents assume a cosmopolitan identity and consciously define themselves as citizens of the world. They consume the city in which they live as if they were tourists. A "reciprocal transgression" occurs which sweeps away distinctions between tourists and residents and between touristic and non-touristic spaces (Maitland 2013, 14). This continuum is analysed by Padua Machado and Allis (this volume), who take as their case study the Minhocão highway in São Paulo, an amorphous, hybrid and multimodal urban object which is simultaneously a motorway, a place to stroll and explore the city and an urban performance space. The hybrid nature of this space offers a striking example of how urban objects can evolve and change to embrace radically different practices. It invites us to re-evaluate tourism on the basis of new spatial and social parameters.

Everyday tourism stakeholders: the emergence of civil society

The traditional "inhabitant-tourist" and "ordinary-extraordinary" dichotomies have now been superseded by two triptychs: the "consumer, practitioner, inhabitant" triptych which "makes it possible to consider hybridisation as a combination of a recreational place and a place to live", and the "visitor, spectator, stakeholder" triptych "which allows us to consider in-between states which occur between recreational practice and work, or between recreational practice and activism" (Berthelot 2012, 167). Tourism development in ordinary places and the transformation of tourist locations into ordinary places involve two different types of stakeholder. While a political element is present, these mechanisms are more wide ranging; to some extent they thwart all attempts at planning, and their dynamics are often created by stakeholders who do not always see themselves as belonging to the tourism field or the tourism economy.

A number of examples demonstrate that a "tourism invention" which owes nothing to political decision-making can function successfully (Herzfled 2017). The "outsider's gaze" plays a particularly important role in the revalorisation of an area: somewhere that may appear to be mundane and unattractive to some may appeal to outsiders, whose interest will further reinforce the allure of this location. This has been the case in rural areas of the Poitou-Charentes region whose tourism profile has been raised by their popularity with British tourists. Second homes, which are often rented out during the holiday season, also reveal the complex nature of the interface of the "formal" and "informal" tourism sectors (Sacareau et al. 2013). Many celebrities have played a role in "discovering" tourist locations – Brigitte Bardot in Saint-Tropez, and the Duc de Monry in Deauville, for example (Knafou 1991).

Local society also plays a critical role in tourism invention. In several contexts, local rather than institutional stakeholders have capitalised on interest in their villages, countryside or coasts from early adopters in order to attract more visitors. Today, residents can take on this role, playing the "tourism" card to enhance their town or village (Hatt, this volume).

Conversely, disengagement on the part of public authorities or other stakeholders involved in changing tourism practices can motivate tourism stakeholders to seek alternatives to tourism, or even to blend into a more "ordinary" landscape, notably by introducing a residential function (Casamayor, this volume).

In these contexts, the involvement of civil society in the tourism sphere accompanies, or is accompanied by, a revival of values shaping tourism practices. Bypassing the commercial tourism system and facilitating direct contact between individuals responds to a desire for "authenticity" or even an ethical element (Priskin and Sprakel 2008):

> By refusing to be a basic "consumer", the tourist will feel "invited", as in the case of couch-surfing, which presents itself as a vector for giving new

meaning to travel – "real" (i.e. non-virtual) contact with people based on exchanges and a reinvented form of hospitality.

(Bourdeau 2012, 38)

In the case of tourism, and urban tourism in particular (as opposed to seaside or mountain tourism, for example), a number of different stakeholders are involved. It becomes more difficult to establish a clear demarcation between tourism professionals (institutional or economic) and members of "civil society". This is the *de facto* position in areas on the fringes of tourism, and particularly in outlying city suburbs where the voluntary sector is often responsible for "tourism development". This is the case, for example, with the Accueil Banlieues association comprising residents of Seine-Saint-Denis, a former industrial suburb north of Paris, "whose passion for the area led them to host visitors staying in the Paris region".[1] Inspired by the "farm stay" model, members of the association adopted a social and solidarity economy and local development approach which is pro-active, or even militant. Its aim is "to give new meaning to tourism which is no longer reduced to dreaming and pleasure" but expresses "travellers' desire to meet and interact intelligently with local people in a way that is respectful of the natural, cultural and social environment" (Sallet-Lavorel 2003). It introduces, by definition, an alternative relationship with tourists, where they are no longer viewed as consumers of a professional service created by professionals to allow them to access a time and space away from the everyday (the fundamental basis for the touristic act; MIT 2005) but as participating hosts. Sallet-Lavorel introduced the concept of "participatory" tourism to describe this new relationship between visitors and hosts (Sallet-Lavorel, idem). Several similar initiatives have appeared in outlying metropolitan areas which have become true laboratories for the involvement of local society in tourism. Big Apple Greeter in New York, StattReisen Berlin in Berlin and Hôtel du Nord in Marseille are examples of local initiatives with their roots in civil society, bringing tourists and local residents together.

However, the term "civil society" is ambiguous here. These initiatives, which claim to represent alternative tourism (Cousin et al. 2015), are not *entirely* "bottom-up". They are often located at the interface of the voluntary sector and the institutional sector and reveal not just civil society's desire to play a role in "alternative" tourism, but also a willingness on the part of regional and institutional partners to become involved in a fresh approach to tourism. Returning to the example of Accueil Banlieues in the Paris suburbs, the non-profit association was initiated by and received support from the Comité Départemental du Tourisme in Saint-Denis, a pioneering area for institutional involvement in inclusive and participatory tourism. What emerges is a complex reading of civil society, combining independent bottom-up voluntary sector approaches with top-down institutional policies, and projects developed in the gaps between the two. Occasionally, institutional stakeholders draw inspiration from voluntary sector initiatives. Tourism Information Offices have introduced a network of "greeters" in Mulhouse and launched "Tof people" in Brussels, where expatriates living in Brussels are invited to become ambassadors for their host city (Condevaux et al. 2016).

This raises questions about the role of civil society in ordinary tourism development on the one hand, and in processes of detachment or diversification, on the other. If we consider that civil society must play a more significant role in tourism activities (notably through the use of new technologies), we must address the issue of whether these dynamics challenge the oppositions underpinning tourism practices. Does the hypothesis of the dedifferentiation of practices and the interpretive framework offered by post-tourism theories (Feifer 1985; Viard 2000, 2006; Bourdeau 2012; Girard 2013) account for the involvement of civil society?

Reinventing tourism practices

The dialectic between the ordinary and tourism and current transformations can be understood through the prism of the spatial dimension and of practices themselves. One of the characteristics of contemporary tourism lies in the extension of the tourist gaze and practices to the whole of society, for which the term "infusion" has been coined by Lussault (2007, 199). Since the form and content of practices are indeed defined by their relationship with the society that produced them (Cuvelier 1997), it is important to consider the structural socio-economic changes which inform them.

These hybrid practices are reflected, for example, in new types of hosting such as couchsurfing. While Girard and Schéou (this volume) issue caveats against idealising the narrative constructed around this practice or service (i.e. couchsurfing and house swaps facilitating authentic travel and relationships, unlike commercial forms of tourism), they highlight the fact that couchsurfing is playing a part in reinventing tourism practices through co-production because "the increase in the social wealth in which the members evolve broadly increases their general capacity for individual and collective action". It also introduces a new element, mutual trust, which is required for this "service" to be provided very cheaply (i.e. free of charge) while being based on prior "real input" to fulfil the duty to offer the other person with a welcoming place to stay (cleanliness, tidiness, information, etc.). This input involves a commitment on the part of the parties involved to forge a form of host–guest relationship which is fundamentally different to a hotel stay, even if this practice is part of an otherwise traditional tourist trip for the guest.

This type of service is also reflected in the growing number of schemes inviting inhabitants of a city to become tourists "in their own living spaces" by viewing the "ordinary" and the "everyday" through the lens of enchantment (Vergopoulos 2013). This is a redefinition of the sociocultural representations of tourism:

> When the geographical displacement imperative is removed it [tourism] becomes a single process of reconfiguring the times and spaces of everyday life by effecting a transformation of the gaze. It is, to borrow Michel

Foucault's terminology, a sort of "technology of the self" which enables the region to be reclaimed and inhabited in a positive manner.

(Vergopoulos 2013, 59)

Tourism is therefore just an "exercise in enchantment" (Vergopoulos 2013, 59).

Disintermediation and dedifferentiation of tourism practices

The dilution of tourism in everyday practices tends to translate into a weakening of the distinction between the "tourist sector" as a structured commercial field and tourism development initiatives with their roots in civil society. New digital platforms have accelerated this phenomenon with "civil society" replacing traditional tourist service intermediaries. This intermediation, which offers flexibility and the aggregation of different elements of a trip as well as a direct relationship with the host in many cases (de Becdelièvre 2015), introduces an element of the everyday into the tourism sphere. Similarly, by using new technologies and collaborative platforms in particular, tourists become stakeholders in the creation of tourism products, often combining production and consumption (Gombault 2011). Practices tend to blur the distinction not only between the commercial and non-commercial and between consumption and production, but also between business and pleasure. Hybridisation is apparent in an increasing fuzziness between business times and places and leisure and tourism times and places. Working in places usually devoted to holidays is not a new phenomenon: hotels have been providing "business centres" for many years (Gault 2016). However, the exponential growth in remote working since the early 2000s linked to the digital revolution has cemented this trend. New offers are encouraging ever greater numbers of remote workers to mix recreational trips with work sessions. Copass, for instance, is an initiative connecting several European co-working spaces to facilitate "working city breaks" away from home (Gault 2016). These forms of mobility providing closely linked recreation and work are defying traditional norms in ever more bizarre ways, with extreme examples such as the CEO of a French company who spent 40 days working on a "desert" island (Gault 2016). In a more mainstream vein,

> more exotic offers have developed, blurring the boundaries between work and holidays even more. Anchor Co-working in Pattaya (Thailand), Coco-vivo in Panama, Box Jelly in Hawaii . . . these co-working spaces are targeted specifically at westerners, sometimes offering accommodation, like Surf Office in Lisbon and the Canary Islands.
>
> (Gault 2016, 31)

Conversely, the "holiday" or "leisure" experience can come to the workplace. Many companies are trying to attract young talent by offering a relaxed working atmosphere and chill-out spaces with couches or table football (Gault 2016), or even a gym, video games, massage space or resistance pool (Marzloff 2016).

These hybridisations also apply to the trajectories of tourists who sometimes opt to move permanently to their former tourist destination. Joly (this volume) analyses the owners of guesthouses in Morocco who fell in love with a place which they discovered as tourists and settled there full time. Their daily professional involvement in the town in which their riad is located means that they are part of the local social and cultural life and can grow their local business network.

These processes sometimes reveal real "exits" from tourism by tourist locations whose virtues (pleasant lifestyle, climate, well-tended environment, abundant leisure opportunities) also make them ideal places to live either in retirement or for a growing number of working people. They have an impact on the location, which gradually develops a wider range of amenities such as schools, health centres, hospitals and administrative services.

Ordinary places and tourism

The concept of an "ordinary" place is difficult to pin down and any attempt at a definition is by its very nature open to challenge. It involves a value judgement which is not neutral – and not "ordinary" at all – as it is achieved via a process of discrimination and, above and beyond that, a projection on the part of individuals or social groups of the mental, affective and practical organisation of the world. According to Segault (2006, 61), "the very fact of describing or writing about ordinary spaces immediately strips them of their 'ordinary' quality".

The *Oxford Dictionary* defines "ordinary" as "normal, customary, usual" and the *Larousse* dictionary as "conforming to the established, normal, common order" (from the Latin *ordinarius*). Ordinary places can be defined more easily if they are contrasted with "hauts lieux" (Micourd 1991) or "prime spots", so dubbed because they "imply the exclusion of all other places" (de La Soudière 1991, 17). A "prime spot" presupposes and entails a process of constructing exemplarity (Micourd 1991). Studying them involves understanding "how they were chosen, transformed and forgotten . . . and who invented and became invested in them" (Micourd 1991, 7).

The notion of ordinary places could account not only for the processes by which prime tourist spots lose their exceptional status to become, or revert to, everyday places, but also the processes by which "ordinary places" are increasingly being sought out by tourists looking for something different.

The term "ordinary places" in the literature refers essentially to everyday places. In the second half of the twentieth century, a body of research spanning all disciplines demonstrated a revival of interest in these ordinary everyday places. In the 1970s, architects became interested in "the ugly and ordinary as a symbol of style" (Venturi et al. 2007, 138). The geographer di Meo (1996) based his territorial theory specifically on these ordinary everyday places. Berger (2008), a geographer, examined ordinary mobilities of everyday life and explored ordinary everyday places with Pousin (Berger and Pousin 2008). The anthropologist Chauvier (2011) encouraged fellow anthropologists to view research areas and topics from a fresh perspective through the lens of the "anthropology of the ordinary". The ethnologist Bromberger (1999) explored the *ordinary passions* of the French today. Museums have developed an interest in simple everyday items and the Musée International des Arts Modestes in Sète in the south of France was created to display "items that are forgotten, non-mainstream, hidden or on the creative periphery".[2] Heritage research has also seen a shift from monuments and their heritage to ordinary heritage. In a wider approach to heritage ranging from "cathedral to teaspoon" (Heinich 2009), there is an interest in micro-heritage, local heritage and the heritagisation of the ordinary (Isnart 2012).

In the tourism field, ordinary places are generally defined in terms of what they are not and in contrast to "hyperspecialised tourist spaces" (Fagnoni 2004, 51) and "because non-tourist territories have not been identified and recognised as such, they are not subject to the structural and functional norms of so-called tourist places" (Vitte 1998, 69). Tourism is deemed to play a part in transforming places, causing them to lose their "ordinary" residents, practices and atmosphere. The term "ordinary place" is synonymous with "non-tourist place" in the sense that there is nothing remarkable about it which makes it attractive.

This raises the question of how to define the paradox of "ordinary" tourist places. Constructing tourist places by subverting ordinary places is as old as tourism itself, but to what extent does the discovery of these ordinary places and their everyday life by tourism today differ from the past? Are we witnessing a new stage in the invention of tourism, a new "place time" (MIT 2005), characterised by the paradoxical recognition by tourism of ordinary places and times which are appreciated for their ordinary qualities?

Geography, and tourism geography in particular, has made the trajectories of places central to its analysis of tourism transformations. Tourism is built on the designation of places deemed/constructed to be *extra*-ordinary (prime spots) or specialised (tourist resorts), whereas ordinary places are dedicated to everyday practices, living, working and/or leisure (Gravari-Barbas and Delaplace 2015). The transformation of ordinary places into tourism places is associated with the history of tourism and has a role in the revival or expansion of destinations. Today, the future of major destinations is being played out on the "fringes of tourism", in places which have very little tourist footfall, as has been demonstrated by ordinary suburban areas which are becoming increasingly involved in promoting Paris as a destination (Gravari-Barbas 2017).

Befores: the discovery of "ordinary" places by tourism

Recognising that a place is ordinary, and therefore somewhere which can potentially be chosen by visitors, would imply moving out of the sphere of the ordinary on the basis of visitor choice. Developing an ordinary place for visitors often occurs via the subterfuge of a change of perspective which gives an "ordinary" place, which is looked at and sometimes even admired or loved, a new identity. The process by which these ordinary places become tourist places has been described by Knafou (1991) as an invention, that is "a new use of an existing place which has the effect of both subverting and developing it" (p. 11). Subversion diverts the place and infrastructures from their usual use, creating a shift from a functional use to a tourist use, shaped by an aesthetic perspective and a desire for relaxation. In development terms, this involves incorporating new areas not previously connected by former uses into the area in question (e.g. linking beaches to coastal villages, or mountain areas to alpine villages). The term "invention", which is used in preference to "discovery" (which suggests exploration) emphasises a change of perspective; "inventors" are people who are able "to suggest an alternative reading translating the emergence of an alternative socio-economic system with new values, and presenting it to their contemporaries" (p. 15).

Hatt (this volume) shows, for example, how Martigues, a town better known for its industrial activities than its tourist appeal, was "invented" as a destination by the combined effects of public policy and spontaneous visitor practices. Radical transformations of imaginaries are required for these places to become tourist destinations. Thus, the development of tourism in Martigues is the result of proactive discourse (as highlighted by one of the author's interviewees), a new self-image and a change of attitude to an industrial past which is now being valorised as a heritage asset.

We can see this orchestration of tourism and its discourse (enchanting storytelling) or tools (contextualised tours) in many residential areas which did not have any tourism activity until recently.

This can apply to peripheral areas characterised by socio-economic problems and a poor brand image. Guerra (this volume) analyses three "ordinary" districts of Turin: *Barriera di Milano*, a working-class area north of Turin; *Porta Palazzo*, the city's former trade district; and *Mirafiori Nord*, a district built in the 1930s around Turin's largest industrial area. Although the city centre has a very high tourist footfall, due in particular to the large number of monuments and museums, these three "ordinary" outlying areas have been the focus of deliberate and proactive tourism development driven by a group of public and voluntary sector stakeholders. The author shows how the narrative framework introduced (*Periferia, non malinconia*: Suburb, not sadness) to offer a different perspective on these districts involved an exercise in resetting and changing people's views.

In the case of New Belgrade, a socialist satellite built on the geographical and touristic periphery of the Serbian capital, and analysed by Nicic (this volume), tourism development is based on the supposed authenticity of the everyday life of the inhabitants of these districts which have not been developed for tourism. This provides the re-enchantment factor in this district which is required to boost local inhabitants' sense of belonging and to play a part in reappraising land and property values.

These analyses can be linked to the analytical study carried out by Auclair, Hertzog and Poulot (this volume) focusing on Cergy-Pontoise, one of the new towns built on the edge of Paris in the 1960s. During its early days as a new town, its development was entirely dependent on its ability to attract new permanent residents, and tourism was seen subsequently as a means of raising the profile of local facilities through the external gaze of tourists. The tourism discourse which has developed there focuses on the site's specific assets, and its natural environment and monumental works of art in the public space in particular.

As in New Belgrade, tours are planned to target both external visitors and local residents keen to (re)discover the places in which they live. These initiatives turn the spotlight on some ordinary places which are overlooked or even marginalised.

These examples show how tourism in these instances moves away from its "traditional" functions and takes on a socio-educational dimension for local residents. Can this be described as tourism development of these places or is this rather an orchestration of the tourism of the ordinary designed to change the way in which residents perceive their districts?

In-betweens: ordinary tourism in extraordinary places

The types of hybridisation which occur between tourist places and ordinary places are many and complex. They depend on the nature of the places visited and their levels of tourism development. The "ordinariness" of the urban peripheries of Turin or the new towns of Cergy-Pontoise and New Belgrade is not the same ordinary as in established urban destinations such as Paris as Chevalier and Lallement and Loisy (this volume) show. In global urban destinations, the aim is to offer a large number of mature, seasoned tourists undiscovered places which will give them the feeling that they are familiar with and even share local people's lifestyles; hence the relationship of foreign second-home dwellers in Paris with local shops and businesses (Chevalier and Lallement, this volume). In this instance, the ordinary, in the sense of everyday places and practices, may seem mundane to host businesses, but is nevertheless extraordinary for people discovering it. The authors highlight how "going shopping just outside one's apartment" offers the satisfaction of a blend of "familiarity and exoticism". Residents fully understand tourists' expectations of "authentic" experiences, as is shown by Loisy (this volume) in relation to Paris. The active involvement of the local population means that the tourism phenomenon can be disseminated in "everyday" places both in the centre and on the periphery of one of the most visited cities in the world. Local amateur guides offer a glimpse of the "authentic backstage areas" of their city, demystifying their inaccessibility and erasing negative and fantasised images.

Not all the contributions in this volume endorse the view that new tourist places will be valued for their truly "ordinary" nature. Infiltrating and experiencing the ordinary reality of others involves a far more sophisticated (or extraordinary?) tourism approach than a standard tourist package. In some respects, tourism in ordinary places may reveal an extraordinary tourism approach often restricted to tourists with substantial tourism and cultural experience looking for distinctive tours.

The hypothesis of the dissolution of the defining oppositions of tourism practice (near/far, exotic/familiar, ordinary/extraordinary) is an important area for inquiry and calls for a degree of nuance which can be provided by other contemporary tourism research in the social sciences (cf. Chabloz 2009; MacCarthy 2017; Stasch 2014).

Afters: different forms of "exit" from tourism

While everyday places can be discovered by tourism, certain tourist places can also become everyday places. Geographers have developed an interest in the trajectories of tourist resorts and in analysing how seaside resorts in particular have become locations for permanent residents. Rieucau chose as his case study the tourist resort of Grande Motte, which was built from scratch in 1968 in the south of France and combines a marina with an area providing technical facilities and a residential complex (privately owned properties, hotel accommodation, social tourism facilities) (Rieucau 2000, 638). The current permanent town developed gradually and was not dependent on seasonal tourism. By the end of the twentieth century, the seaside resort had become a resort town and a complex local social structure (characterised principally by the rise in numbers of permanent and retired residents) has developed over the last 40 years. Rieucau demonstrates this using four indicators: established shops; socio-professional differentiation; the use of very distinctive district names in property development; and the appropriation of certain places by permanent residents, with which they gradually come to identify. Violier (2002) draws similar conclusions for the seaside resort of La Baule on the French Atlantic coast. People who discovered La Baule as summer holidaymakers opted to settle there in retirement. La Baule became an "ordinary" town where an array of services gradually developed, thus drawing a line under the town's monomodal status.

Casamayor (this volume) examines the Interministerial Task Force in Planning for the Aquitaine Coast (MIACA) and shows how prime tourism and leisure spots can be transformed into "everyday" places, that is places used and lived in by their residents.

In the context of ski resorts, Bourdeau (this volume) examines the meaning and forms of recreation practiced by the "new mountaineers" and the transition from "visiting to living". The author views the development of ski resorts as an opportunity to rethink the future of mountain areas in terms of diversification and economic refocusing, in a context in which their dependence on tourism must be re-evaluated. He highlights the development of the Alps as a residential refuge, or a laboratory for a new way of living.

As far as changes in seaside and ski resorts are concerned, "after" tourism is developing gradually and "exits" from tourism are relative. Resorts structured exclusively around a tourism function are becoming multifunctional towns, but they still retain their appeal as leisure destinations (short weekend breaks for neighbouring populations) or for tourism, with a possible differentiation between residential and tourism areas. These former resorts, which are developing into areas for permanent residents, do not, however, always lose their status as tourism spaces. They are characterised primarily by a hybridisation of their functions associated with the appeal of spaces for long and short trips.

However, when tourism places are reclaimed by people using them within the framework of everyday life (leisure), major external causes may be involved. This is the case for a large number of tourism sites deprived of their international visitors by COVID-19, which have had to fall back on local customers. This is the scenario at PortAventura analysed by Clavé, Borràs Nogués, Ayebakuro Orama and Rovira Soto (this volume), a major tourism destination in Catalonia which is increasingly opening up to local and regional populations. However, these "exits" from tourism must be contextualised, and it is difficult at the time of writing to know whether international visitors will return to tourism destinations which have become essentially local or regional.

Sometimes, however, these exits from tourism are permanent and create "tourism wastelands" – areas developed for tourism (resorts or enclaves) that are often permanently abandoned after tourism life cycles of varying duration, such as the "tourism wastelands" of French Polynesia described by Bachimon (this volume).

It is clear from these different analyses that thinking in terms of "before" and "after" is complex. Sudden "entrances" into tourism are actually rare. In most cases, there are complex and non-linear itineraries at play. The complex nature of these approaches is discussed by Freytag, Korff and Winsky (this volume), who suggest that it is reductive to frame the trajectory of the Black Forest in terms of "before" and "after" tourism. They believe that the various components of tourism (stakeholders and practices, materialities and representations) are being continuously reassembled in different ways in time and space. Thus, "before" and "after" can be read iteratively – since "after" can resurface later as "before" and thus be incorporated into a future tourism spatio-temporality. The authors also stress that we need to take the interaction of different geographical scales into account and look at the trajectories of places on a micro, meso and macro level, incorporating global trends such as the impact of the COVID-19 pandemic on tourism.

Conclusion: post-tourism or hyper-tourism?

We cannot examine these dynamics without referring to the broader context of thinking around "post-tourism". This concept, which was introduced in

1985 by Feifer and adopted by a number of authors, is interpreted in a variety of ways, but assumes a radical disruption in the tourism field in recent years. An initial perspective, adopted notably by Urry (2002), situates the "post-tourism" phenomenon in the postmodern global context (Girard 2013). This point of view assumes a rupture between modernity and postmodernity, that is not merely a blurring of distinctions but the renewal of the values on which tourism practices are based. It attempts to account in theoretical terms for far-reaching transformations in society and new trends in tourism practices – the search for "authentic experiences" or new ways of exploiting this authenticity – but also the global criticism which it attracts (Bourdeau 2012). Some people consider that it is doomed to vanish in a world where mobility must be re-evaluated on both environmental and economic grounds (Bourdeau 2012).

The alternative viewpoint, which reflects the position held by Viard (2000, 2006), describes the process of diffusion of the cultural values of tourism in society as a whole. It also aims in more concrete terms to account for what happens after highly touristic places have been developed for tourism. A typical post-tourism scenario would be one in which tourist amenities in an area attract not just tourists but also new inhabitants, who could be considered "post-tourists", such as new residents in the Le Sextant holiday village on the French Atlantic coast (Casamayor, this volume) or in the Massif du Vercors in the French Alps (Bourdeau, this volume). This perspective accounts for the "afters", the extension of tourism development or "post-tourism spirals" to quote Alain Girard (2013).

To sum up, with reference to the terminology employed by Bourdeau (2012), we seem on the one hand to have an approach that highlights the reinvention of tourism through practices that exploit the boundaries between the ordinary and the extraordinary, based on alternative practices and destinations. This "postmodern tourism" is "renewed by phenomena of reinventions and recreational and geotourism hybridisations which emphasize the diversity of sites newly developed for tourism . . . and the new perspectives, practices and links deployed there" (p. 43). On the other hand, "post-tourism" takes on a more literal meaning. It refers to a process of transition and residential repurposing in holiday and tourist regions (Viard 2000, 2006; Violier 2002; Rieucau 2000). In all scenarios, the new "post-tourism" era is characterised by the dilution of tourism as a vector for specific sociabilities, spatialities and temporalities (Bourdeau 2012) and thus by a "dedifferentiation" between the touristic and non-touristic in places, practices and times. The boundaries between "elsewhere" and "here", between the "exotic" and the "everyday", between "ordinary" and "extraordinary" are becoming blurred (Bourdeau 2012). A tourist can no longer simply be defined as "someone who made the periodic, temporary transition from the ordinary space-time of industrial work to the extraordinary space-time of going on holiday" (Girard 2013, 45). This involves reconsidering the fundamental definition of tourism as a time period existing outside everyday life.

Are we witnessing an exit from the dominant tourism model, or conversely are the changes observed simply a new aspect of much older phenomena? Are we seeing a new paradigm, or is this a hyper-sophistication, a more widespread version of phenomena observed since the very beginnings of tourism?

Some contributions argue in favour of the hypothesis of the replacement of the era of traditional tourism by a "new era". Thus, Hatt highlights how the tourism trajectory of Martigues illustrates new dynamics of hybridisation. This hybridisation can be understood not only as a bringing together of touristic and industrial activities, but also as the development and implementation of public policies. In their analysis of free accommodation outside family circles, Girard and Schéou interpret the proliferation of platforms as the product of the emergence of a tourism of co-production. Picking up on Viard's position which describes post-tourism as an extension of tourism values into other fields, they highlight that "We are therefore witnessing an extension, into everyday life, of the relevance of the aesthetic code associated with tourism". However, they advise against an overly naïve vision of the phenomenon and stress that this is not just any type of everyday, but a particular type of everyday which is therefore "associated with the discourse of couch-surfing and home swapping exponents and commentators, we might say that it ultimately represents the pinnacle of the touristic quest and hence the tourism imaginary, and not an exit from it".

In conclusion, the chapters in this volume highlight the many meanings and social dimensions of tourism. They reveal in particular the cross-cutting nature of tourism and the need to study its points of intersection with society as a whole. A significant proportion of tourism practices are shaped by practices which do not stem from the institutional or commercial tourism sectors. They do not show the end of tourism, but rather that the tourism phenomenon permeates all areas of society. Transformations in tourism must therefore be analysed over the long term, taking into account the various strata, issues and specificities of contemporary societies.

Notes

1 Accueil Banlieues website, www.tourisme93.com/document.php?pagendx=661. Retrieved 19 July 2018.
2 Site du MIAM, http://miam.org/fr/l-art-modeste/article/l-art-modeste-68. Retrieved 20 July 2018.

References

Berger, Martine and Frédéric Pousin (dirs.). 2008. "Les espaces du quotidien." *Strates* 14.
Berger, Martine. 2008. "Mobilités résidentielles, mobilités quotidiennes. Une approche des déterminants sociaux des aires de déplacement en région parisienne." In R. Séchet, I. Garat and D. Zeneidi (dirs.), *Espaces en transactions*. Rennes: Presses Universitaires de Rennes, pp. 29–46.
Berthelot, Lebra. 2012. "Vers un après-tourisme?: la figure de l'itinérance récréative pour repenser le tourisme de montagne: études des pratiques et de l'expérience de l'association Grande Traversée des Alpes." thèse de géographie de l'université de Grenoble, Grenoble.

Bourdeau, Philippe. 2012. "Le tourisme réinventé par ses périphéries?" In *Explorando las nuevas fronteras del turismo: Perspectivas de la invetigacion en turismo*, edited by F. Bourlon, M. Osorio, P. Mao and T. Gale. Coyhaique, Chile: Nire Negro, pp. 31–48.

Bromberger, Christian. 1999. "Les monuments ordinaires de la vie quotidienne." In *L'abus Monumental?*, edited by R. Debray. Paris: Fayard, pp. 197–206.

Chabloz, Nadège. 2009. "Tourisme et primitivisme. Initiations au bwiti et à l'iboga (Gabon)." *Cahiers d'Etudes Africaines* 193–194: 391–428.

Chauvier, Eric. 2011. *Anthropologie de l'ordinaire: Une conversion du regard.* Toulouse: Anacharsis, coll. Essais.

Condevaux, Aurélie, Geraldine Djament-Tran and Maria Gravari-Barbas. 2016. "Avant et après le(s) tourisme(s): Trajectoires des lieux et rôle des acteurs du tourisme hors des sentiers battus. Une analyse bibliographique." *Via Tourism Review* 21(9), https://journals.openedition.org/viatourism/409.

Cousin, Saskia, Géraldine Djament, Maria Gravari-Barbas and Jacquot Sébastien. 2015. "Contre la métropole créative . . . tout contre/ Les politiques patrimoniales et touristiques de Plaine Commune, Saint Saint-Denis." *Revue Metropoles* 17, https://metropoles.revues.org/5171.

Cuvelier, Pascal. 1997. "L'économie des pratiques touristiques." Thèse de doctorat en sciences économiques, Université de Lille, Lille, 1.

de Becdelièvre, Geoffroy. 2015. "Le tourisme à l'heure d'Internet et la désintermédiation induite signeront-ils la fin des voyagistes traditionnels?" *Annales des Mines – Réalités industrielles* 3: 80–82.

Delaplace, Marie and Maria Gravari-Barbas. 2016a. "Editorial: Aux marges du tourisme. Utopies et réalités du tourisme hors des sentiers battus." *Via Tourism Review* 9, https://journals.openedition.org/viatourism/415.

Delaplace, Marie and Maria Gravari-Barbas. 2016b. *Nouveaux Territoires Touristiques. Invention, reconfigurations, repositionnements.* Madrid: Sous la direction de, Presses Universitaires du Québec.

De La Soudière, Marin. 1991. "Les hauts lieux . . . mais les autres?" In *Des hauts lieux: la construction sociale de l'exemplarité*, edited by André Micourd. Paris: Editions du CNRS, pp. 17–31.

Deprest, Florence. 1997. *Enquête sur le tourisme de masse: L'écologie face au territoire.* Belin: collection Mappemonde, p. 207.

di Meo, Guy. 1996. *Les territoires du quotidien.* Paris: L'Harmattan.

Fagnoni, Edith. 2004. "Amnéville, de la cité industrielle à la cité touristique: Quel devenir pour les territoires urbains en déprise?" *Mondes en Développement* 1(125): 51–66, www.cairn.info/revue-mondes-en-developpement-2004-1-page-51.htm.

Feifer, Maxine. 1985. *Going Places.* London: Macmillan.

Gault, Franz. 2016. "Hybridation des temps, hybridation des lieux: Travail et vacances: nouveaux rythmes, nouveaux lieux." *Espaces* 330: 30–33.

Girard, Alain. 2013. "Faut-il raccorder une théorie générale de la postmodernité à une théorie à moyenne portée du post-tourisme?" In *Fin (?) et confins du tourisme. Interroger le statut et les pratiques de la récréation contemporaine*, directed by Philippe Bourdeau, Hugues François and Liliane Perrin-Bensahel. Paris: L'Harmattan, pp. 43–52.

Gombault, Anne. 2011. "Tourisme et création: Les hypermodernes." *Mondes du Tourisme* 4, http://tourisme.revues.org/449. Consulté le 05 février 2016.

Gravari-Barbas, Maria. 2013. *Aménager la ville par la culture et le tourisme.* Paris: Editions le Moniteur, p. 159.

Gravari-Barbas, Maria. 2017. "Tourisme de marges, marges du tourisme. Lieux ordinaires et 'no-go-zones' à l'épreuve du tourisme." *Bulletin de l'Association de Géographes Français* 3: 400–418.

Gravari-Barbas, Maria and Marie Delaplace. 2015. "Editorial: Le tourisme hors des sentiers battus." *Teoros* 34: 1–2.

Gwiazdzinski, Luc. 2016. "De l'hybridation territoriale à la créolisation des mondes." In *L'hybridation des mondes.* Grenoble: Elya Editions, pp. 311–334.

Heinich, Nathalie. 2009. *La fabrique du patrimoine: "De la cathédrale à la petite cuillère".* Paris: Edition de la Maison des sciences de l'homme, coll. ethnologie de la France.

Herzfled, Michael. 2017. "Playing for/with Time: Tourism and Heritage in Greee and Thailand." In *Tourism and Gentrification in Contemporary Metropolises: A Comparative Perspective,* edited by M. Gravari-Barbas and S. Guinand. London: Routledge, pp. 233–252.

Isnart, Cyril. 2012. "Les patrimonialisations ordinaires: Essai d'images ethnographiées." *Ethnographiques.org* 24, juillet.

Knafou, Rémy. 1991. "L'invention du lieu touristique: la passation d'un contrat et le surgissement simultané d'un nouveau territoire." *Revue de Géographie Alpine* 79(4): 11–19, www.persee.fr/doc/rga_0035-1121_1991_num_79_4_3624.

Lussault, Michel. 2007. "Le tourisme, un genre commun." In *Mondes urbains du tourisme,* directed by P. Duhamel and R. Knafou. Paris: Belin, coll. "Mappemonde", pp. 333–349.

MacCarthy, Michelle. 2017. *Making the Modern Primitive: Cultural Tourism in the Trobriand Islands.* Honolulu: University of Hawai'i Press.

Maitland, Robert. 2013. "Backstage Behaviour in the Global City: Tourists and the Search for the 'Real London'." *Procedia – Social and Behavioral Sciences* 105: 12–19.

Marzloff, Bruno. 2016. "De s airs et des aires de vacances. Les équipements de loisir pénètrent dans l'univers du travail: Travail et vacances: nouveaux rythmes, nouveaux lieux." *Espaces* 330: 34–36.

Micourd, André. 1991. *Des hauts lieux: La construction sociale de l'exemplarité.* Paris: Editions du CNRS.

MIT. 2005. *Tourismes 2: Moments de lieux.* Paris: Belin.

Pirotte, Gautier. 2007. *La notion de société civile.* Paris: La Découverte, "Repères", p. 128.

Priskin, Julianna and Joris Sprakel. 2008. "'CouchSurfing': À la recherche d'une expérience touristique authentique." *Teoros* 27(1): 68–71.

Rieucau, Jean. 2000. "La Grande-Motte, Ville permanente, ville saisonnière." *Annales de Géographie* 616: 631–654.

Sacareau, Isabelle, Luc Vacher and Didier Vye. 2013. "La résidence secondaire est-elle un objet aux confins du tourisme? Réflexions à partir de l'exemple des résidences secondaires des Britanniques en Poitou-Charentes." In *Fin (?) et confins du tourisme. Interroger le statut et les pratiques de la récréation contemporaine,* edited by Philippe Bourdeau, Hugues François and Liliane Perrin-Bensahel. Paris: L'Harmattan.

Sallet-Lavorel, Hélène. 2003. "Encourager le rapprochement entre visiteurs et Franciliens. Pour un tourisme urbain participatif en Île-de-France." *Cahier Espaces* 78: 118–133, Juillet.

Sauthier, Géraldine. 2011. *Trajectoire de développement touristique et régimes urbains: analyse du cas de Montreux, mémoire de master sous la direction de Christophe Clivaz.* Sion: Institut Universitaire Kurt Bösch, p. 98.

Segault, Marion. 2006. "L'ordinaire des espaces quotidiens." *Urbanisme* 351: 60–62.

Stasch, Rupert. 2014. "Primitivist Tourism and Romantic Individualism: On the Values in Exotic Stereotypy About Cultural Others." *Anthropological Theory* 14(2): 191–214.

Urry, John. 2002. *The Tourist Gaze.* London: Sage Publications.

Venturi, Robert, Scott Brown Denise and Izenour Steven. 2007. *L'enseignement de Las Vegas.* Paris: Mardaga (édition originale en anglais, 1977, MIT).

Vergopoulos, Hecate. 2013. "Etre touriste chez soi. Le tourisme comme modèle socioculturel d'appropriation du territoire quotidien." In *Fin (?) et confins du tourisme. Interroger le statut et les pratiques de la récréation contemporaine*, directed by Philippe Bourdeau, Hugues François and Liliane Perrin-Bensahel. Paris: L'Harmattan, pp. 53–61.

Viard, Jean. 2000. *Court traité sur les vacances, les voyages, et l'hospitalité des lieux.* Paris: Editions de l'Aube.

Viard, Jean. 2006. *Eloge de la Mobilité. Essai sur le capital temps libre et la valeur travail.* Paris: Editions de l'Aube.

Violier, Philippe. 2002. "La Baule de la station au lieu de vie." *Mappemonde* 66: 20–24.

Vitte, Pierre. 1998. "Tourisme en espace rural: le territoire à l'épreuve." *Revue de géographie alpine* 86(3): 69–85, https://doi.org/10.3406/rga.1998.2893.

Part 1

Befores

2 Tourism of the ordinary Paris

An unstaged *authenticity*[1] proposed by the inhabitants

Marine Loisy

For over 300 years, Paris has been a favourite destination for travellers. Compared with Barcelona, which has had a tourist boost with the organisation of the 1992 Olympic Games, Paris became a destination at the birth of tourism. This industry has favoured urban transformations. The capital has a recognised cultural offer, thanks to its heritage, museums and gastronomy. Historically, the city has been able to adapt to tourism changes and has developed, over the years, special attractions. However, Paris is facing increased competition not only from London and Rome but also from Berlin, Prague and Amsterdam.

Tourism development policies recognise the need for a renewal of the offer and bet in particular on a diffusion of the flows towards the outlying districts and beyond the ring road. Gradually, tourist attraction is no longer exclusively focused on the classic monumental aspects or around activities and services designed for visitors. Tourists are now entering areas which were previously devoted to the "ordinary" and daily activities of the inhabitants. In this context of hyper-tourism, Parisians are becoming new actors in the reception and tourist management of their own city. This chapter examines these evolutions which could be seen as signs of a new tourism paradigm.

A few months after the January 2015 terrorist attacks in Paris, the City Council published a video promoting the capital entitled "Paris je t'aime" ("Paris I love you").[2] The objective of this investment: "to re-enchant the destination" and give it a positive image, mainly in the eyes of American and Asian visitors. This two-and-a-half-minute clip directed by Jalil Lespert[3] showed the kitchen of Alain Ducasse's[4] gastronomic restaurant, the corridors of the world's largest museum, the Louvre, an aerial shot of the Champs-Élysées, the haute-couture Balenciaga and Christian Dior fashion shows, the roof of the Opéra Garnier (access to the roof of the Opéra Garnier is normally strictly forbidden) and multiple shots showing the Eiffel Tower from all angles. A concentration of the symbols of luxury, prestige and monumentality associated with the image of the French capital, that was notably broadcast on long-haul Air France flights.

Sensitive to the disparity between the images of a clip encouraging people to "live Paris" and their representation of the city on a daily basis, two young Parisian directors – Maxime Baudin and Léo Bigiaoui – created in just a few days their own version of this promotional film, ironically entitled "Paris, on

DOI: 10.4324/9781003138600-4

t'aime aussi" ("Paris, we love you too").[5] They carry their camera through the stalls of the food markets, behind the counter of a bar in the 13th arrondissement, in the squares and corridors of the metro. Between the croissants on display in a bakery in the early morning and the atmosphere of an overcrowded discotheque, the directors want to show the value of a more "ordinary" facet of the capital, on the fringes of its monuments, its luxury and its starred chefs.

This episode underlines the opposition between, on the one hand, an institutional project focused on an "extraordinary" dimension of Paris and, on the other hand, a local vision where the city's charm is found in its everyday life. However, this contrast is not limited to the promotional framework. It also concerns tourist practices offering some "ordinary" places a new appeal.

The aim of this chapter is not to provide an exhaustive description of what opposes these different representations of the destination, but rather to understand how some inhabitants encourage spontaneous touristification to places of everyday life in the heart and on the fringes of one of the most visited cities in the world: Paris. Indeed, this phenomenon is perhaps based on a paradox, given that opposition movements to tourism have been emerging in several major European destinations since the 2010s. The increase in the number of visitors and short-term rentals are among the main factors behind anti-tourist protests expressed in Barcelona, Venice and Dubrovnik. In Paris, compared withs destinations in the Mediterranean basin, tourists are rarely directly blamed. However, voices are being raised against the expansion of café terraces and the real estate inflation which is said to be linked to tourist rental platforms.

At the same time, a growing number of tour operators are offering a discovery of the capital through the eyes and the account of an inhabitant. With the development of digital technology and the economy of disintermediation, some locals are taking on a new role to become actors in the tourist activities on their own territory. They can host visitors in their homes, suggest their favourite restaurants or guide them on a walk through their neighbourhood (Loisy 2019).

In getting closer to locals, some visitors are looking for an "authentic experience" in the "real Paris", in the sense of the quest described by Dean MacCannell as a desire to go behind the scenes (MacCannell 1989) of the staging (Goffman 1973). For their part, through the desire to share their city, their way of life and their everyday life, some residents participate in a tourism experience of the ordinary. This is notably the case of the members of the association "*Greeters*-Parisiens d'un jour". This group has more than 400 volunteers[6] and is the largest structure among the 200 member associations of the *Global Greeter Network*, which was founded in New York in 1992. The activity takes the form of a free walk in a small group (generally between one and six people) accompanied by a local "*Greeter*", who is not a tourism professional. In Paris, other local, national or international companies offer such activities on a paid basis. This is the case of *Airbnb Experience*, the *Cariboo* platform[7] or *Wide Trip*.[8] Generally speaking, the "amateur guided walk" allows you to discover a district of Paris or its suburbs thanks to the personal anecdotes of the guide and according to the interest of the visitors. The banal and the trivial are thus highlighted by the inhabitant in a rather spontaneous setting that the urban walk in "their" district allows.

From an anthropological perspective, this chapter therefore seeks to understand the incursion of tourism into "ordinary" places and practices which until now have been exclusively devoted to everyday habits. I suggest going beyond the apparent paradox of an expansion of tourism places in a context of rising anti-tourist claims to analyse this participation of civil society. By looking at the framework and content of the activity, the aim is to understand whether the participation of non-tourist inhabitants offers visitors unstaged *authenticity*.[9] What roles do these locals play in the transformation of the tourist field? Does this involvement promote a hybridisation between tourism practices and those of an "ordinary" dimension? Finally, this chapter examines the transformations that suggest the birth of a post- or hyper-tourism era and thus looks at the actors, practices and places newly integrated into tourism.

To accomplish this, the survey is based on a field ethnography carried out between 2016 and 2018 in Paris and its suburbs. It is based on participatory observation and a series of semi-directive interviews. This ethnographic field focused on the practices and discourses produced in the context of tourist activities proposed and supervised by Parisians who are not tourism professionals: this chapter is based more specifically on the case of about 15 Parisians who are amateur guides. Amateur guided walks were favoured for their accessible (often free) dimension and the possibility of multiplying observations in different districts and with different inhabitants. This work has led to a better understanding of the emphasis chosen by the amateur guides-inhabitants for tourists. It also provides information on the meaning given to the places and objects that make up their neighbourhood in spaces that are *a priori* non-touristified.

The local inhabitant: actor of the ordinary tourism city

The value placed on "real" inhabitants

In the context of the amateur guided walks, resident guides play a central role. They show their attachment to the human dimension of tourist activity. They also express a desire to present themselves in a spontaneous context. In his description of the "ville-rencontre" ("meeting-city"), the French anthropologist Marc Augé explains that "the appeal to the senses and aesthetic emotion" is made possible by considering "the city as a person . . . and that the city as a person is obviously the social city, the one where people can meet and interact" (Augé 2013, 145). From the point of view of the researcher, even before the idea of encounter, the observation of "the social city . . . is only possible and meaningful in an environment which is animated by the flows of work or leisure, in the order desired by an active society . . ." (p. 148). In this sense, the initiative of the amateur guide inhabitant enables a personification of the city in the eyes of tourists, giving them the opportunity to see those who, like their guide, live there on a daily basis.

For visitors, calling on the services of a non-professional in the tourism sector is a guarantee that they are dealing with a "real" inhabitant: someone who lives, consumes and sometimes even works there. For Sylvain, who proposes walks in one of the most touristic districts of the capital – Montmartre – the fact that he has grown up and lived there is considered an added value that the *Cariboo* platform does not hesitate to promote. This French platform "likes, precisely, to interact with 'real' locals", says Sylvain. Referring to its guiding activity, he adds: "When I introduce myself at the beginning, I immediately say that I lived 25. . . 27 years in Montmartre, that I was born here".[10] This familiarity also sometimes allows for chance encounters with a neighbour, a friend or a shopkeeper in the neighbourhood. This is the case of Jacques who, in addition to being a long-time resident, was also deputy mayor of the 4th arrondissement of Paris. His *Greeter* walks regularly gave him the opportunity to shake hands and briefly chat with other people in the street.[11] These spontaneous encounters show that the guide is personally integrated in the neighbourhood and gradually shapes his image as a resident. In addition to the work of guiding, the guide is able to satisfy "a more unconscious, if not less explicitly formulated expectation, namely the quest for authenticity" (Sagnes 2010, 97). In this way, the local guide embodies an "Other" who affects the visitor through a sensitive and personal narrative.

Moreover, Paul, a *Greeter* resident guide in Montmartre, thinks that the majority of tourist groups do not take the time to meet the locals. He exclaims: "These people . . . they don't see us, eh, they don't see us!".[12] His involvement with the *Greeters* therefore seems to be positioned as a form of resistance to this context of indifference. It is in this state of mind that, for Isabelle, the interest of the *Greeters* walks she proposes in her town of Boulogne-Billancourt (in the western suburbs of Paris) lies essentially in the fact of showing the places "where people live",[13] far from the tourist circuits of the capital. In highly visited neighbourhoods, monuments and heritage sites shape local identity through their symbolic and emblematic force. But, contrary to appearances, their role is not exclusively rooted in tourist attraction, since they are also linked to personal histories and journeys, to the social trajectories of a population. During a walk in the heart of summer, Cécile, a *Greeters* guide for several years, describes the Christmas masses spent "every year", with her family, at the Basilique du Sacré-Cœur de Montmartre.[14] Jacques, for his part, tells of his weekly habit of coming to read his newspaper in the garden of the Hôtel de Sully, a Louis XIII style mansion in the Marais district.[15] In the link with the monument, autochthony and local identity are highlighted. Thus, through the narrative offered by the amateur guide inhabitant, the Sacré-Cœur, the Hôtel de Sully, caught up in a "patrimonialisation of this heritage which we now like to describe as intangible" (Sagnes 2010, 95), produces local identity. Cécile, Jacques, Sylvain and the other amateur guide inhabitants then embody autochthony by highlighting a daily dimension of their town. Choosing the example of industrial heritage, the French ethnologist Daniel Fabre describes the transformation of the relationship to heritage from an object to a subject:

"Heritage is ours" becomes "Heritage is us". The recognition by UNESCO of communities as guarantors of their own intangible cultural heritage in the 2003 Intangible Cultural Heritage Convention is very significant of this reversal of the foundations of expertise. Who states heritage value? This simple question is enough to shake up the entire system, which is primarily national, built around monumentality. . . . Communities recognise their heritage and the experts are at the service of these communities to tune the various heritage professions to the new purpose entirely defined by those who recognise themselves as heirs. This thesis . . . on reversal is particularly important.

(Fabre 2016, 52)

Spontaneity and personalisation to show an "ordinary" Paris

In the context of amateur guided walks in Paris, the inhabitant does not prevent himself from producing an intimate discourse. Also, the spatial dimension of the walk is partly shaped by this personal life trajectory, the guide's daily habits and affinity places. In this sense, making people discover their neighbourhood on foot consists of attracting visitors to places where the life and existence of the inhabitants take place, in the heart of the places where they live, where they (re)find their "centre of gravity" (Le Breton 2012, 150), their "home".

Marie, a 60-year-old woman who has lived in the Marais since the 1980s, appreciates the opportunity to show her neighbourhood as part of *Greeters'* walks, as she considers herself capable of delivering a personal story:

I want to stay in my neighbourhood because it's natural to talk about my life here. . . . If I were in another neighbourhood . . . first of all, I know less . . . except the third [arrondissement] because I've lived there too and I go there sometimes. And it's also the Marais, eh. It's very close. But if I go, for example, to the Latin Quarter. . . , it won't be the same. These are not neighbourhoods where I lived, so it's not the same . . . it's much less personalised.

(Extract from the interview of 18 December 2017.
Translated from French.)

Also, when she shows her visitors the ruins of Philippe Auguste's wall, particularly highlighted near the Jardins Saint-Paul Street in the heart of the 4th arrondissement, Marie sometimes takes the time to look back to the Lycée Charlemagne to say that her son went to school there. Further on, when she arrives on the Sainte-Catherine market square, she tells us: "We liked to come there, with my husband and my son, to the restaurant or the café . . . because there were no cars and so the children could play without risk".[16] For his part, in Aubervilliers, Louis (73 years old, retired theatre teacher) is happy to mention a few anecdotes related to the history of his ancestors, their life in the neighbourhood and the stories they passed on to him. He notes that these anecdotes are of interest to the visitors: "this, [tourists] will find nowhere else",[17] he explains. For example, during a walk in January 2016, as we pass under the ring road, he says:

> So I'm going to tell you a very [he insists on the word "very"] personal anecdote . . . With my father, we left at three in the morning to get the meat from the abattoirs at La Villette. Then, we had to go to the grocery shops. But, as sometimes we had to wait a little . . . because it was too early in fact, so we would go to a bistro there [he shows me a street corner] and there we ate a super ham-butter sandwich [he stops walking to insist on every syllable] with bread that I never found until today. A bread with a flavour! . . . I'm telling you about my childhood here!
>
> (Extract from the field notes of 25 January 2016.
> Translated from French.)

From Sylvain's point of view, unlike "classic" guided tours, his walk with *Cariboo* allows him to tell "a little more about the personal aspects of [his] life"[18]:

> I walk past this building, and I say "this was my school". One time, I passed by my mother's house, I saw my mother at the window, I said: "ah well, there's my mother!". Stuff like that.
>
> (Extract from the field notes of 7 July 2017.
> Translated from French.)

According to him, these anecdotes bring a "lively, . . . less monotonous" side to the visiting experience. Through the frequent use of "Me" and "I", the amateur inhabitant guide places himself at the centre of the visit. His narrative goes beyond informative and explanatory discourse to expose an assumed affective and personal dimension. However, this personalisation often applies in both directions: visitors and residents call each other by their first names and evoke anecdotes about their children, their work, their leisure activities and sometimes even about more sensitive or intimate subjects such as political opinions or accidents in life.

The value given to the guide-inhabitant's advice

The amateur guide-inhabitant has the role of mediator, but also of advisor. They are the link between the visitor and an environment that the latter considers more or less foreign. Suggestions concerning shops, neighbourhoods to visit or souvenir shops abound during the walk. The inhabitant fully assumes his role as ambassador and becomes aware of the value of his suggestions in the eyes of the visitors. For example, Gérard, *Greeter* in the 2nd arrondissement, tells the following story:

> People come back to the neighbourhood afterwards, as I tell them: "There, that's my butcher, there, that's my baker, my pastry cook, why I come here and not there, I've tested . . . there, the pastry shop in such and such a place. If you like it, I recommend this one". Well, uh . . . so when we visit, we don't have time but I know that the next day, they tell me: 'We came back, we saw, we appreciate . . . thank you very much!". . . . It's authentic in so far as I know personally. Afterwards, I say it, it's all subjective. But hey, that's how they take it.
>
> (Extract from the interview of 5 July 2017.
> Translated from French.)

According to him, tourists do not give the same value to the advice of the amateur guide as they do to the recommendations of tourism professionals. The discourse of Gérard is perceived as impartial. And the personal relationship between the visitor and the inhabitant gives the guide's advice a privileged character. The status of "local" then seems to act as a guarantee of trust. In addition, the guide-inhabitants often adopt a protective, mothering or paternalistic attitude towards those they accompany. This is the case of Gérard when he takes reticent tourists on the metropolitan transport network:

> Some people don't want to take the metro. Well . . . I tell them: "You know, it's still an experience, the metro. We're going to save time . . .", because there were people, uh . . . we had made a visit, I don't know, it was in Montmartre or something else. They were supposed to meet in the Marais. And they had an appointment . . . so I said: "Listen, we're not going to take a taxi, uh . . . Trust me, we'll go together, by metro, and you'll discover the metro". And, well, they actually saw, the people in the metro, how you take the metro . . . it was a real experience. So I was a bit the . . . the . . . not their bodyguard but I was vigilant, I told them to be careful, there can be pickpockets, things like that. But I was very vigilant, I reassured them. They arrived on time.
>
> (Extract from the interview of 5 July 2017.
> Translated from French.)

The inhabitant finally stands as the key to a spontaneous, intimate and privileged relationship of trust with the city. In addition to this figure of the local, the "Paris of Parisians" is also embodied in a materiality and a narrative in which the ordinary city takes precedence over monumentality.

A discursive production around daily concerns

Story of an "ordinary" life and city

Part of the exchanges that take place during the urban walks supervised by the inhabitants relate to current events. It can happen that one of these subjects is approached from a question or comment from tourists, as with the American couple that Diane (*Greeter* in the 11th arrondissement) is expecting on a rainy morning in January 2016. The tourists end up arriving anyway, explaining that they had "a taxi problem". From the beginning of the walk, the conversation was based on a comparison with their country: "Here in Paris, you can wait a long time before getting a taxi. In the United States, there are plenty of them waiting for you!",[19] explains the American. Then the discussion continued for a few more minutes on the taxi strike that has been going on since the day before in the capital, against the Uberisation of the activity. For her part, Isabelle (a retired teacher and *Greeter* in Boulogne-Billancourt) recounts that her visitors ask her about the educational system, about what she thinks of Macron, of Donald Trump: "Euh . . . Trump, that made a lot of people talk, I must say!".[20] Generally speaking, these discussions give the inhabitant and the visitor the opportunity to exchange in a configuration where neither of them is in a situation of domination by the possession of knowledge.

Also, it is not uncommon that exchanges focus on social issues, such as unemployment in France, the role of religion or the leisure practices of Parisians. These questions are sometimes raised by the guide, but when the initiative comes from visitors, the inhabitants do not hesitate to contribute to the exchanges. In Montmartre with Luc, *Greeter* on the Butte, the presence of beehives set up behind the Place du Tertre gives rise to a discussion about the use of pesticides and the public health problems linked to them. In this context, the two adults in the group – parents of three children, who are also present – talk about the case of their town in the west of France, their own experiences and their personal views on the subject.[21] In Seine-Saint-Denis, Louis does not hide the social reality of part of the northern suburbs of Paris. He shows his neighbourhood in all modesty, from abandoned warehouses to low-rent buildings. He speaks of the dilapidated state of many buildings, adding: "We know very well that in some housing, there are ten or fifteen people in a single room. And there are workers who pile up around sewing machines to sell in Chinese shops. . . . But well, that's it too, Aubervilliers, it's part of the town".[22]

In the context of her walk through the covered passages of the 1st arrondissement of Paris, Bénédicte does not devote her speech to the history of the places or to the inspiration of the architects who designed them. On the contrary, she directly evokes the current functioning and daily management of these singular spaces:

> It is a private passage in a public place. It is therefore up to the owners to agree on the maintenance and renovation of the gallery. In return, it is

closed on Sundays and in the evenings until the morning. Some galleries have agreed to open on Sundays, so in exchange, the state will take care of the renovation or maintenance of part of the gallery. This is a negotiation with the Paris City Hall, in fact.

(Extract from the field notes of 8 February 2016. Translated from French.)

Several volunteers from the *Greeter* association note that the majority of visitors seem to be more interested in the day-to-day running of the district than in details about the architecture of its monuments or the history of its heritage. According to Catherine and Diane, two *Greeter* volunteer friends in the 11th arrondissement of Paris, many questions concern everyday objects, such as the functioning of urban facilities: parking meters, self-service cars and bicycles and even gutters. In the public gardens, discussions revolve around the species of flowers that embellish the flowerbeds. Questions about housing and property prices are often asked by visitors, whether French or foreign. Marie, owner of a flat in the very central and touristic district of Le Marais, does not hesitate, during her walk, to stop in front of the window of a *Century 21* real estate agency to show tourists how high the housing prices are there.[23] During another walk with two young women from the north of France, she even mentioned the urban planning standards imposed in the district: "At home, we wanted to change the colour of the shutters. Well, we couldn't have used mimosa yellow or azure blue! We only had the choice between certain pastels!".[24] All in all, these subjects of conversation and the transmission of banal and prosaic information mark the experience of the walk with a very ordinary dimension. Guided by a local resident, visitors take advantage of this privileged opportunity to discuss "trivial" or personal subjects. Then, compared with a professional guide, the amateur guide-inhabitant presents himself as a legitimate interlocutor to address questions about the "ordinary" city.

The spectacle of the "imponderabilia of actual life"

[The imponderabilia of actual life] belong such things as the routine of a man's working day, the details of his care of the body, of the manner of taking food and preparing it; the tone of conversational and social life around the village fires, the existence of strong friendships or hostilities, and of passing sympathies and dislikes between people; the subtle yet unmistakable manner in which personal vanities and ambitions are reflected in the behaviour of the individual and in the emotional reactions of those who surround him.

(Malinowski 2005, 14)

As the methodological recommendations made by Bronislaw Malinowski, the amateur guide-inhabitants pay special attention to certain details of everyday urban life. The latter knows the residents, the shops, the "discrete" details of their district. In Montmartre, for example, Anna comments on the dusty aspect of a children's square, the presence of pigeons and the Sunday animation of the pétanque ground.[25] These elements mark her daily attachment to the neighbourhood. Visitors' interest in these spontaneous scenes contributes to the process of touristification that arises from this ordinary dimension of the district: anecdotal details, simple activities and harmless scenes are then the object of attention and fuel discussions between the visitor and the inhabitant. Moreover, Anna barely speaks about historical references such as the years or periods of construction of the buildings. She remains very approximate when she evokes a significant event in the history of the Butte. However, in her discourse, the experience of everyday life in the district is reflected, made possible by a walk where the insignificant occupies almost all the space.

The questions asked by visitors also play a full part in this highlighting of the "the imponderabilia of actual life". The experience of guiding allows the inhabitants to become aware – often with great astonishment the first few times – of the interest shown in the trivial elements of everyday life. However, the impression of naivety gradually gives way to an awareness of oneself, one's environment and the originality it may represent in the eyes of visitors, especially foreigners. In the context of the amateur guided walk, the objects of the ordinary are thus part of a process of valorisation that does not require staging. Moreover, for the French philosopher Frédéric Gros, the practice of walking takes the spectator back to "pleasures at the level of existence: the enjoyment of the elementary. [This] makes it possible for everyone to regain a certain level of authenticity" (Truong 2018, 52). The inhabitant, whose interest in these objects is confirmed by the curiosity of visitors, draws the discursive elements of his narrative from the daily spectacle of his urban environment. In this context, the walk sometimes highlights new spaces on the fringes of the classic circuits, and sometimes allows one to discover some tourist highlights through an ordinary approach.

Places and sensory experiences of the ordinary city

Show the places of daily life

In the context of amateur guided walks, the places shown by the locals may not have any tourist appeal in their original function. They may be supermarkets or private inner courtyards, for example. By showing and mediating places of daily life, the amateur guide helps to make them attractive to tourists. In November 2017, when her *Greeter* walk in Boulogne has just begun, Isabelle discreetly whispers in my ear:

> With me, it's not very intellectual, eh. We walk around like that. It's not at all . . . We're going to go to Picard [chain of frozen food shops], eh? We're going to go into a pastry shop, we're going to go to the market.
>
> (Extract from the field notes of 8 November 2017.
> Translated from French.)

Like her, the guides highlight, with more or less audacity, places considered banal or even, sometimes, ugly. Near the Porte d'Auteuil, Isabelle explains to the two Texan tourists she accompanies how the ring road is perpetually blocked and that several hours are sometimes necessary to go from one point to another.[26] Later, she doesn't hesitate to take the Americans to a supermarket of the *Picard* brand:

> Isabelle: In Paris, everyone has Picard products in their fridge. . . . It's . . . I would say . . . good and of good quality. Good products. It's not cheap. In Boulogne, there are maybe five or six Picard! You'll see . . . You can buy vegetables, you can buy soup. [The American women seem very interested, they follow Françoise, punctuating her speech with "Ohh" of astonishment, they lean over the freezers from which Isabelle takes out a tin of beans or frozen cooked meals].
> (Extract from the field notes of 8 November 2017.
> Translated from French.)

On leaving this supermarket, she offers American women the opportunity to enter the Notre-Dame de Boulogne church, which is on the opposite pavement. Not showing any particular enthusiasm for the announcement of this proposal, one of them reacts: "Oh no, no, we're going to go to *Monoprix* [another widespread supermarket brand]!". A few months later, Isabelle smiles as she remembers this episode during our interview:

> Yes, that's what amuses me! Because the church . . . I have nothing to say about the church. Apart from Jeann D'Arc who passed through there. . . . Anyway, anyway. But as these are not stories I know well . . . You know, [professional guides] are historians. And, well, I don't know about it. These are things I just read.
> (Extract from the interview of 11 January 2018.
> Translated from French.)

Thus, supermarkets, bakeries, squares, disused factories or collaborative gardens are all spaces that make it possible to spatialise and materialise the ordinary city.

Moreover, the sites shown by the local residents can also concern tourist sites, such as monuments. These are approached with both intellectual information and personal anecdotes, often showing an emotional relationship with the place, as described by the French anthropologist Marc Augé: "Memory and history come together in the city. Each of the city's inhabitants has his or her own relationship with the monuments, which themselves bear witness to a deeper and more collective history" (Augé 2013, 135–136). This is how Charles, *Greeter* in the 6th arrondissement, evokes the schooling of his children in one of the most emblematic districts of Paris: Saint-Germain-des-Prés.[27] This example, among others, reveals that the relationship with the capital's heritage monuments and touristic sites is not systematically established in an extraordinary dimension, as Daniel Fabre describes it:

> The identification of groups and individuals with heritage is no longer necessarily based on approved historical knowledge, university or popularised historical knowledge, as schools used to do. This is what work on inhabited monuments or on heritage emotions has revealed to us.
>
> (Fabre 2016, 52)

Therefore, these observations bear witness to the two directions taken by the trajectories of places which make it possible to analyse tourist transformations: on the one hand, the "ordinary" space becoming a tourist attraction, and on the other, the tourist site no longer apprehended in its "extra-ordinary" dimension but through those who live it on a daily basis.

Access to the "backstage area": towards a hybridisation of places?

The American anthropologist Dean MacCannell asserts that the tourist's quest for authenticity is doomed to failure. The tourism industry is adapting to the demands of visitors seeking access to the "backstage" by offering them increasingly realistic "staging" (MacCannell 1989, 101). But the places, practices and objects made accessible by amateur guided walks seem to pose some limits to this analysis. A simple explanation would be to underline that this type of activity is on the fringe of the tourism industry, in the sense that it is a voluntary practice or not paid well enough to live on it. However, the guide-inhabitants play an essential role in the activity. They are the key – through their knowledge of the neighbourhood, or sometimes even because they physically possess a key – to get through the door of a building, to access a narrow alley or to the back shop of a craftsman. The walk represents the only structuring framework for the activity, which limits pre-programmed staging or acting.

Moreover, the ordinary dimension of the activity is not limited to the actors (the guide, the other local residents, the shopkeepers, etc.), to the story of the inhabitant or to the objects that the latter shows to the visitors. But is also part of the senses mobilised through access to certain places. Urban walking brings together the conditions for a sensory confrontation (not always pleasant) with space, through a set of sensitive elements, such as noise, animation or smells. This is what happens when Isabelle invites visitors to become aware of the presence and proximity of the Paris ring road, its traffic, the noise it generates and its place in the landscape.[28] With Louis, during a walk in the Quatre-Chemins district, in the northern suburbs of Paris, we pass a garage where old cars are repaired. He explains: "I know the boss, so sometimes I go in". We stick our heads through the huge door, and he notices the smell of motor oil, adding: "I had an uncle who was a mechanic. When I was young I thought it stank but now I like the smell!".[29] Thus, by experiencing Paris through exploration in a neighbourhood, in contact with an inhabitant, possibly with shopkeepers, by entering a supermarket, a shared garden, by exploring spaces not specially designed to welcome tourists, by being confronted with unwelcoming, sometimes smelly streets, the visitor gets to know the neighbourhood through walking, through his senses and in the same way as the inhabitants experience it on a daily basis.

On the one hand, access to the "backstage" of the capital, allowed through the intermediary of the inhabitants in their role as guides, concerns private places, such as inner courtyards. On the other hand, this access to the "backstage" of the capital also applies to public places, theoretically accessible to visitors but where they do not venture out to, either because they are unaware of their existence or because they do not imagine they have the right to access. This is the case, for example, of France's oldest public library, the Mazarine, within the Institut de France, where Charles takes a Swiss tourist on a cold January morning in 2016.[30] Through these urban walks, tourism does not focus on places created to welcome him. But can we say that tourism continues its dual function of producer[31] and subverter of spaces? After the monuments and historic city centres, tourist attraction is inserted into new interstices where inhabitants and visitors are increasingly brought to interact (Gravari-Barbas 2013). But the transformation of space does not always take place: a co-ownership that decides to change the access code to the courtyard of the building or the limitation to four visitors imposed by the Mazarine library are all barriers or brakes to the hybridisation of space.

Conclusion

Several researchers have been working on the interpretation of *authenticity* staged in various tourist contexts. Davydd J. Greenwood, for example, sees it as a sign of the weakening of society (Greenwood 1989, 183). In her research work in Florès, Indonesia, Maribeth Erb, for her part, sees the ability of individuals to adapt to the new presence of tourists by developing strategies, while maintaining continuity in their practices and beliefs (Erb 2000). Through the desire to show Paris without staging, in an ordinary and daily dimension assimilated to the practices, places and concerns of the locals, the practice of amateur guided walks consists, for its part, in resisting against the distorted scenery of "classic" tourism. Thus, the inhabitants "fight" peacefully against the invisibility of certain places, people (including themselves) and activities which, in their eyes, constitute Paris, and against the dissemination of fake, fantasised and embellished images of the capital. In this context, civil society seems to be demonstrating its desire to separate from the "classic" tourist activity in Paris. The initiative of these inhabitants allows visitors to enter places that were previously confined to daily practices, without a systematic and simultaneous hybridisation of spaces. But the spread of the tourist phenomenon seems to be confronted here with the limits imposed by the other inhabitants who refuse to see their library, building courtyard or neighbourhood grocery shop transformed to adapt to the expectations of outside visitors.

Therefore, in Paris, the inhabitants seem to have acquired a new role in tourist activity in their own city. Their place is more recognised by the political representatives in charge of tourism development. And their involvement can be observed on the field: the ethnographic analysis of the amateur guided tours is proof of this. The Parisian *Greeters'* association is, moreover, the one with the most volunteers in the world, ahead of the (older) association in New York, for example. Some 50 platforms offer activities supervised by non-professionals from the tourism sector: pastry lessons with a retired pastry chef, a ride on the St-Martin canal on a self-service bicycle with a student in art and so forth. These signs can be seen as characteristic of an "after" of tourism where civil society has acquired a new role. This active involvement of the inhabitants goes hand in hand with the evolution of visitors' expectations. If the romantic, classical and extraordinary Paris still attracts many tourists, the expectations also target other parts of the city not initially conceived for passing visitors.

Finally, these developments in Paris are part of a history of tourism that goes back more than three centuries, but also of the recent movements associated with overtourism. Conflicts and crises are often indicative of social phenomena. The health crisis linked to COVID-19 is, of course, a new example. Restrictions on travel have favoured the development of local tourism. Then, the spread of tourism in the interstices of the city could encourage, in this context, an "exoticism" of the local population. However, although tourism has played an important role in the production and transformation of spaces (Gravari–Barbas 2013), it remains to be seen whether the involvement of the inhabitants will also promote such changes in the "ordinary" places of everyday life.

Notes

1 The term "unstaged authenticity" refers to the "staged authenticity" described and analysed by Dean MacCannell in MacCannell Dean 1989 [First edition: 1976]. *The Tourist: A New Theory of the Leisure Class.* New York: Schocken Books, https://doi.org/10.108 0/11745398.2014.890513.
2 Source: www.youtube.com/watch?v=yV2HSv-dwEI.
3 Jalil Lespert is a French actor, screenwriter and director.
4 Alain Ducasse is a French chef who operates a number of restaurants including one which holds three stars (the top ranking) in the *Michelin Guide.*
5 Source: www.youtube.com/watch?v=e_M807HAe2c.
6 2018 data. Source: Association "Parisiens d'un jour-Paris Greeters".
7 The *Cariboo* company has teamed up with another platform called *Meetrip*, which offers a professional tourist guide service.
8 *Wide Trip* introduces itself as: "Local and new experience to discover France off the beaten track". Source: https://www.widetrip.fr
9 I mobilise the notion of "authenticity" following the approach of the American anthropologist Edward Bruner, who sees it as "a diversion that should only be studied when tourists, locals or producers themselves use the term". The observation of its use in practice and discourse leads to an analysis of its indigenous meanings and representations. In this regard, when the indigenous perspective of a concept (-emic) is considered, it is indicated in quotation marks, while when it is understood as an analytical term

(-etic), it is shown in italics. Bruner, Edward M. 2005. *Culture on Tour: Ethnographies of Travel.* Chicago: University of Chicago Press, p. 5.

10 Extract from the interview of 7 July 2017.
11 Source: Field notes, 5 February 2016.
12 Extract from the interview of 11 July 2018. Translated from French.
13 Extract from the interview of 11 January 2018. Translated from French.
14 Source: Field notes of 12 July 2018.
15 Source: Field notes of 5 February 2016.
16 Extract from field notes of 21 July 2016.
17 Extract from the interview of 21 December 2017.
18 Extract from the interview of 7 July 2017.
19 Extract from field notes of 27 January 2016.
20 Extract from the interview of 11 January 2018.
21 Extract from field notes of 18 February 2016.
22 Extract from field notes of 25 January 2016.
23 Source: Field notes of 21 July 2016.
24 Extract from field notes of 25 July 2016.
25 Source: Field notes of 7 March 2018.
26 Source: Field notes of 8 November 2017.
27 Source: Field notes of 20 January 2016.
28 Source: Field notes of 8 November 2017.
29 Extract from field notes of 25 January 2016. Translated from French.
30 Source: Field notes of 20 January 2016.
31 To the term "production" can be added that of "invention of place" which the geographer Rémy Knafou describes as "a new use of an existing place that results in both subverting and enlarging it". Knafou Rémy, 1991, "L'invention du lieu touristique: la passation d'un contrat et le surgissement simultané d'un nouveau territoire." *Revue de Géographie Alpine* 79(4): 11–19, www.persee.fr/doc/rga_0035-1121_1991_num_79_4_3624, p. 11.

Bibliography

Augé Marc. 2013. *L'impossible voyage. Le tourisme et ses images.* Paris: Éditions Payot & Rivages (First edition: 1997).

Erb, Maribeth. 2000. "Understanding Tourists Interpretations from Indonesia." *Annals of Tourism Research* 27(3): 709–736, https://doi.org/10.1016/S0160-7383(99)00102-4.

Fabre, Daniel. 2016. "L'ordinaire, le familier, l'intime . . . loin du monument." In *Le tournant patrimonial: Mutations contemporaines des métiers du patrimoine*, edited by Christian Hottin and Claudie Voisenat. Paris: Éditions de la Maison des sciences de l'Homme, pp. 43–58.

Goffman, Erving. 1973. *La mise en scène de la vie quotidienne. 1: La présentation de soi.* Paris: Les Éditions de Minuit.

Gravari-Barbas, Maria. 2013. *Aménager la ville par la culture et le tourisme.* Paris: Éditions le Moniteur.

Greenwood, Davydd J. 1989. "Culture by the Pound: An Anthropological Perspective on Tourism as Cultural Commodization." In *Hosts and Guests: The Anthropology of Tourism*, edited by Valene Smith. Philadelphia: University of Pennsylvania Press (First edition: 1977).

Le Breton, David. 2012. *Marcher. Éloge des chemins de la lenteur.* Paris: Éditions Métailié.

Loisy, Marine. 2019. "Tourism and Involvement of Inhabitants in Paris." *International Journal of Tourism Cities* 5(3): 326–337, https://doi.org/10.1108/IJTC-01-2018-0006.

MacCannell, Dean. 1989. *The Tourist: A New Theory of the Leisure Class.* New York: Schocken Books (First edition: 1976), https://doi.org/10.1080/11745398.2014.890513.

Malinowski, Bronislaw. 2005. *Argonauts of the Western Pacific: An Account of Native Enterprise and Adventure in the Archipelagoes of Melanesian New Guinea*. London: Taylor & Francis e-Library (First edition: 1922).

Sagnes, Sylvie. 2010. "Suivez le guide. . .: De l'Autre à soi, ou comment devenir monument." *Ethnologies* 32(2): 81–101, https://doi.org/10.7202/1006306ar.

Truong, Nicolas. 2018. *Philosophie de la marche*. La Tour-d'Aigues: Éditions de l'Aube.

3 Shopping as a tourist spectacle

How Paris's shops blur the edges between tourists, foreign residents and Parisians themselves

Sophie Chevalier and Emmanuelle Lallement

Introduction

What could be more ordinary in Parisian daily life than a market, food shop, boutique or even a department store? All these businesses form part of the urban landscape; they are deeply ingrained in the city's history and architecture, often as the backbone of social interaction between city dwellers. They are also attractive spots for tourists – from department stores that are now set up as tourist destinations, especially for Asian customers, to food markets in the central districts that convey a typical Parisian image, and the various food-related businesses *(commerces de bouche)* that showcase typically French or Parisian *savoir-faire*, such as pastry, cheese and wine shops.

The shops themselves, places of daily or occasional consumption, structure space and time in everyday life. They help understand what is typical of the city. This is why some shops have become tourist "hotspots". This chapter examines how some of Paris's commercial places have become part of the city's cultural heritage.[1] How do the shops and businesses that shape the city's everyday life influence what tourists do? How have these ordinary places become part of how visitors imagine the city? And for whom are they a tourist attraction?

Shops have been attractive destinations for travellers in large European cities such as Paris and London at least since the eighteenth century (Coquery 2011). The shops of pre-revolutionary Paris were not ordinary, but luxury or semi-luxury businesses. We are interested here in a more recent phenomenon which is how everyday shops have begun to attract tourists.

We are anthropologists of urban and contemporary society rather than tourism experts. But any anthropologist interested in cities today cannot ignore the political, economic and symbolic work invested by local authorities in preserving distinctive local identities. This is especially true for the city of Paris. The importance of this city promotion has grown as a result of competition induced by globalisation. As everyone knows, the city is one of the world's prime tourist destinations. In 2019, the Paris metropolitan area welcomed 38 million tourists, a record year. Paris thus ranks ahead of London, which welcomed 21 million tourists in the same year.[2] According to the *Paris Tourism Economic Observatory* in 2018 (Office du Tourisme et des Congrès de Paris 2019), its attractiveness is

DOI: 10.4324/9781003138600-5

due to the traditional cultural heritage on offer. Events too are significant, such as exhibitions at the Musée d'Orsay or the Fondation Louis Vuitton, as well as major sporting events. It notes that Paris has been featured in major films, such as *Mission: Impossible* and *Fantastic Beasts*[3] (Office du Tourisme et des Congrès de Paris 2019).

We came to the question of Paris's tourist attractiveness through our shared research interest in the links between cities and shopping (Chevalier 2007, 2018; Lallement 2010) and the movement of people in contemporary capitals. This chapter draws on a study we carried out for the City of Paris (Chevalier et al. 2013)[4] in the last decade. Our ethnological survey looked at foreign "secondary residents" in Paris outsiders who buy or rent apartments in the city and the local businesses who serve them. They are long-term visitors, as they usually stay in the city longer than ordinary tourists. Sometimes one month, sometimes one week each month, sometimes more . . . they are really different figures of urban tourism which is usually characterised by short-term stays.[5] But we also analysed here a particular population that differed from the *repeater* tourists studied by Tim Freytag (2008). We studied visitors who saw themselves as being beyond mere "tourists" in that they were looking for a more daily type of city's experience by living and behaving like "residents".

We interviewed secondary residents all over Paris, usually in their homes. We concentrated our inquiries on the 4th arrondissement which has a high proportion of these residents. Some real estate agents there claim, based on their sales, that secondary residents account for 70% of local homeowners. This is certainly a hot issue for politics in such areas. Who are the foreigners who buy apartments in Paris? We didn't collect a sample, but we can generalise about some aspects of a common profile. They have many different origins: of course, Europeans and after them, Americans, but also Canadians, Brazilians and Middle Easterners. They are usually upper middle class, but their professional profiles vary considerably. The size, quality and location of their apartments indicate a wide range of income levels. The forms of tenure are equally variable: rental, ownership, condominium, timeshare. Buying an apartment is usually a project for a couple, with children rarely involved. A variety of actors mediate their experience of a neighbourhood, people who offer direct services or otherwise help to construct Paris's image and attractiveness.

These tourism figures do not take account of the fact that Paris is receiving visitors of other types. These may give a miss to the usual places of interest (the Eiffel Tower, the Louvre, etc.), preferring to take part in ordinary city life. Our research on these long-term visitors focused on what they found attractive in *la vie Parisienne*, a life that they contribute to occasionally shape by their use of the city. They are one type of "Parisian". For this reason, we examine social behaviour in concrete space, representations of the city, social interactions, perceptions and dreams that contribute to the Parisian "scene". They play their part in creating the image and "myth" of Paris.

Our study is of tourists who want to "live like the locals". They stay away from popular tourist attractions or go there only when Parisians visit them (in winter or outside the holiday seasons). What makes Paris familiar to them, they hope, is its resemblance to how the permanent residents experience the city. They want to participate in the daily life of the locals and to interact with people outside the tourism economy. Freytag (2008) notes that regular visitors to the capital consider proximity to the local population to be essential to distinguish these "regulars" from other tourists passing through. The aim is to find opportunities as close as possible to "ordinary" behaviour. This can also be seen in the growing appeal of home rentals, which is what *Airbnb* offers to tourists visiting Paris.[6] Since 2015, this phenomenon has become so massive in Paris that it has invited strong regulation of rentals such that an owner who wants to rent out a flat is obliged to declare it for authorisation. This has not prevented *Airbnb* from advertising their Parisian offers on their website and in promotional videos featuring not just flats but entire neighbourhoods, along with "authentic" scenes of everyday life. The experience of Parisian life on offer is more in line with the life of the inhabitants than a tourist visit.

This chapter will show the place and role played by shops as ordinary places in the city and in the commercial practices of foreign secondary residents, whose form of "tourism after tourism" is typical of their life in Paris.

"Re-enchanting" ordinary places

These foreign secondary residents know that they do not live like Parisians, even if this is what they want; but the frequency of their visits and their daily routines in the city set them apart from tourists. In our survey, we were struck by the importance secondary residents attached to shopping: shopkeepers are important actors because they are a distinctive part of a neighbourhood. The idea of a neighbourhood as a village is a central part of Parisian identity. To visit the butcher and walk around a market, to go to the baker to buy some croissants or to take a coffee on the sidewalk are key moments in establishing a relationship with Paris, and in "performing" a Parisian way of life. The city had 28 shops per 1,000 inhabitants in 2017 compared with 18 in London; and City Hall makes much of this when listing Paris's attractions.[7] The same is true for our target population, for whom the social interactions and distinctive places generated by shopping are central to how they imagine their life in Paris.

Visiting small local shops accounts for a large part of these secondary residents' consumption. "As soon as we arrive, we go shopping", explained an Italian couple in their sixties who own a studio in the heart of Paris. Historically a student district because of the Sorbonne University, this area has now been gentrified. As soon as they get off the plane ("Turin – Paris, it's only a few hours!"), "shopping" in their neighbourhood's main street provides a pleasurable mix of familiarity and exoticism. It allows them to feel "at home" in a place that is only occasionally one. They can reconnect with the city and feel comfortable almost immediately. These local errands renew their acquaintance with favourite shops and walks every time: "You know, it's become a habit, I go to buy *Le Monde* newspaper every day, then I sit down somewhere for a coffee or something, and I read it. It suits me perfectly and I have the impression of participating in Parisian life", explains Hillary, an American who comes every year to her vast apartment behind the Champs-Élysées.

The pleasure of frequenting shops, especially food shops, also stems from the fact that they give an "identity thrill" at a small cost, as De la Pradelle (2006) had shown for local residents and tourists in the small-town market of Carpentras in Provence. French food and drink made our informants feel they really were in Paris. "When we arrive, we buy wine and the cheese", Antonella and Fabrizio told us. These are so many clichés, of course, but they score high on the scale of symbolic effectiveness when living the Parisian experience.

Besides shops in the central district that perpetuate a certain local lifestyle, food markets also produce a similar thrill of local experience. "I love it here. We have a wonderful market – you know the market on rue Montorgueil?" asks Doug, an American journalist and food critic in his spare time, who has been visiting this market close to the historic Les Halles for years.[8] Hillary too praises the "wonderful market on Avenue du President Wilson that takes place on Wednesdays and Saturdays", but this one is different because it is located in a posh residential area. Many spoke of discovering stalls where "you can't help but buy a few cheeses", along with the spectacle of stacked goods and the know-how of the vendors.

Paris's department stores are also very popular with tourists. The best known of these are on Boulevard Haussman, behind the Opera; they have been major shopping hubs since their invention in the late nineteenth century. The "Galeries Lafayette" and the "Printemps" department stores are for occasional visits, not daily shopping, but remain a central reference point for purchases considered to be typically Parisian, especially for gifts to take back home. Nicole, a Californian, sometimes goes there for this purpose, choosing brands that she (and the recipients) associate with Paris, like *Longchamp*, known for its leather products. "I also bring back scarves from *Le Bon Marché*", she adds. This department store, the first one in Paris,[9] portrayed by Émile Zola in *The Ladies' Paradise* (1883),[10] is now itself a Parisian souvenir, inscribed on the bag containing the gift. Although French luxury products are now found throughout the world, Parisian luxury bought on the spot still exerts its appeal. A young Emirati woman, whenever she passes through Paris, without fail visits the *Chanel* store on rue du Faubourg Saint-Honoré. In her eyes it is "so Parisian", very different from the same items on sale in Dubai's shopping malls.

All of these shopping venues constitute the fabric of everyday life for Parisians even if they don't shop often in those places! They may seem ordinary to local inhabitants, even if they are thought to be rather chic, but they are gradually becoming Parisian "heritage sites." Department stores form something of a hybrid category for Parisians: they may visit them regularly for everyday items and more rarely for gifts or for the animated window displays at Christmas. For both categories, the big stores are associated with luxury or semi-luxury consumer goods, but they are now often seen as embodying Paris' history and heritage, a process driven in large part by the huge volume of visitors.[11]

These city locations and the behaviour they support appeal to a logic of enchantment, especially for tourists, as Winkin (1996) shows in his study of tourist attractions. Residents can oscillate between participating in the pleasure afforded by familiar habits (as Parisians do) and enchantment by the exotic (as tourists do). Moving between these perspectives allows them, almost at will, to freeze in time places, atmospheres and "eternal" signs of Paris, thereby providing a pool of images to complement their ordinary Parisian lives.

Certain aspects of these ordinary practices – like drinking coffee at a bar counter – constitute images of Paris that circulate globally, as the culture industries and tourism agencies know well. How the secondary residents make *their* Paris conforms to what anthropologist Augé (1997) called a logic of recognition. During each stay, they can pick encounters and activities that afford them pleasure in the city, *their* city.

Is their "Parisian" identity informal, because it lacks institutional legitimacy, so different from what Parisians themselves preserve and promote through their local institutions? What does it say about how ordinary places of business become sites of cultural interest for tourists? And who are the actors involved in this material and symbolic process?

Processes and actors in the "enchantment" of "ordinary" places

Food markets serving "neighbourhood" life

Paris's food markets appear to be local; they contribute to the identity of a neighbourhood, while being very circumscribed in space and time – at least the outdoor ones. Likewise, for many, these are places for neighbourly encounters when mutual acquaintance is strong. In their small way, they produce tourist enchantment, whether local or global.

A telling sign: the City of Paris website does not feature food markets in its "practical life" section, but under "leisure." The tab for marketplaces lists the information for more than 80 "markets and booksellers" in the capital. This category groups together district food markets, the second-hand booksellers along the banks of the Seine, flea markets, flower markets, book markets and garage sales. The logic of this grouping is because they come under the same administrative category, "non-sedentary shops", perhaps also because they reflect the same image of Paris as a "city with eighty villages" (Hazan 2002, 20). This is intended primarily for the Parisians themselves who want to reside in "friendly" neighbourhoods with "good shopping". But it also appeals to tourists, presenting them a local way of life that is authentically Parisian. Food markets are key to this staging of Parisian neighbourhood life. Their places among the "neighbourhood hubs" convey a particular geography of the city, since each district is divided into several areas corresponding to the names of their respective markets. The Raspail market in the posh 6th arrondissement, the Bobillot market in the 13th arrondissement to the south of the city, the Montorgueil market in the central 1st arrondissement, the Batignolles market in the 17th arrondissement, and finally the more working-class La Villette market in the north – all these paint a picture of Paris that seems to respond perfectly to the local and picturesque image. The markets also punctuate time in the city and, depending on whether they are covered or open-air, these have a particular rhythm – usually weekly, but sometimes daily – and this is important in neighbourhood life.

Urban shopping hubs: more than a backdrop?

The shopping hubs in downtown urban areas (mainly shops for fashion or interior design) are found in the main tourist areas and open on Sundays.[12] Tensions sometimes arises between the local inhabitants and outside visitors. This is especially true if the goods on offer – international brands supplied by chain stores – reduces the distinctive character of a neighbourhood. The rue des Francs Bourgeois in Paris's famous Marais district is emblematic of this. It is perceived as being typically Parisian and has a strong cultural presence – museums and townhouses *(hôtels particuliers)*. But tourists gravitate to the possibilities for deep shopping in small designer boutiques offering Parisian brands, while recognising as familiar the chain stores lining the streets. World capitals everywhere and even airport duty free zones share this commercial fabric. Brands like *Kooples, Nespresso* and *Maje* can be found in the Marais in Dubai alike. "Invaded" as they are by strolling crowds of tourists and suburbanites, the local inhabitants admit to "no longer going out in the street at weekends" because they don't feel "at home" anymore (from an interview with a local resident). Permanent residents here compete for control of their territory with crowds of visitors, and they also believe that they own a monopoly of the place's proper image.

Anti-tourist movements have emerged in several European capitals recently,[13] with Barcelona being a prime example. This movement is not noticeable in Paris. But voices have been raised against the transformation of some Paris neighbourhoods into "open-air shopping centres", intended for a non-local population, as one resident put it. Voices are becoming louder and have been a subject of debate, even controversy, for several years. As early as 2011, the weekly magazine *Le Point* provided a little history of shopping establishments in the Marais and noted that "the risk of [this area] becoming another Saint-Germain[14] with its luxury boutiques is real. There is also a speculative madness affecting all areas", according to Dominique Bertinotti, then mayor of the 4th arrondissement. "All the brands want to set up shops here. Yet the district town hall keeps an eye on them. For example, the *Cos* brand had to respect the tradition of the old Turkish baths where its shop is located."[15] In fact, the company just kept the façade but completely destroyed the interior of the building!

The heritage dimension of any neighbourhood is a sensitive matter which the real estate sector tries to turn in its favour by making the conservation of architecture and local memory a marketing point. The *Libération* daily explained in 2014:[16]

> *Uniqlo* is now setting up shop in one of Paris' last factories built on rue des Francs-Bourgeois in 1860. . . . Heritage conservation was one of the keys to its establishment here, a heritage little known to Parisians themselves. If the building had been torn down and rebuilt, *Uniqlo* would have drawn the wrath of its neighbours. The store is now spread out over three floors under a large glass roof and is dominated by a huge red-brick fireplace. The machines are still there, visible through glass floors that the Japanese casual wear "giant" will be happy to show on Heritage Days.

The authenticity of buildings hardly conceals the commercial standardisation at work in all cities. From being places where local norms are expected in everyday life, retail outlets become over time become globalised and filled with images that tend to exclude or alienate the locals. But this widespread phenomenon, following town planner Mangin (2004), shows how shops, the current backdrop for "franchised" town planning, now aim for a clientele of urban tourists with varied profiles: commuters strolling the streets of the Marais on Saturdays, Japanese visitors who come to smell the air of Parisian creativity or North Americans in search of a "shopping experience *à la Parisienne*". The inhabitants yearn to see their streets "empty" again during weekends and the holidays, as they are now only early in the morning before the crowds arrive. All they want is the freedom to enjoy their local familiar places in peace.

Department stores

Finally, Paris's department stores represent heritage landmarks illustrating the increasing significance of retail spaces for tourism. These stores are close together and form typically Parisian "commercial hubs". They contribute to the city's identity as a whole – Paris as the world's shopping capital – in several districts: Boulevard Haussmann, the Hôtel de Ville and the Sèvres district (including *Bon Marché*).

As Chabault reminds us in *Eloge du magasin*:

> In the capital, the department stores have become the showcase of French ready-to-wear, elegance and good taste. Today they are tourist attractions as branding the city seeks to attract an international traffic by means of publicity campaigns and by creating links with tour operators.
>
> (Chabault 2020, 119)

Department stores have become tourist places that are visited in the same way as the Eiffel Tower. Building on the image of Paris, they have positioned themselves as the privileged symbols of French fashion and luxury and have oriented their strategy towards "chic and expensive" goods for years. "Parisian chic", so often highlighted in the tourist image of France, is combined here with international "fashion". Customers from all over the world look to these department stores as temples of consumption, but also of globalisation, with all the international brands.

A study commissioned by Paris's Urbanism Agency in the early 2000s stressed the importance of foreign tourists who see department stores as destinations in themselves. More than shops, they have now become "cultural sites" to be visited like a beauty spot, monument or museum, just as we would go to see a show.[17] The main actors in the "touristification" of department stores are the stores themselves – at *Galeries Lafayette*, foreign customers contribute half of sales. They set up "organised tours" guided by hostesses of different nationalities, carry out promotional activities in target countries and develop duty-free zones. But the city itself also plays a role through the Tourist Office. The weight of department stores in promoting the capital's attractiveness was reflected in 2015 and 2016 when a fall in the number of foreign tourists visiting Paris's stores was mentioned by the press in the same breath as a similar reduction in attendance at museums and monuments: "The attacks in France, the strikes and the feeling of insecurity scared foreign tourists away in 2016. This had a heavy impact on the Parisian luxury trade and the hotel industry" (*L'Expansion*[18]).

Here is another example of tension between local and tourist customers. At the height of the tourist season, coaches pour in with floods of foreigners. As *Galeries Lafayette*'s managing director admits, this doesn't suit the French customers.[19] This store wants to bring back individual Parisian customers. It acquired a commercial space on Boulevard Haussmann for a store aiming to welcome groups of tourists, mainly Chinese, who come to shop in the capital. According to the *Le Parisien* daily:[20]

> Signs in Mandarin. A selection of items sought after by the Chinese. Asian vendors. Welcome to the *Galeries Lafayette* duty-free which opened this Thursday evening. Since the opening, dozens of tourist coaches have offloaded hundreds of visitors from the Middle Kingdom every day into 21 boulevard Haussmann's open doors.

In this entirely redesigned space,[21] the items Chinese are particularly fond of are on sale: jewellery, leather goods, delicatessen, macaroons and souvenirs labelled "Paris." Much like the duty-free shop at Charles de Gaulle Airport, this space represents Paris's most cliched goods, without competing with the original department store. The latter is still considered the "flagship" store, under the famous dome, housing the most expensive luxury brands for an "upmarket clientele", both French and foreign. These are joined by products of its own brand intended for smaller budgets and for more ordinary and local consumption. In this "Ladies' paradise", now as Parisian as it is globalised, the sociology of consumers no longer distinguishes between tourists and local citizens.

Conclusion

Parisian shops play a major part in building up what the inhabitants usually think of as ordinary places as an integral feature of what makes Paris attractive to tourists. This phenomenon is based less on the goods offered, which are very ordinary or standardised because they are globalised, than on the places themselves, sometimes turned into heritage, and on how they fit into the city. They are much more than shops for the long-term visitors we studied. They provide a function that is ultimately as important as those other cultural places that Paris lovers can visit. Secondary residents, with their "in-between" position, highlight the paradoxes and social tensions caused by these contemporary social transformations. They are never fully caught up in the enchantment of places, because they are only half tourists and half resident like their Paris neighbours. Secondary residents are foreigners in the eyes of Parisians, but they remind them of how their familiar world is constructed and above all contingent. As Bégout (2005, 424) explains of the everyday world: "Without even seeking to question them, the foreign world, by its mere presence, puts its finger on the limitation of the familiar world and on the constructed character of its everyday life".

This constructed familiar world is, in Paris as elsewhere, subject to multiple transformations. Its actors and places are many: politicians, shopkeepers, long-term Parisian householders, secondary residents and tourists. All play a role in redefining how a locality is imagined and sometimes spread globally. Most Parisians are proud of their way of life and of the city that makes it possible. They want ordinary (high-quality) businesses in their area to support neighbourly social life and to offer everyday goods. Politicians and shop owners are trying to find a balance between the need to satisfy permanent residents – who vote and consume daily – and to attract as many tourists as possible, so that Paris can remain one of the world's great capital cities.

Notes

1 French *patrimoine* does not translate easily into English, variously as patrimony, legacy, inheritance or heritage. Here, although it sometimes reads awkwardly, we use the term "heritage" throughout.
2 See: www.cityoflondon.gov.uk/things-to-do/tourism-trends-and-strategies/tourism-statistics
3 Mission: Impossible is a series of American action spy films since 1996. *Fantastic Beasts and Where to Find Them* is a British-American fantasy movie with a worldwide commercial success since 2016.
4 This research was carried out with the support of Mairie de Paris as part of the "Paris 2030" research programme between 2009 and 2011. It led to the writing of a research report and to the publication of a monograph.
5 See Christophe Guibert, Mohamed Reda Khomsi and Nicola Bellini (2019).
6 Sixty thousand properties were available on Airbnb in Paris in 2019. With an occupancy rate of 51% (Office du Tourisme et des Congrès de Paris 2019), Paris is the city with the largest number of Airbnb accommodations in the world. See: http://insideairbnb.com

7 Database Apur, L'évolution des commerces à Paris – Inventaire des commerces 2017 et évolutions 2014–2017, www.apur.org/fr/nos-travaux/evolution-commerces-paris-inventaire-commerces-2017-evolutions-2014-2017.

8 *Les Halles*, a fresh-food market in the centre of Paris, was built by architect Victor Baltard in the middle of the nineteenth century and described by the novelist Émile Zola as *The Belly of Paris*. The market was torn down in 1971 despite strong opposition.

9 A first shop was founded in 1838, before moving to its current location in 1869.

10 It was "the cathedral of modern commerce . . . for a nation of customers."

11 The building and decor of the *Galeries Lafayette* are protected in law by the ministry of Culture.

12 International Tourist Zones (ZTI) are geographical areas where businesses are allowed to open on Sundays and late in the evening in order to meet the need to develop France's tourist economic potential. The 12 international tourist areas in Paris were designated in August 2015 by the "Law for growth, activity and equal economic opportunities" with the aim of adapting the conditions for opening shops on Sundays and in the evening to the reality of the tourist frequentation of towns. Source: www.economie.gouv.fr/entreprises/creation-zones-touristiques-internationales-paris-ZTI.

13 See the interview with Maria Gravari-Barbas in Socgéo: https://socgeo.com/2017/08/21/maria-gravari-barbas-le-tourisme-necessite-une-gouvernance-drastique-et-efficace-prenant-veritablement-en-compte-les-interets-des-uns-et-des-autres/

14 This refers to when St Germain des Prés in the 6th arrondissement was no longer home to writers, intellectuals and publishers but became a high-end shopping area with a succession of clothing shops in its streets.

15 *Le Point*, "Le quartier où il faut vivre? Tendance. Le Marais est plus que jamais le quartier parisien à la mode." A. Emery et V. Peiffer, published 15 December 2011 at 02:42.

16 *Libération*, "Uniqlo et H&M se jettent dans Le Marais", M. Ottavi, 9 April 2014 at 12:31.

17 "Asians are the top foreign customers (40%) of Galeries Lafayette Haussmann, ahead of Europeans (35%) and North Americans (11%). Next come Russian and Middle Eastern clienteles. Chinese customers mainly buy perfumes and accessories (Berger lamps, Omega watches) and are particularly fond of the major fashion brands as they embody luxury and French know-how. Japanese customers, the number-one Asian buyers, show a particular interest in the big names specialising in French leather goods such as Louis Vuitton or Christian Dior." *Place et avenir des grands magasins parisiens, éléments clés du patrimoine économique de la capitale*, Apur, April 2006.

18 *L'Expansion*, "2016: Pire année pour l'hôtellerie depuis 2009" 4 January 2017.

19 "Despite the strong presence of tourists in Galeries Lafayette, Parisians remain the main buyers in our stores and their loyalty is very important to us," explains Nicolas Houzé, the group's director. "We believe that the invasion of Asian tourists into our stores can intimidate French customers, which is why we are trying to improve the flow of visitors in our establishments," he added. https://fashionunited.fr/actualite/retail/galeries-lafayette-re-nove-son-image-pour-capter-une-cliente-le-parisienne/201509219952

20 *Le Parisien*, "Paris: les Galeries Lafayette ont ouvert leur annexe . . . pour touristes chinois", C. Henry with C. Robinet, 23 March 2017.

21 By Ito Morabito, also known as Ora-ïto, who designed many such commercial spaces (boutiques, cinemas, etc.).

Bibliography

Apur. 2006. *Place et avenir des grands magasins parisiens, éléments clés du patrimoine économique de la capitale*, April, https://docplayer.fr/867230-Place-et-avenir-des-grands-magasins-parisiens-elements-cles-du-patrimoine-economique-de-la-capitale.html.

Augé, Marc. 1997. *L'impossible voyage: Le tourisme et ses images*. Paris: Payot & Rivages.

Bégout, Bruce. 2005. *La découverte du quotidien*. Paris: Allia.

Chabault, Vincent. 2020. *Eloge du magasin. Contre l'amazonisation*. Paris: Le débat, Gallimard.

Chevalier, Sophie. 2007. *Faire ses courses en voisin: Pratiques d'approvisionnement et sociabilité dans l'espace de trois quartiers de centre-ville*. Paris: Lyon et Besançon, www.revue-metro poles.com.

Chevalier, Sophie. 2018. "Shopping." In *The International Encyclopedia of Anthropology*, edited by Hilary Callan. New York: John Wiley & Sons, https://doi.org/10.1002/9781118924396. wbiea2202.

Chevalier, Sophie, Lallement Emmanuelle and Corbille Sophie. 2011. *Paris 2030, Territoire de Résidences Secondaires?* Paris: Research Report for the City of Paris.

Chevalier, Sophie, Lallement Emmanuelle and Corbillé Sophie. 2013. *Paris résidence secondaire. Enquête chez ces habitants d'un nouveau genre*. Paris: Belin.

Coquery, Natacha. 2011. *Tenir boutique à Paris, au XVIIIème siècle, Luxe et demi luxe*. Paris: CTHS.

Crossick, Geoffrey and Jaumain Serge (eds.). 2019. *Cathedrals of Consumption: European Department Stores, 1850–1939*. London: Routledge.

De la Pradelle, Michèle. 2006. *Market Day in Provence*. Chicago: University of Chicago Press.

Freytag, Tim. 2008. "Making a Difference: Tourist Practices of Repeat Visitors in the City of Paris." *Social Geography Discussions* 4: 1–25.

Guibert, Christophe, Reda Khomsi Mohamed and Bellini Nicola. 2019. "Enjeux et défis du "tourisme urbain." *Téoros* 38(1), 15 January 2019, http://journals.openedition.org/ teoros/3502.

Hazan, Eric. 2002. *L'Invention de Paris*. Paris: Seuil.

Lallement, Emmanuelle. 2010. *La ville marchande. Enquête à Barbès*. Paris: Téraèdre.

Lallement, Emmanuelle. 2013. "La ville marchande: une approche ethnologique." *Espaces-Temps.net*. www.espacestemps.net/articles/la-ville-marchande-une-approche-ethnolo gique-2/.

Masset, Claire. 2010. *Department Stores*. London: Shire Publications.

Miller, Daniel. 1998. *A Theory of Shopping*. Cambridge: Polity.

Miller, Daniel. 2001. *Dialectics of Shopping*. Chicago: Chicago University Press.

Négoces dans la ville. 2005. "Ethnologie Française." https://te.booksc.org/book/27296407/ b0038e.

Office du tourisme et des Congrès de Paris. 2019. "Le Tourisme à Paris. Chiffres clés 2018." https://pro.parisinfo.com/etudes-et-chiffres/chiffres-cles.

Ritzer, Georges. 2010. *Enchanting a Disenchanted World: Continuity and Change in the Cathedrals of Consumption*. London: Sage.

Whitaker, Jan. 2006. *Service and Style: How the American Department Store Fashioned the Middle Class*. London: St. Martin's Press.

Winkin, Yves. 1996. *Anthropologie de la communication: de la théorie au terrain*. Bruxelles: Editions De Boeck.

Zukin, Sharon, Kasinitz Philip and Chen Xiangming. 2015. *Global Cities, Local Streets: Everyday Diversity from New York to Shanghai*. London: Routledge.

Newspapers

Le Parisien. 2017. "Paris: les Galeries Lafayette ont ouvert leur annexe . . . pour touristes chinois." *Le Parisien*, C. Henry and C. Robinet, 23 March.

Le Point. 2011. "Le quartier où il faut vivre? Tendance. Le Marais est plus que jamais le quartier parisien à la mode." A. Emery and V. Peiffer, 15 December, https://fr.wikipedia. org/wiki/Le_Marais_(quartier_parisien).

Sophie Chevalier and Emmanuelle Lallement

L'Expansion. 2017. "2016: Pire année pour l'hôtellerie depuis 2009." 4 January, https://www.challenges.fr/economie/france-2016-pire-annee-pour-l-hotellerie-depuis-2009_445862.

Libération. 2014. "Uniqlo et H&M se jettent dans Le Marais." 9 April, https://www.liberation.fr/mode/2014/04/25/uniqlo-un-pied-dans-le-marais_1004604/.

4 The emergence of co-production tourism beyond commercial tourism?

Alain Girard and Bernard Schéou

The emergence of co-production tourism beyond commercial tourism?

This text addresses the question of "after-tourism" through two different practices of hospitality that are experiencing significant growth thanks to dedicated online platforms. Both meet a criterion of externality to tourism: non-commercial accommodation. They constitute two ways of travelling for leisure without using tourist accommodation, excluding staying with family or friends.[1] By making the ordinary inhabited space of residents a place for "tourists" to stay, these practices also seem to mark a shift of the criterion by which tourism has often been defined in the humanities: that of leaving an ordinary inhabited space in order to experience an extraordinary setting, creating a break from everyday life.

In this chapter we have chosen to use the word "tourism" to designate all leisure travel,[2] whether trips are commercial or non-commercial. Thus, we consider after-tourism not in terms of an "exit from tourism" but of the rise of co-production tourism which would put an end to the hegemony of commercial tourism.

We speak of co-production tourism rather than of "collaboration". We distinguish the collaborative organisation from the co-productive organisation. In the collaborative-economy model, the separation between producers and consumers is maintained, and the model of exchange on a market is renewed.[3] A third party allows individuals (as opposed to businesses) to be producers of market services and enables consumers to benefit from prices that are lower than the standard offer. We can only be sceptical about the transformation potential of this kind of collaborative economy, which in tourism can refer to the "Airbnb" model. Indeed, the massive entry of non-professional individuals into the commercial offer of services is leading to the development of low-quality jobs, which risks eliminating standard full-time jobs. In contrast, co-production avoids separation between producers and consumers, and tends towards creating a community of users where the prevailing forces are usage value and connections between people.

DOI: 10.4324/9781003138600-6

The first type of hospitality practice analysed, frequently referred to as "Couchsurfing"[4] since the mid-2000s, involves accommodating at home travellers who one does not know, and/or being received in a stranger's home. This hospitality takes place between strangers, and with no obligation regarding reciprocity. Any member of the network is free to host and/or be hosted, and can thus enter a chain of "giving – receiving – returning" hospitality; this does not prevent some members from using the network only to "take advantage" of being hosted for free. We link these hospitality practices to the logic of gift giving, because there is neither financial compensation (direct or indirect) for accommodation, nor equivalence in kind (which is the characteristic of non-market exchanges).[5]

The second set of practices relates to reciprocal exchanges of accommodation, for holiday purposes, between people (often families) who, again, do not know each other initially. The two partner households agree on the terms of the exchange beforehand, and each lends the use of their home to the other only because the other does the same. According to the distinction between gift and non-market exchange (Testart 2006), these practices fall under non-market exchange, that is to say "bartering", as was expressed by the name of the French version of HomeExchange until 2018 (www.trocmaison.com).[6] The aim of equivalence, as opposed to gifting, is manifest here. Guestoguest[7] introduced flexibility into this principle of equivalence by allowing non-simultaneous reciprocal exchanges and by introducing a kind of local currency ("guestpoints") that can be used within the community. Any household can agree to lend their accommodation in exchange for guestpoints credit; they can then use this credit to secure a stay in the accommodation of another host on the network. The introduction of this intermediary also gives the exchange partners a clearer idea of the equivalence of the exchange, including when it is reciprocal, since each accommodation has a value in guestpoints. However, the partners can also decide between themselves to equalise the number of guestpoints, or indeed to exchange without using guestpoints, and thus retain the spirit of a reciprocal exchange which would not necessarily be based on a strict equivalence.

While these two types of practice are negligible in the total volume of leisure stays, their geometric progression curve[8] suggests that we could be dealing with something other than a simple niche. However, our interest here is not to study future trends in tourism demand, but to question the social issue that these practices could represent. Are they likely to favour the emergence of co-production tourism, as an alternative to the dominant model of commercial tourism which:

- Is conditioned by the (very unequally distributed) purchasing power of people
- Promotes practices in terms of "consumer" benefit (in contradiction with the calls for ethical responsibility in tourism)
- Reduces the evaluation of the wealth produced to the income generated by tourists' spending[9]?

Our discussion fits into a broader issue of the gift as a dynamic of the social bond, which is undermined by the utilitarian concept of social life and the deployment of the civilisational programme of growth, centred on optimal allocation of human resources. In a tourism based on co-production, the core principle of leisure trips and stays is the well-being and development of individuals. These objectives depend above all on the links forged between people, emotional attachment to places and the pleasure derived from cost-free activities.

In the first section, we will argue that it is not in the opposition between everyday life and the extraordinary that we can pinpoint the transformations taking place within practices of hospitality and home-swapping between strangers. The discourse of valuing a mode of entry into another person's everyday life, which often accompanies these practices and feeds comments on them, can be understood as personal engagement with patterns that we identify, on the contrary, as being at the heart of the tourist imaginary. The latter is structured by the differentiation, in the key locations on the quest for "discovery", between the monument-focused façade made prominent for tourists, and the "backstage" arena that is the lives of local people. This backstage is viewed as the more genuine and profound truth of places, and entering it is endowed with additional value for the traveller.

In the second section, we will identify the potential for breaking free from the commercial tourism hegemony through the capacity of these practices to generate "social wealth" (collective social capital) independently of purchasing power, and without restricting people's leisure accommodation options to their existing networks of family and friends. However, we will see that on this point, we come up against a paradox: uptake of these practices, which enable travel at considerably reduced financial cost, is very low among people in economically deprived social categories. In fact, the practices do not promote a dynamic of democratisation, and can sometimes reinforce social inequalities, which carries the risk that they will mainly operate at the level of social distinction.

As regards Couchsurfing, the empirical basis of our analysis is a series of transcribed interviews, each lasting 40 to 90 minutes, with couchsurfers who lived or travelled in Perpignan in 2009 (five interviews), in 2014 (four interviews) and in 2016 (four interviews) (Girard and Schéou 2016b; Schéou 2010, 2013, 2014). The interviews all deal with experiences of hospitality: the 2009 ones tend to focus on the hospitality relationship and members' motivations for practicing hospitality, while the 2014 and 2016 conversations focus more on the spatial practices of hosts and guests. In addition to these interviews, there are observations provided by participants in couchsurfers' meetings and events held in 2016. In addition, one of the authors of this chapter is an active member of the network and has hosted more than 200 people in his home since 2007. We also consulted the profiles of the 261 couchsurfers who sent to this author an accommodation request between January 2016 and April 2018, enabling us to find out each individual's age, city and country of residence, country of origin and "professional situation".

As regards data on home swapping, we mainly rely on extracts from interviews published in two master's theses from the universities of Gothenburg and Copenhagen, which strongly converge with the only survey interview that we carried out with a French member of HomeExchange. We also use the results of the questionnaire survey conducted at the University of Bergamo (Forno and Garibaldi 2013). Moreover, one of us also joined Guestoguest (now HomeExchange) as a basic member, which has enabled us to generate a set of messages requesting house exchanges, and to gain some knowledge of the practice from a member's perspective. In this process, care was taken to avoid confusing situation-specific, local knowledge with our global and representative knowledge of the practice studied, and also to take into account the militant bias that the position of member can induce.

An erasure of the opposition between living the everyday and leaving the everyday, central to the tourist experience of the world

A whole literature (in particular around the research team *Mobilités, Itinéraires, Tourismes*[10]) affirms that we are witnessing, in the current evolution of tourism, the end of the opposition between the ordinary characteristics of places inhabited by people and the characteristics of the tourist destinations they choose as a means of escape from the routines and/or pressures of everyday life. This opposition, considered fundamental to tourism, is becoming less and less clear-cut, to the point of being erased. Places initially dedicated to tourism are increasingly becoming places of residence, and many places that were residential before any tourist use are themselves becoming visitor destinations for tourists and residents alike.

We have pointed out in previous work (Girard 2013) that one of the tendencies often put forward to illustrate this blurring of the boundaries between the ordinary and the touristy had been qualified as "post-tourist" by (Viard 2000), and also that he rightly argued that this referred not to an exit from tourism but rather to an extension of certain values celebrated in the ways tourists explore and experience the world. Indeed, a growing number of people aspire to endow the fabric of their everyday life with the aesthetic qualities that used to be sought only or mainly in tourist destinations. We are therefore witnessing an extension, into everyday life, of the relevance of the aesthetic code associated with tourism. Thus, all the trends put forward to support the theory of an exit from tourism rather describe an entry into the era of generalised tourism.

On the other hand, since everyday life forms the context of leisure stays in the practices of hospitality and accommodation exchange between "foreigners", these practices seem compatible with the dynamic of exiting the opposition between the ordinary and the extraordinary. In both Couchsurfing and house swapping, the "home", that is the ideal space of everyday life, provides the very framework of the tourist experience. The distinction between the practices of hospitality reserved for relatives, on the one hand, and commercial welcome for tourists, on the other, is blurring. The line between inhabitant accommodation and tourist accommodation is fading or being crossed.

This method of travelling while actually staying in a home environment, either with the householder present or staying in their house while they are absent (staying in yours), is often qualified as "non-tourist" by its practitioners and valued as such by its promoters. Home swapping and hospitality platforms highlight the opportunity to travel not like a tourist but like a local, and to be immersed in a resident's living environment. Example slogans posted on the websites' home pages include "Stay with Locals and Meet Travellers. Share Authentic Experiences" (Couchsurfing); "A way to experience an area as a local, not a tourist" (HomeExchange); "Travel – live like an inhabitant of the country, stay for free" (Trocmaison).[11] Guestoguest seems to have evaluated travel more shrewdly still, as regards the opposition between the ordinariness of everyday life and the extraordinariness of visiting tourist destinations: whereas in tourism terms, home is generally the place to which the trip offers a contrast (i.e. the home vs. elsewhere; the private, intimate space vs. the exterior, public character of tourist destinations), this platform informs you that from now on "your house lets you travel". The themes in these slogans converge and are echoed in the feeling and/or views expressed by the practitioners, who often say that the trip they are taking is "not touristy".

This therefore appears to align with the theory of erasure of the ordinary/extraordinary opposition on which tourism is founded. However, we will bring out two elements that are consistent with the tourist imaginary. First, the current situation remains strongly influenced by the "tourist map": most of the popular destinations for Couchsurfing and home exchanges are places where tourist flows are already well established. Second, the experiential enhancement attained by entering the everyday life of local residents is part of another distinction integral to the tourist imaginary: that between the tourist-oriented façade and people's lives behind the scenes; between "sightseeing" and "lifeseeing".

Practices that fall within the tourist map

The emic and militant discourse on Couchsurfing contrasts tourism-dictated "discovery" of a region (i.e. going to see something that has already been established as a destination by the tourism industry) with a way of travelling that enables entry into people's lives. This access to the "backstage" arena overlooked by the conventional tourist trail is achieved by forging a non-market, and therefore "authentic", relationship with a local person (or several). The notion is one of lifting the veil from a tourist public space to reveal a private, intimate space beyond.

However, out of phase with this indigenous representation, the interviews conducted between 2014 and 2016 show that most leisure visitors chose accommodation in the predominant tourist area(s). Thus, several people expressed the view that the ability to offer hospitality depended on the property's location relative to routes usually frequented by tourists. Anita, a Ukrainian student on Erasmus in Annecy and studying economics in Poland, told us that in Bydgoszcz where she studies, she has never received a request for a stay in her home because people tend not to travel to her city, which lacks recognised tourist attractions. The same was true when she lived in her village of Vinnytsia Oblast, Ukraine, which is totally off the "beaten track". On the other hand, during her time in Annecy, a city well ranked on the tourist map, she was able to host many couchsurfers in her spare room, even having to turn down some requests. Similarly, Sébastien, from Perpignan, accommodated couchsurfers while he was temporarily residing in a small town in New Zealand, located on one of the routes frequented by travellers.

Further examples: most of the requests addressed to Couchsurfing hosts in Perpignan come from members travelling to or from Barcelona. Only a small minority of the 200-plus couchsurfers hosted in Perpignan by one of this chapter's authors had come to visit Perpignan; the others were going to (or coming from) Barcelona. In Barcelona, many couchsurfers deactivate their profiles simply because they are physically unable to respond to the dozens of hosting requests they receive every day. In contrast, the scholar Zuev notes that in small towns "lacking a tourist infrastructure or spectacular tourist attractions", Couchsurfing members compete to offer accommodation to the few couchsurfers who have come this far (Zuev 2012, 235). So, if there is indeed a desire to go behind the scenes, this tends to appeal only if there is a façade of destinations to attract tourists in the first place. One interviewee named Anaïs asserted, "Saint Mark's Square in Venice? Okay, I only saw it once with Rita, one of the coolest girls who hosted me. In four days in Venice, she took me backstage. I haven't seen a single tourist" (Neiman 2012, 53), yet she was in one of the busiest cities in the world. To sum up, it seems rare for couchsurfers to seek hospitality in a place devoid of any tourist reputation.

Likewise, once in a given destination, the observed spatial routes taken by our interviewed travellers are anything but removed from the tourist map. Interviews conducted in Perpignan show that the places visited in Perpignan and the surrounding area are mainly governed by the tourist map of things to see, listed and highlighted on the map handed out at the tourist office. Only a few rare deviations from the tourist map are observed, in particular when the host plans an "outing" involving certain aesthetic, sporting or festive experiences they know in the area, and invites the guest along. Let us add that from surveys carried out with couchsurfers in Paris, Neveu (2017b) affirms that visitors want to see the Eiffel Tower, the Sacré-Coeur, the Louvre and/or even Notre-Dame. She is surprised "that they do not aspire to tourist itineraries off the beaten track, and yet this in no way dampens the couchsurfers' impression that they are engaging in alternative practices" (Neveu 2017b).

The pervasiveness of the tourist map is also verified with regard to home exchanges. Interviews were carried out with a sample of nine families from Sweden and Canada, by Swedish students gathering data for their master's thesis. They show on the one hand that the families questioned seek as a priority to go to southern tourist regions (southern United States for Canadians, southern Europe for Swedes), and on the other hand the difficulty of finding people interested in a house located away from the tourist trail. According to Lydia,

> I couldn't say we get so many offers on our ad. I mean, you have to present Nova Scotia as being good enough for people to be interested. So it's difficult to get people here, too. You have to give them all those additional benefits.
>
> (Arente and Kiiski 2005, 51)

Magnus, who lives in a village in the countryside, several hours from a big city, also emphasises the fact that this hampers his chances of securing an exchange near a city with significant tourist interest or in a large metropolitan centre. He says,

> Like the last two years our advertisement in that home-exchange website attracted just two more families: one from Germany and one from Holland. And they didn't live in those exciting places where we would like to go, so we didn't accept them,
>
> (Arente and Kiiski 2005, 52)

A member of Guestoguest who offers two properties for home exchange notes that over six months, he received three requests for his large apartment in Perpignan (a second-tier city in terms of tourist reputation, 8 km from the Mediterranean coast) compared with 61 requests to stay in his small three-bedroom apartment in a very popular location on the Costa Brava.

So again, the position of the accommodation on the tourist map determines people's options for participating in the accommodation exchange. In other words, this practice that is presented or often experienced as an alternative to tourism is strongly rooted in the established "value" of the places from a tourist perspective (the tourist map).

Reconsidering the link between the ordinary and the tourist

Since its emergence in the West, the tourist imaginary has been constituted by a double valuation, both contradictory and complementary, of the High and the Small, of the extraordinary and the ordinary, of what is part of people's everyday lives. From Sterne's sentimental voyage published in 1768, (Delon 2016) remarks that

> humans interest him more than monuments, people of little consequence touch him more than great people, emotional contact has more human weight than the objects of admiration listed in travel guides. . . . Against

the Grand Tour of his noble compatriots, he praises of the small. . . . He focuses on the details of everyday life.

Alongside the "seeing" of monuments is recurrently asserted the "seeing" of people's lives, both the scenes of their life and the objects emanated from them, which MacCannell refers to as "the second gaze".[12] This desire to go beyond the limits of the first glance, the "institutionalised" gaze, is part of the very structure of the tourist gaze.

This partially contradictory double valuation of the High and the Small, the extraordinary and the ordinary, corresponds to the structuring of the tourist world into different layers, ranging from the monument-oriented façade of a society displaying itself to tourists, to the unglossed lives of ordinary people, independent of any representation for tourists. This is where the behind-the-scenes entry into people's real lives offers value, on the fringes of the simple sightseeing tour of monuments and things to see (MacCannell 1976). And it is finally with reference to this characteristic of the tourist world that MacCannell proposed his controversial definition of the tourist as a "modern man in search of authenticity", where authenticity opposes both the artificiality of everyday life in commercial and industrial societies, and the systems of services and tourist representations sold to tourists. Which amounted in a way to defining the tourist as a leisure traveller who would prefer not to be a tourist, or at least who overvalues temporary exits from his "tourist" status (always deceived in his quest, yet able to be satisfied with the deception without really ignoring it). In this way, entry into the ordinary lives of local inhabitants has always represented the culmination of the tourist quest (with different modalities of investment or engagement of the subject). It follows that Couchsurfing and home exchange form part of this central motif of the tourist imaginary.

Therefore, everyday life is not absent from the conventional tourist world, but celebrated through an aesthetic of people's lives that values the Small. It is there that it touches the deep, hidden level that lies beyond the reach of the superficial tourist visit.

With the exception of stays in tourist bubbles which constitute an abstract environment of any vernacular everyday life, or – in the opposite direction on the experiential scale – treks in natural wildernesses, any leisure trip therefore means frequenting, to a greater or lesser extent, a context marked by another everyday life: a foreign everyday life, that of the inhabitants of another place. In the tourist imaginary, what is valuable is an "everyday life" which is "typical" of a place. The difference from the tourist's own everyday life should correspond to certain characteristics contrasting with those seen in the industrial and commercial worlds. Thus, to be appreciated, a foreign everyday life must present the general characteristics by which it is deemed a "typical" everyday life of that place (signs of a local tradition distinct from the uniformity of industrial products of the consumer society). There is therefore a code of the "typical", which tends to function as a prism in the perception of the vernacular everyday life, and reduces its strangeness (Girard 2004). The appreciation of a foreign everyday life as "typical" of a place is part of an experience of recognition and enchantment, rather than of knowledge (Girard and Schéou 2016a). As a result, everything that is obvious and familiar in the tourist's everyday life remains unharmed, even reinforced. This celebration of the typical is to be differentiated from an experience of strangeness, in which the subject apprehends elements of the cultural codes of a foreign vernacular everyday life, which will destabilise the evidence sedimented in their familiar everyday life and make them aware of their own "strangeness". Thus, it is not through a privileged entry into a "typical" everyday life that one leaves the tourist imaginary, but through the experience of the strangeness of a vernacular everyday life. And if we stick to the discourse of Couchsurfing and home exchange practitioners and commentators, we could say that there is ultimately a consecration of the tourist imaginary, not an exit from it.

On another level, the analysis shows something of a gap between members' militant discourse on the platforms' ability to offer access to a typical everyday life, and the members' actual practices, which are characterised by entry into everyday lives similar to their own. Indeed, before establishing a relationship of hospitality or home exchange, the protagonists rely on a certain amount of information which ensures a certain similarity of settings and lifestyles. In the home exchange, members tend not to seek entry into a "typical everyday life" of a place, or into a life that may be "too foreign", but rather entry into the kind of everyday life that roughly matches their expectations regarding the general characteristics of a "home", while having some specificities. Couchsurfers will tend to connect with guests or hosts by choosing profiles that have similarities to their own or that evoke an interesting travel plan. It is therefore mainly between peers (social and cultural) that home exchanges and hospitality take place. These experiences of a similar everyday life could ultimately provide more possibilities for experiences of strangeness than experiences of a "typical" everyday life. However, the pervasiveness of a militant representation that is misaligned with actual practices certainly promotes a logic of social distinction at the expense of an experience of strangeness; this occurs through the assurance of being in the right practice, that is one that allows entry into the real lives of people as opposed to sticking to the tourist trail.

Factors of a shift from commercial tourism towards co-production tourism?

Home exchanges and hospitality between members of networks give rise to two opposing narratives of analysis. Some scholars point to this type of practice as an obvious manifestation of an exit from the reign of commercial order, allowing people to contact each other to organise their own leisure trips. According to Forno and Garibaldi (2015), Couchsurfing and HomeExchange are, within travel practices, the most accomplished expressions of a collaborative economy, calling into question the workings of the conventional tourism industry. And it is one of the challenges of achieving widespread social change linked to the rise of a sharing economy. Similarly, for Andriotis and Agiomirgianakis (2014, 586): "Contrary to the realm of commodification, home swappers escape the world of money. By exchanging houses outside the market system, transactions take on an element of authenticity, as opposed to strictly commercial exchange". Other scholars argue that on the contrary, especially for home swapping, this type of practice does not threaten to reduce tourists' expenditure in the host regions. Far from being totally external to the market economy, these practices would rather lead to a shift in the *type* of expenditure, with home-swapping visitors ultimately consuming more local wares and services than the average tourist. On this point, the manageress of communication at HomeExchange emphasises the high level of local spending by these tourists: "Non-commercial accommodation does not necessarily mean cheap tourism. Most people who choose a home-swapping holiday are mature tourists, comparatively well-off and cultured, and their on-the-spot spending is high. . . . Members double their purchasing power on vacation" (Origet du Cluzeau 2014, 57).

We find these two types of contradictory discourse to be biased by debatable *a priori*. We do not believe that the only measure of the value produced by practices is the expenditure incurred, and that the only way of redeeming these practices in terms of social acceptability is to show their contribution to economic growth. However, nor do we subscribe to the contrary idea that the value of a practice can be measured by the mere absence of monetary expenditure. In such a case, the redemption ("authenticity") of these practices would be in the simple exit they represent from commercial exchange. Moreover, it is not difficult to detect in Couchsurfing, as in HomeExchange, elements of commercial logic that could then tip them to the "wrong" side. All the more so since the largest and most popular platforms are run by for-profit companies. Besides, home exchanges are based on the possession (or, more rarely, tenancy-based occupation) of a property asset, and therefore indirectly on its market value. The exchange power held by a member is essentially conditioned by their property's asset value. In Couchsurfing, while the (indirectly market) value of the accommodation offered is less of a priority, we can say that the central role played by reviews and comments on individuals, together with the way members present themselves in their network profile, is part of a rationale of managing one's own personality "brand", where positive reputation and connections with others must be maintained as a form of social capital (in the Bourdieusian sense) to be optimised. The Couchsurfing community (as evidenced by a whole corpus of literature already produced on the question[13]) thus functions rather like a market, where the number of positive reviews represents a sort of "price" equivalent, and serves to reduce the uncertainty around entering into an interpersonal relationship with strangers (without a contract). It is as though the capitalist notion that, logically, one ought to optimise any available resource, has been imposed even on interpersonal relations, as if even in the very spheres one might consider separate from the system, someone's personality represents "human capital". Finally, we could also use the approach of analysing social distinction, to read these practices deployed outside a market exchange as a desire to gain prestige ("symbolic capital"), conferred by taking leisure trips that enable the traveller to stand out from simple "tourists". Behind the claimed value of authenticity would thus lie the benefit of social distinction.

For us, criticism of the predominance of the commercial model in tourism should not be confused with the binary diagram juxtaposing the merchant as factitious and artificial, and the non-commercial as genuine. Likewise, unlike activist and promotional rhetoric, we do not assert that Couchsurfing and HomeExchange enable authentic travel while conventional tourism does not.

We propose to identify the issue of a generalisation of hospitality and home exchange practices, based not on this opposition but on two hypothesised contributions from these practices:

1 They generate collective social capital within the meaning of Putnam (2001) or what we will call "social wealth" to avoid any confusion with Bourdieusian social capital.
2 They represent a mode of access to tourism which, by relying more on a certain relational involvement than on the purchasing power of the people travelling, could be a way to democratise tourism.

We take the first contribution for granted: the primary virtue of Couchsurfing and HomeExchange is not to be found in ideas of a more authentic mode of discovery (according to the myth of the genuine trip vs. tourism as a false trip) but in the creation of social wealth. Co-production tourism is based on social wealth, not on economic wealth. Indeed, the two practices are based on a gamble of trust between platform members and establish links between them which allow the self-production of services. The additional "social wealth" resulting from this self-production of tourism services does not only allow access to tourism, independently of the purchasing power of platform users. By casting individuals in the role of platform users rather than as industry consumers, the call for ethical attitudes on the part of tourists is much less contradictory. And finally, the increase in the social wealth in which the members evolve broadly increases their general capacity for individual and collective action. Note: this supposes an end to the belief that progress measured by "GDP" is the main wealth to be taken into account. Social wealth, which is not countable, constitutes a social environment that brings happiness to members and increases their capacity for action (which is not only assessed in terms of their contribution to GDP).

We will discuss the second contribution because its effectiveness seems much more problematic. Indeed, from the point of view of the democratisation of leisure travel and stays, the practices of Couchsurfing and, above all, exchanging accommodation present us with a paradox: the people who engage in these practices are essentially those who have the financial means to travel and who previously used conventional tourist accommodation. Also, adoption of these practices is more a case of increased leisure travel among certain higher educated categories of the middle class, rather than expanding access to tourism for the more modest social categories. We are going to explore this paradox, in order to reflect on the conditions in which this type of trip could also be an opportunity to democratise access to tourism.

Even if there are no systematic surveys on the social characteristics of the members of hospitality and housing exchange networks, the various studies already carried out indicate that home exchangers live in highly favourable social situations (Forno and Garibaldi 2013), while the social situations of couchsurfers are quite favoured.[14] Although we are discussing two distinct hospitality practices and two separate audiences, the difference is mainly linked to two different life stages within the qualified middle classes.

Couchsurfing is first and foremost associated with young people, at an age when they still have minimal income or property assets, and they are not yet settled in a long-term relationship. Mature people are not absent from the community, but often take on a role of youth travel facilitator, with the majority involved in hosting travellers rather than being hosted.

Home exchangers are primarily people from the upper middle classes in couples with young children, or older people with grown-up children and owners of comfortable accommodation.

The two practices differ not only in terms of audiences but also in their logic. Couchsurfing is based on a relational involvement, intended to ensure face-to-face contact during the stay, unlike home swapping where contact can be limited to the prior correspondence. People who accept the hospitality of others in Couchsurfing without spending time getting to know their host are considered, by the members of this community, to be much-discredited "freeloaders": those who want to avoid spending money on accommodation but keep things as impersonal as in a commercial exchange (i.e. one where the parties do not need to talk to each other and establish a relationship). This is someone who adopts the same behavioural logic as a tourist in a hotel, but wants access to free accommodation. This negative figure of the "freeloader" does not fulfil the host's expectation of a return ensuring an equivalence in the exchange, but rather that of being in the spirit of the gift such that their hospitality is not transformed into a free offer of a merchant service. I give you hospitality without expecting in return your hospitality or remuneration in kind, but to establish an interpersonal relationship, and that hospitality can subsequently circulate among members of the network.

The involvement of the partners in a HomeExchange is played out mainly on two levels:

1   The mutual trust that we grant each other: I can trust the other because they trust me, and this mutual trust allows everyone to benefit from a valuable asset (accommodation inhabited by another family) under conditions that are very advantageous (free) for everyone and from which we could not benefit if we did not make this gamble of trust.

2   The work required beforehand to meet the obligation to provide the other with a welcoming space (cleanliness, tidying up, providing information, etc.). Each is more concerned with delivering their house to the other in the required condition than they are afraid of arriving in a dwelling that does not correspond to this condition. And each property holder takes care to facilitate their guests' access to the local tourist amenities by leaving documentation and sound advice; each partner feels involved in helping the other get the most from their visit. Neither hopes to "win" in the exchange at the expense of the other, but also, one would rather not give less than one receives.

In Couchsurfing, the importance of the interpersonal relationship seems to be accompanied by a reduction in the sanctity of the home environment, which is simply a support structure (almost absent in the accounts of practice) for the relationship of hospitality. On the contrary, in HomeExchange, the characteristics of the home environment are essential for the participants. And if allowing strangers to live in a dwelling while its usual residents are absent appears in some way to transgress the private/public borders proper to the sanctity of "home", simultaneously the "magic" of being able to go and stay in the home of someone else, when this is perceived as more than simply a means of staying somewhere for free, is indeed based on a valuation attributed to "home". Finally, the possibility and the desire to exchange will largely depend on each partner's ability to present accommodation that has the characteristics of a pleasant "home", in which the other can feel good. This difference in the importance attributed to the actual housing in the two practices can also be read in the fact that with Couchsurfing, the gift of hospitality is intended for short stays (the unwritten rule is a maximum of three days), whereas for HomeExchange, the tacit duration would be more like two weeks, or longer.

Despite their differences, however, neither of these two practices seems to have much relevance for the working classes. And so we have this economic paradox, where leisure trips requiring no purchasing power are not adopted by low-income social categories. Thus, the demographic groups who could be the main beneficiaries of this co-production tourism are rarely those who choose to engage with it. It is mainly appropriated by classes with a certain cultural capital, hence the fact that the most economically disadvantaged people who utilise Couchsurfing are mainly younger individuals in higher education, most of whom can probably look forward to higher economic capital in the later stages of their biographical trajectory, where this is not already the case through their parents. Thus, the social wealth generated by these practices of hospitality and exchange mainly benefits somewhat privileged classes. Consequently, a concept that has the potential to reduce social inequalities in access to tourism can ultimately exacerbate these inequalities, not by worsening the situation of the most deprived, but by intensifying the tourist activity of social categories who already had access to it. The situation is not so much an exit from the hegemony of commercial tourism, but more a dynamic of hyper-tourism through multiplication and diversification of tourist practices, in which people travel more often, further afield and for longer.

Also, in order to prevent claims about the authenticity of this type of practice from feeding into social distinction strategies, due to the social inequalities evident in access to the practices, it would be necessary to define and actively engage in the conditions that would encourage their appropriation by lower education, lower income groups. If such conditions were to succeed, they could lay the groundwork for a post-hegemony of commercial tourism.

This could be achieved via an ambitious social tourism project, through the development (subsidised, at least initially) of collaborative associative or cooperative platforms, oriented towards developing hospitality practices and housing exchanges between people from working-class backgrounds. Twinning agreements between municipalities could also resolutely include this type of co-production tourism aimed at disadvantaged social groups. From the social wealth generated by this co-production tourism, we could expect not only a democratisation of access to tourism, but also increased self-esteem and capacity for action of weakened people, likely to respond to the symbolic disqualification by self-withdrawal or violent rejection.

Today we often lament the effects of a dualisation of society between on the one hand, its "winners" with their far-reaching mobility, and on the other, its losers or those left behind. This dualisation has many consequences: the populist vote, abstention or social withdrawal by a large part of the population, some people increasingly resorting to violence, and others focusing on security, even with a component of xenophobia. Perhaps we should take more account of the challenges of opening co-production tourism to a broader range of classes. This undoubtedly means, however, that we would need to stop hiding behind the great humanist principles ritually put forward, admit that tourism is valued mainly in terms of its effects on economic growth, and instead reconsider the importance of non-countable social wealth.

Notes

1 In metropolitan France, overnight stays with family or friends accounted for 44% (36.8% and 7.4% respectively) of non-business accommodation in 2017 according to data from the *Direction Générale des Entreprises*. Note the stability of this figure: it was 43% in 1993 and 46% in 2006.
2 Trips and stays away from home for enjoyment, not out of necessity such as paid activity or family obligation, even if strips with a functional aim often take on tourist aspects.
3 From the separation between producer and consumer, Godbout devised the criterion for the institution of market exchange (Godbout 2007).
4 This generic name for the practice is that of the main platform used, which drove the upscaling of this phenomenon.
5 The gift is defined more by the absence of specifying a counterpart than by the absence of a counterpart. This absence makes the return uncertain and leaves the recipient free to give in turn, and to whomever they choose. It is a relationship in which equivalence in exchange is neither guaranteed nor sought (one does not count) (Godbout 2007).
6 "Troc" is a French word for "barter"; "maison" means "house".

7 Guestoguest became the largest house-swapping platform in 2017 with its takeover of HomeExchange, before the two organisations merged under the latter name.
8 Regarding Couchsurfing, there were 17 members in 2004, 396,311 in 2008, and 3,640,994 in 2012. After a change of status of the network in 2012, the overall figures published indicate even stronger growth (seven million in 2013, 12 million in 2016, still 12 million in 2018).
   In terms of home exchanges, the world's leading network HomeExchange was offering 450,000 homes in 2018, that is a twelvefold increase compared with 2014.
9 As in the definition of tourist (and therefore tourism) adopted by the UNWTO.
10 As, for example, in (MIT 2002) and subsequent volumes.
11 Respectively: www.couchsurfing.com. Retrieved 3 July 2018, www.homeexchange. com consulted in March 2017 and www.trocmaison.com/fr/. Retrieved 3 July 2018.
12 "The desire to escape the limitations of the tourist gaze is built into the structure of gaze itself – into the fact that the first tourist gaze requires a second" (MacCannell 2001, p. 31).
13 See Lauterbach et al. (2009), Peterson and Siek (2009), Tan (2010). Teng et al. (2010), Rosen et al. (2011), Germann Molz (2014).
14 The various works focusing on the social profile of members highlight their high level of study, their command of English, as well as their skills to travel, to use new technologies and their belonging to the middle and upper classes. Neveu (2017a) speaks of self-segregation and social homophily to qualify the great social similarities of couchsurfers. We decided to check this among the 261 couchsurfers who sent us a request for accommodation in Perpignan between 1 January 2016 and 30 April 2018. A third did not mention their status or activity in their profile or in the request message. Of the remainder, 42% are students, 49% work and 9% qualify themselves as nomadic travellers. As regards those who are in activity, 10% are teachers, 10% are computer scientists, 9% graphic designers, 9% photographers, 7% artists, 6% engineers, none are in "typical working class" employment (one person in the sample declares himself a gardener).

References

Andriotis, Konstantinos and George Agiomirgianakis. 2014. "Market Escape Through Exchange: Home Swap as a Form of Non-Commercial Hospitality." *Current Issues in Tourism* 17 (7): 576–591.

Arente, Helena and Veronika Kiiski. 2005. "Tourist Identity Expression Through Postmodern Consumption – A Focus on the Home-Exchange Phenomenon." Master, Tourism and Hospitality Management, Göteborg University, Göteborg.

Delon, Michel. 2016. "L'éveil de l'âme sensible." In *Histoire des émotions, vol. 2. Des Lumières à la fin du XIXe siècle*, edited by Alain Corbin, Jean-Jacques Courtine and Georges Vigarello. Paris: Le Seuil, p. 480.

Forno, Francesca and Roberta Garibaldi. 2013. *My House Is Yours*. Bergame: Université de Bergame.

Forno, Francesca and Roberta Garibaldi. 2015. "Sharing Economy in Travel and Tourism: The Case of Home-Swapping in Italy." *Journal of Quality Assurance in Hospitality & Tourism* 16(2): 202–220.

Germann Molz, Jennie. 2014. "Collaborative Surveillance and Technologies of Trust: Online Reputation Systems in the 'New' Sharing Economy." In *Media, Surveillance and Identity: A Social Perspective*, edited by A. Jansson and M. Christensen. New York: Peter Lang, pp. 127–144.

Girard, Alain. 2004. "La reconnaissance/méconnaissance de l'autre dans l'ésthétique touristique: la réduction folklorisante produit-elle la folklorisation des cultures?" In *Les formes de reconnaissance de l'autre en question*, edited by Ahmed Ben-Aoum, Alain Girard, Jean-Louis Olive, Jean Pavageau and Philippe Schaffauser. Perpignan: Presses Universitaires de Perpignan, pp. 227–296.

Girard, Alain. 2013. "Faut-il raccorder une théorie générale de la post-modernité à une théorie à moyenne portée du post-tourisme?" In *Fin (?) et confins du tourisme. Interroger le statut et les pratiques de la récréation contemporaine*, edited by Hughes François, Philippe Bourdeau and Liliane Perrin-Bensahel. Paris: L'Harmattan, pp. 43–52.

Girard, Alain and Bernard Schéou. 2016a. "Fair Tourism and the 'Authentic' Encounter: Realization of a Rite of Recognition in the Context of the Myth of Authenticity." In *Tourism Imaginaries at the Disciplinary Crossroads: Place, Practice, Media: New Directions in tourism Analysis*, edited by Maria Gravari-Barbas and Nelson Graburn. London: Routledge, pp. 130–146.

Girard, Alain and Bernard Schéou. 2016b. "Un espace intermédiaire entre façades et coulisses du monde touristique?" *Espaces vécu et domestique de l'hôte dans le couchsurfing*, Papier présenté au colloque, Prendre position: métissages disciplinaires et professionnels autour de questions spatiales, Strasbourg, 1er Juillet.

Godbout, Jacques. 2007. *Ce qui circule entre nous. Donner, recevoir, rendre. La Couleur des idées.* Paris: Seuil.

Lauterbach, Debra, Hung Truong, Tanuj Shah and Lada Adamic. 2009. "Surfing a Web of Trust: Reputation and Reciprocity on CouchSurfing.com." *Proceedings of the 2009 International Conference on Computational Science and Engineering* 4.

MacCannell, Dean. 1976. *The Tourist: A New Theory of the Leisure Class.* Berkeley: University of California Press.

MacCannell, Dean. 2001. "Tourist Agency." *Tourist Studies* 1(1): 23–37.

MIT. 2002. *Tourismes 1, Lieux communs. Mappemonde.* Paris: Belin.

Neiman, Ophélie. 2012. "J'ai fait le tour du monde en canapé." *Géo* 49–56, Octobre.

Neveu, Pauline. 2017a. "Couchsurfing: La distinction touristique par la rencontre." *Téoros* 36(1). Retrieved 20 April 2018.

Neveu, Pauline. 2017b. "Le Couchsurfing: Une forme d'hospitalité touristique entre familiarité et altérité." *Mondes du tourisme* 13, https://doi.org/10.4000/tourisme.1394. Retrieved 30 mars 2018.

Origet du Cluzeau, Alexandra. 2014. "Homeexchange, leader mondial de l'échange de logement." *Revue Espaces* 316: 55–57.

Peterson, Katherine and Katie A. Siek. 2009. *Analysis of Information Disclosure on a Social Networking Site.* Berlin, Heidelberg: Springer.

Putnam, Robert. 2001. "Social Capital: Measurement and Consequences." *Canadian Journal of Policy Research* 2: 41–51.

Rosen, Devan, Pascale Roy Lafontaine and Blake Hendrickson. 2011. "CouchSurfing: Belonging and Trust in a Globally Cooperative Online Social Network." *New Media & Society* 13(6): 981–998.

Schéou, Bernard. 2010. "Le retour de l'hospitalité, pratiques subversives ou expression d'une conformité postmoderne?" *L'Autre Voie* 6(6).

Schéou, Bernard. 2013. "Réseaux sociaux d'hospitalité et post-tourisme." In *Fin (?) et confins du tourisme. Interroger le statut et les pratiques de la récréation contemporaine*, edited by Hughes François, Philippe Bourdeau and Liliane Perrin-Bensahel. Paris: L'Harmattan, pp. 99–109.

Schéou, Bernard. 2014. "Couchsurfing: l'espace domestique de l'hôte comme espace touristique?" Le tourisme hors des sentiers battus: coulisses, interstices et nouveaux territoires touristiques, Paris, 22 mai.

Tan, Jun-E. 2010. "The Leap of Faith from Online to Offline: An Exploratory Study of Couchsurfing.org." Proceedings of the 3rd international conference on Trust and trustworthy computing, Berlin, Germany.

Teng, Chun-Yuen, Debra Lauterbach and Lada A. Adamic. 2010. "I Rate You. You Rate Me. Should We Do So Publicly?" Proceedings of the 3rd World Conference on Online Social Networks, Boston, MA.

Testart, Alain. 2006. *Critique du don. Etudes sur la circulation non marchande. Matériologiques.* Paris: Syllepse.

Viard, Jean. 2000. *Court traité sur les vacances, les voyages et l'hospitalité des lieux.* La Tour d'Aigues: L'Aube.

Zuev, Dennis. 2012. "CouchSurfing as a Spatial Practice: Accessing and Producing Xenotopos." *Hospitality & Society* 1(3): 227–244.

5 The invention of the ordinary city as a heritage and tourist place

The case of a new town, Cergy-Pontoise (France)

Elizabeth Auclair, Anne Hertzog and Marie-Laure Poulot

Introduction

This book chapter offers a reflection on the emergence of the ordinary city as a heritage and tourist place. We used Cergy-Pontoise as a case study. Cergy-Pontoise is one of the five new towns built at the beginning of the 1970s in the Paris region in the northwest outskirts of the metropolis. Its location in the remote periphery of the world-leading tourist metropolis, its architectural and urban history and its social and political reconfigurations make Cergy-Pontoise a significant field to observe the social construction of the ordinary city as a tourist place.

This case study also demonstrates how different practices and narratives result from the emergence of "alternative tourism" models in the city. Our study is based on the analysis of two projects led by two associations, *Les Voix d'Ici* and *Bastina*, in order to create urban visits and itineraries based on a participatory approach, involving the inhabitants.

We used several methodological approaches: the first part of the chapter, a recontextualisation of the tourism policies and initiatives in Cergy-Pontoise, is based on more than 20 years of research and observations about this territory by one of the co-authors. The second part develops a comparative analysis of two itinerary-making processes, based on field study and discourse analyses. As academics teaching in the local university, we took an active part in *Bastina* itineraries. Therefore, some analyses are based on our observations, experiences and regular encounters with many stakeholders. We attended some meetings, followed participants in the process, developed formal or informal interviews and discussions with them.

First, we will show how, as a new town, Cergy-Pontoise has been viewed from the beginning as an area whose development depended entirely on its ability to attract new inhabitants: it was crucial, therefore, to meet the requirements of a popular destination. Infrastructure and urban developments were not meant to be touristic at first, but local collectivities started to highlight some of its characteristics such as the natural environment or the architectural creations. Second,

DOI: 10.4324/9781003138600-7

we will critically present two recent alternative tourism projects in order to question the entanglement aspects of a tourism that becomes a daily life experience and a tourism that invests in everyday places. These projects are indeed intended mainly for Cergy-Pontoise inhabitants for them to (re)discover their living place, which tends to overlay tourism and excursionist practices. Furthermore, these initiatives allow some ordinary places to be brought to light, if even ignored or marginalised. The Cergy-Pontoise case more specifically questions the space left to civil society and grassroots initiatives in urban tourism contexts.

From an urban project meant to attract new inhabitants to the organisation of an institutional tourism

Producing a new city, fostering attractiveness

> The new towns in Ile-de-France region: breaking with the expansion of the Parisian suburbs and creating "real towns".

In the mid-1960s, the French government decided to restructure the Paris region by creating five new towns located about 35 km from the capital, separated by "natural zones", several of which would later become Regional nature parks (Figure 5.1).

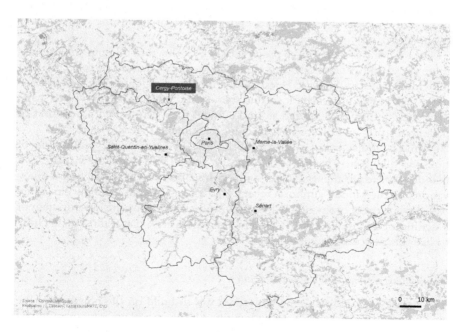

Figure 5.1 Mapping of new towns around Paris planned in the 1960s

The objectives of these new towns were manifold: curbing the oil-stain growth of the Paris region, limiting the anarchic consumption of rural areas, building towns linked to Paris by rail to reduce car use and providing a balance between housing and employment to limit commuting. To appear attractive, these cities had to offer housing and jobs, but also activities, services and urban amenities for the new inhabitants, such as green spaces, public transport networks, educational establishments and cultural, sports and leisure activities (Vadelorge 2005). To implement this important programme, the national government set up, for each of the new towns, a public planning agency (EPA), composed of town planners and architects in charge of steering the urban project. In a context of strong demographic growth, the aim was to offer an alternative to dormitory towns and to build cities offering a pleasant living environment, capable of attracting new populations.

The architectural and urban choices defined by the Cergy-Pontoise EPA (created in 1969) led to the building of a city anchored in its area, enhancing the natural site and using the potential of the Oise loop and the surrounding wooded hillsides. The town planners decided to enhance the existing forests, woods, allotments and individual gardens; they also created new parks and green spaces and laid out a vast natural recreational area, located in a meander of the river Oise in the heart of the urban area. In addition, they encouraged architectural diversity within the city, with the desire to liberate the architects from old models. The aim was to avoid monotony and the repetition of identical architectural forms, and thus to break away from the "modernist" models inspired by Le Corbusier's theories, applied in the large housing estates of the post-war period.

The choice was therefore to propose rather low height buildings, and to promote social and generational mixing through a combination of collective and individual housing. Specific rules were defined for designing the urban space with small living districts built around schools and shops. The aim was to shape dense neighbourhoods located around bus and train stations, with networks of pedestrian paths and footbridges reaching the different areas (Figure 5.2).

While architects were given relatively little freedom in the production of housing, they were given more choices for the schools where new forms and colours were experimented, often with open spaces allowing pedagogical innovations. In the kind of euphoria related to the construction of a new city, there was also a form of utopian new life proposition, marked by the development of a significant community life, steered by the "pioneers", that is those who chose to live this new urban experience.

Shaping local heritage, between past and future

The strategy for designing the new town was to build on the potential of the area but also to enrich the existing identified heritage resources by introducing contemporary architectural elements. The heritage of Cergy-Pontoise designed by the planners is organised around three main themes. The environmental and

Figure 5.2 Several examples of architectures in Cergy Prefecture, surrounding a pedestrian area near the Metro Station

Source: Marie-Laure Poulot

natural heritage is an asset clearly acknowledged by the local stakeholders and the inhabitants. The first documents presenting the new town as well as the successive communication campaigns regularly mentioned the advantages of a "city in the countryside", due to its proximity to the agricultural and forest areas of the neighbouring Vexin region (later integrated into the Regional nature park of French Vexin, created in 1995). The documents and discourses also mentioned the advantages of a "green city", specifying the existence of "ten trees for every inhabitant", unlike Paris, which has twice as many inhabitants and only one tree for every ten inhabitants on the same surface area (Engrand and Millot 2015). Research works carried out recently on heritage issues in Cergy-Pontoise confirm the strong attachment of the inhabitants to their natural environment (Auclair et al. 2016).

The historic built heritage includes elements of the ancient town of Pontoise and the rural villages mainly located around the loop of the river Oise (Figure 5.3).

The challenge, defined by Cergy-Pontoise EPA in the 1970s, was to preserve the former architecture to keep the atmosphere as a "testimony" of what

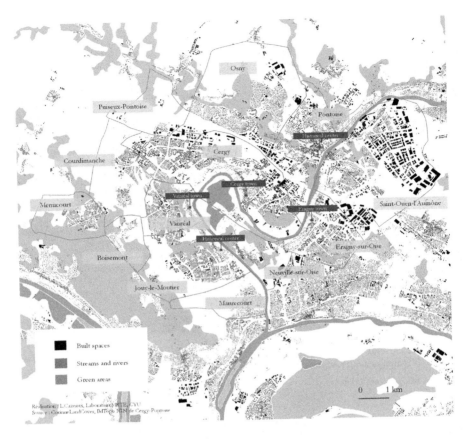

Figure 5.3 Mapping of old villages in the new town area

existed before the new town. The town planners therefore worked with the mayors of the different municipalities to preserve the older urbanised districts and to keep the existing urban structure, while at the same time trying to establish relationships with the new districts. Nevertheless, the physical articulation between the new and the old districts remains today incomplete, and demographic and social segmentation persists.

Creating a new town was the opportunity to launch a sort of "architectural laboratory", contributing to the constitution of a twentieth-century heritage. The evolution of the city's urban and architectural forms followed successive town planning "trends", but also responded to the expectations, demands and new needs expressed by the inhabitants and users. For example, while the initial emphasis was on pedestrian walkways and footbridges to circulate in the city, the planners were later led to develop easier access to the districts by car.

Figure 5.4 The Axe Majeur and the view on the Oise loop and leisure area

Source: Marie-Laure Poulot

Cergy-Pontoise currently presents a kind of open-air exhibition of the recent history of town planning and contemporary architecture. In addition, the planners of the EPA decided to include a major work of urban art, "*l'Axe majeur*", entrusted to an internationally renowned artist, Dany Karavan. This artwork, composed of different elements arranged along an axis, occupies an important place in the town, both physically and symbolically (Figures 5.4 and 5.5). While the axis has become a tourist hotspot in the city, systematically shown to outside visitors, the inhabitants of the neighbourhood regularly used it as a place for leisure.

Attracting new residents, creating a popular destination

Based on the myth of the "new town", the institutional promotion of Cergy-Pontoise has been conceptualised from the start, on paradigms similar to those used in the tourism industry, such as exploration (pioneers), well-being (leisure parks, nature) or innovation (urban, architectural and industrial). The "exploration" myth has been extensively exploited through the use of the "pioneers" notion to characterise the new residents, a term still in use today by some

Figure 5.5 The Axe Majeur and the green urban area of Cergy-Pontoise – the Axe Majeur is one of the touristic spots in Cergy

Source: Marie-Laure Poulot

inhabitants. The artificial lakes surrounded by forests (planned in 1965 by the Ile de France Region) has become one of the most popular spots around Paris, for urban citizens from Cergy-Pontoise but also for the whole Parisian metropolis seeking "space", "green" and "water". Opened in 1987, Mirapolis, a short-lived theme park, described as being "France's first large amusement park", reinforced the image of the city as a popular leisure destination, even if it had to close in 1991 due to lack of profit. Other qualities of the urban landscape also attracted specific social categories of international visitors: from the very beginning, the city became a place attracting architects and urban experts, curious about the new town urban innovations and experimentations. This architectural touristic dimension is still very prevalent.

The emergence of a tourism strategy led by Cergy-Pontoise Agglomeration Council

From the "new town" to the "ordinary city"

At the beginning of the 2000s, considering that the cities had reached a sufficient level of "maturity", the government closed the public planning agencies, and these urban areas lost their specific status of "new towns". The EPA of Cergy-Pontoise closed in December 2002 and the new *Communauté d'agglomération de Cergy-Pontoise*, currently composed of 13 municipalities, was created in January 2004. Nowadays, the city is characterised by its social (more than 100 nationalities), housing (for rent or ownership), urban and architectural diversity (diverse urban forms, buildings of different sizes and shapes, etc.). "Diversity" has therefore become the key notion in the city marketing and is widely promoted through many narratives. However, the urban design and the architectural diversity are sometimes misunderstood by the inhabitants or visitors (difficulties in finding their way around the city, lack of recognition and appropriation of some of the buildings. . .). Other issues and uncertainties concerning the future of Cergy-Pontoise are linked to the place of this conurbation in the "Grand Paris" programme, a development project for the Parisian metropolis including Paris and its nearest surrounding suburbs, initiated in 2007. This large-scale planning project does not concern the outskirts of the region. So Cergy-Pontoise appears somewhat isolated from this dynamic and presents risks of marginalisation (Desponds and Auclair 2016).

Seeking a new image

The end of the "new town" period marked a fundamental shift for the territory, on several levels: political, institutional and economic, but also in terms of its identity and image (Auclair 2003). The 30 years of rapid government-led urban development enabled the town not only to receive strong national financial support, but also to benefit from the image of an experimental urban laboratory, amply observed and visited by elected representatives, town planners and architects from all over the world. It also became the subject of numerous studies and academic works (Dagnaud 1979; Hirsch 1990; De Saint-Pierre 2002). Therefore, by losing this specific status of new town, the city had to face many challenges. One of the major issues for local stakeholders was to build a new identity, in order to avoid becoming a mere suburban city (Auclair 2015).

It was less a question of attracting new inhabitants than promoting the appeal of the city, in order to continue luring in new businesses, but also receiving more visitors. Relying on the potential of the environmental setting and the architectural and urban heritage resources, as well as the local socio-economic dynamics, the institutional actors of the territory developed communication and territorial marketing strategies centred on a modern and dynamic vision of the city turned towards the future. The previous logo of the new town was replaced, and a new slogan was launched: "*Cergy-Pontoise Energies Ouest*".[1] From 2002, a specific programme, "*Histoire à vivre*",[2] was set up to accompany the institutional evolution of the town, including symposiums, exhibitions and various events. Most of these activities aimed at highlighting the city, promoting both its history and its prospects. At the same time, an institutionalised tourism strategy was launched.

Uncertainties in terms of heritage and tourism strategies

Cergy-Pontoise Agglomeration Council initiated many projects at the beginning of the 2000s aiming at developing a global tourism strategy and building a new discourse centred on the heritage resources of the city. However, this overall dynamic was affected by several changes due to some political tensions between the municipalities and various hesitations concerning the approach: several projects were abandoned while others were taken over directly by the municipalities, on a local scale rather than on the agglomeration level. As an example, the city of Pontoise, alone, obtained in 2006 the label "*Ville et Pays d'Art et d'Histoire*"[3] and not the whole agglomeration. Public stakeholders in Cergy-Pontoise never made the choice to implement a metropolitan heritage policy through the creation of a museum for the whole agglomeration.[4] Some attempts of valorising the public art disseminated in the different municipalities also failed. The establishment of an "Urban Initiatives Forum", whose purpose was to be a kind of showcase for Cergy-Pontoise, as well as a place for reflection and debate on current urban forms and practices, has never been completed. The only significant initiative was the reactivation of the association dedicated to the enhancement of the *Axe Majeur*, considered as an international masterpiece, as well as the symbol of the city.

However, the Agglomeration Council published three tourist maps presenting the natural heritage, the historical built heritage and the contemporary architecture of the area. For three years (between 2003 and 2007), the town also took part, together with other partners from the Val d'Oise Department, in the "Tourism Week" event, where stands were set up in the Trois Fontaines Shopping Centre to present the region's tourist attractions to customers.

A kind of complexity or ambiguity appears on the part of the new Agglomeration Council in defining the town as a genuine tourist city. Two documents illustrate these difficulties. The first is a "carto guide" published in 2003 by Gallimard, whose title is "Cergy-Pontoise between Pays de France and French Vexin". Cergy-Pontoise is presented only as one of the elements of the region, in the same way as the Vexin valleys, the Pays de France with its castles and abbeys, the Montmorency valley and its forests, Auvers and its past marked by Van Gogh and the Impressionists. Moreover, the geographical division of Cergy-Pontoise by districts and not by themes does not really allow the emergence of a clear tourist image. However, this guide does provide a lot of practical information, which is mainly of use to the local population. The second document, which is a small booklet called "Guide touristique de Cergy-Pontoise, un air de vacances"[5] illustrates more explicitly the assets and resources of the area. Published in 2007, the book is organised around four themes (the old city, the nature city, the architectural city and finally the cultural city). The section devoted to the "old city" presents the medieval and pre-industrial heritage of Pontoise, St Ouen l'Aumône and the old villages; the "nature city" evokes the neighbouring Vexin, the green spaces, the leisure centre and the loop of the river Oise. The "architectural city" highlights contemporary architecture and the *Axe Majeur*, and finally the "cultural city" deals with museums and exhibitions. Even if the targeted public remains essentially local or regional, the tourist dimension appears here more evidently.

It is only in 2010 that the Cergy-Pontoise Agglomeration Tourist Office was created as a common equipment for the whole agglomeration,[6] nevertheless built in the most touristic part of the territory: the Oise riverbanks in the old city of Pontoise. Numerous visits are now organised in the various municipalities of the agglomeration and its surroundings, trying to valorise the various histories and landscapes of the agglomeration.

These institutional initiatives focused mainly on the built, architectural and natural aspects of the new town. Highlights on the "remarkable" architecture of the city have gradually been combined with the emphasis on the ordinary city and the inhabitants' experiences. This change of perspective is also accompanied by the enhancing of multiple artistic expressions, on the part of artistic figures from Cergy, but also and above all, figures producing a discourse on the city. The exhibition *"Formes et fictions d'une ville nouvelle – Cergy-Pontoise"*,[7] which ran from June to September 2015 in Paris, at the Pavillon de l'Arsenal,[8] thus included meetings with cinema director Céline Sciamma and a concert by Fredo, singer of *Les Ogres de Barback*. Similarly, in 2019, for the event *"Regards croisés sur la ville"*[9] celebrating the fiftieth anniversary of the city, famous writer Annie Ernaux and the director Céline Sciamma were invited to speak about the town in which they used to live or are still living. Through their works, mundane places are described and sometimes re-enchanted, such as the Three Fountains shopping centre mentioned in several writings by Annie Ernaux (1993, 2000, 2014) or the swimming pool and the centre of Cergy-Préfecture district (in the 2007 film *Naissance des pieuvres* translated as *Water Lilies*).

The rise of alternative tourism in Cergy-Pontoise

New categories of actors, critical approaches, alternative models: a renewed vision of tourism

The global context: the emergence of the participatory paradigm

Beyond the dynamics driven by the Tourist Office, new orientations have gradually been put in place, broadening the conceptions and representations of heritage and tourism in Cergy-Pontoise, giving more space to the notion of "ordinary heritage" and "alternative tourism", involving inhabitants' participation. This shift in local tourism is particularly illustrated by several initiatives and research projects led in the city between 2015 and 2019. A research project on "participatory heritage" led by academics from the local university, along with the Regional Office for Heritage Inventory and the support of the Agglomeration Council is one of them.[10] This research project, based on fieldwork in the urban space and the organisation of participatory workshops, aimed at including inhabitants' narratives in the heritage terminologies applied by professional curators.

In the same time period, new types of tourism itineraries were initiated in the city, focusing on the notion of alternative tourism, and involving inhabitants as tourism guides, in order to promote "living heritage", "intangible" and "ordinary" heritage.

The coincidence of these two kinds of initiatives coming from different actors reflects the spread of the participatory paradigm, aiming at looking for "alternative" models for public action in tourism and heritage making.[11] Revealing the diffusion of heritage recognition towards the metropolitan suburbs and peripheries (Cousin et al. 2015), these two initiatives can be seen as the local expression of a global change, characterised by the redefinition of the notion of heritage (Smith 2006) and the growing fascination for the "ordinary" (Fabre 2013; Gravari-Barbas 2017; Condevaux et al. 2019; Condevaux et al. n.d.), in response to new issues such as urban renewal,[12] cultural diversity and local democracy (Delaplace and Gravari-Barbas 2016). Far from being a local or national phenomenon, this participatory paradigm is also part of new international recommendations framing heritage making and tourism at a global scale (UNESCO, EU).

Innovative tourist projects initiated by artistic and cultural associations

The actors who originated these new tourism itineraries are two associations, external to the territory and specialised in creating "urban walks" (a notion preferred to "guided tours" in both cases). While innovative on the local scale, these initiatives can be seen as signs of the circulation of models and concepts already applied and tested in other cities and relocated in Cergy-Pontoise. Also, these actions reveal new actors' games, referring to one of the questions of this book on the place of civil society actors in tourism, and the processes of hybridisation at work between the concepts of "ordinary" and "tourism".

Les Voix d'Ici association, based in the East of France, intervened for the first time in 2015 in a festival, "Cergy Soit!", organised every year in Cergy and dedicated to street theatre. The project of a "sound walk" proposed by this association was integrated into the cultural event's programme, organised by the municipality's cultural service. The concept of the "sound walk" is based on the collection and assembly of pieces of life stories transmitted by the inhabitants on a soundtrack that visitors can listen to with the help of an audio guide (designed as the "inhabitants audio-guide") while walking in the city (Antoine 2018, 247–282). The concept had already been developed in other places: the Paris district of La Goutte d'Or (in 2012) and Saint Laurent du Maroni (French Guiana, in 2013), and then, similarly in other towns such as Ile-Saint-Denis, Mulhouse and Clichy.

Bastina association also appears to be an exogenous actor. When it intervened in Cergy-Pontoise in 2017 at the request of the Agglomeration's

Tourist Office, the association had already four years of experience in creating "intercultural itineraries" in Paris and in several towns in the Parisian suburbs. Since 2014, *Bastina* had also been part of a European network of NGOs and companies specialised in "responsible tourism", within the framework of the European Project *Migrantour*.[13] Close to the concept of "greeters" (Maitland and Newman 2008; Villepontoux 2018) the principle is to train inhabitants from immigrant backgrounds to accompany visitors along urban itineraries they actively shape. According to the European programme frame, the main objective is to promote urban "responsible tourism". Making the "migrant" an active actor of the process, the project also has a clear political objective, which is "to facilitate the integration of citizens of foreign origins, in European metropolises, by encouraging mutual understanding and respect among all residents".[14] The programme is rooted in a critical vision of the global impacts of tourism on societies of the "South" and aims to foster "best tourism practices", avoiding "commercialisation", "exoticisation" and "folklorisation" of ethno-cultural diversity. Encounters, social inclusion and participation are therefore central notions that allow migrants to acquire the "right to self-representation" – and not to be represented – through the elaboration of subjective narratives concerning the city, anchored in their personal experiences and journeys.

The comparison of the two associations shows converging objectives founded on the promotion of encounters and participation between visitors and residents in multicultural, peripheral or stigmatised urban areas, and therefore, similarities in their geographical choices: working-class districts located in suburban areas marked by an important immigrant population of diverse origins.

Militant visions of tourism

These two associations belong to the ever-expanding galaxy of cultural and social activists involved in participatory projects, in working-class or marginalised neighbourhoods over the last decades: artistic companies or multidisciplinary collectives, all performing in different contexts, in response to multiple political and social issues (urban renewal, deindustrialisation, urban violence, segregation, social inequities). *Les Voix d'Ici* team presents itself as a collective of artists rather than a touristic company, even if the notion of tourism can be found in its communication. In that way, the "sound walks" are qualified as "sensitive tourism". *Bastina* is totally assuming being a tourism stakeholder, both through its history (*Bastina* began as a commercial platform selling "fair travels" all over the world) and its promotion, focused on "responsible and solidarity tourism". Unlike *Les Voix d'Ici* whose members are mostly creatives (designers, journalists, sound engineers, etc.), *Bastina* leaders are tourism professionals. The two associations nevertheless have in common the promotion of a militant vision, in their intention to elaborate *alternative* tourism models. In their own words, they define it as a tourism "off the beaten track" (Delaplace and Gravari-Barbas

2015). In this respect, avoiding mainstream categories through the use of alternative terminologies in their narratives is part of the approach: "walk" instead of "visit", "passeur de culture" ("cultural intermediary") instead of "tourist guide".

Grounded on its expertise in the field of local and participative cultural projects, *Les Voix d'Ici* communicates on best practices and a "know how" adaptable to multiple contexts: "preservation of memory (disappearance of industrial wasteland, workers' memory), planning in shrinking areas, cultural events, promotion of social and solidarity-based economies, new forms of tourism and mobility" (Les Voix d'ici website). These multiple objectives show that in the framing of these associations, the constructions of the itineraries in the city are based on values related to sustainability and social innovation: tourism should foster global, social, political and urban changes, redefining the role and objectives of tourism practices, such as "branding" or "discovering the city".

Involving the civil society in alternative tourism projects: an ambivalent process?

The role of institutions in the associative and militant action

Realising participatory tourist itineraries are often seen and studied as the result of grassroots processes, "ground initiatives" and "local actions". The Cergy-Pontoise case brings a different reading. The participatory tourism projects are not only based on exogenous initiatives, but also are institutionalised. They embraced a large set of collective actions and used to involve a wide variety of actors: local activists or cultural actors, members of local associations, inhabitants as well as institutional stakeholders.

Les Voix d'Ici project was launched and supported by agents of the municipal cultural office of Cergy, and organisers of an institutionalised festival. The collective of artists had been selected for the festival, as its work was considered in line with the objectives of the socialist municipality cultural policy, based on the participatory paradigm. Bastina's project (Migrantour in Cergy) had been initiated by the manager of the Agglomeration Tourism Office. He considered that the concept could be a means for diversifying the tourism offer and audience, following tourism management objectives. The choice of *Bastina* to bring some changes in the local tourism can also be explained by his own sensibilities.[15] In his view, tourism should be linked to social and urban planning issues: working with *Bastina* meant "acting" in marginalised neighbourhoods of the agglomeration, representative of its ethno-cultural diversity, to change their image. The project was rooted in social objectives, which was also made clear in the financial partnerships involved. Significantly, this multi-partner project has been financed by the CGET,[16] a State department in charge of social policies in disadvantaged urban districts to promote territorial "equality". Consequently,

Bastina had to develop the concept in limited institutionalised target districts, given the CGET criteria.

The complexity of linking tourism and immigration issues in Cergy-Pontoise

Tourism within the agglomeration has thus undergone a "reterritorialisation" process linked to the perimeters of national and local public policies, with underlying issues related to urban renewal, but also to social integration. However, from the very beginning, *Bastina* could not fully follow the original framework of the European project Migrantour, as, according to several local stakeholders, immigration heritage locally appeared to be a sensitive issue. Some local actors contacted by *Bastina* to set up partnerships[17] declined the offer or showed reluctance, arguing that the project could lead to "stigmatisation" of some neighbourhoods and communities or "instrumentalisation"/ manipulation of the migrants. Some of them pointed out "communitarian temptations" of a tourism project providing more visibility to certain minorities. For *Bastina*, it became a long and challenging process to recruit guides within the migrants living in Cergy-Pontoise.

Consequently, the Migrantour project in Cergy-Pontoise has undergone a notable shift, both in its discourse (less focused on migratory trajectories and "minorities") and in its sociology (fewer migrants among the guides than in the Parisian version of the project). Added to that, the lack of visibility of ethnic neighbourhoods, as most of migrants are scattered in the city rather than concentrated in homogeneous community neighbourhoods, made it difficult to develop walks on a small scale, comparable to those in Paris on the theme of the "Asian Quarter of the 13th district", "the little Mali" or the "Tamil Quarter".

The promotion of the multi-ethnic city through a public discourse based on tourism seems to have had difficulty finding its place in Cergy-Pontoise, within an agglomeration where cultural diversity is often claimed (the "city of 130 nationalities" or "la ville-monde"). Still now, the city branding is largely based on a "tradition of hospitality", a scheme that has long been the basis of the social and political construction of the territorial identity of the "new town". Thus, Cergy-Pontoise remains outside the contemporary trend, which consists in valorising "immigration heritage" in alternative tourism projects, notable in some metropolises such as Paris (Chapuis and Jacquot 2014) or Montreal (Poulot 2017), to promote the cosmopolite global city.

Tourism as a political project

Conceiving the tourist activities as a social and political project finds its expression in the various stages of the process for elaborating the itineraries. This process consists of a great diversity of actions and integrates a variety of devices and events to orchestrate the participation of the inhabitants (workshops, meetings, etc.). In Cergy-Pontoise, *Bastina* initiated a partnership with the university to train the future guides. For two consecutive years, as teachers of a master's degree in cultural project development, we opened our classes to a group of residents from social housing neighbourhoods. Often unfamiliar with the codes of the university institution, they worked on the elaboration of urban walks along with the master's students who could in return be initiated to participative projects. In practice, this collaborative process proved to be difficult and often conflicting, sometimes misunderstood. For all participants however – students, teachers, and guides – this collaboration had been considered as a unique and unprecedented experience.

The acquisition of new skills, of academic knowledge, is only a secondary dimension of the project, beside the symbolic and social impacts of the experience. Not very common in French universities, this approach can be seen as a way of putting in practice the "radical horizontalism" which is at the very centre of both *Voix d'Ici* and *Bastina* methodologies, as well as the desire of their initiators to situate their action "beyond tourism". By including inhabitants in a university curriculum, *Bastina* intended to break down a set of symbolic, social and spatial barriers. While inhabitants were welcomed in university, students were invited by the inhabitants to explore and study their neighbourhood to co-design the itineraries. The "academic knowledge" of the students was to be enriched by the "inhabitants' expertise" and vice versa, according to a principle of "de-hierarchisation" of knowledge and practices. Thus, considering the tourist project as a political and social experience induces certain expectations – some of them fictitious – regarding a complex process having multiple effects on the individual level (recognition, self-esteem, feeling of integration, etc.) and on the collective level (living together, mutual understanding and knowledge, etc.). In the case of *Bastina* and *Les Voix d'Ici*, designing a tourist itinerary in the city refers to a project whose objectives, practices and effects are both within and outside the field of tourism.

The ordinary at the heart of the projects?

Invisible boundaries in the ordinary city: "crossing the line"

Recent academic works suggest "the dissolution of tourism as a field that carries specific sociabilities, spatiality and temporality and therefore [that of] 'dedifferentiation' between tourist and non-tourist, whether in places or practices" (Delaplace and Gravari-Barbas 2015). These works point out that "the boundaries between the 'elsewhere' and the 'here', between the 'exotic' and the 'everyday' are wavering". The concepts developed by the two associations in Cergy-Pontoise led to the formulation of a tourist imaginary where the boundaries between a "tourist" space and a "daily" space are blurred, but also those that would distinguish between practices of urban drift, strolling with friends and tourist visits. Various authors show that these experiences are based on the search for the "extraordinary" in the ordinary and everyday urban environment, both for the inhabitants in their familiar surroundings and for visitors when "the ordinary of the other can become extraordinary for oneself" (Delaplace and Gravari-Barbas 2015).

Les Voix d'Ici and *Bastina* promote the idea of "travelling away from home", their discourse operating as a kind of "relocation" of the confrontation with the otherness that the classic tourist trip implies. To put it another way, alternative tourism makes it possible to operate, without necessarily moving, encounters between different worlds that characterise our metropolises here and there. In this sense, their discourse participates, not without a certain ambiguity, in a social construction of urban otherness (which justifies the exploratory dimension of an urban tourism "off the beaten track"). *Les Voix d'Ici* presents the inhabitants' audio-guide as an "accompaniment" device: "*accompanied, guided, reassured, the visitor thus takes the plunge and sees in these places, that are now familiar*" (translated from the association's website, October 2020). "*Crossing the line*": this rhetoric used in the promotion of the *Voix d'Ici* "sound walk" seems to condense the experimental approach at the heart of the practices; the phrase expresses both the existence of invisible frontiers that cross the ordinary city and the function of alternative tourism practices in crossing them. Walking is a way of discovering the city, which is not a matter of "looking" but of "living and experiencing". The encounter, the confrontation with otherness, passes through the sensory and sensitive experience of the city, and the setting in motion of the body (Jaillet 2016). Walking thus allows this "exercise of transformation of the gaze [which] is, to use Michel Foucault's term, a kind of 'technique of the self' that allows one to reappropriate the territory and inhabit it in a positive way" (Delaplace and Gravari-Barbas 2015).

What is to be experienced in the (too) ordinary city?

The tours initiated by *Bastina* focus on personal stories of the inhabitants and encounters with local actors (shopkeepers, managers of community centres or local cultural institutions, etc.). The itineraries should explore certain urban "interstices", which, until now, had escaped the tourism industry within the agglomeration (social housing estates, homes and hostels, mosques or churches), as shown by three examples[18] (Figure 5.6).

Captions: 1. Town Hall and Grouchy park 2. The Tunnel 3. Coalia centre (refugee centre) 4. Community centre 5. Jean-Pierre Duvergé, Cergy's faces (street art)[19]

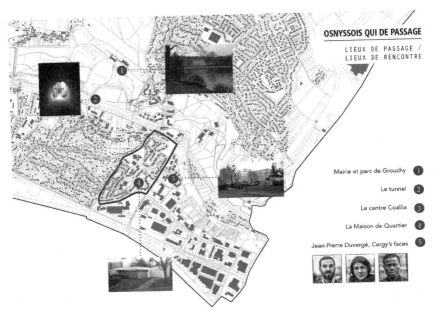

Figure 5.6 This itinerary proposal concerns Osny, one of the municipalities of Cergy-Pontoise, rarely visited by tourists, and is particularly focused on a housing neighbourhood and encounters with local residents and social workers (Migrantour Project, Bastina Project, 2017–2018)
Authors: Pierre Berruer et al. (2018)

Another example of itinerary suggests a walk around The Louvrais, a neighbourhood built in the 1970s in the periphery of the historical town of Pontoise. It makes visitors discover several sport infrastructures and shops and meet residents from different origins.

> The suggested stages of the itinerary are: 1. The Virgin (statue) 2. Pissaro High School 3. The Commercial centre 4. La Place de la Paix (the main square) 5. Le cour des Louvrais (the main avenue) 6. The soccer field 7. The skate park in project 8. Redouane Bougara Avenue 9. Place de la Fraternité (square). Authors: Baron et al. (2019)[20]

The third example is one of the itineraries suggested in Cergy city, around the Axe Majeur. The team of students and "Passeurs de culture" (local residents) present the tour in these terms:

"The prototype of our tour is two km long. It starts at the station of Cergy le Haut, on the forecourt in front of the cinema. From there, we reach the Great Mosque along Hazay avenue. Then, we have a little walk to Jules Verne high school, which is one of the first building built in the area. This will bring us to the Cergy parish on the Nautilus square where we will also visit 'Visage du Monde' [a community cultural centre]. On the way back to the station, we will stop in the wine shop 'Nicolas', a shop that has been around for a long time". Authors: Descoubes et al. (2019)[21]

Figure 5.7 The walks of the Passeurs de Culture Projects in Cergy–Pontoise
Author: Laure Cazeaux

Even if this itinerary leads visitors to walk through sides streets, it also includes the Axe Majeur as a main spot of the visit. Several other itineraries realised during the academic years have been deployed in the old village of Cergy, the modern district of Cergy Prefecture (the original core of the new town in the 1970s), the Axe Majeur and its esplanade and the banks of the Oise river.

One can notice that some of these alternative itineraries, which were intended to be "off the beaten track", still remain close to or "in the beaten tracks". These participatory experiences therefore enhance the value of the "ordinary" city, but they also contribute to overvaluing the places already identified as the agglomeration's better known spots.

Mapping of the heritage sites mentioned by the Tourism Office and of the places chosen by the "passeurs de culture" working with the students for the Migrantour Project (2017 to 2019). We notice that certain itineraries add value to certain peripheral districts making them privileged as opposed to others, concentrating on the places that are already tourism and heritage hotspots.

Certainly, these places are grasped in their daily or ordinary dimension through the subjectivities of the guides and different meanings are given to them, according to each individual story. On the one hand, it reflects the perceptions of the inhabitants about their appropriation of well-known places in Cergy-Pontoise, to which they feel attached or proud of; on the other hand, it shows the objectives of associations (Bastina), wishing to offer "something worth seeing" in a (too) ordinary city.

This raises questions about the limits, in the context of Cergy-Pontoise, of the relevance of itineraries focused on the "ordinary" city: the peri-urban agglomeration might represent one of the last frontiers of the tourist space: socially mixed but not enough "exotic", marked by social inequalities and urban crisis but not "unsafe" enough, that is to say, a (too) ordinary space where, apart from the famous "traditional" spots, it can be difficult to "see" and "explore" the "extraordinary".

Conclusion

As a new town, Cergy-Pontoise has been viewed from the beginning as an area whose development depends entirely on its ability to attract new inhabitants: it was crucial, therefore, to meet the requirements of a popular destination. Based on the myth of the "new town", the institutional promotion of Cergy-Pontoise from the start has been based on registers similar to those used in the tourist industry, such as exploration (pioneers, etc.), well-being (leisure parks, nature, etc.) or innovation (urban, architectural, and industrial). Since the mid-2010s "alternative tourism" initiatives brought a shift in the local tourism development and promotion of the city. More institutional initiatives are attempting to spread tourism to little frequented places; the initiatives of urban walking associations are also part of this shift in perspective. Furthermore, these initiatives show the "infusion" of tourism into the practices of local people. Inaugurated in September 2015 during the "Charivari au Village" event and the Cergy, Soit! festival, the Voix d'Ici walk is primarily dedicated to the inhabitants of Cergy-Pontoise. Likewise, the three visits organised in 2015 by the CAUE[22] around the Grand Centre, Cergy St Christophe and Axe Majeur[23] attracted residents who are concerned about their living environment and want to share their experiences. This example shows the two parallel aspects of a tourism that becomes "daily" and a tourism that invests in everyday places (Lussault 2007, Larsen 2019).

We can underline the permanence of centre-periphery logic in these actions: the town of Cergy seems to be privileged to the detriment of the other towns belonging to the agglomeration, symbolic places (Axe Majeur, Prefecture district) to the detriment of other more interstitial spaces. On another scale, that of the Parisian metropolis, certain initiatives are part of the same logic, while expanding the places visited. This is the case of tourist trails that seek to encompass the ordinary territories of large metropolises. After the GR®2013 around the metropolis of Aix-Marseille-Provence, a similar initiative is under-way for the Paris agglomeration, with the Greater Paris Metropolitan Trail project,[24] including photographers, illustrators, sound designers, journalists and writers. The objective is to "question the limits and go beyond the bounda-ries" and to encompass with "the same look the strategic territories, the inter-stices and the surroundings that surround and constitute them".[25] The route from Cergy-Pontoise to Saint-Denis thus once again passes through several districts of Cergy. However, the routes from Cergy to Pontoise, from Pontoise to Herblay and from Conflans-Sainte-Honorine to Cergy also pass through less "extraordinary" or at least more confidential areas in the other towns of the agglomeration.[26]

These initiatives have contributed to enhance new urban spaces (including marginal spaces) and promote more democratic conceptions of heritage in an activist spirit, even if this last dimension is less important in the case of Cergy-Pontoise than in other tourist actions, such as Hôtel du Nord in Marseille, for example (Hascoet and Lefort 2015). Following a new globalised paradigm, these initiatives have attempted to set the local inhabitant as a central figure of urban tourism, and the ordinary and multicultural city as a new archetype of the authentic tourist place. In Cergy-Pontoise, participatory tourism, as a new model of tourism is an imported concept, brought by professional "outsiders", who had already applied their methods in other territories, and sincerely hope to produce a new perspective on the ordinary and multicultural city. However, initiatives and choices of these associative actors have been conditioned by protocols and methodologies, shaped by partnerships and networks and con-strained by financing arrangements. The ephemeral nature of these supports has prevented the prolongation of certain initiatives. Ultimately, these experiences are therefore part of institutional policies in response to various local challenges and haven't really been given room to flourish. They remain highly regulated and dependent on public policies linked to the inherited control mechanisms set up for tourism and image branding in the (post) new town. Moreover, what can be underlined is the limited social appropriation of these tours in Cergy-Pontoise. *Les Voix d'Ici* audiotours remain little used in Cergy-Pontoise. The *Bastina* Migrantour itineraries seem far more successful in Parisians districts or other suburbs and cities. These tours, sold by the Tourism Office, aren't really appropriated, either by tourists visiting the city, or by inhabitants. More traditional guided tours are mostly preferred by external visitors, and inhabitants do not seem really aware or attracted. This raises the question of the future of these kinds of initiatives and their potentialities in a post-COVID-19 world.

Notes

1 Cergy-Pontoise West Energies.
2 Stories to be experienced.
3 Created in 1985, this national label "City and Country of Art and History" is given by the Minister of Culture and Communication. The implementation of the label is based on a partnership between the State and local authorities, formalised, after the label is awarded, by the signature of a renegotiable agreement every ten years. The local authority must include the "City or Country of Art and History" project in its local public policy. This label is supposed to help the local players to the enhancement of architecture, heritage, landscape and the tourist development.
4 Unlike the memorial and museum initiatives of Saint-Quentin-en-Yvelines (with its previous eco museum created in 1977 and transformed in 2000 into a museum of the city, dedicated to contemporary periods and the study of the construction of the new town and the lifestyles of its inhabitants; Guiyot-Corteville 2003).
5 Cergy-Pontoise tourist guide, a holiday atmosphere.
6 Before 2010, only Pontoise had its own municipal tourism office.
7 Forms and fictions of a new town.
8 The Pavillon de l'Arsenal is an information, documentation and exhibition centre for urban planning and architecture of Paris and the Paris metropolis.
9 Mixed views on the city.
10 The research led by the authors of this chapter, entitled "Patrimonialisation process, between institutional expertise and inhabitants' expertise", was financed by the programme "Interculturality in Heritage Institutions" the Ministry of Culture and Heritage. Its aim was to develop a new approach to heritage and an attempt to "share" expertise. It raised several issues: setting a collaboration between inventory experts and academic researchers, developing cross-methods (heritage diagnostics, qualitative interviews with residents, urban walks and participatory workshops) and identifying the heritage of a former new town located on the outskirts of Paris. See Auclair et al. 2016.
11 In an article (Condevaux et al., n. d.) recall that the categories "used by the literature to account for these new forms of tourism are: off-track tourism (Maitland, Newmann 2004); alternative tourism (Breton 2009; Butler 1990, 1992; Cohen 1987; Stephen 2004); experimental tourism (Urban 2002); interstitial tourism (Urban 2002), which adds a transgressive dimension to the innovative character of the previous one; slow tourism (Fullagar and Markwell 2012); participative or collaborative tourism (Coquin 2008; Ferrary 2015); creative tourism (Gombault 2011)".
12 In the French context, urban renewal is used to describe processes of urban renovation in order to control a crisis situation (urban, economic, social).
13 See www.mygrantour.org/en/.
14 See presentation brochure of Migrantour: https://issuu.com/fondazioneacra/docs/migrantour_fr.

15 Very sensitive to participatory paradigm in heritage and tourism, he was also involved in participatory projects as part of the decentralised cooperation led by Cergy-Pontoise with Haiti Palestine and Benin.

16 CGET: Commissariat Général à l'Égalité des Territoires – General Commission for Territorial Equality.

17 For instance, a local NGO in charge of refugees in Cergy city, another one involved in actions of inclusion of Roms. But also ethnographers working in local public offices in charge of collecting living memories (Atelier de restitution du patrimoine et de l'ethnologie of Val d'Oise Department).

18 These three examples are taken from the academic works realised by students and "Passeurs de culture" under the supervision of Anne Hertzog and Stéphane Buljat (Bastina Association) as part of the Migrantour Project developed in collaboration with the master degree 'Développement Culturel et Valorisation des Patrimoines', CY Cergy-Paris University, in 2017–2018 and 2018–2019.

19 Pierre Berruet, Marius Bonane, Adrian Buisson, Thomas Carrières, Carole Ethève, Lucile Gounin, Mathilde Lull (2018). *Osnyssois qui de passage*, Cergy-Pontoise University, Migrantour Project, Bastina, 2017–2018.

20 Chloé Isabet, Amandine Laurent, Clémentine Pillet, Gisèle Baron (2019), *Les Louvrais, un lieu-dit et raconté*, Cergy-Pontoise University, Migrantour Project, Bastina, 2018–2019.

21 Carla Duret, Cheick Diakate, Lucas Richard, Sarah Descoubes, Victoria Vermeulen, François Petitjean, *Des Hauts et Débats. Promenade dans le quartier des Hauts de Cergy*, 2019, Cergy-Pontoise University, Migrantour Project, Bastina, 2018–2019.

22 CAUE is a local institution implanted in every Department, devoted to counselling in architecture, urbanism and environment.

23 www.pavillon-arsenal.com/fr/hors-les-murs/10209-promenades-urbaines.html.

24 www.lesentierdugrandparis.com/.

25 Dossier de presse, « Faites-nous marcher ! », 2011.

26 https://lesentierdugrandparis.com/de-versailles-a-cergy-pontoise

References

Antoine, Mélanie. 2018. "Les Voix d'ici, Balades sonores de quartier guidées par les voix des habitants." In *De la participation à la co- construction des patrimoines urbains. L'invention du commun?* edited by Elizabeth Auclair, Anne Hertzog and Marie-Laure Poulot. Paris: Editions du Manuscrit, collection Devenirs urbain, pp. 267–282.

Auclair, Elizabeth. 2003. "Le développement culturel comme outil de promotion d'une identité territoriale ou comment les acteurs se saisissent de la culture pour faire émerger un territoire." In *Lieux de culture, culture des lieux*, edited by Maria Gravari-Barbas and Philippe Violier. Rennes: Presses Universitaires de Rennes, pp. 95–101.

Auclair, Elizabeth. 2015. "Si on n'est plus une ville nouvelle, qu'est-ce qu'on est?" In *Cergy-Pontoise, formes et fictions d'une ville nouvelle*, edited by Lionel Engrand and Olivier Millot. Paris: Editions du Pavillon de l'Arsenal, pp. 56–57.

Auclair, Elizabeth, Anne Hertzog and Marie-Laure Poulot. 2016. *La patrimonialisation en question: entre culture experte et culture habitante*. Paris: Rapport de Recherche financée par le Ministère de la culture et réalisée en partenariat avec le Service Patrimoines et Inventaire de la Région Ile de France.

Chapuis, Amandine and Sébastien Jacquot. 2014. "Le touriste, le migrant et la fable cosmopolite. Mettre en tourisme les présences migratoires à Paris." *Hommes et Migrations* 1308(4): 75–84, doi:10.4000/hommesmigrations.2999.

Condevaux, Aurélie, Francesca Cominelli, Géraldine DjamentTran, Edith Fagnoni, Maria Gravari-Barbas and Sébastien Jacquot, n.d. "La mise en tourisme de lieux ordinaires et la déprise d'enclaves touristiques: quelle implication de la société civile? Etat de l'art." *PUCA*, www.pantheonsorbonne.fr/fileadmin/IREST/Colloques/PUCA-EIREST_Etat_de_l_art.pdf.

Condevaux, Aurélie, Maria Gravari-Barbas and Sandra Guinand. 2019. *Lieux ordinaires, avant et après le tourisme*. Paris: Collection "Recherche" du Puca n°239.

Cousin, Saskia, Géraldine Djament-Tran, Maria Gravari-Barbas and Sébastien Jacquot. 2015. "Contre la métropole *créative* . . . tout contre. Les politiques patrimoniales et touristiques de Plaine Commune, Seine-Saint-Denis." *Métropoles* 17, doi:10.4000/metropoles.5171.

Dagnaud, M. 1979. *La banlieue autrement. Vie sociale à Cergy-Pontoise*. Paris: Fondation des villes.

Delaplace, Marie and Maria Gravari-Barbas. 2015. "Introduction Le tourisme urbain 'hors des sentiers battus', Coulisses, Interstices et nouveaux territoires touristiques urbains." *Teoros* 34: 1–2. URL: http://journals.openedition.org/teoros/2790

Delaplace, Marie and Maria Gravari-Barbas. 2016. "Editorial." *Via* 9, http://journals.open edition.org/viatourism/417, https://doi.org/10.4000/viatourism.417.

De Saint-Pierre, Caroline. 2002. *La fabrication plurielle de la ville: Décideurs et citadins à Cergy-Pontoise, 1990–2000*. Paris: Créaphis.

Desponds, Didier and Auclair Elizabeth. 2016. "The New Towns Around Paris Forty Years Later: New Dynamic Centralities or Suburbs Facing Risk of Marginalization." *Urban Studies* I(16).

Engrand, Lionel and Olivier Millot. 2015. *Cergy-Pontoise, formes et fictions d'une ville nouvelle*. Paris: Editions du Pavillon de l'Arsenal.

Ernaux, Annie. 1993. *Journal du dehors*. Paris: Gallimard.

Ernaux, Annie. 2000. *La vie extérieure 1993–1999*. Paris: Gallimard.

Ernaux, Annie. 2014. *Regarde les lumières mon amour*. Paris: Seuil.

Fabre, Daniel. 2013. "L'ordinaire, le familier, l'intime . . . le patrimoine loin du monument." Conférence donnée au PREAC, http://preac.crdp-paris.fr/ressources/patrimoines-familiers-patrimoine-universel/lordinaire-le-familier-lintime-le-patrimoine-loin-du-monument/.

Gravari-Barbas, Maria. 2017. "Tourisme de marges, marges du tourisme. Lieux ordinaires et 'no-go zones' à l'épreuve du tourisme." *Bulletin de l'association de géographes français* 94(3), https://doi-org.ezpupv.biu-montpellier.fr/10.4000/bagf.2097.

Guiyot-Corteville, Julie. 2003. "L'écomusée de Saint-Quentin-en-Yvelines, acteur ou témoin de la ville nouvelle?" *Ethnologie française* 33(1): 69–80, doi:10.3917/ethn.031.0069.

Hascoet, Yannick and Isabelle Lefort. 2015. "Au détour des barres et des tours." *Teoros* 34(1–2), http://journals.openedition.org/teoros/2768.

Hirsch, Bernard. 1990. *L'invention d'une ville nouvelle, Cergy-Pontoise 1965–1975*. Paris: Presses de l'École nationale des Ponts et Chaussée.

Jaillet, Marie-Christine. 2016. "Réaménager la ville pour y faire place à la marche 'ordinaire'." *Sciences de la société* 97, https://doi.org/10.4000/sds.4133.

Larsen, Jonas. 2019. "Ordinary Tourism and Extraordinary Everyday Life: Re-thinking Tourism and Cities." In *Tourism and Everyday Life in the City*, edited by Thomas Frisch, Christoph Sommer, Natalie Stors and Luise Stoltenberg. London: Routledge.

Lussault, Michel. 2007. "Le tourisme, un genre commun." In *Mondes urbains du tourisme*, edited by Philippe Duhamel and Rémy Knafou. Paris: Belin, coll. "Mappemonde", pp. 333–349.

Maitland, Robert and Paul Newman. 2008. "Visitor-Host Relationships: Conviviality Between Visitors and Host Communities." In *City Spaces – Tourist Places: Urban Tourism Precincts*, edited by Bruce Hayllar, Tony Griffin and Deborah Edwards. New York: Elsevier, pp. 223–242.

Poulot, Marie-Laure. 2017. *Le Long de la Main cosmopolite. Promouvoir, vivre et marcher le boulevard Saint-Laurent à Montréal*. Québec: Presses de l'Université du Québec, collection Patrimoine urbain.

Smith, Laurajane. 2006. *The Uses of Heritage*. London and New York: Routledge.

Vadelorge, Loïc. 2005. "Action culturelle et villes nouvelles, des histoires croisées." In *L'action culturelle dans les villes nouvelles*, edited by Loïc Vadelorge. Paris: La documentation française.

Villepontoux, Stéphane. 2018. "Le tourisme participatif ou l'invention du guide habitant, nouvel enjeu pour la mise en tourisme des territoires. L'exemple du phénomène Greeters en France." In *Le touriste et l'habitant*, edited by Dominique Crozat and Daiane Alves. Saint-Denis: Connaissances & Savoirs.

References of the "Passeurs de culture" and students' works

Baron, Gisèle, Chloé Isabet, Amandine Laurent and Clémentine Pillet. 2019. *Un lieu-dit et raconté: Les Louvrais, Pontoise*. Migrantour: Université de Cergy-Pontoise.

Berruer, Pierre, Marius Bonane, Adrian Buisson, Thomas Carrieres, Carole Etheve, Lucile Gounin and Mathilde Lull. 2018. *Osnyssois qui de passage: Parcours urbain alternatif*. Migrantour: Université de Cergy-Pontoise.

Descoubes, Sarah, Cheick Diakite, Carla Duret, François Petitjean, Lucas Richard and Victoria Vermeulen. 2019. *Des hauts et débats. Promenade dans le quartier des Hauts de Cergy*. Migrantour: Université de Cergy-Pontoise.

Websites

www.bastina.fr/
www.lesvoixdici.fr/
www.mygrantour.org/fr/
www.ot-cergypontoise.fr/en/welcome-homepage/

6 Feeling home, promoting home

Cultural heritage, community building and participatory tourism in Barriera di Milano (Turin, Italy)

Mariachiara Guerra

Introduction

Barriera di Milano is a nineteenth-century working-class suburb, located in northern Turin, inhabited by approximately 53,000 inhabitants. It became the most recent and emblematic case of transformation in a city undergoing long-term regeneration, and which has experienced tourism-led urban policies since the end of 1990s.

Turin could be considered a significant case, in which both top-down public actions and bottom-up private initiatives coexist in order to generate an innovative touristic development. While today the historic centre already seems to be a tourism place, the inner suburbs are still experimenting with programmes and practices to attract outside visitors to ordinary urban areas (Salone et al. 2017).

Favouring a historic perspective, the chapter analyses two main factors affecting local touristic development: architectural heritage and community engagement. It stresses how the first element drives public regeneration policies while the second assumes a key role in bottom-up actions.

Turin was considered the country's industrial capital for most of the twentieth century, but when the industrial sector fell into a definitive recession, local institutions found themselves at a crossroads, forced to choose between an epochal new deal or an unavoidable decline (Berta 1998).

Actually, the 1990s crisis worked as an engine for change (Allasino et al. 2000), and ambitious strategic urban policies, as well as widespread valorisation of monument sites, were set in motion. In 2006, during the XX Olympic Winter Games, these efforts produced the very first outcome of a tourism-led top-down urban regeneration process.

However, the impacts were essentially reserved to the historic centre, and the peripheral suburbs did not follow the same development progression.

The topic of tourism effectively explains the temporal gap between the adoption of urban policies on the metropolitan scale and the actual effect on ordinary neighbourhoods. While the historic and richest districts seem to be the most receptive ones, the inner suburbs require a slower and more complex approach. The regeneration process often creates a phase shift between the city centre and peripheral areas.

DOI: 10.4324/9781003138600-8

Thus, in 2014, since the touristic aptitude of the historic city seemed saturated, the municipality was ready to go beyond the previous regeneration approach by launching *Torino 2025*, an additional strategic plan, driven by the keywords "education", "food" and "smart innovation" (The European House-Ambrosetti 2014). *Torino 2025* faced the academic questions on the real capability of cities in attracting long-term tourist flows, aiming to chase the most recent wave of gentrification (Semi 2015).

At the same time, Barriera di Milano was starting to capitalise on the very first touristic outcomes of European urban regeneration programmes, albeit with a ten-year gap in comparison to the historic centre.

Therefore, the following study connects the overall framework of Turin's policies to the particular context of Barriera di Milano, comparing it with the neighbourhoods of Porta Palazzo and Mirafiori Nord. This approach analyses the various ways in which similar tourism-led regeneration programmes can be affected by the presence of different endogenous factors (e.g. cultural heritage, nearness to city centre as reported on Figure 6.1).

Indeed, the effects are so different that Turin appears to be a collection of "scattered pieces of city" (Gardini 2011, 230). In general terms, it testifies how hard the strict systematisation of urban regeneration processes is.

To reinforce the argument, it is important to mention different Italian experiences following a top-down approach, in which city planners designed a leading urban image *a priori*, not always driven by the survey of local community needs. These interventions are often kick-started both by international events (e.g. Genoa European Capital of Culture 2004 or Expo 2015), or by the economic necessity to convert empty urban spaces into cultural, scientific or tourist facilities.

Several examples could be referred to: the regeneration of Bari's historic centre through the European initiative Urban I (Fanizza 2015), the controversial reconversion of the *Italsider* brownfield site in the western seaside district of Bagnoli in Naples (Gardini 2011) as well as the "student conquest" of the old city in Genoa or the "filtering of young and well-educated residents" into Milan's Isola district (Semi 2015). In Bagnoli, *Città della Scienza* (the City of Science) was inaugurated in 1996 on the former industrial site. Since its inauguration, it has attracted thousands of students and scholars. However, in 2020, the district seems very far from the stereotype of the Roman emperor's paradise envisioned in the original strategic plan (Bull 2005). In Bari, the Urban I interventions consisted mainly in the restyling of the façades of historic buildings in a limited pedestrian area, identified as a social and cultural gathering place for middle-class residents and curious tourists. The neighbourhood's centre is still experiencing crime and a low quality of life.

On the other hand, experiences that privilege a bottom-up approach testify that a deeper coherence between "place-telling" and actual state of change can be reached if recipients are directly involved in the transformation process. For instance, a successful case is that carried out by *Migrantour*, an international network of migrant-driven intercultural routes founded in Turin in 2010. It

Figure 6.1 The districts of Porta Palazzo and Aurora, Mirafiori Nord and Barriera di Milano, compared with the historic baroque core.

Note: Author's elaboration on a 1/25,000 general plan

spread to ten Italian cities and several European capitals, including Paris, Brussels and Lisbon.

This NGO designs new urban itineraries in active cooperation with foreign inhabitants, asking them to guide hundreds of tourists around ordinary neighbourhoods (Rabbiosi 2016).

A participatory methodology has also been adopted in the small, disadvantaged village of Favara (Sicily), where two architects, Andrea Bartoli and Florinda Saieva, opened *Farm Cultural Park* in 2010. The architects transformed seven neglected courtyards, located in the very historic centre, into outdoor galleries and artistic residences. Since its opening, special attention has been given to community engagement and to its younger audience.

In 2016, *Farm Cultural Park* inaugurated *SOU – Scuola di Architettura per Bambini* (School of Architecture for Children), and the *Opp Festival* (a festival of creativity for teenagers) was launched in 2017. Thanks to this dense public programme, Favara now welcomes 120,000 visitors per year.[1]

Furthermore, in summer 2020 the *SOU* was exported in Ostuni (Apulia), on the initiative of *Officine Tamborrino – Scaffsystem*, a metal system construction company which has been deeply involved in local development since its foundation in 1957. Officine Tamborrino traditionally supports important cultural events like the *Apulia Land Art Festival* in Alberobello, and the *MAS Week*, an architecture and design festival held in Taranto.[2] Its commitment in the field of education has been proved by its sponsorship of *CREA Summer Academy*, a design thinking school promoted by the Politecnico di Milano, in Ostuni.[3]

Inevitably, the COVID-19 pandemic has stimulated new participatory practices, often finding the solution in digital platform meetings. In contrast, *Sinopie*, a Rome-based cultural association, launched the *Cultura in balcone* (culture from the balcony) challenge, asking tourist guides to go onto their own balconies and tell their neighbours about the urban heritage around them.[4]

All these heterogeneous examples provide terms of comparison in different conceptual categories: top-down vs. bottom-up approach, scale and solidity of urban policies, local and international resonance.

Turin meaningfully reflects the effects produced when each of these factors interact with one another. The following sections propose an analysis of the municipality's strategic actions carried out since 1997, narrowing the scope to the representative cases of Porta Palazzo and Mirafiori Nord.

The concluding part of the chapter investigates the recent regeneration process in Barriera di Milano, presenting field research carried out in the district by the author, focusing on children as a crucial target and as stakeholders for local development.

Turin: beautiful to see, beautiful to live: building the shape of a touristic city

On an international scale, Turin started to reposition itself as a tourist destination after hosting the XX Olympic Winter Games in 2006. The former capital of the Italian industrial sector discovered a new and unexpected vocation.[5]

In 2015, a report by the Regional Observatory on Tourism disclosed that 6,673,770 visitors came to Turin and its metropolitan area, which is 200% more than in 2006.

The figures are all the more impressive when compared with the improvement of the tourist flow in the whole region. Piedmont experienced an average increase of just 23.32% in visitors, and Turin continues to hold a leading role, doubling the regional percentage.

After receiving the nomination for the 2006 Olympic Games, Turin's local authorities and research institutions started working together to insert tourism into the Regional Strategic Plan, anticipating it could become a lever for development, and one of its main economic axes.

In 2010, two specific regional agencies *(Sviluppo Piemonte Turismo* and *Osservatorio Culturale del Piemonte, 2010)* published the results of *Destinazione Torino*, a survey carried out to investigate tourist expectations, in both international markets and as part of the national scenario. The sample highlighted that Turin was a cultural and artistic destination for more than 80% of interviewees and summarised their perception of the city with the motto "Beautiful to see, beautiful to live".

The cultural inclination has been confirmed by annual figures released by the Ministry of Cultural Heritage and Tourism (MiBACT, 2020). In 2019, the Museo Egizio and the Venaria Reale royal palace were both visited by almost 850,000 tourists, holding the sixth and seventh positions on the national list of most visited cultural locations, right after the archaeological areas of Rome and Pompeii, the Uffizi Galleries and the Galleria dell'Accademia in Florence and Castel Sant'Angelo. In the last decade, Turin has finally confirmed its place among the most important Italian tourist destinations.[6]

However, the development of tourism in Turin has been confined to very specific, dignified urban areas, within the perimeter of the baroque capital. This image has been defined thanks to a long series of restoration sites, constantly improved since 1997, when the residences of the Royal House of Savoy were added to the UNESCO World Heritage List.

To sum up, "historical heritage" and "cultural tourism" became the keywords, driving this early phase of touristic development.

Beyond the baroque: tourism as an opportunity for peripheral areas

In the meantime, Turin underwent a significant transformation of its peripheral suburbs. In those areas, industrial decline coincided with a new influx of foreign immigrants, who took up residence in the same districts where the older generations of migrants from southern Italy had arrived after the Second World War.

In 1997, in order to regenerate them, the municipality set up a strategic plan for the peripheral districts *(Actions for participatory local development)* and devoted a specific office to the regeneration of the inner neighbourhoods (Città di Torino 1997). Over the past two decades, almost 20 urban projects have been launched all around the metropolitan area. They include European programmes, local initiatives, participatory community agreements and refurbishment plans (Città di Torino 2005).

This long-term vision is explored in the guidebook *L'altra Torino (The Other Turin)*, published in 2011 with the support of the municipality (Bergamin et al. 2011). It describes 24 tourist itineraries, leading the visitor beyond the city centre. Emphasising the motto *Periferia, non malinconia* (periphery, not melancholy), the authors define the existence of fragmented parts of the city and promote each of them as a specific destination for other local residents moving from central districts to the "ordinary" city. *L'altra Torino* should be considered one of the several literary outcomes of a long-lasting academic survey of the built heritage. This 30-year research was driven from the 1980s on by the municipality and curated by the History and Cultural Heritage centres at the Politecnico di Torino (Comoli and Viglino 1984; Davico et al. 2014).

In view of this, the next section of the chapter narrows the scope to the experiences of Porta Palazzo, the old central commercial district, and Mira-fiori Nord, the peripheral neighbourhood built in the 1930s around the largest automotive industrial settlement in Turin. Quite significantly, the former was not included in *L'altra Torino*, while the latter was described in detail.

Although the growth of the tourism sector was one of the expected goals in both suburbs, a comparison of the two cases proves that specific endogenous factors affected the outcomes appreciably.

Porta Palazzo: the multicultural face of the city

In 1996, the municipality presented *The Gate – living not leaving* to the European Regional Development Fund. The Gate was a pilot project conceived to improve quality of life and working opportunities in Porta Palazzo, the historic suburb located just across the northern fringe of the baroque city centre. Actually, the first plan of the area was designed in 1729 by the royal architect Filippo Juvarra, contemporary to the *corona di delitie*, the "crown" project of the Royal House of Savoy residences spread around the territory (Comoli 1995).

During the nineteenth century, Porta Palazzo affirmed its role as the commercial core of the city, and today it hosts the biggest outdoor market in Europe, with a considerable number of the 5,000 commercial licenses held by Maghrebian and Chinese merchants (Black 2012).

In 1998, *Comitato Progetto Porta Palazzo*, an operative local committee created by public and private interested parties, started testing various innovative approaches and original practices to engage different generations of immigrants, in order to solve the heavy conflict existing between the older generation of southern Italian residents and the new foreign inhabitants (Allasino et al. 2000). In 2002, the municipality turned the committee into *The Gate*,[7] a permanent local development agency, and broadened the scope of interventions bordering the suburb of Barriera di Milano (Briata 2014).

The committee, and later on the agency, managed to turn the main critical weakness, that is the presence of different communities of immigrants, into the most characteristic and positive distinguishing feature of the area. Today the project's official website introduces a rich catalogue of tourist proposals, collected under the motto "*Discover Porta Palazzo. Le Ventre de Turin*".[8] Porta Palazzo is now considered the heart of the multicultural city and an autonomous tourist destination in its own right, thanks to the fusion of historical estates and international cultures (Gilli and Ferrari 2017). It is evident therefore that the effectiveness of these strategies was strongly facilitated by two factors: the proximity to the baroque area and the historic value of its buildings.

In 2016, two important acknowledgements were made: describing Turin as one of the 52 places to go, the *New York Times* suggested a visit to Porta

Palazzo (Wyner 2016), while *Lonely Planet* described it as "frantic, fabulously multicultural and fun".[9]

Mirafiori Nord: the industrial district beyond the factory

In 2000, the municipality of Turin chose Mirafiori Nord, a blue-collar neighbourhood of 25,000 inhabitants, to be nominated for the European programme Urban II. Mirafiori Nord is located 5 km south of the historic centre, close to the 3,000,000 m³ FIAT factory, which hired 22,000 workers and attracted thousands of immigrants from southern Italy. Today, those same workers raise the average age of residents, since 32% of inhabitants are over 60.

The FIAT settlement became the symbol of the Italian industrial capital, but during the 1980s it fell into progressive disuse, and the whole area started to lose its peculiar identity (Giusti and Tamborrino 2008).

Consequently, the district faced unemployment, impoverishment and a general decrease in its social and cultural level. Therefore, after years of debate between local authorities, associations and citizens, the municipality proposed a project structured into three main axes of intervention: *recovery and sustainability*; *economic development*; and *social integration, contrast to exclusion and cultural growth*. The project was granted more than 28 million Euros of public funds.[10]

In January 2002, authorities officially started carrying out interventions like the improvement of waste sorting, the refurbishment of public social housing and the restoration of *Cascina Roccafranca*,[11] a historic 2,500 m² farmstead (a rare example of the agricultural past of the territory, now hosting a job centre, 80 non-profit associations, 100 different courses, 40 workshops and 160 events per year). Moreover, in order to collect the memories of the elderly, several specific initiatives were planned.[12]

Furthermore, also in 2002, with the support of the *Fondazione Adriano Olivetti*, the public art programme *Nuovi Committenti Mirafiori Nord* was set up, following the French model of the *Nouveaux Commanditaires* (Revelli 2004). In 2008, after a slow process of engagement, involving children, teenagers and residents of social housing complexes, the needs and expectations of the inhabitants were translated into four works of public art.

The interventions included the restoration of a small baroque chapel facing the FIAT site, which was transformed by a group of primary school teachers into the main Mirafiori archives (Comitato Urban 2 2008).

Furthermore, after six years of research, 1,300 original pictures and 100 interviews were collected and published by the non-profit cultural association *AQuMe – il Quartiere e la Memoria*, in the book *Da Miraflores alla Roccafranca. Turismo urbano a Mirafiori Nord*, a choral historical guide, describing not only the architectonic environment but also the intangible heritage (Robotti and Zanlungo 2008). Despite these efforts, Mirafiori did not become an actual tourist destination, and although some important and concrete local goals were achieved in the improvement of life quality, the district is not well known outside the perimeter of a limited specific audience.

Barriera di Milano: the tourist experience, between old industries and new inhabitants

The district of Barriera di Milano lies between the two cases presented earlier and merges the industrial past of Mirafiori Nord with the multicultural presence of Porta Palazzo. Additionally, it holds the record as the youngest neighbourhood in the city and has the highest concentration of foreign families (ISTAT 2011), with schools enrolling almost 75% non-Italian-born pupils.

From 2011 to December 2015, Barriera di Milano experienced *Urban Barriera*, the most recent regeneration programme, led by a public committee. The following sections analyse the mutual relationship between historic architectonic shape, urban policies and participatory touristic development in that specific context.

Workers and migrants: the district of the past

Barriera di Milano derives its name from the city gate of the 1853 customs wall, standing on the main route to Milan. Indeed, in the second half of the nineteenth century, Turin set new strategies for industrial development, privileging the northern area, since it was tax-free and rich in canals. These facilities rapidly attracted several investors and generated early industrial production settlements. Consequently, the number of inhabitants living in the neighbourhood rose from 1,901 in 1881 to 17,791 in 1901 (Gambino and Lupo 2011). In the late 1970s, concurrently with the peak of industrial production, and after two huge influxes of migrants from the eastern regions and from the south, the population of Barriera di Milano reached almost 61,000 (Miletto and Sasso 2015).

The early and widespread presence of workers' unions and mutual societies made the participation of residents a constant feature of the district's history. Since the beginning of the twentieth century, the community has been strongly committed to guaranteeing essential public services, above all education and healthcare. The inhabitants' awareness was likewise a crucial factor of the Italian resistance movement partisan brigades during the Second World War (ISTORETO 2003), and it let the immigrants maintain their own cultural heritage in the post-war period. For instance, residents from the Apulia region in the south of Italy reinforced their social presence in the district, maintaining their hometown traditions and religious rituals (Cacciatori and Seminara 2011).

However, a new migrant influx took place in the decades of the late twentieth century, and in 2011 Barriera di Milano reached the highest incidence of foreign population (28.9% compared with the average 13.6%) and the highest concentration of foreign minors (40% compared with the average 26%) in the city. These migrants came mainly from northern African countries (Maghreb) or from recent EU member states (especially Romania). The unemployment rate (10.5%) testifies that these residents often live in conditions of social and economic marginalisation (Comitato Urban Barriera 2016). In fact, they paid the ultimate price of the long-lasting recession (as well as that related to the COVID-19 pandemic).

In 2011, the municipality launched the *Urban Barriera* regeneration programme to face the consequences of recession, aiming to create an original participatory asset. At the same time, a comparable number of cultural, social and economic actions were launched by private interested parties (Salone et al. 2017).

Both public top-down interventions and private bottom-up initiatives are reported ahead, stressing that they both work to promote Barriera di Milano as a tourist destination.

Urban policies and public investments for a new phase of local development

In technical terms, *Urban Barriera* is a PISU,[13] jointly promoted by the municipality of Turin, the Piedmont region and the European Union, financed by 35 million Euros of public capital. Covering an area of 2.3 km², the project is articulated along four axes: physical-environmental, economical-employment, social-cultural, and communication and community support.

Within the first axis, a huge renovation plan concerned 78,000 m² of built and environmental estate, providing 40,000 m² of new collective spaces, and adding 62,000 m² of green areas. It also included the restoration of the *Bagni Pubblici*, a public baths facility, inaugurated in 1956 and reopened in 2006, to face the needs of new incoming residents. It was transformed to host additional social functions and cultural associations, including bodies committed to promoting free guided historic tours of the district. The *Bagni Pubblici* was redesigned to underline its symbolic role as a crossroads for different generations of inhabitants.

In 2017, along with other cultural hubs such as the aforementioned *Cascina Roccafranca*, it was included in the *Rete delle case del quartiere* (the network of district houses). The *Rete delle case del quartiere* is a standing committee promoted by the municipality and the *Compagnia di San Paolo* (the principal bank foundation located in Turin), in order to connect the main community hubs located all around the suburbs of the ordinary city. Each *casa* shares the manifesto and acts as a local development agency.[14]

Nevertheless, the *Bagni Pubblici* was not the main physical-environmental intervention in the programme. At a cost of 23 million Euros, the regeneration of the 23,000 m² of the former INCET industrial site aimed to transform a huge, abandoned factory into both a community centre and a fine culinary tourist destination. However, this project has never really taken off, and today the high-quality food pole is already experiencing a severe crisis.

As part of the communication actions, in 2014 the *Urban Barriera* committee and the municipality of Turin launched B.*ART*, an international call for artists to create a new urban art tourist itinerary featuring 13 façades located around the neighbourhood. The artworks were chosen by a public panel made up of experts and inhabitants. The initiative was reported in almost 100 articles in the international press, including the *New York Times* (Wyner 2016). B.*Art* cost 44,000 Euros and was a successful tour, promoted by local associations as well as by external tourism organisations, although the local inhabitants were not well informed about it.

The other main communication initiative was launched in late 2016, when *Urban Barriera* was coming to the end of its term. In order to present the outcomes of the regeneration, Barriera di Milano was described in *A Barriera c'è il mare* (The sea in Barriera), a tourist map edited by the committee, the *Bagni Pubblici* and other private bodies with the sponsorship of the *Fondazione CRT* (a local bank foundation) and the support of several unions of tourist agencies and guides.

A Barriera c'è il mare is a collection of the impressions of 600 residents, interviewed (in Italian) during public meetings. They were asked to identify particular places in five categories (culture, food, art, spare time and photography) to give tourists a feeling of home.

Twenty thousand copies were distributed for free at tourist info points all over Turin, and all content was made permanently available on the website www.turinbarriera.it. Nevertheless, the choice to publish the guide only in Italian seems to be a lost opportunity for this multicultural district. It does not let foreign residents read the content, and it does not let international visitors discover Barriera.

In conclusion, after this synthetic review of the public top-down actions, the most significant long-term impacts seem to be produced by the most participatory initiatives, not always related to the biggest budget.

The internal engine of regeneration: private investments and individual initiatives

In Barriera di Milano, private investments make up the core of bottom-up actions carried out over the last decade. Taking advantage of the low rents, the empty real estates and its nearness to the city centre (2 km away) as well as Turin's reputation as an international contemporary arts capital, several entrepreneurs and companies have been investing in cultural projects, art galleries, new museums and innovative multifunctional venues.[15] In this section, an overview of the most relevant cases will be provided.

First of all, the experience of the artist Alessandro Bulgini will be shown, to attest how effective an individual initiative can be in the promotion of a territory. In 2008, he transformed Barriera into an open studio and declared the district "*Opera Viva*", affirming his intention to consider Barriera as a living work of Art, and to take care of the most fragile area in the city. His performances are supported by *Flashback*, one of the main Italian art fairs. Every year, from May to November, he curates *Opera Viva – Cartellone*, a six-month exhibition which takes place on a billboard standing on a traffic circle in the ancient suburb. He has also led hundreds of students in artistic performances and guided tours (Figure 6.2). Bulgini's experience was reported in more than 100 articles in international magazines, and, in the late summer of 2020, he became the head of the *Artista di quartiere* (district artist) school, supported by the Ministry of Cultural Heritage and Activities, in order to transfer his practice to young artists.[16]

In 2014, Bulgini also set up one of the inaugural exhibitions of the *MEF – Museo Ettore Fico*, a new private contemporary art museum, located in a disused

Figure 6.2 Students viewing the *Opera Viva – Cartellone*, the Alessandro Bulgini exhibition in Barriera di Milano, Turin (2017 edition)

electrical–mechanical factory. By the end of 2016, the museum had already attracted 50,000 visitors and more than 6,500 students, involving the inhabitants in important special initiatives and promoting local audience engagement. For instance, in 2016, with the support of *Compagnia di San Paolo*, the museum launched *MEF in Market*, a curatorial programme devoted to the merchants of Piazza Foroni, the oldest outdoor marketplace in the district. After a participatory educational training course, the merchants themselves planned a public programme.

Three months before the opening of the *MEF*, very close to that marketplace, a new community hub was inaugurated on the initiative of *Sumisura*, a local cooperative enterprise. Located in a former printing factory, the hub named *Via Baltea 3 – Laboratori di Barriera*, since 2014 has hosted a social café, a jazz school, co-working offices and a bakery staffed by migrants and refugees. Furthermore, some activities for elderly people and children are hosted for free, while other specific initiatives (e.g. community kitchen, social carpentry) respond to the will to engage the inhabitants. The *Via Baltea* staff say: "We cannot imagine our work without improving the world we are living in. We will continue serving beers to provide community services."

This motto best summarises the bottom–up approach of the private actors in Barriera di Milano.

Atelier Héritage: *experimenting a new model of urban workshop*

Shortly after opening, *Via Baltea* welcomed *Atelier Héritage*, a permanent urban workshop founded by the author: it is based on the key idea that cultural heritage knowledge can be an effective tool to make children lead players in participatory practices. Its core business consists of activities for children (6–13 years old), featuring a cultural heritage school in summer, and a weekly workshop from October to May.

Located in the very inner heart of the nineteenth-century borough, where the buildings are old and degraded, *Atelier Héritage* engages pupils whose parents are often outside the processes of social inclusion, due to their linguistic difficulties and economic marginalisation.

The assumption is that architectural heritage can be the meeting point for people from different countries and cultures. In fact, according to the *Osservatorio sulla scuola a Torino*, foreign pupils make up almost 74% of the enrolled population in the *"Aristide Gabelli"* school district, the closest to Via Baltea.[17]

Therefore, *Atelier Héritage* invests in making today's foreign children tomorrow's Italian citizens. It fosters a common identity, built through the knowledge of urban history, assuming that they have all found the same shared home in Barriera di Milano even though their families came from different countries, different histories and a different culture.

The children, in fact, were nearly all born in Turin, and they speak and understand Italian perfectly. As a matter of fact, they represent a strategic human capital for the future of the city. Moreover, their involvement in social and cultural life is an extraordinary opportunity to engage the kind of adults who often feel inadequate to take part in the urban community.

Atelier Héritage inaugurated its activities in spring of 2014, with free workshops all around Barriera di Milano. The following summer, the first school was launched and attended by 20 participants originally from China, Morocco, Romania and Peru.

The four-week programme included urban walks around the district, design workshops, activities in collaboration with artists like Alessandro Bulgini and meetings with the merchants in Piazza Foroni. The summer school ended with *Turisti per casa* (Tourists around home), a guided tour promoted with the *Bagni Pubblici*, and led by the children. The tour involved 50 relatives and visitors in a special itinerary around the historic streets of Barriera.

The following autumn, the weekly workshop was inaugurated. On one hand, *Atelier Héritage* starts its activities making children explore the history of the neighbourhood, and on the other hand, it works to build a network of partnerships with local organisations and associations.

In February 2015, *Atelier Héritage* became a cultural partner of the *MEF*, organising a special initiative to welcome residents and strengthen *MEF*'s role in the territory. In spring of 2017, they involved 150 families and 280 children in *ConTeStudio*, a free educational after-school programme sponsored by *Compagnia di San Paolo*, established in partnership with the *Bagni Pubblici* and the '*A. Gabelli*' school district. The participants acquired a progressive familiarity with cultural places around the district, having the opportunity to learn the history of Barriera, share their own story and experience art workshops.

These families also gave their personal contribution to the construction of a collective archive of contemporary memories. Actually, *Atelier Héritage* has worked on this topic since 2016, when the summer school pupils started to interview both elderly people and their foreign parents, collecting the testimony of urban change through the voices of its inhabitants.

In 2021, the interviews will be donated and organised in a special archive, stored at the *Institute for the History of the Resistance and Contemporary Society* (ISTORETO), and officially presented during *Archivissima*, the national archives festival.

Atelier Héritage, indeed, set up a cooperation with ISTORETO in 2017, when a special visit programme was designed for summer school attendees. After discovering the archives heritage, they wrote the guide of the institute, now available in both printed and digital versions.

In 2019, the pupils contributed to the knowledge of ISTORETO, publishing a second guide in which they traced an itinerary of the places of the resistance movement in Barriera di Milano. Each child adopted the biography of a local partisan, and on 25 April 2019 (*Liberation Day* in Italy), they led a free guided tour for almost 150 visitors. In 2020, due to the COVID-19 lockdown, the tour moved to the web and the children broadcast the virtual itinerary live on their Facebook page. The broadcast was followed by almost 500 users.

In six years of activities, *Atelier Héritage* has consolidated a practice consisting of three main educational phases: knowledge of place, creation of content and presentation of outcomes to external audiences through tours and guidebooks (Guerra, 2015).

This methodology has been applied in Barriera, where the very first guide was created in 2016. Shortly afterwards, it was exported to two further suburbs – San Donato (2017) and Lucento (2019). *Atelier Héritage* has since established projects there (Figure 6.3).

In the spring of 2020, during the lockdown, the children produced self-made Instagram videos to promote their district. In 2021, the National Museum of the Italian Risorgimento guide will be presented in both printed and digital versions.

Each edition maintains the expression '*è casa nostra*' (it is our home) as a common part in the title (e.g. *Barriera è casa nostra, ISTORETO è casa nostra*). Quoting a famous Italian book *(Torino è casa nostra)*, the title merges the children's feelings with the will to make tourists experience home in that place.

For the same purpose, considering the high percentage of foreign communities living in Barriera, *Atelier Héritage* translated *Barriera è casa nostra* into Arabic, Chinese, Romanian, French and English, and *La Stampa*, one of the principal Italian newspapers, published a special report in the national edition. The aim for the future is to publish each guide in a multilingual edition.

Moreover, another important mission of *Atelier Héritage* is the dissemination of its methodology within the network of local disadvantaged schools. In

Figure 6.3 Children discovering a wall painting by the artist Alessandro Rivoir, during the Atelier Héritage summer school (2019 edition)

fact, a special educational project called *Flashback Lab* has been designed with the support of Flashback Art Fair since 2015, starting during the International Contemporary Week in November, and lasting until May. It is attended by 250 students per year, from primary and secondary schools.

In conclusion, after six years of activities, the figures testify that *Atelier Hérit-age* has involved approximately 1,500 pupils and almost 500 families coming from several countries, including Italy, Syria, Nigeria, Morocco, Peru, Senegal, China and Romania.

This experience proves that educational contents can be used as an extraordinary tool of audience engagement, especially for the most fragile population. This approach implies that the production of culture moves from formal institutions towards urban spaces, with the support of interested parties, working together to train future citizens in a long-term process.

It seems to be a strategic challenge, particularly in a suburb like Barriera di Milano, where children can become the main promoters of their own territory.

Conclusion

Strategic planning points to tourist development as a possible outcome of urban regeneration programmes, both in the case of public/collective policies and in the presence of private/individual initiatives.

Nevertheless, while in the dignified historic city public investments produced a linear return in terms of tourist benefits, in the ordinary suburbs, community engagement is a crucial factor for long-term effective outcomes.

Actually, in the case of Barriera di Milano, the investment of considerable public funds generated results comparable to those achieved by private stakeholders using fewer resources.

Furthermore, if the designers do not adopt a participatory approach from the very preliminary phase of planning, the refurbishments of a few thousand square meters of disused areas could be irrelevant to life quality, and the tourism engine could stay turned off.

Without community engagement, the effectiveness of the practices risks ending along with the expiration of each regeneration programme, and the ordinary city will remain ordinary.

On the contrary, the strength of suburbs like Barriera is the presence of a stable network of cultural and social bodies, supporting residents in becoming the main characters of local development. Actually, their committed presence mends the social fabric and contributes to raising the awareness of citizens.

This statement should be the starting point for any tourist programme in peripheral areas: otherwise, if the residents stay outside the process, guided tours could likely be a sort of urban safari, without any economic benefits or social impact on the district (Semi 2015). For example, visitors enjoy the *B.Art* experience going around Barriera di Milano in private buses, without even coming into contact with residents or places.

On the other hand, private/individual actions put down meaningful roots among inhabitants, stimulating their participation. The experiences are shared and the citizens themselves become content creators.

Although it is clear that these stakeholders do not have the financial capability to promote immediate results on a large scale, this bottom-up approach testifies that the main key point lies in the alliance between promoters and recipients, both shaping the same vision of the place.

In conclusion, inhabitants should be considered the very first tourist guides in a territory, since they have a deeper commitment to promoting their home place, even when the physical experience is forbidden.

Therefore, tourist development must aim for the engagement of citizens and the tangible improvement in their quality of life.

Notes

1 www.farmculturalpark.com. All the websites quoted in the present chapter have been verified and retrieved 10 March 2021.
2 www.officinetamborrino.com
3 www.creasummeracademy.eu
4 www.sinopie.it
5 For figures and touristic studies regarding the Piedmont region, the main source is the specific section of the official website of the Piedmont region. Since 2001, the *Osservatorio turistico* has provided annual reports, thematic analysis and market research on tourist fluxes, typologies and strategies (regione.piemonte.it/turismo).
6 https://storico.beniculturali.it/mibac/export/MiBAC/sito-MiBAC/Contenuti/MibacUnif/Comunicati/visualizza_asset.html_1272433589.html
7 www.comune.torino.it/portapalazzo
8 https://scopriportapalazzo.com/
9 www.lonelyplanet.com/italy/turin/shopping/porta-palazzo/a/poi-sho/424727/359924
10 http://ec.europa.eu/regional_policy/it/atlas/programmes/2000-2006/european/urban-ii-torino
11 www.cascinaroccafranca.it/
12 www.comune.torino.it/urban2/asse_rosso_10.html
13 An integrated local development programme.
14 www.retecasedelquartiere.org
15 The following analysis makes use of data and figures directly provided by the referents of each mentioned project, action, institution or association. Moreover, an essential scientific contribution is the research "Cultural production in peripheral urban spaces: lessons from Barriera, Turin (Italy)", (Salone et al. 2017), surveying 18 cultural initiatives, including *Atelier Héritage*, the one carried out by the author.
16 www.artistadiquartiere.com
17 www.comune.torino.it/servizieducativi/direzione/osservatorio/alba.html

References

Allasino, Enrico, Luigi Bobbio and Stefano Neri. 2000. "Crisi urbane: che cosa succede dopo? Le politiche per la gestione della conflittualità legata all'immigrazione." *Polis* 3: 431–449, doi: 10.1424/2849

Bergamin E. et al. 2011. *L'altra Torino*. Torino: Express.

Berta, Giuseppe. 1998. "Torino città opaca." *Il Mulino* 6: 1071–1079, doi:10.1402/805.

Black, Rachel. 2012. *Porta Palazzo: The Anthropology of an Italian Market*. Philadelphia: University of Pennsylvania Press.

Briata, Paola. 2014. *Spazio urbano e immigrazione in Italia. Esperienze di pianificazione in una prospettiva europea*. Roma: Franco Angeli.

Bull, Anna. 2005. "Democratic Renewal, Urban Planning and Civil Society: The Regeneration of Bagnoli, Naples." *South European Society & Politics* 10: 391–410.

Cacciatori, Orlandina and Carmelo Seminara. 2011. *Barriera di Milano*. Torino: Graphot.

Comoli, Vera (ed.). 1995. *Itinerari juvarriani.* Torino: Celi.

Comoli, Vera and Viglino Micaela. 1984. *Beni culturali ambientali nel Comune di Torino.* Torino: Celid.

Davico, Pia. et al. 2014. *La storia della città per capire, il rilievo urbano per conoscere. Borghi e borgate di Torino.* Torino: Politecnico di Torino.

Gambino, Roberto and Giovanni Maria Lupo (eds.). 2011. *Borghi e borgate di Torino, tratutela e rilancio civile.* Torino: Celid.

Gardini, Emilio. 2011. "La trasformazione urbana dell'area dismessa ex-Italsider di Bagnoli. Uno sguardo sociologico sull'immagine dello spazio fisico in mutamento." *Rassegna Italiana di Sociologia* 2: 229–252, doi:10.1423/34987.

Gilli, Monica and Ferrari Sonia. 2017. "Tourism in Multi-Ethnic Districts: The Case of Porta Palazzo Market in Torino." *Leisure Studies* 6: 1–12, doi:10.1080/02614367.2017.1 349828.

Giusti, Maria Adriana and Tamborrino Rosa. 2008. *Guide to Piemonte: Architecture of the 20th century.* Torino: Allemandi.

Miletto, Enrico and Sasso Donatella. 2015. *Torino 900. La città delle fabbriche.* Torino: Edizioni del Capricorno.

Moralli, Melissa. 2015. "Metropolitan Development and Responsible Tourism: The Case of Italian Mygrantour." In *Metropolitan Tourism Experience Development*, edited by István Tózsa and Anita, Zátori. Budapest: Department of Economic Geography and Futures Study, Corvinus University of Budapest, pp. 188–200.

Moralli, Mellissa. 2016. "Fostering Interculturality in Urban Ethnic Neighbourhoods: Opportunities and Limits of the Responsible Tourism Approach." *Journal of Mediterranean Knowledge* 1: 165–183.

Revelli, Marco et al. 2004. *Nuovi committenti. Torino Mirafiori Nord.* Roma: Luca SossellaEditore.

Robotti, Diego and Zanlungo Laura. 2008. *Da Miraflores alla Roccafranca: turismo urbano a Mirafiori Nord.* Torino: Hapax.

Salone, Carlo, Sara Bonini Baraldi and Pazzola Giangavino. 2017. "Cultural Production in Peripheral Urban Spaces: Lessons from Barriera, Turin (Italy)." *European Planning Studies* 12: 1–21, https://doi.org/10.1080/09654313.2017.1327033.

Semi, Giovanni. 2015. *Gentrification. Tutte le città come Disneyland.* Bologna: Il Mulino.

Electronic sources

(verified and accessed 10 March 2021)

Black, Rachel. 2005. "The Porta Palazzo Farmers' Market: Local Food, Regulations and Changing Traditions." *Anthropology of Food* 4, https://aof.revues.org/157.

Città di Torino. 1997. *Deliberazione del consiglio comunale. Progetto speciale periferie: azioni di sviluppo locale partecipato.* Torino: Città di Torino, www.comune.torino.it/rigenerazioneurbana/documentazione/deliberaperiferie.pdf.

Città di Torino – Servizio centrale Comunicazione, Olimpiadi, Promozione della città. 2005. *Periferie 1997–2005.* Torino: Città di Torino, www.comune.torino.it/rigenerazioneurbana/documentazione/periferie9705.pdf.

Coccorese, Paolo. 2017. "I bimbi stranieri mappano la periferia Cari genitori, questa è anche casa nostra." *La Stampa* 20, 9 April, www.lastampa.it/2017/04/09/societa/i-bimbi-stranieri-mappano-la-periferia-cari-genitori-questa-casa-nostra-tIdzOVove4xBhwwz9WJNgN/premium.html.

Comitato Urban 2. 2008. *Nuovi committenti a Mirafiori Nord.* Torino: Città di Torino, http://www.comune.torino.it/urban2/download/news/nc_definitivo.pdf

Comitato Urban Barriera. 2016. *Urban Barriera di Milano. 2011–2015. Final Report.* Torino: Comitato Urban Barriera, www.comune.torino.it/urbanbarriera/news/urban-barriera-report-2011-2015.shtml#.Wgm7gIZry7Y.

The European House – Ambrosetti. 2014. "Torino 2025. Il processo di trasformazione di Torino e la nuova visione per il futuro del territorio metropolitano." www.ambrosetti.eu/wp-content/uploads/TORINO-2025-Documento-di-orientamento-strategico.pdf.

Fanizza, Fiammetta. 2015. "Indifferenza e assenza di affettività: il Programma Urban I a Bari Vecchia." In *Urbanistica Informazioni – Special Issue.* Roma: INU Edizioni, pp. 34–36, www.urbanisticainformazioni.it/IMG/pdf/08_viii_sessione.pdf.

Guerra, Mariachiara. 2015. "Atelier Héritage: Didattica dei beni culturali e storia urbana come strumento di creazione di cittadinanza in Barriera di Milano, Torino." In *Urbanistica Informazioni – Special Issue.* Roma: INU Edizioni, pp. 40–43, www.urbanisticainformazioni.it/IMG/pdf/08_viii_sessione.pdf.

ISTAT. 2011. "8mila Census. Indicatori per aree di censimento." *Torino,* http://ottomilacensus.istat.it/fileadmin/download/01/subcomunali/subcomunali_001_001272.pdf

Istituto Piemontese Per La Storia Della Resistenza. 2003. *La città delle Fabbriche.* Torino: ISTORETO, www.istoreto.it/to38-45_industria/pdf/citta_industria.pdf.

Ministero dei Beni e delle Attività Culturali Press Office. 2020. "2020. Musei, top 30: Colosseo, Uffizi e Pompei superstar nel 2019." https://storico.beniculturali.it/mibac/export/MiBAC/sito-MiBAC/Contenuti/MibacUnif/Comunicati/visualizza_asset.html_1272433589.html.

Rabbiosi, Chiara. 2016. "Il turismo partecipativo a Milano. Un'analisi critica di due iniziative." *Via@* 1, https://viatourismreview.com/wp-content/uploads/2016/11/2016-19-ART8-EN.pdf.

Sviluppo Piemonte Turismo and Osservatorio Culturale del Piemonte. 2010. "Destinazione Torino, RegionePiemonte." www.piemonte-turismo.it/wp-content/files/Destinazione Torino.pdf.

Wyner, Andrea. 2016. "Turin, Italy: Renewal in a Former Industrial Capital." *The New York Times,* 7 January, www.nytimes.com/interactive/2016/01/07/travel/places-to-visit.html?_r=4.Websites

(verified and accessed on 10 March 2021)

www.cascinaroccafranca.it
www.comune.torino.it/portapalazzo/com
www.comune.torino.it/rigenerazioneurbana/documentazione
www.comune.torino.it/servizieducativi/direzione/osservatorio/alba.html
www.comune.torino.it/urban2/asse_rosso_10.html
www.creasummeracademy.eu
http://ec.europa.eu/regional_policy
www.farmculturalpark.com
www.officinetamborrino.com
www.piemonte-turismo.it/documenti/market-research-statistics
www.regione.piemonte.it/turismo
www.retecasedelquartiere.org
https://scopriportapalazzo.com
www.sinopie.it
www.turinbarriera.it

7 Post-socialist cities and the tourism of the ordinary

Milos Nicic

Introduction[i]

Post-socialist studies may be understood as an umbrella term for numerous disciplinary, inter- and trans-disciplinary studies focusing on various types, levels and impacts of changes that occurred in Eastern Europe and elsewhere after 1989. Changes included three major sectors: political (transformation from single party system to multiparty parliamentary democracy), commercial/economical (transformation from planned to market economy) and social (transformation from socialist to capitalist social structure). Common ground for these studies is understanding how these changes "have been played out in everyday life of the people who live in these regions . . . whilst trying to show diverse ways in which political changes are understood as well as created through everyday practices", as Simić (2018, 145) puts it in her recollections on teaching about post-socialism in a post-socialist country.

One of many recent research interests of post-socialist studies are changes that occurred in urban and public spaces, interest that was until recently shadowed for two reasons. First, the problem of transformation has been seen as mainly both a political and an economic matter and second, urban built environment is much less prone to changes than the social institutions, as illustrated by Sýkora (1999, 79): "Political change took only a few weeks and the core institutional transformations of economic system were accomplished within a few years, however, the change of settlement structures will take many years or decades". For this particular reason, research that brings into dialog urban post-socialist transformations and tourism are scarce and require further analysis. At the same time, although it might be seen as a form of a dissonant heritage (Tunbridge and Ashworth 1994), the existence of the built environment from the socialist era in post-socialist times proves to be particularly important for the development of the tourism of the ordinary.

---

i This paper was published as a result of the work on the project No 47021, financed by the Ministry of Education, Science, and Technological Development of the Republic of Serbia.

DOI: 10.4324/9781003138600-9

Post-socialist transformation, along with many others, swiftly brought out an additional change and that is from the industrial to the post-industrial, information society (Castells 2011). It is no wonder how this came to be, as socialist cities were, more than their counterparts in Western Europe,[1] dependent on and defined by belated but rapid modernisation and industrialisation during the second half of the twentieth century. One of the distinctive features of socialist urban development was the excessive role of industrialisation with simultaneous negligence of the service sector and the infrastructures (Vujović 2004, 154). Industry (sometimes even heavy industry) in socialist cities regularly overshadowed consumer and retail functions (Tosics 2005), and it was only expected that post-socialist transformation will bring vast deindustrialisation, followed by privatisation which included even parts of public space (Hirt 2012). Parallel to the loss of industrial function of space in urban centres, the real estate market was gaining foot, after being almost suspended during the socialist times (Tsenkova and Nedovic-Budic 2006) and was strongly dependent on vacant plots freed from derelict industry plants and sites, situated in rather attractive parts of the city. In many cases, the value of the land left behind the derelict industry skyrocketed – profits available through property development were higher than they would be in reinstating industrial production, which attracted "risk seeking investors" to the newly established housing market (Stanilov 2007, 10). In Belgrade alone, more than 60% of former industrial sites went through such urban reconstruction (Krstić 2015; Stanilov and Hirt 2009).

The changes and impacts of urban spatial reconstruction in post-socialist cities carried both positive and negative characteristics, as recognised by Stanilov (2007, 9) (Table 7.1), many of which will be important for the development of the tourism of the ordinary, especially the greater role of public participation and NGO, retreat from planning, revitalisation of some of urban districts and the existence of derelict industrial areas.

Former Yugoslavia was a particular case in the world of socialist countries, as its political regime, led by Josip Broz Tito, pursued a path of socialism independent from the Eastern Bloc and dominance of Moscow. Its symbolic political and social position between East and West (Bakic-Hayden 1995), its crucial role in the development of the Non-Aligned Movement (Rubinstein 1970), the abundance of Western popular culture present in everyday life (Vučetić 2012) to its own take on planned economy via the autochthonous developed system of self-management meant that Yugoslavia was also trailblazing in the domain of urban development and city building too. One of the most ambitious projects undertaken was the creation of New Belgrade, a novel political and administrative centre of the newly formed Socialist Yugoslavia. As early as 1944 began the construction of a whole new city adjoining the Old Belgrade and just on the opposite banks of the Sava and Danube rivers, which grew to become the most populous municipality in contemporary Serbia, with more than 200,000 inhabitants.

New Belgrade has been chosen as the centrepiece of this case study for its unique disposition within socialist and post-socialist urban context of

Table 7.1 Characteristics of spatial reconstruction from socialist to post-socialist city

Positive characteristics	Negative characteristics
URBAN MANAGEMENT	
reestablishment of private property rights	retreat from planning
reestablishment of real estate markets	lack of institutional coordination
decentralisation of power	insufficient financing
rise in entrepreneurship	reduction in public service provision
greater role of public participation and NGOs	poor implementation of laws and regulations
URBAN PATTERNS	
break-up of the mono-centric model	chaotic development patterns
diversification of mono-functional areas	suburban sprawl
revitalisation of some urban districts	depopulation of city centers
redevelopment of brownfield sites	decline of socialist housing estates
improvements in building standards	derelict industrial areas
	surge in illegal construction
URBAN IMPACTS	
increase in individual standards and choices	decline in communal living standards
increase in home ownership rates	loss of open space
diversification of market choices	decline in public service provision
increase in shopping opportunities	privatisation of public realm
increase in personal mobility	increased congestion, air and noise pollution
	the costs of sprawl
	social stratification

Source: Stanilov (2007, 9)

Yugoslavia – it went through most evident and significant changes, both in terms of built environment and social structure, in another words thorough transformation from its genesis to the contemporary times. Though this trans- formation denotes primarily civic and functional features, significant changes have been noted in the interest about its past, heritage, cultural and touristic value from both locals' and visitors' perspectives. The contradictions and twists that will be presented here are mostly connected to the intrinsic features of New Belgrade and the way it came to be. Often described as a brainchild of a new and potent ideology of a strong socialist state, a greenfield project of a well-defined characteristics, New Belgrade was (and is) none of that and much more (Kulić 2012, 2013, 2014; Blagojević 2007; Le Normand 2014; Waley 2011). Another reason for choosing New Belgrade for this study, beside its distinctive genesis and decentred urban character, is its rather non-existent position within the map of Belgrade's tourism, despite the size, wealth and urban significance. New Belgrade is an urban story made of unexpected plots, abrupt turns, planned and extorted changes and represents a "complex urban collage", as Kulić (2014) characterised its tumultuous past.

Theoretical sources of the ordinary in this chapter rely heavily on the traditions of cultural studies and sociology and its understanding of the term (Lefebvre 1947; Hoggart 1957; Williams 1958; de Certeau 1980; Fiske 1989). The affirmation of bottom-up agency among the most mundane sections of everyday life (e.g. visiting the shopping mall, watching television and even people-watching in the neighbourhood) is what tourism of the ordinary is all about. Ordinary spaces, therefore, in this sense are constituted out of a plethora of everyday and mundane practices revolving in and around them and not by the existence of certain architectural, built-up features or lack thereof. The research network has been concentrated around primary and secondary literature about the development of New Belgrade, its position and significance for the capital city of Belgrade in both an urban and a tourist sense. Emerging heritagisation (Harrison 2013) of the built environment and social significance of New Belgrade, together with its potential for participating in the tourism of the ordinary, have been analysed using relevant data from websites of Tourist Organization of Belgrade and the Institute for the Protection of Cultural Monuments of Serbia - Belgrade, two official bodies of great importance for the city-tourism nexus.

Without going into various criticisms of the concept of rebuilding cities for tourism consumption, failed attempts to achieve architectural, creative and cultural uniqueness (cf. Maitland 2013; Sudjic 2005; Teedon 2001), it is my intention to show how these particular processes, originating in the transformation of Belgrade from socialist to post-socialist city, laid foundations for the emergence of the tourism of the ordinary. This chapter presents an account of tourism development in places *not* created to host it specifically (cf. Condevaux, Gravari-Barbas and Guinand, this volume) and as a direct consequence of social relations occurring in the places that *are* created to host it. The extensions of tourism to ordinary places and people signify the *afters* of general assumptions regarding travelling principles, in which shifting roles of actors, their relations and outcomes for both locals and tourists lead to complex hybridisation. Main causes and characteristics of these changes are discussed in relation to the process of post-socialist urban transformation that is seen as central to this hybridisation, so relevant for the understanding of the contemporary tourism dynamics.

Peripheral position, multitude of landmarks and possibilities for one-of-a-kind experiences bring forward New Belgrade to anyone interested in "tourism of the ordinary" or new urban tourism. Reasons for it are explored in depth in this chapter and for making the reader appreciate them fully, it is essential to introduce New Belgrade in its entire urban, social, cultural and commercial complexity.

New Belgrade: stronghold of ideology, bureaucratic paradise and neoliberal playground[2]

Newly liberated Belgrade in the autumn of 1944 was in dire need of infra-structural renewal, with particular focus to rebuilding/repairing the residential buildings and bringing back the basic functions of a city to life, as almost 50% of its residential structures – 12,889 out of 30,000 – were partly or completely destroyed (Somborski 1951, 51). Newly formed city administration directed its efforts to clearing out the debris while simultaneously forbidding any new constructions on empty plots or those left behind the collapsed buildings. It was in fact illegal to commence with any construction work (Petranović 1970). It was clear that authorities had another urban project in mind, one that did not include the complete restoration of an old city, like it was done with Warsaw and Dresden.

Erecting New Belgrade from ground zero on the marshlands confined by the Sava and Danube rivers was as much a political act as it was an urbanistic undertaking, since the parallel streams of priorities flew throughout all phases of the project. The necessity to construct a city which will extend the existing urban borders of capital Belgrade and house most significant party and state structures was constantly followed by a notion that by creating a new city, we create a new society. Hence, the role of New Belgrade in immediate post-war years was twofold – functional and symbolic. The party, state and federal government edifices planned along its wide avenues, elaborate monuments serving as *lieux de memoire* and vast amounts of public space (that in socialism was the privilege of the people, not the commerce, and thus always invokes political connotations; cf. Banerjee 2004; Le Normand 2014) meant symbolic shifts from the old capital city to the new one and a clear sign of the power of the newly formed state.

Internal political and economic changes during the 1950s, and severing the links with the Soviet Union, brought the wind of change to the construction of New Belgrade. The production-focused economy gave way to more balanced consumption-oriented behaviour; diminishing Soviet influence in urbanism meant that imaginaries for New Belgrade were about to change and ideas about magnificent administrative centre dropped out. Instead, New Belgrade became one of the largest state laboratories for the most pressing issues of the time – housing. This change echoes the shifts on the political stage, westward swings of the Yugoslav state and consequent affirmation of the (socialist) individual with his or her needs acknowledged. These needs were most vocally expressed in square meters, and New Belgrade became one of the largest housing construction sites of Europe.

Housing quickly took primacy over many other functions of a city – transportational/modal, societal, cultural and educational, to name a few. Skyscrapers were envisioned and built to include as many living units as possible, and interviews of first New Belgrade inhabitants testify about the diminishing attention for additional services and amenities that go hand in hand with the urban lifestyle. Lack of hair salons, low number of bakeries, far away libraries and reading rooms were common complaints of the dwellers. "New Belgrade during this period could be better described as an isolated and under-equipped dormitory settlement than as the new centre of a socialist capital city", stated Le Normand (2014, 81), describing the pattern of inhabitants' behaviour in relation to hotels and guests – "They lived in New Belgrade as if in a hotel, only staying there to eat and sleep" (p. 198). This in a way echoes Szelényi (1996) when he states that socialist cities were missing the spontaneity of spaces and people that make the core of what it means to be urban. Instead, "they projected an image of unity and orderliness that only a regime with extraordinary power to control space could produce" (Hirt 2012, 37).

The rise of market socialism in Yugoslavia was witnessed following the decades of the 1960s and the 1970s, a fact that disrupted the housing issues of New Belgrade even further, along with the proclaimed idea of egalitarian approach to accommodation. This meant that new apartments are not exclusively provided free of charge to workers but could be acquired on the market. Archer et al. (2016) illustrates that in a very complex system of loans, company-owned apartments and clientelist practices, higher quality apartments were given to white-collar workers, at the expense of blue-collar workers who were often neglected.

During the 1980s, the last decade of socialist Yugoslavia, New Belgrade was paying the price for the failed promises it was supposed to uphold. Vocal opinion by Henry Lefebvre after his visit to Belgrade sums it up:

> The planification of Novi Beograd has failed, both in its attempt at global coherence and in its political will to create a city. The conceptual and morphological schematism of the zoning and grid could lead only to failure, social and urban. What remains of the desire for ordered functionalism and summary purism . . . towers and bars of ominous dimension, lost in a deserted space where neither the public nor the intimate find their place. . . . The bars and towers, progressively abandoned, would become the ruins of another time, a museum in a memory of a former era where individuals were not entitled to be citizens in full measure.
>
> (quoted in Bitter and Weber 2009, 4–5)

The decade of 1990s, along with the disruptive dissolution of Yugoslavia, was even gloomier for New Belgrade than the past ones. With no funds or political will to continue with the development, New Belgrade was failing in both its intentions – a representative space and successful example in social housing for all. As Kulić (2013, 57) notes, New Belgrade was going backwards: "It is hard to imagine a more emphatic denial of a city's symbolic meanings than what happened in New Belgrade during the 1990s. The city of rational socialist planning became a city of small-scale gray economy".

However, it would be misleading to state that New Belgrade consists of nothing more than housing units. One of the largest buildings in Serbia, and an architectural marvel in its own right, the Federal Executive Council building (nowadays called *Palace Serbia*), is just 1 km away from Communist Party Headquarters (nowadays business tower *Ušće*), along other buildings of political and cultural importance. With the exception of the recently reopened Museum of Contemporary Art, all structures seem to be as out of context or non-engageable (cf. Le Normand 2014). It is not feasible to enter a building, no matter how famous it might be (as Genex Tower surely is) and no permanent exhibitions regarding such wonders of "brutalist" architectural style exist. This existence marked by non-existing interpretation or valorisation, hence consequent touristification, make these structures mere reference points on a landscape of a passing individual.

As such – the unfinished, fragmented, complex urban collage of New Belgrade became an ideal playground during the turbulent years of post-socialism in Serbia. Nowadays it hosts multinational companies from the world of finance, IT, heavy industries and so forth. It is one of the largest housing construction sites in Serbia, but this time for another clientele – luxury penthouses and vista-marketed skyscrapers form an area with one of the most expensive square meters of newly built apartments in the whole country. The complaints about the missing activities, amenities and services from the socialist era were, paradoxically (or not) met during the post-socialist times via small-scale entrepreneurial initiatives. However, such an uneven development created urban and contextual space for reconfigurations, reinterpretations and reconceptualisation, a much needed environment for the rise of the tourism of the ordinary and travelling practices oppositional to the attraction-driven tourism.

Touristification in the post-socialist city and the tourism of the ordinary

When describing stark differences between socialist and post-socialist cities and typology of change, Hirt (2012, 38) brings out that one of the most significant elements within the aesthetics category are pluralism and importation of Western styles; postmodernism and "Las Vegas-isation" of the built environment. Rise of tourism, thinking through and by the tourist gaze (Urry 2002) and consequent touristification of the built environment were oftentimes the easy way to achieve these changes. The arrival of international hotel chains meant instant westernisation of neighbourhoods, if not always in architectural style, then in symbolic presence – shining neon signs and logos were replacing the obsolete messages of public interest, informing the public (and its space) that the long-awaited change has arrived (cf. Kincheloe 2002).

The rise of inbound tourism in Serbia as one of the markers of post-socialist transformation provided not only much needed economic benefits but also and more importantly a sense of symbolic renewal among its citizens. A decade of violent break-up of Yugoslavia during the 1990s brought along with it international sanctions and suspended mobility for many of the citizens of Serbia, a shared sense of *fall from grace* (Simić 2014) – a specific gloomy feeling of sudden rejection by the international community, the very one socialist Yugoslavia actively created. Being of cosmopolitan disposition (Simić 2010) was one of the integrative elements of identity for many citizens of Serbia born and raised during socialist Yugoslavia and the sudden inability to practice this cosmopolitanism and relate to it via travel and consummation of (mostly western) foreign popular culture carried strong negative features. Henceforth, the development of tourism and arrival of foreign tourists[3] is seen as a rather positive and upward trend. This message is taken very seriously by contemporary city and state urban planners, whose activities in alternations to urban tissue follow this line. Touristification of the city centre became one of the defining features of urban change in Belgrade in the past 20 years.

Changes to Belgrade's city centre echoed Harvey's (1989) notion of entrepreneurial city, in which urban redevelopment is directed towards achieving a competitive position on the world stage of global consumerism. Beside land fragmentation that attracts overseas investments, tourism is one of the most potent phenomena that locally links revenue from foreign visits, international presence and image making, important for such a position. For this particular reason, the built-up environment is altered to foster tourism growth and enhance consumption. Accommodation units are added and diversified; restaurants, bars and other commercial places are given more public space; festivals created; and tourists' info points opened, while old public and industrial buildings are reshaped into museums, galleries, conference spaces, concert halls and multifunctional cultural centres. Concentrated in narrow confines of urban cores, these changes necessarily bring (re)aestheticisation and revalorisation (Clark 2003) of what urban is and oftentimes leads to the creation of tourist bubbles (Judd 2003). Belgrade is indeed trying to rebrand itself and become attractive to foreign capital, tourists, global nomads and other mobile elites. In this key one should contextualise regular public announcements of Mr. Goran Vesić, city manager, like the one he gave as 2020 New Year's announcement, titled *"Belgrade is being developed and is becoming a real and orderly European city"*, in which he stressed that *"Belgrade is already some sort of business, tourist and cultural capital of this part of Europe and it is evident that all more companies are moving their HQ to Belgrade"*, while pointing out that *"we should live out of services, become the city of start-ups, creative industry"* (Objektiv.rs 1.1.2020.).[4]

This development, "Europeanisation,"[5] and imposition of orderly character of Belgrade is predominantly being laid out through various forms of grandiose strategies directed to its old city centre and pre-Second World War urban core. Many, if not all of those, should be understood as complex processes of "beautification" that render the urban environment (more and more) attractive, as the creation of stages for constant consumption of spectacle (Debord 1967), be it in forms of changes to the built surroundings, multisensory installations, pop-up events and so forth.

In the course of the past ten years, the centre of Belgrade has been significantly altered in accordance with the mentioned beautification. The oldest parts of the city, around Kalemegdan Park and Fortress have been pedestrianised,[6] arguably lowering accessibility for the local population, while providing much needed space for many new restaurants, bars, ice cream parlours and other entertainment-based services. Pedestrianisation is conceived and carries a signature by Boris Podrecca, which yet again echoes known steps in creation of tourist bubbles – the invitations to star architects to monumentalise a city

(Smith 2007). Exoticisation of urban core continued with introduction of palm trees along the oak-tree lined avenues of Kalemegdan Park in 2020. The same park is destined to host one side of Belgrade's first cable car, intended to connect the area around the Sava–Danube confluence with Belgrade Fortress. This idea was rendered ravaging to the architectural and urban heritage of Belgrade, with organisations such as Europa Nostra warning about the devastating consequences this might have on the potential future of Belgrade's applications for UNESCO protected sites lists.[7] These changes, along with complete remodelling of Belgrade's main Republic Square to expand its open spaces in order to include more commercial and entertainment pop-up events, were met by popular protests in many ways. Main concern was uncontrolled touristification of the city and requests for returning to citizen-oriented urban planning, as voiced by many other European cities battling the balance between the existing (dwellers) and future (visitors) (Colomb and Novy 2017).

In its expansion period, tourism was constituting spaces of its own (Gravari-Barbas 2013), shaping built-up environments and natural landscapes to the purpose of schematic tourist consumption (hotel resorts, theme parks, heritage villages, etc.). Tourism was happening on the scene specifically constructed for its consumerist libretto, simultaneously creating supply by "discovering" new attractions to be visited and managing demand by creating various actions that followed (built and human tourism infrastructure such as inbound agencies, tourist guides, maps, billboards, etc.). However, such expansionistic type of tourism progress revealed a multitude of intrinsic difficulties, from security (Hall et al. 2012) and environmental problems (Mowforth and Munt 2015; Liu et al. 1987), overcrowding and saturation (Navarro-Ruiz et al. 2019), loss of cultural identity and spirit of a place (Nunkoo and Gursoy 2012), to clear voices expressing exit from tourism on local and municipal level (Seraphin et al. 2018). These problems were influencing changes on the side of tourists' themselves, be it to get away from spaces designated specifically for them or to avoid spaces subverted by other tourists (Delaplace and Gravari-Barbas 2016). In a world characterised by rapid growth in international travel and problems associated with it, ordinary locations began gaining momentum and became focal points for all actors in contemporary travel (Gravari-Barbas and Jacquot 2016; Novy and Huning 2008; Andersson 2007; Butler 1990). Seeking alternatives to mass and pre-designed tourism based on attractions began long ago (Eadington and Smith 1992), but the full potential of the *ordinary turn*[8] could be achieved just recently, with the digital revolution, Web 2.0 systems and sharing economies platforms (Ničić and Iguman 2016), bringing new actors, places and practices into the tourism arena (Delaplace and Gravari-Barbas 2016). Alternative was (in) ordinary!

As a consequence of and contrary to the expansion period, non-tourism space began shaping tourism, forming a phenomenon of *tourism of the ordinary* or *new urban tourism* (Maitland 2008; Fueller and Michel 2014). In the long quest for authenticity in the overwhelming consumerism of the globalised culture (Gilmore and Pine 2007), it is the everyday that carries the aura of the "real", while the lived, ordinary life of the urban citizens (locals) carries the aura of the authentic and worth visiting/experiencing. It is the lived and temporary what constitutes the genuine genius loci, not the built attractions and pre-arranged tourist spaces; simply said "areas not planned for tourism are valued as offering distinctiveness" (Maitland 2010, 3).

Novel actors brought tourism into new stage, where tourist offer is not conceived, managed and executed by established players of the industry; it is actually not conceived, managed and executed almost at all, and if it is, it is done by temporary, impromptu, unstable and tourism-decentred actors such as NGOs, student associations, citizens' organisations, volunteers, political and local initiatives and actions. Stage in which tourist resorts are turning into permanent settlements (Stock and Lucas 2012), accommodation shifts from objects built for the purpose of welcoming tourists to private rooms and apartments shared among travellers via platforms such as Airbnb and Couchsurfing (Guttentag 2015; Germann Molz 2011), so change the spaces of tourism that move away from attractions to mundane and "ordinary" settings (Gravari-Barbas and Fagnoni 2013). Fluid character of tourism and its ability to blur borders (Urry 1995) has been particularly important when observing the disputed division between tourists and locals, residents and visitors (Salazar 2010) and ability of meaning-assigning practices to transform almost any space (especially ordinary) into a tourist place (Young 1999). These ordinary places are the loci of hope for the contemporary tourists, places in which the mentioned division could be overcome and attractions avoided, while still maintaining the thrill of travel and satisfaction related to tourism.

Thus, ordinary is used in this chapter to detonate spaces, places and practices standing in opposition to attractions and established ways of tourism consumption. This is a rather specific understanding of ordinary, as it is not presupposing the mandatory mundane character of its objects, people and processes, but rather a relational status – ordinary is everything that is not labelled as attraction, no matter how everyday or unique it can actually be, as will become evident in the case of New Belgrade.

New Belgrade and the ordinary tourism

Almost all of Belgrade's tourism sites, activities, pop-up events, walking tours, pedestrian zones and other points of interest are located in the old, historical core of the city. This distribution is set not only by physical and morphological characteristics of the city, but also by practices of various actors in the city's tourism – from tour guides (Rabotić 2010) to official tourism promoting agencies and bureaus. The Tourist Organization of Belgrade and its alignment with state-approved strategies for the development of Belgrade tourism is seen as one of the driving forces behind such a concentration – the majority of the suggested places to visit are located in the historical core.

Belgrade is noting a steady rise in all tourism-related development parameters, from number of international arrivals, overnights and expenditure, with its attractions, organic and constructed, becoming ever more busy. Despite that, New Belgrade is not featured as a suggested site to visit while in the capital of Serbia, according to the Tourist Organization of Belgrade. At its website, within the webpage *Attractions*, out of 13 entries, 12 are historic sites and one is an outdoor recreational area. The discrepancy is clear, and New Belgrade's existing and future visitors are profiting from it. Thus New Belgrade is gradually being discovered by a particular type of tourists, those seeking mundane and ordinary locations and unmediated contact with local population, gaining access to non-touristy spaces in which authentic genius loci can be perceived (Figures 7.1 and 7.2).

The principal consequence of such a concentration is a specific tourist-zoning of the city, in which some areas are designated for tourism consumptions, while others are left out. Concentration of places and activities (attractions) designed for tourism consumption within a narrow space of the old core of the city makes other neighbourhoods exposed and ready for different forms of tourist consumption, with an attraction-opposite form of tourism involvement. Belgrade's urban core as an attraction-saturated area makes New Belgrade an area off the tourism's grid, rendering it fit for the various practices of the new urban tourism. Its peripheral position to the attraction-based Old Belgrade, variety of landmarks and dense housing area with ordinary people living ordinary lives as local inhabitants constitute New Belgrade as an ideal place to visit for those searching for "everyday and mundane activities of city residents as significant markers of the real" (Maitland 2010, 3).

What plays a great role in the many potential ways a built environment might be used in tourism is the valorisation of such an environment, and New Belgrade holds a paradoxical position in this sense. As a city built in accordance with principles of modernism and Corbusian vision, characteristically modern in its visage, New Belgrade awaits proper local valorisation, after it has been internationally acclaimed, most recently and potently throughout a major exhibition in Museum of Modern Art in New York titled *Toward a Concrete Utopia: Architecture in Yugoslavia, 1948–1980* (Stierli and Kulić 2018). This particular position of semi-valorised neighbourhood allows New Belgrade to feature stunning pieces of architecture and public space, while retaining an atmosphere of ordinary and offering a great stage for the development of the *new urban tourism*.

Mentioning landmarks, it is rather important to offer a distinction between an urban location as a landmark and as an attraction, in which a principal division is the level of tourism attractiveness and consumption associated with it. Landmarks carry inherently present distinctive qualities found in an object – including location, symbolic significance, size and shape, architectural style and so forth that distinguish it from the nearby environment and give it either functional, aesthetical or symbolic value. Attraction is, though, permanently in firm association with tourism (Harris and Howard 1996; Lew 1987, 2014), while at the same time not possessing any physical ability to attract tourists by itself (Leiper 1990), always relying to the mind and imagination of the tourist

Figure 7.1 High-rise in New Belgrade's Blok 30

Figures 7.2 and 7.3 Hotel Jugoslavija district of New Belgrade, seen from the Danube river

Source: Author

Figures 7.2 and 7.3 Continued

to draw its appeal from (Lew 2014, 363). This note is of great importance for the neighbourhood of New Belgrade, as it is dotted with landmarks, both in built and natural environment. Its locations, such as world-famous Genex Tower, "brutalist" housing Blocks 23 and 70 or Sava river island Ada Medjica are by all accounts splendid landmarks, places of great value that have not been subjected to the process of beautification by either local authorities or the local tourism market. Its surroundings are in a way pristine, with no tourist offices, info points and billboards available to interfere with its mundane and everyday character and *pace* of the ordinary.

Realising the potential of the tourism of the ordinary and that there is more to a city than its proclaimed attractions, mentioned independent actors on the tourist stage started offering walking or cycling tours around New Belgrade, focusing mainly on the "lifestyle of ordinary people" (belgradefreetour.com). Yet again, foreign gaze (Urry 2002) sparked these creative assemblages between visitors, knowledgeable locals and ordinary spaces – *The Guardian* named "New Belgrade bike tour" one of the ten best alternative city tours in Europe in 2016 (Coldwell 2016) and *Evening Standard* published its coverage, not forgetting to mention must-see sites: Genex Tower, Sava Centar, Hotel Jugoslavija and several residential blocks (Tierney 2016). Complimentary to these *ventures into the ordinary*, expat-owned rent-a-car agency (Yugotours) offers rides around New Belgrade in Yugoslav cars, contributing to specific creative multisensory experience of consuming legacies of communism.[9] Media agency and cultural association Tačka komunikacije (Point of communication) executes walking tours intended for both foreign and domestic tourists called "Residential New Belgrade: From the brutalist bastion to the garden city", focusing on the everyday life of the local residents, while yet another cultural association Still in Belgrade leads two bike tours that include architecture and beach (riverside) and a written guide to self-led walking tour around New Belgrade (Zuza and Pavlicevic 2014).

All the mentioned tours are designed and conducted by local residents and associations whose main area of activity is outside of tourism or its mainstream avenues, thus guaranteeing that the aura of ordinary character maintains intact. All organised efforts to showcase New Belgrade to foreign visitors meet in one focal point – there is no singular set of "attractions" or must-see destinations within New Belgrade, none of its landmarks have been made attractions and its complex heritage involving chimeras of both socialism and post-socialism stalls local valorisation and consequential heritagisation. For that reason, every visit to New Belgrade falls in the category of the new urban tourism. The lack of attractions – places and practices associated with prefabrication for tourism consumption – and the lack of commodification of urban infrastructure towards tourist use make New Belgrade ideal setting for the tourism of the ordinary.

New Belgrade as an ordinary destination can exist only in relational context to the attractiveness (abundance of attractions) of the old city core. As in Tuan's (1977) understanding that "space" and "place" require each other in order to exist as separate entities, the same goes with ordinary and attractions – one requires another in order to be distinct. They are defined in terms of relatedness via social actions. After discursively making something an attraction, its corresponding Other is automatically becoming ordinary, no matter how unique its physical features might be, as it is the case in New Belgrade. In Belgrade, the majority of objects and activities labelled as attractions praise its pre-Second World War built environment and favour its pre-communist past,[10] consequently leaving New Belgrade as the protagonist of the times spent under socialism in the pleasant position to foster the scene for growing interest in new urban tourism forms. This division between attraction-laden pre-communist past and non-valorised past of the socialist times should be contextualised along the ever-present post-socialist transformation of Serbia, where legacies towards the communist rule of Serbia are still debated and articulated (Simić 2014; Jansen 2005). As per the Institute for the Protection of Cultural Monuments of Serbia - Belgrade, various locations and structures in New Belgrade are placed under the protection of the city, signalling their significance and value. However, their nominal status as protected is not reflected in any actual care, as the majority of built environments is not properly conserved and revitalised. In addition, none of the protected listings are part of the tourism offer of Belgrade, as per the Tourist Organizations of Belgrade and Serbia.

As it was shown in the previous remarks about New Belgrade, it is not the intrinsic characteristics of the environment that makes it ordinary, rather it is the practices of those who inhabit it and visit it. Being placed peripherally to the centres of tourism consumption in Belgrade, New Belgrade depends on its visitors to partake in the consumption of its spaces and activities, and this consumption is of the *ordinary* nature. This in a way aligns New Belgrade to those tourists who venture into neighbourhoods that have not been purposely equipped for tourism, in order to feel the perceived authenticity of everyday life among its inhabitants.

Another link between New Belgrade and tourism of the ordinary, besides being a space not constructed with the purpose of tourism in mind, is the human component – there are very few other tourists in sight, compared with the abundance of local population. The non-existence of traditional tourism actors, tourism infrastructure, promotion and general multilingual accessibility render New Belgrade particularly fitting for the settings of the new urban tourism. This mix of characteristics is ideal for attracting the cosmopolitan consuming class (Fainstein et al. 2003), as for them "what's there, who's there and what's going on combine to form high quality of place" (Maitland 2010, 3). This echoes a shift from tangible to intangible resources, from museums and monuments, to lifestyle and creativity (Richards and Wilson 2007).

The position of New Belgrade as an ambiguous neighbourhood between international recognition and local shunning, its central location within the city confines, yet lack of links with the tourism world, abundance of landmarks and absence of attractions make it rather appropriate for the participation in the practices of new urban tourism. Practices of its tourism consumption are oftentimes associated with individual explorations of everyday life, its local customs and ways, oftentimes aided by written or digital resources provided by the tourists themselves and coming from non-tourism-related sources.

Such practices should be contextualised as part of framework developed by de Certeau (1980), in the relation between urban actors and *strategies* and *tactics*, as mentioned earlier. Initially developed in Nicic and Iguman (2019), this idea brings forward a notion that tourist practices of Belgrade work as strategy in de Certeau's terms, and position the core of the city at the centre of travellers' attention, simultaneously setting New Belgrade aside. New Belgrade's lack of attractions is evident only when perceived in the relation to the city centre, the same as the practices of tourism consumption of New Belgrade stand in relation as tactics to the proclaimed attractions of the old core. Tourism practices of the ordinary thus position the place in the contrast to the attraction, regardless of the inherent properties of such a space. Furthermore, in de Certeau's terms, creativity of the everyday practiced by the tourists of the ordinary takes form of tactics and stands contrary to the strategies of tourism industry.

Yet another feat that brings New Belgrade into line with the tourism of the ordinary is the fact that none of its built environment is designed by a starchitect. Although this proves more difficult for its proper valorisation and both bottom-up and top-down appreciation, it renders it most eligible for visits by the tourists in search of the authentic lived experience away from the attraction-laden city centre. By tackling the palimpsest of meaning behind its contemporary appearance and exploring its spaces untouched by tourism, visitors are likely to get in touch with the local inhabitants and share their perceptions of the everyday. This is enforced by the fact that not a single structure is made with tourism in mind and with no available services and products to cater for a large number of tourists, visitors are *nolens volens* directed towards establishing communication with the locals.

Conclusion

Post-socialist cities went through specific changes during their transformations, and many of them are still in such a process. These changes, some which are the same as in the cities of the West, brought along specific conditions in which urban environment, concentration of the attraction-based tourism in the city centres and ambiguous stance towards socialist heritage laid fertile ground for the emergence of the tourism of the ordinary or new urban tourism. This also applies to New Belgrade – its mixed character and shifting functionalities, staggering differences in skyline, complex valorisation and the fact that it is still being heavily developed in both housing and commercial ways inform its position in the framework of Belgrade's tourism landscape. Not being exclusively residential, not cultural, not commercial, New Belgrade leaves ample space for opposing the world of attractions and indulging in many creative practices of tourism of the ordinary.

In this chapter I have tried to show in which ways tourism of the ordinary is being conducted in a setting that lacks no tangible resources and whose built environment in another regime of tourism valorisation might easily be considered attractions. This presents an interesting addition to the discussions regarding the evident emergence of new tourism paradigm (post-tourism or hyper-tourism) in which the dynamics will revolve well beyond or *after* the established roles and divisions (tourism/civil, amateur/professional, even foreign/domestic), in which hybridisation will lead the way, not compartmentalisation. This insight might have lasting impact on how attractions in tourism context are understood, maintained and (un)made, inevitably impacting the urban tissue in general. Nevertheless, in the particular mix of characteristics, from disputed socialist past to contemporary neoliberal developments, New Belgrade remains in the *fog of war* for much of the mainstream tourism, keeping its allures for the creative visitors, whose interest in the everyday indeed brings them closer to the destination.

Notes

1 For the theoretical and conceptual difference upon the existence of "socialist city", compare with Hirt (2012, 34).
2 Certain parts of this and other sections of this paper have been discussed in *Post-socialism and "ordinary" tourism: New Belgrade* (2019) and I thank my co-author Sanja Iguman for the permission to bring them to the attention of the readers of this volume.

3 For detailed evaluation of urban residents' attitudes towards tourism development in Belgrade, see Tournois and Djerić (2019).
4 https://objektiv.rs/vest/12753/vesic-beograd-se-razvija-i-postaje-pravi-uredjeni-evropski-grad/
5 For historical review of changes intended to make Belgrade an European city, see Arandjelović et al. (2017).
6 For various aspects of ever-expanding pedestrian zones in Belgrade, see Vukmirović (2020).
7 www.europanostra.org/stop-harmful-cable-car-project-on-the-belgrade-fortress/
8 The term "turn" mimics the multitude of turns within the field of anthropology, among which linguistic, reflexive and ontological are most important. They signify deep change of perspective and consequent alterations to the field itself (Simić 2020).
9 Legacies of communism are commoditised and consumed in various spheres of touristic offer along a multitude of post-socialist cities. For details on local particularities, see Velikonja (2009), Light (2000) and Rabotić (2012).
10 With the exception of the mausoleum of Josip Broz Tito and the Museum of Yugoslavia in which it is situated.

Bibliography

Andersson, Tommy. 2007. "The Tourist in the Experience Economy." *Scandinavian Journal of Hospitality and Tourism* 7(1): 46–58.
Arandjelović, Biljana, Milena Vukmirović and Nikola Samardžić. 2017. "Belgrade: Imaging the Future and Creating a European Metropolis." *City* 63: 1–19.
Archer, Rory, Igor Duda and Paul Stubbs. 2016. *Social Inequalities and Discontent in Yugoslav Socialism*. London: Routledge.
Bakic-Hayden, Milica. 1995. "Nesting Orientalisms: The Case of Former Yugoslavia." *Slavic Review* 54(4): 917–931.
Banerjee, Tridib. 2004. "Beijing, Berlin, and Bucharest: Legacies of Socialist Modernity at the End of History." Paper presented at the Biannual Conference of the International Planning History Society, Barcelona.
Bitter, Sabine and Helmut Weber. 2009. *Autogestion, or Henri Lefebvre in New Belgrade*. Vancouver: Fillip Editions and Stenberg Press.
Blagojević, Ljiljana. 2007. *Novi Beograd: Osporeni Modernizam*. Beograd: Zavod za udžbenike.
Butler, Richard. 1990. "Alternative Tourism: Pious Golden Hope Trojan Horse?" *Journal of Travel Research* 20: 40–45.
Castells, Manuel. 2011. *The Rise of the Network Society: The Information Age: Economy, Society, and Culture*. New York: John Wiley & Sons.
Clark, Terry. 2003. *The City as an Entertainment Machine*. San Diego, CA: Elsevier.
Coldwell, Will. 2016. "10 of the Best Alternative City Tours in Europe." www.theguardian.com/travel/2016/aug/01/10-best-alternative-city-tours-europe-warsaw-reykjavik-barcelona. Retrieved 30 September 2020.
Colomb, Claire and Johannes Novy. 2017. *Protest and Resistance in the Tourist City*. London, New York: Routledge.
Debord, Guy. 1967. *The Society of the Spectacle*. London: Bread and Circuses Publishing.
de Certeau, Michel. 1980. *L'invention du quotidian*. Paris: Union générale d'éditions.
Delaplace, Marie and Maria Gravari-Barbas. 2016. *Nouveaux territoires touristiques: Invention, reconfigurations, repositionnements*. Canada: Presse de l'Université du Québec.
Eadington, R. William and Valene L. Smith. 1992. *Tourism Alternatives: Potentials and Problems in the Development of Tourism Publication of the International Academy for the Study of Tourism*. Philadelphia: University of Pennsylvania Press.

Fainstein, Susan, Lily Hoffman and Dennis R. Judd (eds.). 2003. *Cities and Visitors: Regulating People, Markets and City Space.* Oxford: Blackwell.

Fiske, John. 1989. *Understanding Popular Culture.* Boston: Unwin Hyman.

Fueller, Henning and Boris Michel. 2014. "Stop Being a Tourist!' New Dynamics of Urban Tourism in Berlin Kreuzberg." *International Journal of Urban and Regional Research* 38(4): 1304–1318.

Germann Molz, Jennie. 2011. "CouchSurfing and Network Hospitality: 'It's Not Just About the Furniture'." *Hospitality and Society* 1(3): 215–225.

Gilmore, James and Joseph Pine. 2007. *Authenticity: What Consumers Really Want?* Cambridge, MA: Harvard Business School.

Gravari-Barbas, Maria. 2013. *Aménager la ville par la culture et le tourisme. coll., "Ville-aménagement".* Paris: Le Moniteur.

Gravari-Barbas, Maria and Edith Fagnoni. 2013. *Métropolisation et tourisme: Comment le tourisme redessine Paris.* Paris: Belin.

Gravari-Barbas, Maria and Sebastian Jacquot. 2016. "No Conflict? Discourses and Management of Tourism-Related Tensions in Paris." In *Resistance and Protest in the Tourist City*, edited by Johannes Novy and J. Claire Colomb. London: Routledge, pp. 45–65.

Guttentag, Daniel. 2015. "Airbnb: Disruptive Innovation and the Rise of an Informal Tourism Accommodation Sector." *Current Issues in Tourism* 18(12): 1192–1217.

Hall, Colin Michael, Dallen Timothy and David Timothy Duvall. 2012. *Safety and Security in Tourism: Relationships, Management, and Marketing.* New York and London: Routledge.

Harris, Robert and Joy Howard. 1996. *Dictionary of Travel & Tourism Hospitality Terms.* Melbourne: Hospitality Press.

Harrison, Rodney. 2013. *Heritage: Critical Approaches.* New York, Milton Park, Abingdon: Routledge.

Harvey, David. 1989. "From Managerializm to Entrepreneurialism: The Transformation of Urban Governance in Late Capitalism." *Geografiska Annaler B* 71(1): 3–17.

Hirt, Sonia. 2012. *Iron Curtains: Gates, Suburbs and Privatization of Space in the Post-Socialist City.* London: Wiley.

Hoggart, Richard. 1957. *The Uses of Literacy.* London: Penguin Books.

Jansen, Stef. 2005. *Antinacionalizam.* Beograd: XX Vek.

Judd, Dennis. 2003. "Urban Tourism and the Geography of the City." *Eure* 29(87): 51.

Kincheloe, L. Joe. 2002. *The Sign of the Burger: McDonald's and the Culture of Power.* Philadelphia: Temple Uni Press.

Krstić, Iskra. 2015. "Džentrifikacije Beograda, Budimpešte i Praga." *Kultura* 146: 86–103.

Kulić, Vladimir. 2012. "East? West? Or Both? Foreign Perceptions of Architecture in Socialist Yugoslavia." *The Journal of Architecture* 14(1): 129–147.

Kulić, Vladimir. 2013. "National, Supranational, International: New Belgrade and the Symbolic Construction of a Socialist Capital." *Nationalities Papers: The Journal of Nationalism and Ethnicity* 41(1): 35–63.

Kulić, Vladimir. 2014. "New Belgrade and Socialist Yugoslavia's Three Globalisations." *International Journal for History, Culture and Modernity* 2(2): 125–153.

Lefebvre, Henri. 1947. *Critique de la vie quotidienne.* Paris: L'Arche.

Le Normand, Brigitte. 2014. *Designing Tito's Capital: Urban Planning, Modernism, and Socialism in Belgrade.* Pittsburgh, PA: University of Pittsburgh Press.

Leiper, Neil. 1990. "Tourist Attraction Systems." *Annals of Tourism Research* 17(3): 367–384.

Lew, Alan. 1987. "A Framework of Tourist Attraction Research." *Annals of Tourism Research* 14(4): 553–575.

Lew, Alan. 2014. "Introduction: Tourist Attractions: Places, Spaces, and Forms." In *The Wiley Blackwell Companion to Tourism*, edited by Alan Lew, Colin Michael Hall and Allan M. Williams. London: John Wiley & Sons, pp. 3–24.

Light, Duncan. 2000. "Gazing on Communism: Heritage Tourism and Post-Communist Identities in Germany, Hungary and Romania." *Tourism Geographies* 2(2): 157–176.

Liu, Juanita, Pauline Sheldon and Turgut Var. 1987. "Resident Perception of the Environmental Impact of Tourism." *Annals of Tourism Research* 14: 17–37.

Maitland, Robert. 2008. "Conviviality and Everyday Life: The Appeal of New Areas of London for Visitors." *International Journal of Tourism Research* 10: 15–25.

Maitland, Robert. 2010. "Everyday Life as a Creative Experience in Cities." *International Journal of Culture Tourism and Hospitality Research* 4(3): 176–185.

Maitland, Robert. 2013. "Backstage Behaviour in the Global City: Tourists and the Search for the Real London, from Research to Practice." Asia Pacific International Conference on Environment-Behaviour Studies, University of Westminster, London, 4–6 September.

Mowforth, Martin and Ian Munt. 2015. *Tourism and Sustainability: Development, Globalisation and New Tourism in the Third World*. New York and London: Routledge.

Navarro-Ruiz, Sandra, Ana B. Casado-Díaz and Josep Ivars-Baidal. 2019. "Cruise Tourism: The Role of Shore Excursions in the Overcrowding of Cities." *International Journal of Tourism Cities*, ahead of print, https://doi.org/10.1108/IJTC-04-2018-0029.

Ničić, Miloš and Sanja Iguman. 2016. "Technological development and Sharing economies: implications on tourism destinations." In *SITCON 2016*. Belgrade: Singidunum University, pp. 37–42.

Nicic, Milos and Sanja Iguman. 2019. "Post-Socialism and 'Ordinary' Tourism: New Belgrade." *International Journal of Tourism Cities* 5(3): 307–325.

Novy, Johannes and Sandra Huning. 2008. "New Tourism (Areas) in the New Berlin." In *World Tourism Cities. Developing Tourism Off the Beaten Track*, edited by Robert Maitland and Peter Newman. London: Routledge, pp. 87–108.

Nunkoo, Robin and Dogan Gursoy. 2012. "Residents' Support for Tourism: An Identity Perspective." *Annals of Tourism Research* 39(1): 243–268.

Petranović, Branko. 1970. "Obnova u Beogradu 1944–1945. godine." *Godišnjak grada Beograda* 17: 165–185.

Rabotić, Branko. 2010. "Tourist Guides in Contemporary Tourism." International Conference on Tourism and Environment, Philip Noel-Baker University, Sarajevo, Bosnia and Herzegovina, pp. 353–364, 4–5 March.

Rabotić, Branko. 2012. "The Tomb as Tourist Attraction: The House of Flowers in Belgrade." 1st Belgrade International Tourism Conference: Contemporary Tourism – Wishes & Opportunities, Belgrade, Serbia, pp. 249-262, 22-24 March.

Richards, Greg and Julie Wilson (eds.). 2007. *Tourism, Creativity and Development*. New York: Routledge.

Rubinstein, Alvin. 1970. *Yugoslavia and Nonaligned Movement*. Princeton, NJ: Princeton University Press.

Salazar, Noel. 2010. *Envisioning Eden. Mobilizing Imaginaries in Tourism and Beyond*. London: Berghan Books.

Seraphin, Hugues, Paul Sherean and Manuela Pilato. 2018. "Over-Tourism and the Fall of Venice as a Destination." *Journal of Destination Marketing & Management* 9: 374–376.

Simić, Marina. 2010. "Locating Cosmopolitanism: Practicing Popular Culture in Post-Socialist Serbia." *Der Donauraum* 51(3–4): 345–363.

Simić, Marina. 2014. *Kosmopolitska čežnja: etnografija srpskog postsocijalizma*. Beograd: CSK FPN i Čigoja štampa.

Simić, Marina. 2018. "Teaching Postsocialism in a Postsocialist Country: Everyday as a Source of the Political." *Genero* 22: 143–161.

Simić, Marina. 2020. *Ontološki obrt: uvod u kulturnu teoriju alteriteta.* Novi Sad: Mediteran.

Smith, Andrew. 2007. "Monumentality in 'Capital' Cities and Its Implications for Tourism Marketing." *Journal of Travel & Tourism Marketing* 22(3–4): 79–94.

Somborski, Miloš. 1951. "Razvoj Beograda između dva rata." In *Beograd: Generalni urbanistički plan 1950*, edited by Oliver Minić. Beograd: Izvršni odbor N.O. Beograda, pp. 40–51.

Stanilov, Kiril. 2007. "Taking Stock of Post-Socialist Urban Development: A Recapitulation." In *The Post-Socialist City*, edited by Kiril Stanilov. Dordrecht: Springer, pp. 3–21.

Stanilov, Kiril and Sonia Hirt (eds.). 2009. *Twenty Years of Transition: The Evolution of Urban Planning in Eastern Europe and the Former Soviet Union, 1989–2009*. Nairobi: U.N. HABITAT.

Stierli, Martino and Vladimir Kulić. 2018. "Introduction." In *Towards a Concrete Utopia: Architecture in Yugoslavia 1948–1980*, edited by Martino Stierli and Vladimir Kulić. New York: MoMA, pp. 7–9.

Stock, Mathis and Leopold Lucas. 2012. "La double révolution urbaine du tourisme." *Espaces et sociétés* 151: 15–30.

Sudjic, Deyan. 2005. "Can We Still Build Iconic Buildings?" *Prospect* 111: 22–26.

Sýkora, Ludek. 1999. "Changes in the Internal Spatial Structure of Post-Communist Prague." *GeoJournal* 49: 79–89.

Szelényi, Ivan. 1996. "Cities Under Socialism – and After." In *Cities after Socialism: Urban and Regional Change and Conflict in Post-Socialist Societies*, edited by Gregory Andruzs, Michael Harloe and Ivan Szelényi. Oxford: Blackwell Publishers, pp. 286–318.

Teedon, Paul. 2001. "Designing a Place Called Bankside." *European Planning Studies* 9(4): 459–481.

Tierney, Paul. 2016. "Belgrade: Where to Explore the Serbian Capital's Brutalist Architecture." www.standard.co.uk/lifestyle/travel/belgrade-where-to-explore-the-serbian-capitals-brutalist-architecture-a3253406.html. Retrieved 30 September 2020.

Tosics, Ivan. 2005. "Post-Socialist Budapest: The Invasion of Market Forces and the Response of Public Leadership." In *Transformation of Cities in Central and Eastern Europe: Towards Globalization*, edited by F.E. Ian Hamilton, Kaliopa Dimitrovska Andrews and Natasa Pichler-Milanovic. Tokyo: United Nations University Press, pp. 248–280.

Tournois, Laurent and Gordana Djerić. 2019. "Evaluating Urban Residents' Attitudes Towards Tourism Development in Belgrade (Serbia)." *Current Issues in Tourism* 22(14): 1670–1678.

Tsenkova, Sasha and Zorica Nedovic-Budic. 2006. "The Post-Socialist Urban World." In *The Urban Mosaic of Post-Socialist World*, edited by Sasha Tsenkova and Zorica Nedovic-Budic. Heidelberg: Physica Verlag, pp. 349–366.

Tuan, Yi-Fu. 1977. *Space and Place: The Perspective of Experience.* Mineapolis: University of Minnesota Press.

Tunbridge, J. E. and G. J. Ashworth. 1994. *Dissonant Heritage: The Management of the Past as a Resource in Conflict.* London: Wiley.

Urry, John. 1995. *Consuming Places.* London and New York: Routledge.

Urry, John. 2002. *The Tourist Gaze 3.0.* London: Sage.

Velikonja, Mitja. 2009. "Lost in Transition: Nostalgia for Socialism in Post-Socialist Countries." *East European Politics and Societies* 23(4): 535–551.

Vučetić, Radina. 2012. *Koka kola socijalizam.* Beograd: Službeni glasnik.

Vujović, Sreten. 2004. "Akteri urbanih promena u Srbiji." In *Društvena transformacija i strategije društvenih grupa – Svakodnevnica Srbije na pocetku milenijuma*, edited by Andjelka Milić. Beograd: ISI FF, pp. 151–193.

Vujović, Sreten and Mina Petrović. 2007. "Belgrade's Post-Socialist Urban Evolution: Reflections by the Actors in the Development Process." In *The Post-Socialist City*, edited by Kiril Stanilov. Dordrecht: Springer, pp. 361–385.

Vukmirović, Milena. 2020. "Pedestrian-Friendly Belgrade." In *Belgrade: The Urban Book Series*, edited by Biljana Arandjelović and Milena Vukmirović. Dordrecht: Springer, pp. 273–296.

Waley, Paul. 2011. "From Modernist to Market Urbanism: The Transformation of New Belgrade." *Planning Perspectives* 26: 209–235.

Williams, Raymond. 1958. *Culture and Society*. London: Chatto and Windus.

Young, Martin. 1999. "The Social Construction of Tourist Places." *Australian Geographer* 30(3): 373–389.

Zuza, Maja and Bojana Pavlicevic. 2014. "Guide to Modern Yugoslav Architecture." http://stillinbelgrade.com/guide-modern-yugoslav-architecture/. Retrieved 30 September 2020.

8 New approaches to urban tourism

Living with a "big worm" in central São Paulo (Brazil)

Ana Carolina Padua Machado and Thiago Allis

The President João Goulart Elevated Highway, in São Paulo, popularly known as *Minhocão*, was inaugurated in 1971 – during the military dictatorship in Brazil – and it is a consequence of the road culture of the time, when automobility was seen socially and politically as paramount. Today, while closed for cars at given periods of the week, *Minhocão* also works as an elevated park. In these moments, a wide range of practices and sociabilities take place: physical activities, street vending, social encounters, strolling, outdoor pop-up parties. Departing from this study case, this chapter aims to discuss urban tourism amidst the routines at one of the largest metropolises in the world. To this purpose, a set of semi-structured interviews was carried out in 2018 and 2019, aiming to unveil how this urban structure is perceived as a tourist space.

Introduction

When it comes to tourism in large cities, it is quite common that tourism experiences take place in spaces that were not exclusively designed to serve tourists – except for specific services, such as accommodation or local tours. Therefore, understanding the evolution of urban tourism requires looking at how urban landscapes and practices evolve over time. In other words, in order to grasp how tourism is spatialised in urban daily life, one needs to understand the urban *milieu* itself.

City spaces become tourist spots when specific groups of people attribute them meanings and values, though tourism is part of a broader range of activities, and, because of that, it may not be so evident. Thus, city residents and tourists interact and make use of the same services and, at certain times, it becomes difficult to differentiate them (Aldrigui 2017; Allis 2016, 2012; Hayllar et al. 2011; Pearce 2001).

In what ways, then, does urban tourism take place? Since 1990, literature shows that this happens in many ways: it ranges from the development of new corporate districts – which stimulates business tourism and events – to urban heritage restoration and the promotion of cultural districts – leading to the development of cultural tourism and its variants (Ashworth 1992; Roche 1992;

DOI: 10.4324/9781003138600-10

Judd and Fainstein 1999; Pearce 2001; Law 2002; Selby 2003; Spirou 2011; García-Hernández et al. 2017; Shoval 2018, to name a few).

As in other neoliberal contexts, in Brazil, economic and political changes that took place since the last decades of the 20th century led to transformations of urban landscapes, as well as economic activities. This makes tourism emerge as an alternative in the rebirth of former industrial economies. The tertiarisation of economies points to a socio-spatial (re)arrangement, bringing about possibilities of new urban businesses, be they related to cultural activities, creative economy, corporate and business events, *haute* cuisine, artistic life and entertainment, shopping or simply the dynamism of city life itself (Alcantara 2020; Lugosi and Allis 2019; Arantes 2000).

This transition from a non-touristic "before" to a touristic "after" is key for understanding urban tourism. This refocusing can occur in the most unusual spaces and situations, depending on the complexity and diversity of a given city. Urban tourism can emerge in the least obvious spatial and symbolic interstices. Particularly in São Paulo, Allis and Vargas (2015) showed the importance of metropolitan and regional visitors to São Paulo, stressing the importance of considering short-distance or even local demands when planning urban tourism and leisure policies. Also, one can note that, regardless their geographic origins, visitors experience the *ambience* of Korean bakeries in central São Paulo – that is "engaging in certain representations and embodiments, visitors to Bom Retiro perform certain spatial behaviours that would hardly be framed as purely leisure [of local] or conventional tourism" (Leite and Allis 2020, 138).

Traditionally, tourism scholarship has focused on the relationship of urban tourism with materiality and transport, but its approaches lack of a deeper theoretical analysis from the field of mobilities (Hannam 2009; Sheller and Urry 2004). However, with the consolidation of globalisation, it is becoming increasingly entangled, and this brings new rhythms to large cities and its complex routines. The concept of tourism mobilities – of people, ideas, goods and communication – reveals how contemporary mobile lives are organised and it emerges as a tool for unveiling other dimensions of tourism as a complex socio-spatial phenomenon (Elliot and Urry 2010; Urry 2002). Sheller and Urry (2006) argue:

> Mobilities of people and objects, airplanes and suitcases, plants and animals, images and brands, data systems and satellites, all go into "doing" tourism. Tourism also concerns the relational mobilisations of memories and performances, gendered and racialized bodies, emotions and atmospheres. Places have multiple contested meanings that often produce disruptions and disjunctures. Tourism mobilities involve complex combinations of movement and stillness, realities and fantasies, play and work.
>
> (p. 1)

Thus, the boundaries between tourists and non-tourists in the city life are becoming blurred: *tourists* looking for the "authentic" and "real" tastes of places (e.g. Airbnb motto is "live like a local") and *residents*, on the contrary, being seduced to explore the city during their time there (Maitland 2013, 14).

Indeed, tourism in large cities is not as visible as in seaside resorts, for instance (see Mullins 1991, on "tourism urbanization"), which makes it more challenging to analyse tourism in urban spaces. As residents and tourists share the same spaces and services, it is hard to differentiate them accurately (Vargas and Paiva 2016; Henriques 2003). City dwellers can perform "extraordinary" activities, behaving "as if" they were tourists. Even without travelling away from their hometown, a change of ambience and landscape can occur at the level of an individual's perceptions when he or she discovers new perspectives on what seems familiar to him or her. This makes room to discuss the so-called end of tourism (Urry 2002), that is when tourism-like performances mix with the domains of everyday practices, being no longer possible to discern from other ways of being and moving around the world. Thus, (de)differentiation of tourism emerges from a wide range of mobilities carried out by individuals, which are difficult to classify in pure and exclusive definitions (such as locals, tourists, travellers and others) (Urry 2000; Germann-Molz 2018).

New urban cultures and lifestyles are key components in the contemporary city marketing, whose purpose is to boost urban economies and business. In this sense, while city dwellers and all sorts of "city users", regardless of their origins, pursue special activities, several sectors of the urban economy can benefit (Condevaux et al. 2016; Ashworth and Page 2011; Maitland 2010; Franklin and Crang 2001; Judd 2003; Martinotti 1994).

Given this context, we ask: how does a concrete and massive road structure, the result of controversial car-oriented urban policies in the 1970s, contribute to new tourist narratives and practices in São Paulo? What does that "before" (i.e. an expressway for individual transport) indicate for a potentially "after" in terms of tourism (new performances and embodiments in unforeseen spaces and moments of leisure)? Under what terms and with what conditions?

Today, the President João Goulart Elevated Highway, popularly known as *Minhocão* (or "big worm" in Portuguese), in São Paulo (Brazil), extrapolates its traditional uses, playing additional roles other than this of an urban expressway. *Minhocão* is an output of an emerging road culture, when car circulation was privileged in the urban planning mindset in Brazil. It has brought remarkable urban transformations to its surroundings, illustrating one of the reasons that make *Minhocão* subject to endless discussions in the present time and in the future.

Despite all the enthusiasm of public officials, *Minhocão* became a source of concern since its construction, being closed to car traffic during nighttime shortly after its inauguration to avoid noise and other environmental disturbances (Silva et al. 2017). Today, this expressway also works as an uncommon elevated park, open for pedestrians only during nighttime and weekends. In fact, *Minhocão* depicts an urban setting where encounters between visitors, locals and tourists re-create and shape social and political issues, from a broad array of person-to-person interactions, such as walking, contemplation, eating, shopping and jogging, to other activities that differ from merely crossing the city in a car at high speed.

Amidst intense debate, currently two different views emerge: on the one hand, a future opportunity to transform the viaduct into an elevated park and, on the other hand, a claim to dismantle it, as a final solution for a long-standing problem. In this sense, tourism comes to the fore as an important narrative to justify and legitimise some space transformations, in combination with other topics of city life.

In this context, *Minhocão* represents an opportunity to understand current challenging urban phenomena, based on new attributes of public spaces and tourism. Increasingly, urban and everyday situations mingle each other and illustrate the importance of re-discussing tourism based on new parameters. This study draws upon on fieldwork carried out at *Minhocão* Park in 2018 and 2019,[1] using unstructured observation techniques and semi-structured interviews. In particular, interviews were conducted with two different groups: first, multiple actors directly involved with the future of *Minhocão* (such as city councillors, members of the "Minhocão Park Association" and the "Dismantle *Minhocão*" movement), and, second, general users of the Park (143 valid interviews), from October to April, split into weekdays (58 interviews) and weekends and holidays (85 interviews).

The methodological framework also comprised a literature review on urban tourism and contemporary urban planning, as well as a mapping and an inventory in grey literature, official publications and tourism websites (Booking. com, TripAdvisor and Airbnb).

Stretching the worm out: from a brutalist urban highway to a controversial elevated park

As an heir of the road lobby in Brazil, *Minhocão* – along with Rio-Niterói Bridge (Rio de Janeiro) and Itaipu Hydroelectric Power Plant (Paraná) – is one of the various massive structures built across the country to spread a message of modernity and development (Zaidler Junior 2014).

The elevated road is 3.4 km long, 5 m high, with two lanes on each side. Its construction was justified as a solution to connect the east and west sides of the city of São Paulo, relieving the increasing, chaotic traffic in central São Paulo. When the project was announced, the structure was labelled as one of the largest concrete construction sites in Latin America and a great solution to the city's growth (Bertoni 2016; Anelli and Seixas 2008).

Despite the enthusiasm of public agents, several problems emerged given the obvious fact that *Minhocão* disrupted an immense sector of the urban fabric. The structure stands very close to residential buildings that already existed there, bringing remarkable environmental changes to the landscape, as well as worsening problems such as noise and air pollution. Not surprisingly, numerous complaints and controversies arose since its beginnings (Campos 2008; Luna and Magalhães Júnior 2008). In 1976, the expressway was closed to car traffic at night as one of the first responses to tackle its harmful effects – a measure expected to reduce noise and prevent accidents (Luna and Magalhães Júnior 2008).

In 1987, local ordinances from the Municipality of São Paulo anticipated the idea for a linear park over the viaduct. That was considered a "project to save the expressway and to transform it into the largest hanging garden in Latin America", as well as to "transform *Minhocão* into a tourist spot" (Pitanga do Amparo 1987). That was the first time when an explicit discourse linking tourism to *Minhocão* emerged as a real possibility, opening a new phase to rethink its urban functions.

After 1989, *Minhocão* was closed for a longer interval – from 9:30 p.m. to 6:30 a.m. – and in 1990, that was extended to Sundays, followed by the installation of protective fences for safety reasons, since the structure was not originally designed for pedestrians. Since then, *Minhocão* went on to confirm its non-road functions when people spontaneously started to access its upper sections (Machado 2019) (Figure 8.1).

Years later, the second edition of the Prestes Maia Urbanism Award (2006) challenged architects and urban planners to present alternatives to the "problem" imposed by the expressway. The winning project proposed the maintenance of the road but tunnelling it into a metallic structure and bringing to light a park–like space, which included a tourist information centre (Artigas et al. 2008).

Reverberating the diversification of intentions relating to alternative uses, in 2013, the Minhocão Park Association was created, aiming at gathering proposals for the future of *Minhocão* and to forming a representative front for its conversion into a leisure area. In the same year, the association hosted an exhibition

Figure 8.1 The *Minhocão* as a park: closed to cars, open to people

Source: Thiago Allis (2019)

as part of the 10th Biennial Architecture Exhibition of São Paulo about the High Line Park (New York), intending to bring ideas and incentives to transform *Minhocão* into something else (Machado 2019). In a different direction, another group was established: the movement *"Desmonte do Minhocão"* ("Dismantle *Minhocão*") called for the demolition of the structure to make way for a park at the ground level or an avenue with a promenade. Composed of volunteers, nearby residents and merchants, the movement claims for tearing *Minhocão* down in favour of a renewed urban environment, inspired by examples from Seoul (Cheonggyecheon), Rio de Janeiro (Perimetral), Boston ("Big Dig": Central Artery/Tunnel Project) and Montreal (Autoroute Bonaventure).

In 2014, a significant milestone in the history of *Minhocão* was set: the new urban Master Plan for São Paulo was approved, in which it was stipulated a progressive deactivation of *Minhocão* as an expressway in three possible scenarios: keeping its current situation (a combination of park and expressway, in alternate periods), dismantling it completely or implementing a park on the viaduct, but eliminating car traffic permanently.

In March 2016, a new law was passed recognising *Minhocão* officially as a "park". In structural terms, nothing changed. However, this meant that, when the viaduct was closed to cars and open to people, it legally came to be known and called as the *Minhocão* Park. This action marked, in legal terms, a legitimation of this structure as a leisure area and opened for people only, in addition to the public recognition of a new function of the structure: an urban park. In December 2017, a new law (16.833) was approved, stipulating that cars would be allowed from 7:00 a.m. to 8:00 p.m., and the road would be open for pedestrians on Saturdays (full day), Sundays and holidays.

Between 2017 and 2019, a legal confrontation took place, having City Hall as a supporter of the park and other counter-voices questioning the project at the courts. Though not implemented, a project was announced by the mayor, aiming at initiating landscaping interventions on 0.9 km (out of 3.4 km) of the expressway, making part of the road structure closer to what could be recognised as a green area (Figure 8.2).

Amidst the COVID-19 pandemic, in September 2020, when pedestrians were prohibited from accessing *Minhocão* due to lockdown, a plebiscite was approved by the São Paulo City Council, transferring the decision on the future of *Minhocão* to public consultation. As a way to feed this debate, a 2019 public survey pointed out that 47% of the respondents are in favour of dismantling the *Minhocão*, while 39% support the current maintenance of the structure and 14% prefer its transformation into a park (PIU Minhocão 2019).

"Taming the worm": elevated urban park or clearing the ground for a new boulevard?

Over the last couple of years, *Minhocão* went global: while some urban sectors discussed its uses and futures, international eyes also were placed on this bizarre and unusual structure (Mead 2017). Linking the future of *Minhocão* (as a

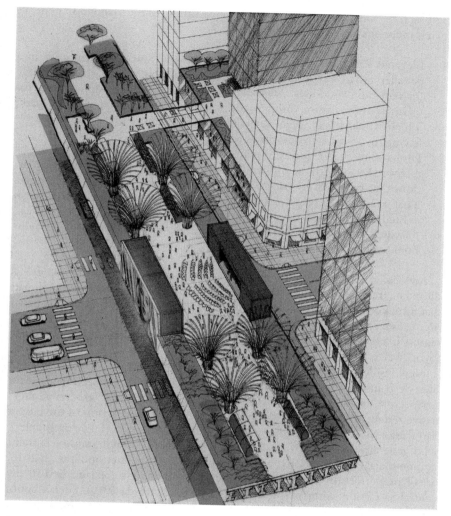

Figure 8.2 The project of the *Minhocão* Park (Lerner Arquitetos Associados, 2019)
Source: https://vejasp.abril.com.br/cidades/minhocao-capa-projeto-verde/

park) to international experiences, such as the High Line (New York) and the Promenade Plantée (Paris) (Benghida and Benghida 2017; Bouvet et al. 2019; Heathcott 2013) is commonplace in the local press.

Though *Minhocão* has been a controversial topic, from a political, urban and environmental perspective, in the twenty-first century new discourses and practices began to merge with the "back to downtown" trend. In this context, political positions and demands start to take shape, sometimes reinforcing the park option, sometimes claiming for the dismantling of the viaduct. In general, two standpoints are predominant:

1   Elevated Park: this claims for more leisure and tourism spaces even in a peculiar urban environment, maintaining the expressway structure only for non-motorised uses. *Minhocão*, therefore, is seen as an opportunity for urban transformation through the implementation of an elevated park, which would boost urban revitalisation in its immediate surroundings – having, in a way, tourist visits as part of the strategy.
2   Dismantling the viaduct: this is an understanding that urban quality will be recovered only with the dismantling of the structure, followed by interventions that would bring back a sense of "promenade" to São João Avenue. That would make way to a boulevard on the ground floor similar to what existed until the mid-twentieth century. *Minhocão* is seen as an urban scar, to which the only solution would be its dismantling to improve air conditions and the overall urban quality.

Advocates for both standpoints represent different views on how *Minhocão* should be treated. In one way or another, different positions question the threats that future decisions on *Minhocão* would pose to the surroundings, mainly based on the risk of increasing rents and gentrification. Real estate speculation in that region is evolving, taking advantage of and reinforcing the "back to downtown" wave.

New residential developments compete with the old ones, while a different lifestyle is insufflated by real estate companies and, from a more independent perspective, small business (coffeeshops, bio and organic food groceries, alternative restaurants, etc.) with special interest in the central region of the city of São Paulo. Most of these businesses target young consumers (single or couples), who generally do not own a car and seek the benefits of living more centrally, despite social issues associated with central zones in large metropolises. In 2018, 5,544 properties (in new vertical residential buildings) were launched in the central São Paulo, compared with 3,144 in 2010 (Lacerda 2019). Such a boom can be partially attributed to – but it is also a result of – an ongoing process of "hipsterization" (Santos 2018; Alcantara 2020; Paiva and Schicchi 2019), over the last 20 years in central neighbourhoods (namely República, Liberdade, Bela Vista, Consolação, Vila Buarque, Santa Cecília and, more recently, Bom Retiro).

In fact, the first stretch of *Minhocão* Park overlaps with an area that faces a steady real estate boom, including recent launchings of new developments targeting mainly middle and upper-middle classes (Santoro 2018). Paradoxically, this area is legally recognised as Special Social Interest Zones (ZEIS), an urban management tool that claims portions of the space for future social housing, aiming at avoiding land prices to be inflated, high rent values and potential gentrification. Indeed, based on a comprehensive press analysis, Santos (2018) noted that "rental values in the area [Santa Cecília] are increasing and rehabilitation or retrofit initiatives . . . are often cited as a way of making aesthetics and commercially attractive run-down or outdated buildings" (p. 34). The urban changes in this area unveils, indeed, the "return of the population [mainly middle-classes] as well as the economic and symbolic revalorization of the region, which is also felt . . . in demand for commercial spaces" (p. 43).

In different ways, leisure, culture, entertainment and tourism emerge as arguments to explain how central São Paulo is changing. In any case, there is a dispute of narratives, in which urban tourism is included – sometimes explicitly, other times more abstractly – and *Minhocão* is another actor on the stage.

Elevated urbanism: leisure and tourism at the upper level

"Elevated urbanism" is an expression of "post-industrial urbanism", stimulating practices of converting obsolete transport structures – mainly old railways – into new urban spaces, such as parks, greenways and boulevards, enhancing "neighborhood quality and [increasing] land value" (Dupre 2017, 115). These new urban spots would promote a unique city experience, not at ground level and following a linear architectural style.

International examples are mentioned to support this argument, which confirms that, in a way, the principles of elevated urbanism are "in motion", travelling from contexts where projects have been already implemented to others where "good practices" are wanted. This, indeed, seems to be an opportunity for tourism development in an unprecedented way, echoing the idea of "urban policy tourism" (González 2011): students, professionals and policymakers travelling to São Paulo and paying visits to *Minhocão* to understand (and, further, spread) urban experiences related to it.

In the 1990s, *Minhocão* started to take on a new meaning when it acquired – spontaneously and with no specific incentive – new uses as a park (in addition to its primary functions as an expressway, which in fact still exist). Following that, Minhocão Park Association lobbied in favour of the park, arguing that, despite the approval of the law that acknowledges *Minhocão* as a park, it is already perceived as a park by users. For its president, "be they users, tourists or local residents, their visits are opportunities to get to know and experience the city".

> I have already seen . . . some publications, some tour guides in São Paulo that already mentioned Minhocão Park [as a tourist attraction]. . . . in several magazines, they have already published that it is an attraction, that it is a big deal, especially when this discussion was "in vogue". So, I would say yes, it is an interesting site for foreigners . . . And it is a tourism location [for many] people . . . but it is a type of tourism in which, I guess, many of them [visitors] are actually from São Paulo.

For him, formal definitions do not make any difference, but in his opinion, tourists attending Minhocão Park can be classified into three groups: (i) "tourists who live in the city of São Paulo, but not in the surroundings of *Minhocão*", who stroll and seek to discover spots of the city where they live; (ii) "Brazilians, non-residents of the city of São Paulo", mainly attracted by the unique features of *Minhocão* and (iii) "foreign tourists" who appreciate such an unusual place that provides a series of unprecedented experiences. This classification does not necessarily meet conventional concepts of tourist and tourism, but rather highlights the interaction between different types of visitors with a given urban spot that makes room to re-discuss and reshape concepts based on emerging urban practices.

Another member of the *Minhocão* Park Association reflects – in a semi-structured interview in 2019 – on tourist activities resembling a search for urban experiences, which can be enjoyed by different actors: *"People are attentive to city experiences, you know? People are thirsty for urban experiences. I've seen people stop the car to get up in Minhocão. People who come from elsewhere"*.

For a city councillor (who participated in a semi-structured interview, in 2019), author of the law (16.833/2018) that created *Minhocão* Park and provided for its "gradual deactivation", *Minhocão* should be a permanent topic on the urban planning agenda of São Paulo. His argument in favour of the park is that it is already being "created collectively and spontaneously by its users", which is a legitimation to transform it into a park designed by urban and landscaping professionals ensuring better and safer use.

The diversity and spontaneity of the activities that take place in *Minhocão* Park illustrate an ongoing process. Among the main uses identified, one may list sports and physical activities, socialising, observation and contemplation, walking pets, playing with children, meetings, selling goods, access, sunbathing, photographing and strolling. On weekdays, physical activities are predominant, while on weekends they are quite varied, including small events and groups meetings, street vending and so forth.

> *People come to sunbathe, have a picnic, I've seen the guys having a barbecue up here . . . there are dance classes, there's a lot of things that [regular] parks sometimes don't offer, because a park has 'n' prohibitions. Here is a space for the population to enjoy the way they want and people have been busy and innovating here. Everything happens and I feel more encouraged to come here.*
>
> (interviewee #61)

In fact, among all respondents, 95% live in São Paulo, mainly in the central region and in the surroundings of *Minhocão*. The frequency of visits depicts a lot about how interaction with Minhocão is embedded in peoples' daily lives, thus exercising less strangeness typical of tourists: 33.6% of the interviewees visit Minhocão Park every weekend and 18.9% visit every day.

On the other hand, assuming that the elevated expressway – particularly when on park mode – is part of a process of urban transformations that embeds tourism, the view of current users brings a set of reflections on the tourist nature of this space. In their statements, although the idea of Minhocão as a tourist space is not precise, some interviewees refer to it as a leisure and tourism space due to some characteristics.

A resident of the surroundings (interviewee #1) characterises his experiences in *Minhocão* as everyday leisure. However, reflecting on possible other uses by a greater variety of people, he mentioned the possibility of tourism practices based on a known marker that is not yet exclusive: "I think more on residents . . . but tourism, also, because we know that there are a lot of people who love to come and take pictures here". This reflection can be complemented by other interviewees:

> *Interviewee (A):* Tourism is already happening here.
> *Interviewer:* How do you perceive this?
> *Interviewee (B): We can tell by the movement,* right?
> *Interviewee (A):* They are never the same people, right? It always changes . . . You have to think on both sides, right? Not only at leisure, too, right?
>
> (interviewee #41)

Interviewee #4 illustrates an alternative conceptualisation of tourism, based on time-distance measures, strangeness and regularity of activities undertaken within the vast metropolis spaces:

> In a way, *I come from an outlying region*, there in the capital, to get to know *something that is not part of my life*, in my daily life, so it is tourism in quotes, right? But I still haven't stopped to think about it, but I think so. It makes sense, right? Because I think *it is no longer tourism when you have it on a daily basis,* I believe, right. For example, a carioca[2] who is on the beach every day, for him, that is normal. But if I lived in a region that was not beachy in Rio and went to the beach, I would still be in my city, but I would be a tourist there in that beach region. It's interesting, right?
>
> (Emphasis added)

In this sense, the idea of such practices that take place in a very particular space in the city of São Paulo starts to resemble – within the scope of these reflections of the interviewees – a kind of "internal tourism", as interviewee #27 stated: "*I think that it's much more about internal tourism than something that will bring someone here to São Paulo. I don't believe it is just for this, for the people who live here*".

Interviewees #11 and #16 classify their experiences in *Minhocão* as that of a tourist from an anthropological perspective: "*I think there is that type of tourism of the people who live here, right? . . . It is a discovery, because I have lived in São Paulo for three years, so for me it is tourism*" (interviewee #11). Interviewee #16 adds: "*It ends up being more of an anthropological, sociological tourism, so to speak, you know? To reveal the characteristics of the city*".

The overlapping senses of leisure and tourism practices are also identified by interviewee #24. When explaining what he sees in terms of practices undertaken at the park, he ends up bringing these practices together in the same activity, understanding them as a single experience: "*Here we see leisure that allows a kind of tourism, of living, of leisure, somewhat different . . . that maybe it is the proposal that we believe in, that brings together both those who come from elsewhere and the residents*".

The double character of *Minhocão* – of elevated expressway and an urban park – is constantly emphasised at TripAdvisor, a tourism and leisure reviews online platform. When operating as an expressway, its environment depicts chaos and speed, but, when closed to car traffic (park mode), it becomes calm and peaceful. Thus, there is also the opportunity to escape the urban chaos through experiencing the park, making it possible, according to reviewers, to observe everything that is not achieved when it opens again for cars.

On the other hand, a TripAdvisor visitor classifies the experience at *Minhocão* as "roots of São Paulo" – an expression used to designate original, traditional activities and actions of specific group or person. For this visitor, *Minhocão* seemingly brings authentic experiences, truly translating the essence of the city of São Paulo. In this sense, *Minhocão* seems to reflect an imaginary that comes close to the local reality, in a context in which ordinary and extraordinary situations may coincide, within the discussion about the "end of tourism" (Urry 2002).

Regaining the ground floor: claiming back a boulevard to central São Paulo

From 1900 to 1950, the population of São Paulo went from 240,000 inhabitants to 2.2 million, reverberating a robust industrial development associated with stark migratory flows (including domestic) (Jannuzzi 2004). Thus, the process of urban densification led to the consolidation of a polynuclear metropolis, in which the historic centre and surrounding neighbourhoods were neglected in favour of other regions, especially in the southwest direction: Paulista Avenue, Brigadeiro Faria Lima Avenue and, more recently, Marginal Pinheiros, the highway alongside Pinheiros river, with the latter being the current Central Business District of this global city.

São Paulo downtown, as usually occurs with large cities, suffered from urban, economic and social decay. However, since the 1970s, local government initiatives were put in march aiming at an urban recovery, generally attached to cultural agendas and, in some cases, cultural tourism. Drawing upon the concept of "cultural anchors", in 1994 an old railway station was converted into one of the major concert halls in the world (*Sala São Paulo*) and, in the early 2000s, the Monumenta Program, funded with loans from the Interamerican Development Bank, channelled investment in the requalification of the historic central market (*Mercado Municipal*) and in the cultural quarter around Luz station, including *Pinacoteca do Estado de Estado* (Figure 8.3) (Allis 2012; Kara-José 2007; Sandler 2007; Tozzi 2007).

In this context, *Minhocão* – which half-circumvolves the historic centre – has always been seen as an urban blow in a region already suffering from residential exhaustion and loss of symbolic prestige. Therefore, when discussing its future, one of the most radical solutions is its complete dismantling, which would cut off "the root" of an unresolved historical problem, leading the way to recovering urban and environmental qualities along São João Avenue.

A local city councillor is one of the clearest voices against the creation of a park and in favour of the dismantling of *Minhocão*. For him, the dismantling represents the best solution for the city, for several reasons: a moderate dependence on the expressway for the traffic, possibility of implementing alternative transport infrastructures (such as bike lanes and bus corridors), high costs to maintain the elevated park (mainly from the public treasury), the precarious structural conditions of the viaduct and the need to reduce air pollution. He is the author of a local law (PDL 93/2019) that provides for a plebiscite in which three options will be given: park, partial dismantle and total dismantle (Machado 2019).

On a similar note, for the eyes of the "Desmonte do Minhocão" movement, the construction is compared to a scar, the result of a "madness" of the mayor of the time, which is why the structure has always been contested given the irreversible degradation brought to the area. In turn, the possibility of a park there is seen as a whim, superficially and inappropriately compared to the High Line Park (New York), which would result in gentrification, thus reinforcing existing social inequalities: "on the top, a cool and hype green park; underneath, the same problems: poverty, homelessness, noise and air pollution, traffic".

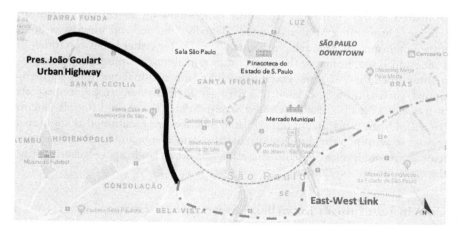

Figure 8.3 Central São Paulo and its expressways

Source: Authors on Google Maps base

Figure 8.4 Marechal Deodoro Square, before the expressway

Source: https://br.pinterest.com/pin/256845984975871945/

One can perceive, in this argument, a hint of nostalgia of a city life before the expressway (Figure 8.4). The dismantling, in this sense, could be questioned for its naïveté, insofar as it seems to be a simplistic solution to more complex social and urban problems that emerged in the last decades.

Regarding tourism potential, here the relations are tied more subtly when compared to the creation of an actual park following an elevated urbanism scheme. Dismantling *Minhocão* would allegedly "rescue" and improve a good urban environment, favouring urban experiences for either locals or visitors in a renewed space, in line with several other requalification programmes implemented since the 1970s in central São Paulo. International examples are mentioned, such as those associated with large-scale urban redevelopment projects in Barcelona (Spain), Seattle (United States), Seoul (Korea) and Rio de Janeiro (Brazil). Urban tourism and other related practices are mentioned as additional reasons to reinforce the dismantling solution, and a large and extensive promenade at ground level would enhance attractive urban landscapes – where, today, the environment is repulsive.

Conclusion: futures for urban leisure and tourism

Minhocão, as a contested urban space and object of endless debate (tourism included), faces current conflicts, especially in the context of the COVID-19 pandemic. In 2020, it was fenced off and pedestrians were no longer allowed, remaining open to car traffic during the day. This situation generated reactions of frequent users – usually residents of the surroundings. Despite the fact that users were not able to access the viaduct in the "park mode" (nights and weekends), unusual practices have been observed: newspapers reported families playing cards and sunbathing in the corners near the park's forbidden spaces, exercising in flower beds and groups of cyclists insisting on entering the park.

Even if concrete plans for its future are uncertain, *Minhocão* illustrates an urban situation that embeds multiple practices and movements in a large city, challenging the logic of traditional differentiation of tourism: ordinary spaces for locals and extraordinary spaces for tourists.

In 2011, Urry and Larsen wrote:

> We need somehow to dispense with the "exotic gaze" which drives so much contemporary tourism and instead favour discourses, schemes and funding which develop what we might term a "local gaze", to keep people in places rather than roaming across the globe.
>
> (Urry and Larsen 2011, 236)

Prophetically or not, at the beginning of the pandemic (first half of 2020), images of residents interacting with their surroundings or visiting places that they did not usually attend because they were often crowded with tourists also became commonplace. It seems that the dynamics of cities began to be reshaped: a kind of awakening, more attentive to what is close, at the level of the eyes, which take on new tones and question the previous practices of excessive tourism. While popular destinations such as Barcelona, Amsterdam and Venice were emptied of tourists, they started to be revisited by locals.

This is what could be a trend for urban tourism: from one's own balcony to short trips, is it possible that the geographic reach of post-pandemic tourism mobilities enable new meanings and possibilities for urban experiences? Reverberating over 20 years of debates on slow tourism, "proximity tourism" and "staycation" come (back?) to fore as a demand for experiences that combine the anxiety to take the road with the aversion to risk. In the first years of the twenty-first century, slow tourism and staycation – a term coined in 2003 to refer to vacations "requiring little or no travelling" (De Bloom et al. 2017) – emerged along with the concern of some sectors with environmental and social impacts of mass tourism. That does not seem to be the case of post-pandemic tourism trends though.

If urban middle classes are dreaming of escaping from the risky conditions of large cities, it does not mean longer trips are possible or recommendable – also because medical assistance tends to be poorer in smaller towns. In this sense, shorter concentric circles – having home as zero point – are emerging as new frontiers for tourism during and probably after the pandemic.

Airbnb recently launched on its website a new space for travellers to seek accommodation for their periods of social isolation and home office (away from home!). The message clearly describes a possibility in everyday life, of discovery at the level of the environment, work and leisure ("Give your routine a new home. Settle in a new place. Find out nearby. Stay to live, work or just to relax"). Another widely used online travel service, Booking.com has also launched a new section on its website, encouraging customers to book accommodation in the logic of "working where they want", combining work and fun in a non-daily and permanent environment (even if provisionally, for specific periods of isolation).

At the urban level, new apps launched in 2020 combine gamification with the promise of alternative urban experiences, in "tours with no social interaction" (Capuchinho 2020). Drawing upon Pokémon-like activities, these apps bring people – locals or tourists – to interact with unusual urban spots, providing information in a playful – and safe – way.

Amidst (re)interpretations of urban spaces and routines, questions arise about what would be the possible consequences for large cities. As a manifold urban spot, *Minhocão* has been a place where familiarity and strangeness bonded together – even before the pandemic – depending on the personal background and interests of the ones who visit it.

In this context, practices and concepts that were already being debated seem to be even more under dispute, based on the evolution of practices, expectations and experiences in the urban scenario. Will cities' routines change with likely post-COVID-19 mobilities patterns? How will spaces be perceived and experienced by the local population and by temporary visitors? What are the feelings and desires of being in the public space?

Notes

1 These interviews were conducted for a master's thesis research (Machado 2019). All interviews were recorded and carried out with the consent of the interviewees. For further details and full manuscript, see: www.teses.usp.br/teses/disponiveis/100/100140/tde-02122019-160313/en.php.
2 Expression used to describe people who live in the city of Rio de Janeiro (Brazil).

References

Alcantara, M. F. 2020. "A Vila Buarque torna-se hipster: conceitos globais, efeitos locais." *Iluminuras* 21(54): 642–659.
Aldrigui, M. 2017. "Turismo Urbano: Um olhar para o quase invisível." *Revista do Centro de Pesquisa e Formação* 4: 131–143.
Allis, T. 2016. "Em busca das mobilidades turísticas." *Plural, Revista do Programa de Pós-Graduação em Sociologia da USP* 23(2): 94–117.
Allis, T. 2012. "Projetos urbanos e turismo em grandes cidades: o caso de São Paulo." Phd thesis (Urban and Regional Planning), University of São Paulo, Brazil.
Allis, T. and H. C. Vargas. 2015. "Turismo Urbano em São Paulo: Reflexões teóricas e apontamentos empíricos." *Revista Turismo em Análise* 26(3): 496–517, doi:10.11606/issn.1984-4867.v26i3p496-517.

Anelli, R. and A. Seixas. 2008. "O peso das decisões: o impacto das redes de infraestrutura no tecido urbano." In *Caminhos do elevado: Memória e projetos*, edited by R. Artigas, J. Mello and A. C. Castro. São Paulo: Secretaria Municipal de Planejamento, pp. 59–73.

Arantes, O. 2000. "Uma estratégia fatal: A cultura nas novas gestões urbanas." In *A cidade do pensamento único: desmanchando consensos*, edited by O. Arantes, E. Maricato and C. Vainer. Petrópolis: Vozes, pp. 11–73.

Artigas, R., J. Mello and A. C. Castro2008. "2° Prêmio Prestes Maia de Urbanismo: As propostas para o Minhocão." In *Caminhos do elevado: Memória e projetos*, edited by R. Artigas, J. Mello and A. C. Castro. São Paulo: Secretaria Municipal de Planejamento, pp. 13–16.

Ashworth, G. 1992. "Is There an Urban Tourism?" *Tourism Recreation Research* 17(2): 3–8, doi:10.1080/02508281.1992.11014645.

Ashworth, G. and S. Page. 2011. "Urban Tourism Research: Recent Progress and Current Paradoxes." *Tourism Management* 32(1): 1–15.

Benghida, D. and S. Benghida. 2017. "La créativité dans la réhabilitation urbaine: Le Viaduc des Arts à Paris". *Association Culturelle Franco-Coreenne* 35(2): 215–243.

Bertoni, E. 2016. "O que é e para que serve o Minhocão." www.nexojornal.com.br/expresso/2016/10/11/O-que-%C3%A9-e-para-que-serve-o-Minhoc%C3%A3o. Retrieved 20 October 2020.

Bouvet, R. et al. 2019. "Promenades végétales: Pour une approche interdisciplinaire." *Enjeux et société* 6(2): 277–288, https://doi.org/10.7202/1066700ar.

Campos, C. M. 2008. "Eixo da ambiguidade: a região da Avenida São João nas inversões do tempo." In *Caminhos do elevado: Memória e projetos*, edited by R. Artigas, J. Mello and A. C. Castro. São Paulo: Secretaria Municipal de Planejamento, p. 144.

Capuchinho, C. 2020. "Apps transformam turista em detetive e animam roteiros urbanos na pandemia." www.uol.com.br/nossa/noticias/redacao/2020/10/29/aplicativos-de-enigmas-propoem-turismo-urbano-em-tempos-de-covid.htm. Retrieved 30 October 2020.

Condevaux, A., G. Djament-Tran and M. Gravari-Barbas. 2016. "Before and After Tourism(s). The Trajectories of Tourist Destinations and the Role of Actors Involved in: A Literature Review." *Via Tourism Review* 9: 1–24, https://doi.org/10.4000/viatourism.413.

De Bloom, J. et al. 2017. "Holiday Travel, Staycations, and Subjective Well-Being." *Journal of Sustainable Tourism* 25(4): 573–588.

Dupre, K. 2019. "Trends and Gaps in Place-Making in the Context of Urban Development and Tourism: 25 Years of Literature Review." *Journal of Place Management and Development* 12(2): 102–120, https://doi.org/10.1108/JPMD-07-2017-0072.

Elliot, A. and J. Urry. 2010. *Mobile Lives*. London: Routledge.

Franklin, A. and M. Crang. 2001. "The Trouble with Tourism and Travel Theory?" *Tourist Studies* 1(1): 5–22, https://doi.org/10.1177/146879760100100101.

García-Hernández, M., M. De la Calle-Vaquero and C. Yubero. 2017. "Cultural Heritage and Urban Tourism: Historic City Centres Under Pressure." *Sustainability* 9(8): 1346, https://doi.org/10.3390/su9081346.

Germann-Molz, J. 2018. "After the End of Tourism." In *Mobilities and Complexities*, edited by O. Jensen, S. Kesselring and M. Sheller. London: Routledge, pp. 101–106.

González, S. 2011. "Bilbao and Barcelona 'in Motion': How Urban Regeneration 'Models' Travel and Mutate in the Global Flows of Policy Tourism." *Urban Studies* 48(7): 1397–1418.

154   *A.C. Padua Machado and T. Allis*

Hannam, K. 2009. "The End of Tourism? Nomadology and the Mobilities Paradigm." In *Philosophical Issues in Tourism*, edited by J. Tribe. Bristol: Channel View Publications, pp. 101–113.

Hayllar, B., T. Griffin and D. Edwards. 2011. *Turismo em cidades: Espaços urbanos, lugares turísticos*. Rio de Janeiro: Elsevier.

Heathcott, J. 2013. "The Promenade Plantée: Politics, Planning, and Urban Design in Postindustrial Paris." *Journal of Planning Education and Research* 33(3): 280–291, https://doi.org/10.1177/0739456X13487927.

Henriques, Eduardo. 2003. "A cidade, destino de turismo." *Revista da Faculdade de Letras – Geografia* 19(1): 163–172.

Jannuzzi, P. 2004. "São Paulo, século XXI: A Maior metrópole das Américas." *Ciência e Cultura* 56(2): 30–32.

Judd, D. R. 2003. "El turismo urbano y la geografía de la ciudad." *Revista Eure* 87(29): 51–62.

Judd, D. R. and S. S. Fainstein (eds.). 1999. *The Tourist City*. New Haven: Yale University Press.

Kara-José, B. 2007. *Políticas culturais e negócios urbanos: a instrumentalização da cultura na revitalização do centro de São Paulo (1975-2000)*. São Paulo: Annablume.

Lacerda, F. 2019. "Novos negócios hipster valorizam imóveis do centro de São Paulo." https://www1.folha.uol.com.br/mercado/2019/11/novos-negocios-hipster-valorizam-imoveis-do-centro-de-sao-paulo.shtml. Retrieved 20 October 2020.

Law, C. M. 2002. *Urban Tourism: The Visitor Economy and the Growth of Large Cities*. London: Continuum.

Leite, E. P. and T. Allis. 2020. "Migration and Tourism Mobilities: How Younger Koreans Are Enhancing New Urban Experiences in São Paulo. In *Neolocalism and Tourism: Understanding a Global Movement*, edited by L. J. Ingram, S. L. Slocum and C. T. Cavaliere. Oxford: Goodfellow Publishers, pp. 123–142.

Lugosi, P. and T. Allis. 2019. "Migrant Entrepreneurship, Value-Creation Practices and Urban Transformation in São Paulo, Brazil." *Revista Brasileira de Pesquisa em Turismo* 13(1): 141–163.

Luna, F. and M. Magalhães Júnior. 2008. "Uma cicatriz urbana." In *Caminhos do elevado: Memória e projetos*, edited by R. Artigas, J. Mello and A. C. Castro. São Paulo: Secretaria Municipal de Planejamento, pp. 7–9.

Machado, A. C. P. 2019. "Para além de um viaduto: análises de usos e discursos sobre o Parque Minhocão." Master's thesis, University of São Paulo, São Paulo, Unpublished.

Maitland, R. 2010. "Everyday Life as a Creative Experience in Cities: International Journal of Culture." *Tourism and Hospitality Research* 4(3): 176–185, https://doi.org/10.1108/17506181011067574.

Maitland, R. 2013. "Backstage Behaviour in the Global City: Tourists and the Search for the 'Real London'." *Procedia – Social and Behavioral Sciences* 105(3): 12–19, https://doi.org/10.1016/j.sbspro.2013.11.002.

Martinotti, G. 1994. "The New Social Morphology of Cities." www.unesco.org/most/wien/guido.htm. Retrieved 20 September 2013.

Mead, N. 2017. "Taming 'the Worm': How the Minhocão Is São Paulo's Soul." www.theguardian.com/cities/2017/dec/01/taming-worm-minhocao-elevated-highway-sao-paulo. Retrieved 20 October 2020.

Mullins, P. 1991. "Tourism Urbanization." *International Journal of Urban and Regional Research* 15(3): 326–342, https://doi.org/10.1111/j.1468-2427.1991.tb00642.x.

Paiva, M. and M. C. Schicchi. 2019. "O conceito de resiliência urbana: uma ferramenta para a análise de intervenções recentes no centro histórico de São Paulo". *Seminario Internacional de Investigación en Urbanismo* 11, https://doi.org/10.5821/siiu.6760.

Pearce, D. 2001. "An Integrative Framework for Urban Tourism Research." *Annals of Tourism Research* 28(4): 926–946, https://doi.org/10.1016/S0160-7383(00)00082-7.

Pitanga do Amparo. 1987. "Jornal da Tarde". http://pitangadoamparo.com.br/jornaldata rde87.htm. Retrieved 20 October 2020.

PIU Minhocão. 2019. "Projeto de Intervenção Urbana (PIU) Minhocão". https://gestaour bana.prefeitura.sp.gov.br/piu-parque-minhocao/. Retrieved 20 October 2020.

Roche, M. 1992. "Mega-Events and Micro-Modernization: On the Sociology of the New Urban Tourism." *The British Journal of Sociology* 43(4): 563–600, https://doi.org/doi:10.2307/591340.

Sandler, D. 2007. "Políticas Culturais E Negócios Urbanos: A instrumentalização Da Cultura Na revitalização Do Centro De São Paulo, 1975–2000." *Revista da Pós* 22: 213–215, https://doi.org/10.11606/issn.2317-2762.v0i22p213-215.

Santoro, P. F. 2018. "Novos empreendimentos no centro de SP: tudo diminuiu, menos o preço!" www.labcidade.fau.usp.br/novos-empreendimentos-no-centro-de-sp-tudo-diminuiu-menos-o-preco/. Retrieved 20 October 2020.

Santos, C. A. 2018. "Representações da gentrificação na imprensa de São Paulo: o caso do distrito de Santa Cecília." Master's thesis, University of Lisbon, Unpublished.

Selby, M. 2003. *Understanding Urban Tourism: Image, Culture and Experience.* London and New York: I. B. Tauris.

Sheller, M. and J. Urry. 2004. *Tourism Mobilities: Places to Play, Places in Play.* London: Routledge.

Sheller, M. and J. Urry. 2006. "The New Mobilities Paradigm." *Environment and Planning* 38: 207–226, https://doi.org/10.1068/a37268.

Shoval, N. 2018. "Urban Planning and Tourism in European Cities." *Tourism Geographies* 20(3): 371–376, doi:10.1080/14616688.2018.1457078.

Silva, I. et al. 2017. "Espaço urbano, fluxos e direitos: percursos no Elevado João Goulart (Minhocão)." *Abstrato: Revista Eletrônica dos Discentes da Escola de Sociologia e Política da FESPSP* 9(1): 64–74.

Spirou, C. 2011. "A evolução da área funcional do turismo." In *Turismo em cidades: Espaços urbanos, lugares turísticos*, edited by B. Hayllar, T. Griffin and D. Edwards. Rio de Janeiro: Elsevier, pp. 9–22.

Tozzi, D. 2007. "Primavera de estações: o Programa Monumenta e as políticas de preservação do patrimônio cultural da região do bairro da Luz, São Paulo." Master's thesis, University of São Paulo, Unpublished.

Urry, J. 2000. *Sociology Beyond Societies: Mobilities for the Twenty-First Century.* London: Taylor & Francis.

Urry, J. 2002. "Mobility and Proximity." *Sociology* 36(2): 255–274, https://doi.org/10.1177/0038038502036002002.

Urry, J. and J. Larsen. 2011. *The Tourist Gaze 3.0.* London: Sage.

Vargas, H. and R. Paiva. 2016. *Turismo, arquitetura e cidade.* Barueri: Manole.

Zaidler Junior, W. 2014. "Ratículas: As superfícies mudas como lugar de fabulação." Master's thesis, University of São Paulo, Unpublished.

9 The hybridisation of tourism policies

Between the development of seaside resorts and the promotion of "ordinary" urban and industrial development: the case of Martigues, a coastal town in the South of France[1]

Emeline Hatt

Introduction

The coastline, which has now become France's leading tourist destination in terms of overnight[2] stays, has been the centre of significant emotional and symbolic investment since the eighteenth century, embodying the function of pleasure and renewal based on the desire for seashores and "balnearity" (Corbin 1988; Urbain 2002). Since the beginning of the tourist phenomenon, tourism has played an important role in the production and shaping of spaces (Gravari-Barbas 2013). However, the dynamics of the evolution of these regions must be questioned. Analysing the relationship between tourism and the coast, Philippe Duhamel and Rémy Knafou (2003) attempted to renew the idea that a coastline is touristic because it inevitably leads to tourism (the so-called tourist vocation of certain places, an approach that they criticise) provided that it is accessible (neither occupied by industries nor situated in very high latitudes). To this end, they observed the processes that favour the transformation of a space into a tourist destination. Following up on these studies, we will analyse the touristification process (Lanfant et al. 1995; Jansen-Verbeke 2007),[3] in a context marked both by globalisation and the increased attention to the environment and to sustainable development. These developments are also favouring hybridisation processes that bring new actors, places and practices into the tourism arena (Delaplace and Gravari-Barbas 2016). We therefore propose to observe the forms of hybridisation[4] of urban and tourist policies in coastal resorts.

Specific local conditions provide globalisation with elements that give it its own[5] momentum. The challenge of both urban and touristic development strategies is to grasp the identity of the region clearly in order to mobilise it more directly. In this regard, François Ascher (2000, 149) speaks of the

DOI: 10.4324/9781003138600-11

"*hybridisation*" of the global and the local, and considers that "*from this point of view, globalisation is more reflective because it returns to a space and transforms it*". The heritage argument is therefore the sign of an overinvestment in the region. For Emmanuelle Bonerandi (2005, 92), a region is a "*cultural* mediator":[6] "*Beyond support, the region,* [which is] *both a place and a link, builds identity.*" Heritage therefore plays a central role because it participates in the territorial legitimisation by building meaning. In the field of tourism, the relationship to heritage is considered to be complementary. Tourism and heritage reinforce each other's actions, acting as instruments that develop spaces and promote the area. Transforming an area into a tourism attraction zone occurs through the reactivation of heritage features. On the coastline, although the proportion of swimming/beach activity has significantly increased, there has also been a significant diversification of tourist practices and expectations both in terms of leisure activities (such as walks which are the most commonly practised activity) and cultural activities (especially city and market visits), or – to a lesser extent – sports activities (especially hiking[7] and cycling). Natural and cultural assets contribute in this sense to the choice of tourist destination. As a result, the modes that were used to determine the value of generic resources on which the attractiveness of coastal destinations was based (the triptych: the sea, sand and sun of an unrevisited mass tourism, Turner and Asch 1975) no longer suffice to ensure the success of the attraction to tourists of a coastline whose multiple regional[8] resources have become essential.

This phenomenon of "revealing" specific resources is a major challenge, especially because a resource is always dependent on how the actors involved take ownership of it. Regional resources are perceived as a product of history, an emanation of the community and the expression of a regional system. The specificity of the regions lies as much in the existing regional resources as in their original combination (Francois et al. 2006, 696). This chapter thus questions how institutional actors redefine their public policy guidelines by mobilising what they consider to be "regional resources" specific to the spatial structure and sociocultural atmosphere of coastal stations. In this context, we analyse the forms of hybridisation of urban and tourist policies that draw on this movement which seeks to gain entry back into the region, and their roles in the construction and evolution of the identity, image and attractiveness of the coastal region. The analysis of the processes for selecting and promoting regional resources thus allows us to highlight the games played by the actors involved and the potential conflicts of use and governance associated with these processes. This chapter questions the way in which institutions redefine their public policy guidelines (Muller 2005), by mobilising what they consider as regional resources specific to the spatial structure and sociocultural atmosphere of seaside resorts. An insight is gained into the conditions necessary for this movement of regional "re-registration" to succeed by identifying the levers that managers have developed and their role in the construction and evolution of identity, image and attractiveness of coastal areas.

Drawing on a specific case study, this chapter discusses the processes of the hybridisation of tourism and urban policies. It questions how Martigues, an industrial and coastal town in southern France, was transformed into a tourist destination (Hatt 2017). The analysis therefore focuses on a coastal town at the beginning of its "tourism area life cycle" (Butler 1980) and views tourism development as a process, from both a diachronic and a dynamic perspective. We examine the movement of ordinary places that start to take on a tourist dimension. It also looks at the process of hybridisation between tourism practices and ordinary practices. Located in the highly touristic Sud Provence-Alpes-Côte d'Azur region,[9] Martigues is a historic industrial town at the edge of the Berre lagoon, which took the decision in the 2000s to showcase their tourist resources, as can be seen from their classification as a seaside and tourist resort in 2008. In this case, creative tourism practices have become an integral part of the valorisation of regional resources, where transformation into heritage is one of the processes co-constructed by the actors involved. This chapter will present the tensions and paradoxes inherent in this evolution – between the "ordinary" transformation of an area in the context of seaside resort tourism and the promotion of "ordinary" urban and industrial development – which falls within the second urban revolution of tourism (Stock and Lucas 2012). The study addresses the forms of regulation supported by public actors involved in the organisation and management of territories and practices. Echoing the growing hybridisation of tourism and "ordinary" practices (Bourdeau 2012; Gravari Barbas and Delaplace 2016), the hybridisation links between tourism (seaside and heritage) and urban policies (directed towards both permanent residents and visitors) are analysed.

The data production method of this empirical study was undertaken between 2013 and 2016. It was based on the analysis of municipal archives, *in situ* observations, semi-structured interviews with 23 institutional actors (local elected representatives and local, department, regional and government technicians) and photo-based surveys conducted with 84 users (primarily visitors, but also inhabitants). This chapter notably addresses the questions and paradoxes highlighted during the interviews regarding the transformation of ordinary places into tourist areas. It emphasises the role public actors have played and the tensions inherent in the choices and processes of tourism development over the last ten years. To address these issues, this chapter will therefore attempt to:

- Understand the processes of hybridisation of urban and tourism policies driven by public actors and visible in the design of public spaces and the representations they raise.
- Analyse the links between the tourist invention of "ordinary" places and how they are identified as heritage. The decision to award the town the City of Art and History label[10] is also analysed. Specifically, the tensions between the directorates of tourism and cultural bodies in determining which territorial resources are enhanced is highlighted.

Transforming an industrial town into a contemporary tourist town

Martigues: a coastal town with late tourism development

The relationship between industry and tourism is evident in the Martigues town, which lies on two seafronts: one on the Berre lagoon,[11] marked by the image of the petrochemical industry,[12] and the other on the Mediterranean Sea, which is touristy (Figure 9.1).

Although Martigues is the only town at the interface of the Mediterranean Sea and the Berre lagoon, its tourism development occurred later than that of other coastal areas in the Sud Provence–Alpes–Côte d'Azur region. Between the 1960s and 1970s, public actors initially chose to promote industrial development. The steel and port complex of Fos-sur-Mer is constructed in the 1960s (Figure 9.2).

Tourism was then perceived as an activity contrasting with this sector and seemed less aligned with the expectations of the local electorate, composed primarily of the working class. The municipality, which since 1959 was under communist rule without interruption, relegated tourism to the background.

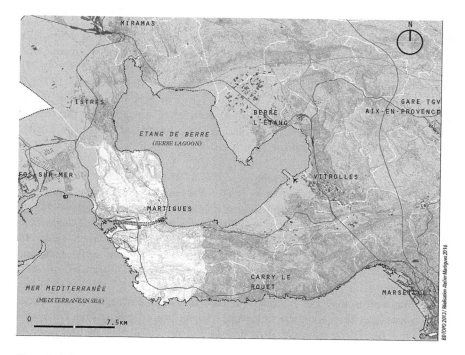

Figure 9.1 A town at the interface of the Mediterranean Sea and the Berre lagoon

Source: Cautellio et al. (2016)

Figure 9.2 The industrial port of Lavéra (sky view)

Source: Photo taken by Hatt (2015)

However, reflections on the creation of seaside facilities and the development of marinas began in the late 1960s. In the municipal archives we found this project which is presented, in particular, in the Delaugere study (1969–1972) entitled "*Operation d'urbanisme – ZOTO*" (Commune de Martigues 1972).[13] This perspective of a "ZOne TOuristique" (tourist zone) focused on social tourism was never accomplished. Indeed, preference was given to the town's industrial development, with the installation of a power plant on the site. Lastly, as the deputy assistant for culture summarised:

> *Tourism in Martigues is something very old and at the same time something very new. . . . There has been a rather belated awareness of this tourism, and it has also been prevented by the highly industrial vocation of our heritage: smoke chasing away tourists. For a large part of the 20th century, this town was hardly destined to nonchalance and strolling and, if one may say so, laziness, but rather to work. All this took quite some time to assert itself. It involved long political work, conviction.*
> (translation ours)

This observation may be extended in part to the department of Bouches-du-Rhône, as evidenced in the following excerpt from the Regional Development Directive (Préfecture des Bouches-du-Rhône 2007):

> Two factors, which are gradually disappearing, have meant that, in the Bouches-du-Rhône, tourism has not always been viewed as an economic activity in its own right: it was long taken for granted; it was also perceived

as "non-noble". Only recently has tourism began to be considered a priority of the department, [and] for two reasons: tourism helps diffuse images and attractiveness and strengthens the relationship between inhabitants and their city when the latter are directly involved in this development; the tourism economy generates jobs.

(translation ours)

The role of civil society actors is clearly visible here insofar as one of the objectives assigned to tourism development is the strengthening of ties between the inhabitants and their town.

Recognition of the tourism factor through classification and labelling in the 2000s

It was not until the 1990s that the issue of tourism development found its way back to the policy agenda. This was because of the difficulties the industrial sector had encountered during the previous decade as a result of oil shocks.[14]

At the same time, at the end of the 1990s, observations in the field led the municipality to engage in a policy to manage tourism development. Recreation and tourism practices across the town had developed in a rather spontaneous and somewhat uncontrolled manner.[15] Parking management was therefore a strategic issue. As the head of the tourism and events department of the municipality highlights, "*Usage conflicts made us act on tourism. . . . We therefore set up a tourism approach to channel usage conflicts, in particular to control parking*" (translation ours). Eventually, tourism development occurred gradually and followed a "*constant evolution*",[16] making "*slow progress until the 2000s*".[17] The town expanded its offer of accommodation and tourist facilities and succeeded in meeting several criteria that allowed it to apply for different rankings and labels. Martigues, for instance, has a high capacity for tourist accommodation at the metropolitan level, particularly in the field of open-air accommodation[18] (Figure 9.3).

The shift towards a more accepted tourism development (also evidenced by the desire to set up a thalassotherapy centre in the town) finally led to the initiation of a strategy for the external promotion of the territory. The town has therefore received the national prize for floral displays since 1996 (the Four Flowers label since 2012), the tourist office and several structures obtained the Tourism and Disability label at the beginning of the 2000s,[19] the classification as a seaside and tourist resort was obtained in 2008 and the municipality took the City of Art and History label in 2012.

The town's classification as a tourist resort was made possible because of the shift in the representations of this industrial territory. According to the director of the local public society of tourism and entertainment events:

> *It might have appeared a bit presumptuous at some point to identify oneself as a tourist city, perhaps even absurd or unrealistic. But this too is a voluntary, assertive discourse that also fits within a strategy, which I think sought to develop other activities.*

(translation ours)

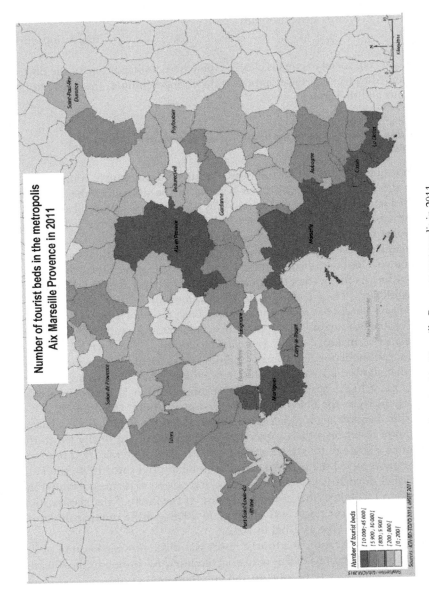

Figure 9.3 Number of tourist beds in the Aix-Marseille–Provence metropolis in 2011

Source: Carli et al. (2015)

Thus, in the 1990s, emphasis was on diversifying the economic activities of the town by proposing, if not an alternative, at least something complementary, that is complementing historical industrial development by tourism development. This clearly shows the evolution of the representation system initiated by the local actors. As the geographer Nicole Girard (former elected member of the city council of Martigues) points out, *"Claims were made with regard to potential. I mean that there's a self-image, an image of the town's representation of itself that was developed, gradually. This. . . . did not exist in the 1960s and 1970s"*. While the industrial crisis led to the relocation of businesses, tourism development, through the creation of territorial resources that could not be relocated, appeared as an asset likely to provide local jobs, thus leading to a change in attitude in this regard.

Development of public spaces: a marker of hybridisation process in urban and tourism policies

The gradual (although fairly measured) opening of this communist town to tourist development follows on from the promotion of the beauty of the landscapes and local heritage begun in the 1980s, at the same time as the industrial sector was experiencing difficulties. As pointed out by the head of the Urban Planning Directorate:

> *An evolution occurred with the arrival of the concept of heritage at the time of the RHI [measure to remove substandard housing, introduced from 1985–1990]. There was a shift in the heads of elected officials, the town was no longer just an oil town, there was also the question of its heritage. . . . A turning point was reached in the 1990s which resulted in a period of redevelopment.*[20]

(translation ours)

As a result, the city gradually became aware of its assets and the quality of its landscapes, earning it the name "Provençal Venice" (Figure 9.4). The "Martigues in colour" operation conducted between 1988 and 2013 and consisting of improving the negative image of the old centre, enabled the rehabilitation of 1,567 façades, 1,234 houses and 353 shops. It was among the urban development strategies initially implemented to improve the living environment of the town's inhabitants.

The vision of a development strategy primarily targeting the inhabitants and likely to benefit visitors indirectly is a strong element of Martigues's planning policy. The urban development plan, carried out under the authority of the Urban Planning Directorate, takes note of this element by stating, *"Above all, the satisfaction of the people of Martigues is the town's main concern, without ignoring the attractiveness of these riches for visitors"* (Commune de Martigues 2015). Finally, as the chief architect of the city pointed out, in Martigues, *"The city project and the tourism project were carried out simultaneously. The aim was to develop a project for the inhabitants and the new inhabitants, and this is also favourable for temporary*

Figure 9.4 The Miroir aux Oiseaux in the city centre of Martigues, symbol of Provençal Venice

Source: Photograph taken by Hatt, April 2013

inhabitants such as tourists". Initially, the town council's redevelopment policies did not primarily target affluent or "visiting" classes (Eisinger 2000).

This hybridisation of urban and tourism policies ultimately echoes the growing hybridisation of tourism practices and "ordinary" practices, analysed in terms of post-tourism and the heterogeneity of new places transformed into tourist areas (Bourdeau 2012). As Maria Gravari-Barbas and Marie Delaplace (2016) point out with regard to the "off the beaten track" urban tourism phenomenon, and drawing in particular on the studies undertaken by Erik Cohen (2008):

> *Tourist categories become blurred, become uncertain, are produced and consumed in contexts that fall under categories that are much more difficult to identify, describe and quantify than in the past. They are much more porous, less bound by time and space. They thus help renew reflections on tourism as an object of study and its role in contemporary society. . . . Unlike modern tourism, which favoured major destinations, the post-tourist questions the uniqueness of the places visited and appreciates everyday living spaces.*

(translation ours)

While this research does not focus directly on the analysis of practices and practitioners, it questions the forms of regulation driven by the public actors involved in the organisation and management of towns and practices. The interviews made it possible to highlight certain local actors' awareness of the developments unfolding in the world of tourism. For example, the chief architect of the city, who we mentioned previously, spontaneously referred to the idea of "*temporary inhabitant*", a concept formalised notably by Mathis Stock (2001) in his analysis of tourist practices. In the same vein, the deputy assistant for culture underlined:

> People work less so they have more time. So the first tourists, one must not forget, are the people living close by, the people here. Being a tourist of your city is something that goes hand in hand with everyday life and that is why cultural policies are essential. . . . Tourism policy must already take into account this awareness of the people who live [here] and take into account their vision of things. . . . Tourism policies can no longer be pursued as they were done before. People have changed, they have expectations, they are no longer focused only on collecting knowledge and information, they are also . . . and this is clear with the forms of tourism that are developing, they are more aligned with people's lives.
>
> (translation ours)

The discourse of the actors in charge of urban and cultural policies developed in Martigues thus takes the form of a demand for an alternative urban and tourism development designed primarily for and with the inhabitants.

The challenge of tourism development can, however, also be reflected in a more entrepreneurial dimension, as evidenced by the choice of the town to be classified as a tourist resort and the desire to create a thalassotherapy centre on the territory. The town council now acknowledges and affirms its desire to attract the "visiting" class. For example, in 2007, the former mayor of the town published the following message in the town's magazine (Reflets 2007):

> For several years we focused on placing the priority on the comfort of our inhabitants, on improving their living environment and well-being. Now (while continuing to offer equipments and facilities for the local community) we can focus on developing the tourism sector . . . an ideal complement to the sustainable development of our town.
>
> (translation ours)

The issue of the quality of the living environment and the attractiveness for both residents and tourists led the town council to pay attention to the development and beautification of public spaces. The creation of the Figuerolles Park in 2005 also reflects the evolution of this industrial territory in search of a new urbanity. The town had acquired this 130 hectares wooded area in 1998 in order to transform it into a leisure and discovery park (horse riding, hiking, mountain biking, an educational farm, etc.) to meet the new recreational expectations of its inhabitants and visitors. These developments are appreciated by the various users of the town, as evidenced by the results of the photographic survey carried out among 84 users of the Martégal coastline[20] (Hatt 2010, 2017). Each of the two corpora presented consists of a set of 30 photographs relating to various French coastal stations, then 30 photographs of the station of Martigues (Hatt 2017). To analyse urban and landscaped environments, it was necessary to identify the representations of each photographed landscape, based on the analysis of the discourse and the ranking of the photos based on their (un)attractiveness. The surveys showed that the quality of the layout of public spaces is undeniably an attractive factor for users, irrespective of whether they are permanent or tourist. Among the 12 photos of Martigues identified as the most attractive, five referred to the upgrading of public spaces (such as Figures 9.5 and 9.6) and were considered to be as attractive as images of "wild" natural spaces.[21]

The enhancement of the coastline of the Berre lagoon[22] appears as an excellent opportunity to expand the range of territorial resources towards local recreation. In recent years, several towns around the lagoon have developed beaches in order to promote their inhabitants' accessibility to the shores and to encourage local leisure activities made possible by the presence of the lagoon

Figures 9.5 and 9.6 Photos of public spaces appreciated in Martigues

Source: Photographs taken by Hatt, 2015

Figures 9.5 and 9.6 Continued

(such as the beaches of La Romaniquette and Ranquet in Istres). Civil society plays an important role here, as evidenced by the investment made by the "L'étang nouveau" association in Martigues, which advocates the redevelopment of Ferrières bay in order to provide the city centre of Martigues with an urban beach. The hybridisation of urban policies, to enhance attractiveness for both residents and visitors, is thus promoted by the inhabitants who come together and demand the development of local recreation spaces.

Thus, the objective of heritage and tourism policies has been twofold, that is with both an entrepreneurial and a social component. This double objective is particularly visible in the context of the tensions sparked by the town's classification and labelling processes and by the decision concerning which of the town's resources get promoted.

The tourist invention of ordinary places and their heritage-making

Seaside tourism vs. heritage tourism: two visions, one town

The relationship between tourism and industry may be considered from three angles relating to the evolution of the tourism trajectory of this town. Initially marked by some form of opposition in the 1960s, the relationship between industrial and tourism developments took the form of complementarity between the 1960s and 1990s.[23] This issue was then increasingly acknowledged and discussed from the 1990s. Among other things, the formalisation of tourism development gave rise to the creation of a tourism and events department. Lastly, the industry-tourism duo (Figures 9.7 and 9.8), which some considered as opposed, gave way to a form of complementarity in practical reality.

The paradox, if there is one, is that ultimately it is the industrial development that has promoted both the protection of nature and the development of local leisure facilities, and then tourism. According to the director of the local public society of tourism and entertainment events:

Martigues' uniqueness is the juxtaposition of the wealth of the town, both industrial and tourist. There has always been a tendency to oppose things, to oppose tourism and industry rather than to address these dimensions in a complementary way. Things are slowly beginning to change, but this culture of opposition is firmly rooted in local mentalities.

(translation ours)

This "culture of opposition" is now implicitly reflected in the manner in which this complementarity is managed. Local actors differ on the degree to which these tourism and industrial dimensions should be connected. While the municipality has taken the decision to exploit its heritage resources in order to promote its attractiveness,[24] the question still remains as to the resources selected and staged as internal conflicts that were revealed with reference to the choices made. Several local actors seem to identify a contradiction in policies between the tourism and the culture departments, which appear to be in confrontation, whereas they could more easily act to their mutual advantage. The tension revolves around the choice of the images of the town projected outwards. As Bernard Debarbieux (2003) points out, the production of graphic representations of towns is a critical moment in initiating reflection about the project and in its establishment. Among the two groups of spatial production created by tourism (Chadefaud 1988), beyond the physical, built and landscaped spaces, we analysed the immaterial spaces represented by the images developed by the local actors responsible for tourism and heritage promotion. The example of the City of Art and History label reflects this tension between the two visions of the towns defended and promoted by these actors. The choice fell to the joint valorisation of the seaside town and the historic town, over the industrial town, according to a process of "narrative reduction" (Vlès et al. 2005), which was to the regret of some members. The deputy assistant for culture reflects on the creation of the City of Art and History label dossier that he supported and points out:

Between the resort and tourism labels, I'm saying this deliberately, which didn't want to see the factories, which erased them from the landscape by showing the classified natural landscapes and not the industry, I wanted

Figures 9.7 and 9.8 Martigues, between beach and industry

Source: Photographs taken by Hatt, 2015

to show, through our dossier, that this contradiction on which we were working between nature and industry exists . . . When we developed this dossier and this way of seeing things, there were several objections, especially from the people who had developed the seaside resort dossier who said, "You're going to completely change our image, our beautiful image of blue skies with gulls and pines lying on the sea". But it is the combination of factors that shows an original town that has many things to say, one which has more to say than the Epinal town which is classified and stereotyped.

(translation ours)

The tourism and events department had a different vision of tourism development which focused on the architectural heritage of the city centre as well as on the town's natural heritage. The head of the department believed in *"industrial tourism for cities which have nothing else to promote (like Dunkirk). But in Martigues, there are coasts, there is a rich heritage, the historic centre has led us to be recognised as the Provençal Venice"* (translation ours). This opinion was shared by the director of the local public society of tourism and entertainment events, who was rather unfavourable to the image developed by the cultural directorate. He believed that this image participated in disseminating conflicting images likely to harm the destination's clarity. The elected representative of tourism admitted that he was in disagreement on this point with the elected representative of culture:

> *Industry remains a part of Martigues' heritage; we cannot sweep away the industry, but I believe that placing it at the forefront of the tourism industry is a mistake. . . . It doesn't provide the most value, it is not what the tourist expects today.*

(translation ours)

Parallel to the introduction of ordinary tourism at the seaside, the event "Marseille-Provence 2013, European Capital of Culture" (MP2013) participated in the reinvention of "the ordinary" in this industrial town. What role, then, did this event play in the contemporary tourist invention of this territory, and what forms has it taken?

MP2013 European Capital of Culture as a path towards the reinvention of the ordinary

Within the framework of the polycentric Aix-Marseille-Provence metropolis, which hosted the European Capital of Culture event,[25] the spread of the tourist phenomenon also occurred in the outskirts of the metropolitan area and in other towns. In Martigues, the tourist promotion of the "ordinary" relies on the industrial culture of the town.

This phenomenon reflects a form of redevelopment of downgraded spaces (Gresillon 2008). In this context, whatever was perceived as giving a repulsive image of the territory was improved. Petrochemical industries were visited during "industry nights" or brought closer as part of urban walks, while live shows were held at the Berre lagoon. These events were hugely successful, demonstrating a certain maturity of tourism practices. Tourists feel the need to venture outside the designated tourist enclaves imagined for them, or far from places subverted by other tourists (Delaplace and Gravari-Barbas 2016). In an article published in 2014, Sophie Bertran de Balanda, then chief architect of the city, noted:

> The city of Martigues is comfortable with its duality between a petrochemical economy and tourist city. We are only at the beginning of the cultural recognition and the recognition of the attractive value of this "impressive" (and impressionist?) industrial landscape.
>
> (translation ours)

On the occasion of the MP2013 event, the municipality developed a number of events associating tourism and industry, including the "industry night" which, initiated on 31 August 2013, was the high point.[26] As Sophie Bertran de Balanda points out, it is questionable whether these projects will remain ephemeral or whether they will help make this development sustainable in the town: "*Doesn't this artistic reconciliation between industry and city provide hope for the future of this laboratory of modernity?*" The policy promoting the town's heritage and tourism occurs in a period where there seems to be intensified concern for the past. In today's complex world, marked by the internationalisation of exchanges and by information overload, the heritage argument reflects the desire to refocus investment efforts at the local level.[27] Heritage plays a central role as it gives a place meaning and participates in a territory's legitimisation. To address the changing expectations and tourist practices, territories now promote their heritage, considered as a resource for tourism development. A shift towards the recognition and promotion of industrial heritage seems possible in Martigues. Sophie Bertran de Balanda questions, however, the lack of recognition of industrial heritage as a challenge for future projects and attempts to identify the causes. She notes (Bertran de Balanda 2014, 38), for instance, that:

> It seems that the value of the forms inherited from this adventure is yet to be recognised as something that will enrich future industrial projects. The following questions thus arise: The industry is still alive: isn't this the right time to promote it? Is it the apprehension associated with the end of the oil cycle, which has marked the life of this town for almost a century, or the familiarity with the "factory" that prevents the consideration of other uses? Lastly, can the recognition of the heritage value of a place come from the outside alone, from a scientific perspective free of empathy?
>
> (translation ours)

Ultimately, this transition may occur gently, gradually settling in spaces and minds. The recognition and promotion of the industrial heritage of Martigues may perhaps be part of the more global dynamic of the redevelopment of the space that supported it and remains the symbol of this redevelopment: the Berre lagoon.

Conclusion

This study has made it possible to highlight the different ways in which the ordinary has been implemented in the tourism development of the town of Martigues. Echoing the growing hybridisation of tourist practices and "ordinary" practices, this study focused specifically on the role public actors have played in this evolution. This reinvention of the ordinary is reflected in a certain hybridisation of urban and tourist policies that target both permanent residents and visitors. Along with the municipal policy in favour of valorising urban and natural heritage for the residents and indirectly for potential visitors, Martigues became a tourist place. The interviews pointed the extent to which local actors were aware of the changes taking place in the world of tourism, which they attempted to integrate into the different forms of regulation and management of their town. However, the approaches privileged by local public actors differed on this point, and tensions emerged in how the region is promoted to outsiders. These tensions are particularly reflected in the double classification of the Martigues town as a tourist resort (2008) and as a City of Art and History (2012).

While the focus of this study was on public actors, it also highlighted the role civil society plays in this hybridisation process. Strengthening ties between the inhabitants and their city is thus one of the objectives assigned to tourism development in the Regional Development Directives of Bouches-du-Rhône (2007). Similarly, at the Martigues level, urban policies are promoted both as territorial issues for the inhabitants and as means of ensuring tourist attractiveness. This has been the case with the town's decision to upgrade the public spaces of the city centre. The role of civil society may also be a driving force in this form of reinvention of the ordinary. The hybridisation of public policies is thus promoted by the mobilisation of inhabitants who demand the development of local leisure activities that can also contribute to the tourist attractiveness of the territory.

Lastly, in these changes relating to the reinvention of the ordinary that seeks to increase the territorial attractiveness, the role played today by creative resources and creative tourism must not be forgotten (Richards 2020). Martigues is a witness to this in that it has become a privileged site for the shooting of films and television series.[28] Although the 2015 urban development plan did not anticipate this evolution, the emerging film economy is beginning to take shape in the town. The management of the cultural directorate since 2014 by the former chief architect of the town undoubtedly ensures the future development of creative tourism promoted by the mixing of urban and cultural dimensions within the town.

Notes

1 This work is a result of the research undertaken within the framework of the Valolitto project "Tourism development in coastal areas: analysing regional representations and their impact on environmental governance". Funded by the Fondation de France (2014) call for proposals "What will the coastlines of tomorrow look like?", this project made it possible to analyse three coastal areas in the south of France: Lacanau, Biarritz and Martigues. The report written after the completion of this project is available online (Hatt et al. 2018).

2 As the top tourist destination with 118 million overnight stays in 2017 (38.5% of all overnight stays) and 22.2% of trips, tourism in coastal resorts is largely stable (www.entreprises.gouv.fr/fr/tourisme/developpement-et-competitivite-du-secteur/tourisme-littoral).

3 Understood as *"the transformation of spaces for tourism purposes"*, touristification is an often ill-defined concept, which has been analysed by Kadri et al. (2019). These authors particularly highlight the different approaches and uses of the concept in the studies published in French and English.

4 This hybridisation is understood in its primary meaning, that is a mixture that does not erase the origins but rather combines and gives them a new course (notably defined by Ascher 2000).

5 As a tool for a certain homogenisation of practices and statutes (through the dissemination of the same products and practices on a global scale), globalisation is, in parallel, a source of diversification that can increase the variety of choices available in each place. *"Globalisation, which is both homogenisation and diversification, generates dynamics of differentiation that, among other things, invent or reuse specificities based on physical proximity, on the 'local'"* (Ascher 2000, 147).

6 The concept of culture is defined within the meaning of Paul Claval, that is as *"everything people receive as a legacy, or that they invent . . . all the representations on which is based the transmission of sensitivities, ideas and norms from one generation to another, or between partners of the same age"* (Bonerandi 2005, 91).

7 In the PACA region, swimming/beach activity was practised by 33% of visitors surveyed, walks lasting several hours by 41%, shopping in the city by 22%, city visits by 33%, market visits by 17% and hiking by 7% of visitors (Atout France 2014). In terms of overall changes across the metropolitan coastal area (Atout France 2014, 170), there was an increase between 2005 and 2010 in city-visiting practices (from 19% to 27%), shopping in the city (from 0% to 20%), market visits (from 11% to 17%) and hiking (3% to 9%).

8 A regional resource may be defined as *"a specific resource that may be revealed through an intentional process, involving a collective dynamic of ownership by the actors of the territory, differing in nature depending on whether or not it takes the path of valorisation"* (François 2007, 65).

9 According to INSEE (2018), in the Sud Provence-Alpes-Côte d'Azur region, tourism consumption accounts for 12.5% of regional gross domestic product, second behind Corsica (33%) and far ahead the national average of 7.4%. On average over the year, 116,000 jobs are directly related to tourism; in 2011, they accounted for 6% of regional employment. In 2014, the total tourism consumption reached 18.9 billion Euros. The region is ranked third behind Île-de-France and Auvergne-Rhône-Alpes.

10 Created in 1985, the "City or Country of Art and History" label is awarded by the French Minister of Culture to municipalities who are committed to a policy of raising awareness among residents, visitors and young people of the quality of heritage, architecture and living environment.

11 This coastal lagoon ("l'étang de Berre") is the second largest salt pond in Europe after the Mar Menor in Spain.

12 Industrial development in Martigues dates back a long way. Initially revolving around shipbuilding, the salt mining industry and the chemical industry (caustic soda and

sulphuric acid) in the nineteenth century, it then turned to the oil industry (refining and petrochemicals) from 1920 (e.g. the oil port of Lavéra constructed in 1952).

13 This study aimed to test the assumption of the establishment of a *"social tourist zone"* around the town of Martigues and anticipated, in the first phase of development, the creation of 10,000 tourist beds.

14 As mentioned in the presentation report of the city's Local Urbanism Plan (PLU) (Commune de Martigues 2015), there was a steady decline in the number of jobs generated by the industrial sector; while in 1983, it stood at 49.5% of total employment, it had fallen to 30.5% in 2007.

15 The tourism management of coastal areas, initiated between the 1980s and the 1990s (notably with the organisation of the Verdon beach and the development of the municipal camp site), really gained momentum in the 1990s and 2000s when larger operations aimed at limiting motorised access and prioritising pedestrians on the coastline were implemented. The construction of the landscaped parking lot on Verdon beach is a good example of this change in tourism development policies.

16 Interview with the 6th Assistant, Tourism – Events – Agriculture – Fishing – Hunting and Commemoration, 27 May 2013.

17 Interview with the city's chief architect, 13 December 2013.

18 In terms of the number of tourist beds, with 14,895 tourist beds, Martigues is ranked fourth in the metropolis Aix-Marseille Provence, after Marseille, Aix-en-Provence and La Ciotat (8% of tourist accommodation). Above all, it is placed first at the metropolitan level in terms of beds in the open-air hotel industry, with 4,368 tourist beds (21% of the hotel beds in the metropolis), according to data from the National Institute of Statistics and Economic Studies (INSEE).

19 The national label provides a guarantee of efficient reception adapted to the essential needs of people with disabilities.

20 The surveys took place from 19 to 23 July across three beaches in Martigues. Regarding the geographical origin of the respondents, more than 20% of the 84 people surveyed were Martégals, almost 50% were from the Aix-Marseille-Provence metropolis (excluding Martigues) and almost 30% were from areas outside this metropolitan area (and approximately 20% were from outside the PACA region). Sixty-five percent of those surveyed were also same-day visitors.

21 Two types of comments were made in reference to Figure 9.5 relative to the public space redeveloped in the city centre with flower beds and statues in the background: while some highlighted the authenticity and uniqueness of this representative image of Martigues and Provence, others remarked on the quality of the layout, its originality and its attractiveness. The comments relating to Figure 9.6, which illustrates a landscaped space between the parking lot and the Verdon beach, all referred to the aesthetic dimension of the layout and its functionality.

22 It may be noted that then mayor of Martigues, Gaby Charroux, announced the nomination to make Berre lagoon a UNESCO World Heritage Site, proposed after the official launch of the call for nominations in October 2017. After having been the territorial project for the industry sector, Berre lagoon became a territorial project for heritage and tourism development.

23 The resources provided by the industry have enabled the regional authority to develop tools for the development and protection of natural spaces, reinforcing the region's tourism attractiveness in a spontaneous manner.

24 The municipality obtained the City of Art and History label in 2012, four years after the town was classified as a tourist resort.

25 The European Capital of Culture is a city designated by the European Union for a period of one year during which a programme of cultural events is organised.

26 The "industry night" was organised by the Théâtre des Salins, the national scene of Martigues, around night tours accompanied by performances by actors and musicians

in factories and in the water. In parallel, several artists drew on this industrial heritage. There was, for instance, Mathieu Immer, who worked on the sound landscapes of the industry from the EDF plant (the French multinational electric utility company plant), and the photographer, Alain Sauvant, who, at the request of the Théâtre des Salins, laid large tarpaulins on which industrial forms could be perceived as works of art in the city centre of Martigues (Bertran de Balanda, *op. cit.*: 39–40).

27 The concept of heritage is defined in the meaning of Paul Claval (cited by Bonerandi 2005) as "*the whole of what men receive as inheritance, or that they invent . . . All the representations upon which depend the transmission of sensitivities, ideas and norms from one generation to another, or between peers*".

28 Representative of this movement, the shooting of the Camping Paradis series took place in Martigues in 2009. According to the deputy assistant for culture, the town hosts ten to 12 shootings per year (films, commercials, video clips).

References

Ascher, François. 2000. *La société hypermoderne. Ces évènements nous dépassent, feignons d'en être les organisateurs*. Paris: Editions de l'Aube, p. 300.

ATOUT France. 2014. *Panorama du tourisme littoral. Cahier 1: analyse de l'offre et dynamiques d'évolution France métropolitaine*. Paris: Atout France, p. 212.

Bertran de Balanda, Sophie. 2014. "Paysage industriel et imaginaire à Martigues." *Rives méditerranéennes* 47, http://rives.revues.org/4578.

Bonerandi, Emmanuelle. 2005. "Le recours au patrimoine, modèle culturel pour le territoire?" *Géocarrefour* 80(2): 91–100.

Bourdeau, Philippe. 2012. "Le tourisme réinventé par ses périphéries?" In *Explorando las nuevas fronteras del turismo. Perspectivas de la invetigacion en turismo*, edited by Fabien Bourlon, Mauricio Osorio, Pascal Mao and Trace Gale. Coyhaique: Nire Negro, pp. 31–48.

Butler, Richard W. 1980. "The Concept of the Tourist Area Life-Cycle of Evolution: Implications for Management of Resources." *Canadian Geographer* 24(1): 5–12.

Carli, Andréa, Cyrielle Dally, Camille Fieux and Matthieu Prietto. 2015. *Carro, noyau villageois balnéaire d'une commune industrielle*. Aix-Marseille Université: Diagnostic de Master 1 "urbanisme et aménagement", supervised by Emeline Hatt, p. 47.

Cautellio, Florent, Charly Davoust, Khalil Djazouli, Léo Girard and Marie Hanastasiou. 2016. *Le littoral, une force pour penser le territoire martégal*. Aix-Marseille Université: Atelier de projet de Master 2 "Urbanisme durable, projet et action opérationnelle", supervised by Emeline Hatt, Frédérique Hernandez and Emmanuel Matteudi.

Chadefaud, Michel. 1988. *Aux origines du tourisme dans les pays de l'Adour. Du mythe à l'espace: un essai de géographie historique*. Pau: Cahiers de l'Université de Pau.

Cohen, Erik. 2008. "The Changing Faces of Contemporary Tourism. Symposium: Touring the World." *Society* 45(4): 330–333.

Commune de Martigues. 1972. "Opération d'urbanisme – ZOTO." Etude Delaugere (1969–1972), archives de la ville de Martigues.

Commune de Martigues. 2015. *Plan local d'urbanisme. Rapport de présentation, Tome 2 Evaluation environnementale*. Paris: Éditions de l'Aube, Approuvé par le Conseil municipal le 21 février.

Corbin, Alain. 1988. *Le territoire du vide: l'Occident et le désir de rivage (1750-1840)*. Paris: Flammarion, p. 403.

Debarbieux, Bernard. 2003. "Neuf enjeux de l'iconographie de projet et de prospective de territoire." In *Les figures du projet territorial*, edited by Bernard Debarbieux and Sylvie Lardon. Paris: Éditions de l'Aube, p. 20.

Delaplace, Marie and Maria Gravari-Barbas (dirs.). 2016. *Nouveaux territoires touristiques. Invention, reconfigurations, repositionnement.* Québec: Presses de l'université du Québec Coll. "Tourisme".

Duhamel, Philippe and Rémy Knafou. 2003. "Tourisme et littoral: Intérêts et limites d'une mise en relation/Tourism and Coastline: Interests and Limits About a Relationship." *Annales de Géographie* 629: 47–67, https://doi.org/10.3406/geo.2003.891, www.persee.fr/doc/geo_0003-4010_2003_num_112_629_891.

Eisinger, Peter. 2000. "The Politics of Bread and Circuses: Building the City for the Visitor Class." *Urban Affairs Review* 35(3): 316–333.

François, Hugues. 2007. *De la station ressource pour le territoire au territoire ressource pour la station: le cas des stations de moyenne montagne périurbaines de Grenoble.* Grenoble: Thèse de géographie – aménagement, Institut de Géographie Alpine, p. 352.

François, Hugues, Maud Hirczak and Nicolas Senil. 2006. "Territoire et patrimoine: la co-construction d'une dynamique et de ses ressources". *Revue d'Economie Régionale & Urbaine* 2006(5): 683–700.

Gravari-barbas, Maria. 2013. *Aménager la ville par la culture et le tourisme.* Paris: Éditions Le Moniteur (coll. "Ville-aménagement").

Gravari-barbas, Maria and Marie Delaplace. 2016. "Éditorial." *Via* 9, http://journals.openedition.org/viatourism/415.

Gresillon, Boris. 2008. "Ville et création artistique. Pour une autre approche de la géographie culturelle." *Annales de géographie* 660–661: 179–198, doi:10.3917/ag.660.0179

Hatt, Emeline. 2017. *Valorisation touristique des territoires littoraux: quelles représentations territoriales pour quelle gouvernance environnementale? Le cas de Martigues.* Aix-en-Provence: LIEU. Rapport intermédiaire du projet de recherche pour la Fondation de France.

Hatt, Emeline. 2010. "Les enquêtes photographiques auprès des touristes: un support à l'analyse des représentations microterritoriales des stations balnéaires." *Mondes du tourisme* 2: 24–44.

Hatt, Emeline et al. 2018. *Valorisation touristique des territoires littoraux: Quelles représentations territoriales pour quelle gouvernance environnementale?* Aix-en-Provence: LIEU. Rapport de recherche pour la Fondation de France, https://hal-amu.archives-ouvertes.fr/hal-01738598.

INSEE. 2018. "L'économie du tourisme en Provence-Alpes-Côte d'Azur." *Dossier Insee Provence-Alpes-Côte d'Azur* 8.

Jansen-Verbeke, Myriam. 2007. "Cultural Resources and the Tourismification of Territories." *Acta Turistica Nova* 34, in The Tourism Research Agenda: Navigating with a Compass, www.researchgate.net/signup.SignUp.html?hdrsu=1be.

Kadri, Boualem, Maria Bondarenko and Jean-Phariste Pharicien. 2019. "La mise en tourisme: Un concept entre déconstruction et reconstruction." *Téoros* 38: 1, http://journals.openedition.org/teoros/3413.

Lanfant, Marie-Françoise, John B. Allcock and Edward Bruner. 1995. *International Tourism: Identity and Change.* Londres: Sage, p. 246.

Muller, Pierre. 2005. "Esquisse d'une théorie du changement dans l'action publique. Structures acteurs et cadres cognitifs." *Revue française de science politique* 55: 155–187, doi:10.3917/rfsp.551.0155.

Préfecture des Bouches-du-Rhône. 2007. "Directive territoriale d'aménagement des Bouches-du-Rhône." Approuvée par Décret 2007–779 du 10 mai 2007, JO du 11 mai, https://www.notre-environnement.gouv.fr/spip.php?page=fond-documentaire&id=124478&title=Directive+territoriale+d%27am%C3%A9nagement+des+Bouc

hes-du-Rh%C3%B4ne+%28Mai%C2%A0(.   .   .)&lienretour=https%3A%2F%2Fwww.
notre-environnement.gouv.fr%2Frecherche%3Frecherch.

Reflets. 2007. "Un tourisme durable." *Le magazine de la ville de Martigues* 7.

Richards, Greg. 2020. "Designing Creative Places: The Role of Creative Tourism." *Annals of Tourism Research* 85: 11.

Stock, Mathis. 2001. "Brighton and Hove: Station ou ville touristique? Etude théorico-empirique." *Géocarrefour* 76(2): 127–131.

Stock, Mathis and Léopold Lucas. 2012. "La double révolution urbaine du tourisme." *Espaces et sociétés* 151: 15–30.

Turner, Louis and Josh Asch. 1975. *The Golden Hordes: International Tourism and the Pleasure Periphery.* Editor: Constable, p. 319.

Urbain, Jean-Didier. 2002. *Sur la plage: mœurs et coutumes balnéaires (XIXè-XXè siècles).* Paris: Editions Payot & Rivages, 3rd edition.

Vlès, Vincent, Vincent Berdoulay and Sylvie Clarimont. 2005. *Espaces publics et mise en scène de la ville touristique.* Paris: Ministère délégué au Tourisme, direction du Tourisme – Rapport de recherche, laboratoire SET UPPA-CNRS n° 5603.

Part 2
Afters

10 Reassembling spatio-temporalities of tourism in the Upper Black Forest

Tim Freytag, Cornelia Korff and Nora Winsky

Introduction

Tourism development and the history of tourism are often framed as a linear process. From this perspective, it can be argued that European tourism was shaped by the Grand Tour and the emergence of summer resorts, before it started to attract a wider public in the early twentieth century and subsequently turned into the mass tourism that has today become a dominant phenomenon at a global scale. Similarly, we can look at particular places that were ordinary places of everyday life before they came into the focus of travellers and tourism professionals who regarded them as an (economic) resource for local and regional tourism development, and who transformed them into tourist destinations. Drawing upon Butler's tourism area life cycle concept, it is possible to identify several stages in the development of tourism (Butler 1980, 2006). However, in the long run it is not clear where tourism is leading to, how it will end or what a place will look like "after" tourism. These questions are particularly prevalent in a world that has experienced severe problems related to overtourism during the past few years, and that is currently confronted with the COVID-19 pandemic and its devastating impact on tourism and mobility.

In this chapter, we suggest conceptualising tourism in a slightly different way: not as a historical path or a tourism area life cycle, but as an ongoing reassembling of spatio-temporalities. We understand tourism dynamics as a process of co-construction involving tourism professionals, visitors and residents. Looking into these dynamic spatio-temporalities it is possible to explain how new types of tourism emerge, while others are marked by change or disruptions. This allows us to conceptualise how ordinary places of everyday life are transformed into tourist places and vice versa. In this light, the "before" and "after" of tourism are inherent in the process of reassembling the spatio-temporalities of tourism. The main aim in this chapter is to introduce our conceptual approach and illustrate it by drawing upon the Upper Black Forest, which is one of the leading tourist destinations in Germany today. Since the first summer resorts were installed in the Upper Black Forest, this area has been widely shaped by shifting tourism-related and other dynamics for more than two centuries.

DOI: 10.4324/9781003138600-13

Firstly, we lay out the background and conceptual framing of our study. On the basis of tourism statistics and additional sources – such as research literature, tourism marketing reports, historical paintings and Instagram posts – we identify some key characteristics that shape the present situation in the Upper Black Forest. Although this tourist destination is marketed under one umbrella, we find it important to point out that the Upper Black Forest embraces a variety of tourism-related settings, sights and activities. This diversity of tourism articulations is reflected in the conceptual framework that is adopted in the main part of this chapter. Accordingly, we reconstruct a chronology of tourism in the Upper Black Forest with a focus on reassembling spatio-temporalities. Drawing upon several examples, we demonstrate how the "before" and "after" of tourism converge in the transformation of tourist places. Further, we show how ordinary places are shaped by tourism, and how tourism itself is shaped by the ordinary life of people in such places.

Background and conceptual framework

Situating the Upper Black Forest as a tourist destination

The Black Forest is a forested mountain region and a leading tourist destination in the state of Baden-Württemberg in southwest Germany (Korff 2008). Its highest peaks range from almost 1,200 m above sea level in the northern part to nearly 1,500 m in the southwestern part (notably, the Feldberg, Belchen, Schauinsland and Kandel). In 2018, almost 22.8 million overnight stays were registered in the Black Forest (Ehrhardt and Merther 2020). Our focus in this chapter is on the Upper Black Forest, an area that is usually not referred to as a clearly defined geographical unit, but as a branded tourist destination embracing two separate cultural landscapes: on the one hand, the highest peaks of the Southern Black Forest with deeply cut valleys and steep, forested slopes (that are particularly attractive for nature sports), and on the other hand, the wider and more gentle vales and plateaus of the Central Black Forest, forming a cultural landscape that is shaped by cattle farming and single farmsteads within extensive meadows and pastures. The name Upper Black Forest goes back to the restructuring of the administrative territorial units in 1956, when the Landkreis Hochschwarzwald was established (Hitz 2011). The core region of the Upper Black Forest, which roughly stretches from the Schauinsland and Feldberg peaks to the "Three-lakes-area" (Drei-Seen-Gebiet between Titisee-Neustadt and Schluchsee), and the peaks of Hochfirst (near Lenzkirch), Brend and Rohrhardsberg (near Schonach and Schönwald), has become a famous tourist destination. Progressively, the Upper Black Forest has been constructed as a comprehensive region by the residents in their everyday activities, and by tourism marketing initiatives. In 2008, the municipal tourism and business development agencies were privatised and transformed into the Hochschwarzwald Tourismus GmbH (HTG), a regional tourism marketing organisation that was founded by ten Upper

Black Forest municipalities (Stadelbauer 2009). From then on, the name "Upper Black Forest" was used for branding this tourist destination.

As a result of the highly successful tourism development in the Upper Black Forest, more and more neighbouring municipalities have sought to become part of this destination and decided to join the HTG. The ongoing marketing and branding activities have sparked a process of territorial expansion to the extent that by now the HTG members have doubled (20 municipalities). The Upper Black Forest as a tourist destination now extends far into the Southern and Central Black Forest, and even includes Löffingen, a municipality that joined the HTG, although geographically it is located outside the Black Forest natural region (see Figure 10.1).

According to the HTG (2019), the Upper Black Forest accounted for nearly four million overnight stays in 2018. However, tourism development and the prevalent types of tourism are unevenly distributed over the different parts of the Upper Black Forest. The tourist destination encompasses, on the one hand, a spatially concentrated cluster of frequently visited and highly successful tourist locations (e.g. Feldberg, Hinterzarten, Schluchsee and Titisee). On the other hand, the Upper Black Forest contains other locations (such as Frieden-weiler, Löffingen or Eisenbach), which adhered to the HTG in the hope of more efficient tourism marketing, but which have not attained any significant growth of tourism as a result (see Figure 10.1). Important industrial locations are situated in Schonach and in Eisenbach, which is called the centre of the "gear-valley" (Zahnrad-Tal). However, an economic basis that is clearly shaped by industry and commerce can also be found in slightly touristified cities, such as Todtnau, and in the community of Neustadt.

Historically, the summer season is more important than the winter season for tourism in the Upper Black Forest (Mohr 1993). For many years, approximately two-thirds of the overnight stays have been registered in the summer season from May to October. The main attractions of the tourist destination are outdoor activities and the natural scenery. As winter sports form the main activities in the winter season from November to April, the general weather conditions, and in particular the availability of snow, have a strong impact on the number of overnight stays. Despite considerable variation from one year to the next, and the expected consequences of global warming, the number of overnight stays in the winter season has been relatively robust since the 1990s. In the Upper Black Forest, and even more so in the Black Forest as a whole, the majority of overnight stays are generated by German tourists (HTG 2019). However, the number of international visitors (mainly from Switzerland, France and the Netherlands) has increased in recent years and accounted for approximately 30% of visitors to the Upper Black Forest in 2018.

The Upper Black Forest not only is an important tourist destination but also serves as a local and regional recreation area for day visitors from places located on the fringes of the Black Forest, including the Stuttgart metropolitan area, as well as places in Switzerland and France. The sight-seeing hotspots and the locations that are most attractive for outdoor sports and recreation because of

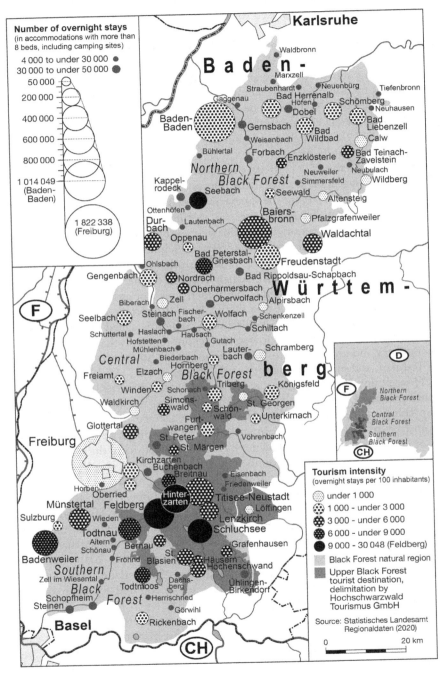

Figure 10.1 Tourism in the Black Forest and delimitation of the Upper Black Forest tourist destination

Note: Modified and updated after Korff and Mohr (2008, 280)

their spectacular natural scenery (such as Hinterzarten, Titisee, Feldberg and Schluchsee) are increasingly confronted with the challenges of overtourism caused by day-trippers and short-break tourists. These places are also popular stopovers for international coach tour travellers, such as visitors from Asia on group tours across Europe. Titisee and Feldberg are probably the hotspots that are most affected by overtourism.

Reassembling spatio-temporalities of tourism: a conceptual framework

The history of tourism in the Upper Black Forest has been shaped by the interplay between advancements and innovations in tourism and broader economic, social, cultural and political transitions. The highly diversified tourism profile prevailing in this destination in the early twenty-first century is the result of complex developments and disruptions that have occurred in the Upper Black Forest over the past two centuries. Although we can identify several patterns, relationships and dependencies over time and space, it would be reductionist (if not deterministic) to present the history of tourism as a linear chronology. Consequently, our aim in this chapter is to show that tourism development is a complex and open set of transitions and disruptions. We will point out that tourism can be understood as (re-)assembled spatio-temporalities, in other words particular constellations that emerge, stabilise or disappear in various ways over time and space. Further, we will underline the interplay between tourism and the everyday life of the local residents. Against the backdrop of the tourism area life cycle model (Butler 1980, 2006) and the criticism related to this concept – including approaches that consider tourism developments as chaotic and that draw upon complexity theory to carry out tourism policy research (Stevenson et al. 2009) – we look upon "before and after tourism" as an ongoing process of becoming. We suggest conceptualising tourism not as a linear path, but rather as a continuous and complex process of transformation. Reassembling the spatio-temporalities of tourism can be used as a conceptual framework to assess incoherent, spatially and temporally different tourist developments and disruptions as they can be traced in the Upper Black Forest.

Richard Butler initially presented the tourism area life cycle (TALC) model in 1980, and more than 40 years later this concept is still influential in tourism studies. The TALC model has been applied to a wide range of tourist areas on a global scale. Based upon the product life cycle concept known from business studies, the TALC model sketches out how the number of visitors in a tourist destination has changed over time. In the beginning, a few pioneers visit little known places that are not equipped with tourist infrastructures. Over the years, as the places become better known, more and more visitors are attracted, tourist facilities are built and local residents become increasingly dependent on the tourism sector. These developments are divided into the exploration, involvement, development, consolidation and stagnation stages. Once the limits of the carrying capacity are reached, tourist areas face development stages ranging from rejuvenation to decline (Butler 2006).

In 2006, Butler published an edited volume consisting of various chapters by researchers who had used and modified the original model. In this volume, the authors point out that not all tourist areas follow the ideal-type model and that they experience the stages in different intensities (Butler 2006, 9). Consequently, the shape of the graph (typically an asymptotic curve) has to be modified for each tourist area as "rates of development, numbers of visitors, accessibility, government policies, and numbers of similar competing areas" (Butler 2006, 10) come into play. Thus, it is clear that local circumstances are central to tourist transformations. Besides the author's own critical assessment of the model, further criticism has come from the scientific community (e.g. Chapman and Light 2016; Ivars i Baidal et al. 2013; McKercher and Wong 2021). A predominant critique of the TALC model is that it treats a destination as a homogeneous unit without taking internal differentiation into account and that it fails to "examine the complex interaction of internal and external factors which affect [a] destination" (Chapman and Light 2016, 255). Besides local specifics, regional, national and global circumstances, such as "globalization, crisis, and changes in tourist behaviors" (McKercher and Wong 2021, 4), have transformational power. Thus, we argue that tourism is strongly influenced by broader sociocultural, economic and environmental changes. By contrast, the TALC model is conceptualised rather narrowly and has difficulties in describing and explaining complex relationships affecting destinations. Moreover, complexity theorists argue in favour of a research methodology encompassing "the inter-relationships, interactions and communications involved in developing and delivering policy" (Stevenson et al. 2009, 217). Accordingly, it is fundamentally important to take human interactions and agencies into account in order to describe and analyse complex tourist policymaking processes, which in turn influence and shape tourist environments.

Following up on this, and as an extension of the TALC model, we understand tourism dynamics as a process of co-construction involving tourism professionals, visitors and local residents as equally relevant actors. In this approach, the human actors and their practices, as well as non-human actors such as materialities and representations, continuously come together and build a co-constitutive network. There is an ongoing interaction between the various components of this network. We agree with tourism scholars who conceptualise tourist processes as a set of assemblages (Darbellay and Stock 2012; Edensor 2011; Farías and Bender 2011). A diachronic perspective is inherent to the conceptual framework, as it captures the ways in which new types of tourism emerge, while others disappear, and shows how ordinary places are transformed into tourist places and vice versa. This allows us to differentiate between continuities, disruptions and branched sequences. Instead of a clear separation between "before" and "after" tourism, or between the different stages identified in the TALC model, we suggest a more nuanced perspective that enables us to understand tourism as an ongoing process: reassembling the spatio-temporalities of tourism. While it may be reductionist to associate the "before" and "after" of tourism with a particular tourist destination, it is possible to identify a set of specific components which emerge or disappear within the assemblages, for example as a result of technological or other innovations, or due to societal or political change. As Edensor (2011, 238) puts it: "[T]he figure of the assemblage . . . can account for the complex, mutable and entangled processes through which place is continuously transformed and stabilized."

Ongoing dynamics of before and after tourism in the Upper Black Forest

From the precursors of tourism to the Second World War

The mountain range of the Upper Black Forest was traditionally shaped by agriculture, forestry, mining and handicrafts (woodworking, clocks, glass, etc.). The proximity to larger trade routes facilitated the marketing of the manufactured goods – and the inns providing food and accommodation along these routes can be regarded as precursors of the tourism industry (Hitz 2011). In the nineteenth and early twentieth centuries, several sites of industrial production emerged, while the rise of tourism was limited to a few places and only started to gain greater importance in the course of the twentieth century. Consequently, both the regional economy and the cultural landscape of the Upper Black Forest have a rich and multifaceted profile with several local specificities and a long-standing cultural heritage. Before the rise of tourism, the prevailing settlement pattern in the sparsely populated lower parts of the Upper Black Forest (in the Hofgütergebiet, which is part of the Central Black Forest) was primarily shaped by isolated farmsteads, with just a few villages. The huge farm buildings are integrated in the surrounding landscape that reflects the characteristic mixed-use pattern of alternating arable land and pasture (crop-pasture rotation), dairy cattle and forestry (Mohr and Laule 2002; see also Dischler's historical landscape painting in Figure 10.2). The heights of the Feldberg mountain range remained almost unsettled (except for a few cattle sheds and herdsmen's huts) and were used as commons or by peasant cooperatives for grazing young cattle during the summer. Until the 1930s, the Feldberg and its pastures did not form an independent community, but belonged to the surrounding municipalities (Rieple 1965).

Landscape paintings by Hermann Dischler (1866–1935) and other artists have been instrumental in constructing the imaginary of the Upper Black Forest with an emphasis on nature, idyllic scenes, calm and good health. The style of landscape painting in the early twentieth century has played an important role in the development of the Upper Black Forest as a tourist destination, as it has been taken up, reproduced and reframed by visitors and tourism professionals (see Figure 10.2). In other words, tourism draws upon and mobilises landscape imaginaries as a resource and unique selling point.

The advent of tourism goes back to the mid-nineteenth century, when the first travellers and hikers looked for huts and cabins where they could find shelter in the upper mountain ranges of the Black Forest. This trend

Figure 10.2 Landscape imaginaries of the Upper Black Forest

was accompanied by the emerging *Alpenromantik*, a fundamental turn in the perception and evaluation of natural landscapes and, in particular, the Alps. While wild mountain ranges with inaccessible forests and uncultivated land were formerly considered as dangerous places, from that time on they were looked at from a different perspective: people started to see natural landscapes as something desirable and established a new type of landscape aesthetics that is reflected in the "romantic gaze", a particular type of tourist gaze with emphasis on "solitude, privacy and a personal, semi-spiritual relationship with the object of the gaze" (Urry and Larsen 2011, 9). The rise of tourism was supported by the construction of improved roads (Höllentalstraße established in 1847) and the creation of a network of hiking trails spurred by the Black Forest Club (Schwarzwaldverein founded in 1864). In 1887, the Höllental-bahn railway link between Freiburg and Neustadt was completed. Although its original purpose was to serve agriculture, the construction business and the lumber trade, the fast and affordable train connection was increasingly used for passenger transportation, especially at weekends (Hitz 2011). Gradually, the railway attracted more and more travellers – both day-trippers and visitors who stayed for several weeks – and it substantially contributed to enhancing the development of tourism in the Upper Black Forest. A further step was taken by a group of pioneers in the 1890s who practised skiing and laid the ground for winter sports and the introduction of a second tourist season (Korff and Mohr 2008).

Hinterzarten, Schluchsee and St Blasien, which are located in the lower heights, can be regarded as the first tourist destinations in the Upper Black Forest. However, hikers and skiers were also attracted by the heights of the Feldberg mountain range and its picturesque scenery. Consequently, the Feldberg started to be touristified, with cattle-sheds being transformed into countryside inns to serve meals to the tourists, and this emblematic change of use was reproduced in many other places. The Feldberger Hof hotel opened in 1864 and as a result of the improved road infrastructure and the rise of skiing in the late nineteenth century, the Feldberg area gained increasing importance as a tourist location. It has gradually developed into a tourist resort, hosting visitors for long vacations and recreation purposes. Interestingly, the Feldberg municipality did not exist before the rise of tourism and was established only in 1939 (forming a joint municipality with Altglashütten and Bärental). Overall, the establishment of summer resorts and the rise of winter sports in the late nineteenth and early twentieth centuries assembled the comprehensive set of three key elements constituting Upper Black Forest tourism. These were further differentiated, transformed and specified in the following decades and have kept their predominant role in the twenty-first century: (i) nature/landscape/aesthetics, (ii) recreation/well-being/health and (iii) outdoor activities/nature sports.

In the first half of the twentieth century, several summer resorts were built, and hiking as well as winter sports became increasingly popular. The growth dynamics of tourism have transformed several communities with an increasing number of guest rooms, boarding houses and hotels. Both the First World War and the Second World War caused temporary disruptions, but they did not have a major impact on tourist activities or tourism-related services in the Upper Black Forest. Although the First World War led to a massive decline in tourism, in particular with regard to international visitors, the 1920s were marked by a rapid recovery that was reinforced by a growing interest in winter sports. This was stimulated in part by popular contemporary films set in such mountain regions. According to Semmens (2005, 89) a "normal" tourist culture prevailed in the Black Forest during the Third Reich:

> The Black Forest's timeless, rural landscapes and its inhabitants' traditional lifestyle seemed to offer an escape from the present. Local tourism officials recognised what tourists were after and therefore promoted the region's ancient customs, buildings and dress alongside the natural attractions in countless brochures, guides, advertisements and postcards. The presence of swastikas or ideological discourse would thus in many ways have been entirely out of place; it would have disturbed the Black Forest's tourist aesthetic.

This does not mean that the Nazi regime and its supporters were absent in the Upper Black Forest. But the hegemonic national ideology was embedded in a quiet and peaceful environment (Mohr and Laule 2002), while demonstrations and unrest occurred primarily in the larger cities in Germany.

Tourism during the second half of the twentieth century

In the decades following the Second World War, tourist activities in the Upper Black Forest were expanded, with a persistent focus on traditional recreation holiday features, such as hiking, regeneration and health, natural landscapes and related aesthetics. In addition to this predominant profile, a few new trends came up in specialised segments, such as farm holidays (from the 1950s) or health resort and spa tourism (that has its beginnings in the first half of the 20th century and was subsequently enlarged and extended). From the mid-1960s, holiday housing complexes, apartments and second homes, and an increasing number of hotels were constructed (Korff and Mohr 2008). In some places, this led to a densification of the single farm settlement structure – a village centre was formed at that time in Hinterzarten (Mohr and Laule 2002) – and to the extension of existing settlements. Although there was an overall growth of tourism into the 1980s, with a majority of visitors spending several weeks in the Upper Black Forest, the region was shaped by uneven territorial development: the tourism economy was concentrated in tourist hotspots, while only a small number of the more remote communities slowly started to promote individual farm holidays or to set up holiday villages, and the industrial sites continued to operate independently of the development of tourism.

New forms of travel and tourist demands have become more prominent since the late 1980s. Resulting from societal changes and technical innovations (such as advances in the rail and road transport infrastructure), there was an increasing demand for short-break holidays, and a growing number of tourists took spontaneous decisions and articulated more individualised preferences in respect of leisure activities (Korff 2008). Consequently, the traditional hiking and recreation holiday of several weeks came to be considered as old-fashioned, boring and not very appealing to the majority of tourists (including more advanced age groups, from then on referred to as "best agers") who were primarily interested in international travel and city tourism. Hence, after several decades of tourism growth, the Upper Black Forest was confronted with declining numbers of visitors and overnight stays. The crisis was particularly severe in health resort and spa locations, which had to cope with the consequences of national health reforms that dramatically cut the budget for convalescent care (Korff and Mohr 2008). To cope with the general decline in Upper Black Forest tourism (which was aggravated by a lack of investment in modernisation), and to avoid the collapse of specialised tourist resorts, it was important to invent and implement new types of tourism and tourism marketing. Transcending the idea of a tourism area life cycle, there was a need for innovation, specialisation and flexibilisation of tourist infrastructures and services in order to completely reassemble, reimagine and reframe tourism.

In the new Upper Black Forest tourism that emerged in the 1990s, the tourist experience plays a key role and binds together highly differentiated types of tourism. This has also increasingly attracted the so-called best agers, older people who look for activities that make them feel they are still young at heart. Some outdoor activities are more sport oriented (such as hiking, trekking, mountain biking, skiing and snowboarding), while others are more leisure oriented (slow walking, enjoyment of nature, heritage, culture, and corresponding thematic trails). In the tourism segment of health and regeneration, the differentiation process with a focus on experience has led to the emergence of innovative health and wellness services that offer comfort, relaxation and a chance to indulge oneself. With respect to nature and landscape aesthetics, the new focus on experience has provoked a renaissance of landscape imageries and related stereotypes. Upper Black Forest landscapes are being staged and reframed according to a new rurality paradigm (i.e. idyllic scenes of staged rurality) that corresponds to a contemporary societal trend that is particularly popular with people living in urban areas. Similar to the continuities in landscape imageries, there is a long-standing tradition of cultural folk costumes. On the occasion of festive events and religious celebrations, many residents of the Black Forest wear traditional dress *(Trachten)* to "embody and express meaningful cultural identities such as connections to their heritage, family values, and their home" (Hughes et al. 2015, 9). Their practices are an expression of local belonging and social cohesion, which people in postmodern societies often miss. Especially urban dwellers associate rural areas with such qualities, which increases the Black Forest's popularity as a destination. The experience-led and highly differentiated new Upper Black Forest tourism is reflected in, and promoted by, innovative concepts and strategies in tourism marketing.

The ongoing process of differentiation in tourism is reflected in various specialisation trends at the local scale. Titisee, for example, has become a tourist hotspot attracting large numbers of international visitors and many day-trippers. As a result of successful marketing campaigns, this location is a very popular stopover for coach tour travellers and international visitors, in particular from Asia. This has led to an extension of the local tourist infrastructure. In addition to several souvenir shops, restaurants and accommodation facilities, the lakeshore tourist resort offers an indoor water park, a golf course and extensive spa and wellness facilities. Hinterzarten, by contrast, shows a tourism profile that is particularly appealing to visitors seeking the experience of nature (sports), well-being and a chance to pamper themselves. Drawing upon staged ruralities and landscape aesthetics, Hinterzarten has found a way to offer a "modernised recreation holiday" for target groups that include families and more affluent tourists. Meanwhile, Feldberg has specialised in the experience of nature sports in the summer and winter seasons; in addition, a nature and heritage experience centre was established in 2001. The concentration on skiing, hiking and other nature sports is to some extent owed to the fact that Feldberg is a relatively young municipality that did not exist before the rise of tourism and does not have a historical centre or local tradition to be used for developing tourism. Its location in the subalpine zone, which is particularly important for nature conservation, is a specificity that has made Feldberg a centre for conservation, and has led to the establishment of a nature park with strict principles and guidelines for nature protection. The Southern Black Forest Nature Park, established in 1999, has not only reinforced the focus on the cultural landscape and related images, but also enhanced activities for ecological awareness and environmental education (Stadelbauer 2009).

Tourism in the early twenty-first century and challenges for future developments

During the past few years, tourism has pursued an ongoing process of diversification and specialisation with a focus on experience-led outdoor activities, wellness offerings and events. However, it would be wrong to understand these transformations as a linear process. In the gastronomy sector, for example, many restaurant owners fear they will have to close down as a result of the skilled labour shortage in a harshly competitive business. On the other hand, there is a small number of emerging high-end gourmet restaurants, as a concentrated cluster in the Northern Black Forest around Baiersbronn (Ottenbacher and Harrington 2013) and at single – and therefore significant – locations in the Upper Black Forest.

A major challenge for the Upper Black Forest is the ongoing competition not only within the region, but also with outlying tourist destinations. Here, the introduction of the *KONUS Guest Card* in 2006, which allows free use of public transport in the Southern and Central Black Forest, and which was extended to the entire Black Forest in 2008, gave the area an important advantage (Korff and Mohr 2008). The Hochschwarzwald Card was established in 2010 for visitors who spend at least two nights in registered hotels or guesthouses in the Upper Black Forest. This card gives such visitors free (or substantially reduced) access to more than 100 tourist attractions, museums, cultural events, sports and wellness facilities during their stay in the Upper Black Forest

(HTG 2019). The Hochschwarzwald Tourismus GmbH (HTG) was established in 2008 to promote integrated professional tourism marketing of the Upper Black Forest for initially ten communities (increased to 16 communities in 2019; see Figure 10.1). Looking at its marketing tools and strategies, we see a growing importance of digital marketing and in particular social media. Marketing initiatives tend to draw upon the traditional imaginaries of the Upper Black Forest (traditional costumes, the *Bollenhut* – a hat topped with pom-poms – and the famous cuckoo clock which serves as the official marketing icon of the HTG, as well as the typical Black Forest farm houses and iconic valley and mountain views) which were promoted and diffused in the late 1860s by the Schwarzwaldverein in travel guidebooks and later in the monthly papers of this club (Hitz 2011). In the social media, these images are often reframed in a slightly different way to construct a young and future-oriented imaginary of the Upper Black Forest (see Figure 10.2). The reframing of images and their diffusion in social media such as Instagram, for example, forms an important part of the professional strategic initiatives implemented by the destination marketing organisations (DMOs). Similarly, travellers and day-trippers actively engage in the ongoing (re- and co-)construction of the Upper Black Forest as a tourist destination by placing traditional motifs in a new light in the social media (Winsky and Zimmermann 2020).

With regard to the future development of tourism in the Upper Black Forest, another major challenge is climate change and its expected impact on winter tourism (Endler et al. 2010). Due to global warming, the snow season will be shorter, and it is likely that only the highest parts of the mountain range will have enough snow. Meanwhile, winter sports have already started to decline on the lower slopes of the Upper Black Forest. The area between Schonach, Titisee, Hinterzarten and Schluchsee (see Figure 10.1) is affected by the uncertainty of upcoming winter seasons, which makes it impossible for decision-makers on the supply side of winter sports to engage in long-term planning and investments. The well-established international winter sports competition events – ski jumping and cross-country skiing in Titisee-Neustadt and Schonach, and biathlon at Notschrei – play an important role in HTG's marketing initiatives, but they will be increasingly difficult to maintain in the future. Consequently, there is a growing need to diversify and expand tourist activities that do not depend on snowfall. This means promoting wellness offers and (high-end) gastronomy, but also outdoor sports such as mountain biking and hiking. For example, the Westweg, established in 1900 as Germany's first long-distance trail, can attract young people who are looking for adventures and are prepared to stay overnight in a mountain hut (Knoll 2014).

However, winter sports providers tend to argue that there is an increasing need to install additional technical equipment, such as snowmaking systems, to ensure suitable conditions for skiing and snowboarding. Among opponents of plans to enhance winter sport infrastructures in the Upper Black Forest, there is increasing awareness of environmental issues and a controversial debate between tourism professionals, politicians, activists and the civil society. At the centre of this debate is a set of questions concerning future land use: how to adequately respond to the need for nature conservation, on the one hand, and the economic interests of professionals in tourism and the hospitality sector, on the other? How to imagine and promote a future winter season with winter sports activities that are not dependent on snowfall? Should there be a transitional period or an immediate withdrawal from snow-based winter sports? Abandoning ski and snowboard activities in the Feldberg area, which will undoubtedly occur sooner or later, means nothing other than destroying a central pillar of tourism in the Upper Black Forest. At present we can observe a desperate clinging onto snow-based winter sports, with professionals planning to expand the existing infrastructures in the Feldberg area, but it is clear that this cannot be a sustainable long-term strategy.

Another point with regard to future tourism developments is related to long-haul travellers. During the past few decades, the number of international tourists from non-European countries has increased. In particular, Titisee and Feldberg have developed into tourist hotspots for these target groups. The severe impacts of the COVID-19 pandemic in 2020 have underlined the vulnerability of the tourism sector (Gössling et al. 2021). Notably, long-haul travellers can be regarded as an unstable target group, not only because of pandemics, but also with regard to political changes, shifts in currency exchange rates and purchasing power or uncertainty due to natural hazards or terrorist attacks. Against this backdrop it will be important to enhance the resilience of the Upper Black Forest as a tourist destination by diversifying the activities offered and thus the profile of incoming regional and national visitors.

Focusing on reassembled components of tourism spatio-temporalities

Within the conceptual framework of tourism spatio-temporalities, it is possible to identify a set of (re-)assembled components. While it is difficult to conceptualise the "before" and "after" of tourism in the Upper Black Forest as a whole, we can focus on its various components. In doing so, we see that the components tend to (re-)assemble over time and space. The temporal dimension is closely related to change and innovation, which can be used to determine the "before" and "after" with regard to a specific component.

Transport and mobility play a double key role in the (re-)assembled spatio-temporalities of tourism. Firstly, transport infrastructure enables and regulates access to the tourist destination, and secondly, tourist activities involve transport and mobility practices. Drawing upon the example of the Upper Black Forest, we can see that transport facilities are closely related to the development of tourism. An early example of the close relationship between transport and tourism infrastructure is the establishment of inns along major trade routes to provide food and accommodation for travellers. Similarly, the construction of the railway, the modernisation of roads, individual car traffic and long-haul travellers who arrive in Europe by air and then move around by coach or train all have a considerable impact on the way tourism is (re-)assembled. We can identify a wide range of mobilities connected with tourism in the Upper Black Forest: all the different kinds of hiking, (cross-country) skiing, snowboarding and mountain biking, for example, but also e-biking, paragliding, and so on. Future trends in transport and mobility may include integrated smart transport systems and self-driving cars.

The digital age is marked by great advancements in the use of digital and smart technologies, including the internet, social media, smartphones and mobile communication networks. This trend affects tourism, leisure and ordinary everyday life. Tourists use digital devices to get information and to book services before, during and after their trip. This is not limited to route planning and booking transport, accommodation and events: travellers also use social

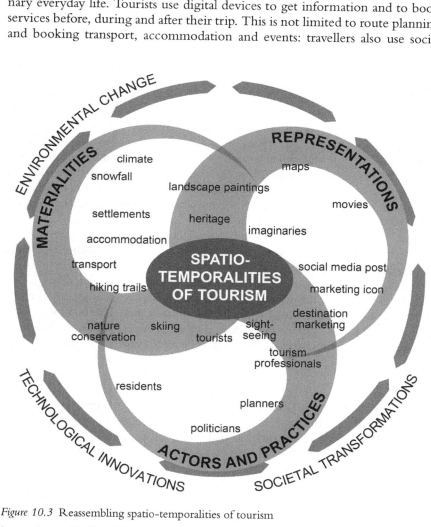

Figure 10.3 Reassembling spatio-temporalities of tourism

Source: Freytag, Korff, and Winsky

media to document and share their tourist activities. Here, tourists become trend-setters and act as "prosumers" complementing professional destination marketing activities. Displaying tourist spots or hiking and biking routes in social media or other digital tools can rapidly increase the attractiveness of such places, and may lead to overtourism or land use conflicts, for example if the recommended sites are located within a nature conservation area with restricted or prohibited access.

Spatio-temporal assemblages of tourism (Figure 10.3) involve various actors, such as tourism professionals, all kinds of tourists and day-trippers, local residents, planners and politicians and activists. All these actors operate and interact within varying geographical dimensions. The territorial dimension is reflected in the marketing initiatives of the HTG and the STG (Schwarzwald Tourismus GmbH), for example, and in the zoning of the KONUS Guest Card and the Hochschwarzwald Card. Visitors may either identify themselves with, or distinguish themselves from, specific types of tourists or tourist practices. The first travellers and hikers in the mid-nineteenth century, who looked for mountain huts and cabins where they could spend the night in the Black Forest, shared a group spirit and were bound together by their common perception and appreciation of natural landscapes. In a similar way, "best agers" today identify with a particular lifestyle and aim at drawing a line between themselves and elderly people in former generations. Thus, the current trend towards experience-led tourist practices links into the use of digital devices, the possibility of spending a night in a mountain hut and other components that together form a newly assembled spatio-temporality of tourism.

Last, but not least, materialities and representations play an important role in the spatio-temporal assemblages of tourism. As a result of climate change and global warming, for example, tourism professionals need to prepare for less snowfall in the winter season, and to readjust their technical equipment, tourist offers and marketing initiatives. Likewise, the material dimension and its representations are addressed in natural and cultural landscapes, settlement structures, cultural heritage and (regional) products prepared and served in hospitality venues, themed museums or family holidays on a traditional Black Forest farm.

Conclusions

The reassembled spatio-temporalities of tourism in the Upper Black Forest allow us to conceptualise tourism as the interplay between various components that form specific constellations in time and space. Although tourism has played an important role and has taken different forms in the Upper Black Forest over the past two centuries, we prefer not to draw upon the tourism area life cycle model which frames tourism development as a chronology in the sense of a linear history. And we believe it is reductionist to try and determine a point in time that is "before" or "after "tourism. Our focus is on the various components of tourism – actors and practices, materialities and representations – that are constantly being (re-)assembled in different ways over time and space. Moreover, we see that individual components may be transformed over time due to technological or other innovations. Consequently, it is possible to determine the before and after of a specific component, such as a guidebook, for example. A guidebook might be abandoned after a while, and later rediscovered and newly edited to re-emerge as part of a new tourism assemblage. In other words, the "before" and "after" of a tourism component may occur simultaneously, or the "after" may later have its renaissance as an upcoming "before" to be integrated in a future spatio-temporality of tourism. The ongoing reassemblages of tourism involve the interplay of various geographical scales. This concept makes it possible to capture tourist practices at a micro-level, tourist destinations, the home regions or countries of the visitors and global trends, such as the impact on tourism of the COVID-19 pandemic.

A specificity of the concept of spatio-temporalities in tourism consists in its openness and flexibility. Similar to current contributions to complexity theory, tourism is not conceived as an isolated or closed system, but is considered within a broader framework that takes into account the interplay between tourism and various other economic, social, political and cultural trends and structures. This is also true of the interrelations between tourism and the everyday life of the local residents, which is important in new urban tourism, for example. Likewise, the concept presented in this chapter may be used to further explore dark tourism and other types of themed tourism, but also eco-tourism, ethno-tourism and many more types and facets of tourism. The notion of the spatio-temporal assemblages of tourism can be mobilised as a conceptual framework to reveal interrelations and disruptions, and to question, for example, the "history of tourism" that has often been described from an exclusively European perspective, starting with the gentry doing the Grand Tour, subsequently expanding to tourists from the middle and working classes and finally resulting in mass tourism and overtourism.

References

Butler, Richard W. 1980. "The Concept of a Tourist Area Cycle of Evolution: Implications for Management of Resources." *The Canadian Geographer* 24(1): 5–12.

Butler, Richard W. (ed.). 2006. *The Tourism Area Life Cycle: Vol. 1, Applications and Modifications.* Clevedon: Channel View Publications.

Chapman, Anya and Duncan Light. 2016. "Exploring the Tourist Destination as a Mosaic: The Alternative Lifecycles of the Seaside Amusement Arcade Sector in Britain." *Tourism Management* 52: 254–263, https://doi.org/10.1016/j.tourman.2015.06.020.

Darbellay, Frédéric and Mathis Stock. 2012. "Tourism as Complex Interdisciplinary Research Object." *Annals of Tourism Research* 39(1): 441–458, https://doi.org/10.1016/j.annals.2011.07.002.

Edensor, Tim. 2011. "Entangled Agencies, Material Networks and Repair in a Building Assemblage: The Mutable Stone of St Ann's Church, Manchester." *Transactions of the Institute of British Geographers* 36(2): 238–252, https://doi.org/10.1111/j.1475-5661.2010.00421.x.

Ehrhardt, Christine, and Jeanette Merther. 2020. "Jahresbilanz 2019: Landestourismus erreicht vor Corona erneut Rekordwerte." *Statistisches Monatsheft Baden-Württemberg* 6–7:

3–10. www.statistik-bw.de/Service/Veroeff/Monatshefte/PDF/Beitrag20_07_01.pdf. Retrieved 11 December 2020.

Endler, Christina, Karoline Oehler and Andreas Matzarakis. 2010. "Vertical Gradient of Climate Change and Climate Tourism Conditions in the Black Forest." *International Journal of Biometeorology* 54: 45–61, https://doi.org/10.1007/s00484-009-0251-2.

Farías, Ignacio, and Thomas Bender (eds.). 2011. *Urban Assemblages: How Actor-Network Theory Changes Urban Studies.* London and New York: Routledge.

Gössling, Stefan, Daniel Scott and C. Michael Hall. 2021. "Pandemics, Tourism and Global Change: A Rapid Assessment of COVID-19." *Journal of Sustainable Tourism* 29(1): 1–20.

Hitz, Rüdiger. 2011. *Entstehung und Entwicklung des Tourismus im Schwarzwald: Das Beispiel Hochschwarzwald 1864–1914.* Freiburg: Schillinger.

HTG [Hochschwarzwald Tourismus GmbH] (ed.). 2019. "Jahresbericht 2018." *Hinterzarten.* www.hochschwarzwald.de/content/download/23602/291494/version/1/file/HTG_Jahresbericht_2018.pdf. Retrieved 11 December 2020.

Hughes, Amy S., Susan J. Torntore and Jennifer Paff Ogle. 2015. "Persistence and Change in the Black Forest Ethnic Dress Tradition." *International Journal of Costume and Fashion* 15(1): 1–18, https://doi.org/10.7233/ijcf.2015.15.1.001.

Ivars i Baidal, Josep A., Isabel Rodríguez Sánchez and José Fernando Vera Rebollo. 2013. "The Evolution of Mass Tourism Destinations: New Approaches Beyond Deterministic Models in Benidorm (Spain)." *Tourism Management* 34: 184–195, https://doi.org/10.1016/j.tourman.2012.04.009.

Knoll, Gabriele M. 2014. "Eine typische Mittelgebirgslandschaft." In *Landschaften geographisch verstehen und touristisch erschließen*, edited by Gabriele M. Knoll. Berlin: Springer, pp. 85–95.

Korff, Cornelia. 2008. "Entwicklungen im Tourismus." In *Geographie Baden-Württembergs: Raum, Entwicklung, Regionen*, edited by Hans Gebhardt. Stuttgart: Kohlhammer, pp. 153–159.

Korff, Cornelia and Bernhard Mohr. 2008. "Der Schwarzwald: Landwirtschaft, Forstwirtschaft und Tourismus." In *Geographie Baden-Württembergs: Raum, Entwicklung, Regionen*, edited by Hans Gebhardt. Stuttgart: Kohlhammer, pp. 271–283.

McKercher, Bob and IpKin Anthony Wong. 2021. "Do Destinations Have Multiple Lifecycles?" *Tourism Management* 83: 104232.

Mohr, Bernhard. 1993. "Der Schwarzwald." In *Geographische Landeskunde von Baden-Württemberg*, edited by Christoph Borcherdt. Stuttgart: Landeszentrale für politische Bildung Baden-Württemberg. (= Schriften zur politischen Landeskunde Baden-Württembergs, 8), pp. 169–207.

Mohr, Bernhard and Josef Laule. 2002. "Touristisches Angebot, Infrastrukturausbau und Siedlungswachstum." In *Hinterzarten im 20. Jahrhundert: Vom Bauerndorf zum heilklimatischen Kurort*, edited by Helmuth Schubert. Konstanz: Stadler (= Hinterzartener Schriften, 6), pp. 159–184.

Ottenbacher, Michael C. and Robert J. Harrington. 2013. "A Case Study of a Culinary Tourism Campaign in Germany: Implications for Strategy Making and Successful Implementation." *Journal of Hospitality & Tourism Research* 37(1): 3–28, https://doi.org/10.1177/1096348011413593.

Rieple, Max. 1965. *Der Hochschwarzwald: Heimatbuch eines Landkreises.* Konstanz: Rosgarten.

Semmens, Kristin. 2005. *Seeing Hitler's Germany: Tourism in the Third Reich.* London: Palgrave Macmillan.

Stadelbauer, Jörg. 2009. "The Black Forest Tourist Region: Actual Changes of Demand, Supply and Organization." *Geographical Sciences (Chiri-Kagaku)* 64(3): 151–167.

Stevenson, Nancy, David Airey and Graham Miller. 2009. "Complexity Theory and Tourism Policy Research." *International Journal of Tourism Policy* 2(3): 206–220, https://doi.org/10.1504/IJTP.2009.024553.

Urry, John and Jonas Larsen. 2011. *The Tourist Gaze 3.0.* Los Angeles, London: Sage, 3rd edition.

Winsky, Nora and Gisela Zimmermann. 2020. "Insta-Research zum #westweg im Schwarzwald – wie digital repräsentierte Wandererfahrungen auf Instagram mittels quantitativer und qualitativer Methoden untersucht werden können." *Zeitschrift für Tourismuswissenschaft* 12(3): 317–342, https://doi.org/10.1515/tw-2020-0022.

11 From tourism to art of living?

Residential utopia and after-tourism in the French Alps

Philippe Bourdeau

Introduction

After having been a lever for economic development during the twentieth century, Alpine tourism is facing structural, sectoral and global change factors which simultaneously concern tourism demand, environmental and economic sustainability and the impacts of climate change (Bourdeau 2007; Gauchon 2010; Achin and George 2013; Clivaz et al. 2015). Faced with an uncertain future, the affirmation and acceptance of a new development model of transition addresses fundamental questions about the status and place of tourism.

Visiting, which is one of the basic acts that define tourism, involves specific social practices and planning policies as well as a distinct culture, and has long been defined in opposition to dwelling, referring to everyday living. This clear distinction is becoming less and less appropriate due to the increasing mix between recreational and residential functions in most tourist areas. What has been referred to as Amenity migration (Moss 2006) offers new functions and identities to traditional tourist destinations (Bourdeau 2009). This phenomenon contributes to a process of tourist-residential convergence, which places recreational practices at the heart of the habitability of these places. By re-articulating these practices with the residential notion, multiple intersections are produced by establishing continuities where spatial, temporal, cultural and functional cleavages or fragmentations prevailed: city/nature, near/far, interior/exterior, natural/artificial, tourist/non-tourist, work/leisure, everyday/vacation.

This residential-recreational in-betweenness contributes to the practical and symbolic reconfiguration of the relationship between "Here" and "Elsewhere" (Bourdeau 2013). The search for a perfect place to live replaces the search for tourist paradises, and unexpectedly updates the former situationist project of "*transfiguring everyday life*" (Debord 1967). With the search for "*year-round living in a holiday home*" (Viard 2000), everyday life and places are increasingly being thought out in terms of quality and sustainability. The "*good life*" is then considered as a continuous holiday (Urry 2002), at least for the more privileged social classes who are involved in phenomena that the social science literature mainly

DOI: 10.4324/9781003138600-14

describes as amenity migration (Moss 2006) and lifestyle migration (Benson and O'Reilly 2009).

This chapter cross-references elements drawn from case studies in the French Alps, based on the conceptual level on collective work on leisure migration (Moss et al. 2009; Martin et al. 2013). Empirically, it is based on a comprehensive approach to the phenomena and practices observed in the Vercors Massif, chosen for its illustrative capacity and its emblematic character of residential migration in a (post)tourist context. This long-term approach, developed over approximately 14 years (2006–2020), is based firstly on field observations and involvement in the activities of the scientific council of the Vercors Regional Nature Park; secondly on semi-directive interviews with local inhabitants, actors and elected representatives within the ANR TerrHab research programme "From habitability to territoriality (and back)" (2013–2017); and finally on nearly 20 workshops and round tables organised with local inhabitants and local actors over the entire period concerned.

With attempts to generalise on the evolution of the relationship between tourism and the art of living: is the dominant status of tourism relativised by the residential utopia function of the mountains in the face of constraints linked to climate change and social or health crises? What is the contribution of this new residential utopia in the transition of development models in mountain areas?

Residential transition in the Alps: a silent revolution?

At the scale of the Alpine region, demographic decline has sometimes seemed to be an "emptying" of permanent inhabitant populations. However, different phases of repopulation have been observed since the 1980s. The phenomena involved are very heterogeneous, with marked geographical variations depending on the regional context. The arrival of new residents does not prevent further departures, and the different forms of migration present variable advantages and disadvantages according to the type of development expected, particularly in relation to urban spaces.

At a time of *happycracy* (Illous and Cabanas 2018) the search for a decent everyday life implies a "perfect" place to live. In considering the best place to live, tourist destinations benefit from numerous advantages, given that their development and desirability appear as a standard of reference. John Urry (2002) notes that the "good life" is thought of as "*as a continuous holiday*", and Jean Viard (2000) postulates that "*living all year round in a holiday home*" is a major residential utopia. In this quest for a residential Eden, tourism makes it possible to test places to assess their habitable qualities (Ceriani et al. 2004). All over the world, tourist destinations are those that "gain" the most inhabitants. In the Alpine region, the phenomenon concerns both urban and rural areas, from the most touristic to the most marginalised. Although many different configurations should be considered, three examples (among others) are proof of this.

In the Vercors Massif (Prealps, France), the population of the Four Mountains sector doubled between 1962 and 2007, and in 2014, the share of the population arriving in the last ten years was 66% in Lans-en-Vercors and 60% in Saint Nizier-du-Moucherotte and Villard-de-Lans.[1] At the same time, the price of vacant building lots has risen from 59 Euros per m^2 in 2004 to 160 Euros per m^2 in 2018.[2] In Chamonix, the proportion of inhabitants of English nationality was estimated at between 12% and 15%, and 11 out of 18 children attending nursery school in Argentière were of English nationality in 2010 (Martin et al. 2013, 394). In Italy, in the northeast of Friuli, the settlement of new inhabitants since the early 2000s has even contributed to a revitalisation of the "ghost towns" of the Canal del Ferrol region, which had been deserted by their inhabitants in the 1980s following an earthquake (Löffler et al. 2014).

Even second homes are now a component of residential trajectories: some of them are occupied well beyond holiday periods, including in the professional context. They can also be converted temporarily or permanently into a main residence, due to retirement or generational transmission. In order to account for these phenomena and also for the increasingly inextricable cohabitation between temporary residents (Stock 2005) and permanent tourists (Jaakson 1986), researchers are competing with concepts that have been forged over the past 20 years: *"amenity migration"* (Moss 2006), *"lifestyle migration"* (Benson and O'Reilly 2009), *"residential tourism"* (McWatters 2008), and *"recre-residents"* (Lajarge 2006). These are all but some categories on the subject, given the diversity of the motivations, circumstances and modalities of these demographic movements. The planned or unforeseen stages of personal life (separation, divorce) and professional life (*burn out*, redundancy, reconversion, retirement) are all opportunities to reshuffle the maps of residential strategies. This is especially significant when the question of where to live is linked to the question of the meaning of life and work. While the explanation of residential movements through the quest for a better quality of life may seem obvious, it nevertheless overturns the classic explanation of voluntary population migration through the search for economic advantage: hierarchical promotion, higher wages and so forth. On the contrary, the literature on leisure migration emphasises that the decisions made between income and lifestyle choices are far from anecdotal: abandoning professional progression, reducing working hours, retraining with loss of wages. The engineer who chooses to become a craftsman, market gardener or bed and breakfast owner is not (just) a myth! Nevertheless, the profile of the neo-alpine residents is very diverse (Perlik 2011): re-immigrants returning to their region of origin, secondary residents who have become permanent residents, hypermobile multi-residents, seasonal workers who are more or less settled, retired people in search of a *"green paradise"* (Urbain 2002).

According to Manfred Perlik (2011), three main types of convergent migration towards the Alps can be distinguished: firstly, *integral* migration which corresponds to a permanent residential settlement, combined either with an economic activity carried out on the spot, or with access to a redistributive income such as retirement. Secondly, *relative* migration in the case of mountain settlements combined with daily shuttles to the workplace in the city. Finally, *partial* migration in the context of multi-residential practices (Elmi and Perlik 2014), from second homes occupied for a variable part of the year to systematic bi-residences on a weekly or monthly scale, including long-distance shuttles via infrastructures that reduce journey times: motorways, tunnels, high-speed rail lines, airports. An emblematic case in point is the widespread use of low-cost flights from Chamonix to London via Geneva airport for around 100 Euros, and sometimes less.

As Jean-Paul Guérin and Hervé Gumuchian (1979) have clearly shown, the figure of the "rurban", an urban dweller living in the mountains, emerged at the end of the 1970s. This led to an exploration of lifestyles that re-examine local resources and identities. For the new residents, it is also the learning of cultural codes, practices and relationships that give rise to a wealth of literature designed to facilitate the introduction to rurality: *"Leaving the city, instruction handbook"*, *"Living in the countryside, the essentials"*, *"How to milk a chicken?"*. This learning process is not without its tensions: driving on snow, parking in hamlets, picking mushrooms and so forth. At the local level, the settling of new inhabitants contributes in a very basic way to the sustainability of public services, to the revival of trade and local crafts and to the dynamism of social and community life. The rise of a so-called residential economy complements or relays the conventional tourist economy. Demographic data are not always very conclusive, with natural and migratory balances, which can sometimes remain negative. However, research conducted in northeast Friuli (Italy) highlights that a small number of immigrants contribute to the revitalisation of depopulated mountain territories (Löffler et al. 2014). Other studies show that, once settled, new highlanders act to strengthen the environmental, traditional and social quality that attracted them to the area. They multiply initiatives oriented towards local cultural and community living, short food channels (Community Supported Agriculture), soft mobility, social and solidarity economy (recycling, repair-cafés, shared gardens), the collaborative economy (third-places, activity cooperatives), teleworking (co-working spaces), to the point of engaging in local debates on issues of environmental transition, participatory democracy, development projects or urban planning procedures.

However, according to many authors such as Perlik (2011), far from revaluing rurality in the manner of counter-urbanisation, new residential dynamics amplify the urban model by ending up with the attribution of an aesthetic and recreational function to the mountains, and thus their dependence on the city. This may be the case even if the peace and the landscape, the immediate accessibility of nature, the quality of life offered to children and a peaceful sociability facilitated by a strong social homogeneity are all ways of expressing an escape from urban constraints and turbulence. *"Pollution seen from above is frightening!"* says a resident of Saint-Nizier-du-Moucherotte in a document announcing a participatory workshop of the Grenoble Urban Community held in 2012. In a survey conducted in Saint Nizier in 2011 by students from the Institute of Alpine Geography, the main reasons given by the new inhabitants for moving to the mountains were, in descending order, *"to leave the urban environment"* (52%), *"to not put up with pollution"* (36%), *"access to property"* (33%) and *"fear of insecurity for children"* (13%).

The most privileged social classes are those who have the most autonomy in the choice of where they live. Their exodus to the mountains began a long time ago. It is accelerating against a backdrop of climate change since "sleeping in the cool" has become a sought-after privilege for a good part of the year, so much so that in March 2017 the cover of the local satirical newspaper *Le Postillon* depicted an uninterrupted line of 4×4s descending the slopes surrounding the conurbation with the headline *"Grenoble cannot welcome all the world's engineers"*. Paradoxically, this residential gentrification is above all marked by the quest for a "simple" way of life and recreational uses of the outdoors: leaving home on snowshoes or mountain bikes, integrating into local cultural and sports networks. Many neo-alpine residents have a profile of "alter-gentrifiers" (Richard et al. 2014) or "cultural creatives" (Ray and Anderson 2001). Let us not forget, however, that there are migrations linked to poverty or even forms of exclusion, such as those observed in the Diois valley (France) by Françoise Cognard (2006). Residential mobility is thus motivated by the hope of a less costly and more autonomous life than in an urban environment, with the search for access to non-market resources which come from nature.

Recreational practices at the heart of habitability

The place of recreational practices in habitability has been explored as part of the research programme *"From habitability to territoriality (and back)"* conducted from 2010 to 2015 with the support of the French National Research Agency (Bourdeau 2016). The results presented here come from a case study carried out in two municipalities – Saint Nizier-du-Moucherotte and Engins – located on the edge of the Vercors Massif, 40 minutes from the Grenoble urban area. If the trajectories of these two communities are clearly distinct – post-touristic in the case of Saint Nizier (Bachimon et al. 2014), post-agricultural for Engins – they have both welcomed new residents of urban origin for the last 20 years. About ten comprehensive interviews (Kaufmann 1996) were conducted with these new residents, in addition to semi-directive interviews with development agents and elected officials, and long-term observations in the field. It should be noted that the socio-demographic and recreational profile of the interviewees proved to be very homogeneous without this having been a particular choice at the start of the research. Let us cite five outstanding characteristics: between 40 and 50 years of age, family life with children, higher intellectual professions, intensive practice of mountain sports, strong local community investment.

It is possible to notice that journeys to Grenoble are an un-thought-out but structuring component of residents' relationship to their living space, even when the repetition of these trips is experienced as a constraint. They punctuate an alternation between up and down, the mountains and the city, free time and work. In this respect, the dream – often evoked by our interlocutors – of building a cable car between Grenoble and Saint-Nizier-du Moucherotte seems to be experienced both as a promise of a temporal shortcut in the link with the valley, while preserving a discontinuity which is the foundation of the city-mountain otherness. The effect of the mountainous character of the cable car, which makes an implicit reference to the imagination of winter sports, is coupled here with an expectation of a reasonable environmentally legitimisation of the choice of residential migration to the mountains, both near to and far from the city.

The settling of our interlocutors in a space with a liminal status, invested with hybrid practices and representations that are both recreational and residential, is conducive to a redefinition of the contours between urban and mountain spaces and lifestyles. The respective habitability of the city and the nearby mountain appears to be a direct result of the crossed relational processes, which are established between these geographical entities (Bourdeau et al. 2011; Bourdeau 2016). The relationships between rootedness and mobility, work and leisure, residential, productive and recreational functions, daily and non-daily life, urban-ness and rurality are reworked according to a wide variety of *modus operandi*: neighbourhoods, telescoping, superimposition, contamination, interweaving, hybridisation. From forms of urbanisation to building styles, from tags to signs for heritage or recreational use, this process manifests itself through ostentatious or, on the contrary, very discreet markers.

In these movements we find the figure of in-betweenness, worked on by Daniel Sibony (1991) in order to rethink the new paths and passages elaborated between the two terms that make up a relationship. This perspective appears to be a fruitful tool for exploring and translating multiple relational patterns of a socio-spatial order which are marked by dualities, ambiguities or cross-breeding, in which differences are replayed, and boundaries are blurred *"by transcending the fragmentation of the spatial order"* (Jeudy 1977). Within the city-mountain dialectic, betweenness is also a space of tensions, even of *"conflicting solidarity"* (Laplantine 2005), as shown by the issues of orientation and management of urbanisation; the reception of new inhabitants; the conciliation of agricultural, environmental, residential and recreational functions.

Recreation as a central component of a local lifestyle

The results of the interviews conducted with the new inhabitants of Saint-Nizier-du-Moucherotte and Engins lead us to approach these places as a space for seeking a local art of living: it is a question of living as a family in a pleasant resident setting, within which a social and cultural anchoring is sought, by transposing an intensive recreational practice into daily life up till now reserved for the most sought-after destinations visited during weekends and holidays, at the cost of long journeys by car.

Recreational practices – effective or possible – are then a key factor of territoriality and habitability through the investment of time, places and relationships at the local level. The challenge of such a life project is the ability to activate a repertoire of mountain practices accessible from home, thanks to a fine temporal sequencing between work, family life and leisure time.

We should bear in mind that this recreational centrality often remains relative or *in progress*: in some cases, it is still defined in contrast to the reference exteriority of prestigious recreational sites; whether through a comparison in the background with previous life experience, and/or through contact with friends and work colleagues. Similarly, it should be noted that, in addition to the residents of Saint Nizier-du-Moucherotte and Engins, the inhabitants of the Grenoble conurbation can also benefit from this proximity effect due to the short access times to the places concerned, including through the use of public transport: excursions, ascents and descents for half a day or even before or after the working day.

The centrality of recreational practices in life choices does not fail to impact on the relationship with working life. Rapid access to the Grenoble conurbation (30 to 50 minutes depending on the destination, the travel mode and traffic conditions) allows residents of Saint-Nizier-du-Moucherotte or Engins to organise their lives around daily or regular shuttles to work. However, in a certain number of cases, the choice to live "in the mountains" is not a neutral one in terms of work, and implies adaptations and reorientations of working life that appear to be chosen. These may even include forms such as refusing promotions or avoiding responsibilities that would be incompatible with intensive sports practice and the search for a local lifestyle, following a model well described in the literature on Amenity migration. Some of the new inhabitants also create economic activities on the spot, to allow and strengthen an attachment to the local community, and to limit mobility experienced as inconsistent with the relocated life model that they idealise. More frequently, working from home a few days a week appears to be a compromise conducive both to personal fulfilment and to reducing travel to town, with regard to criteria of personal comfort and environmental responsibility. In the same spirit, trips to the Grenoble conurbation are presented as being regularly subject to car-sharing practices, and even trips by bicycle, including on the uphill journey. The utilitarian aspect of travel is often combined with sports training to "optimise" the journey.

Against a backdrop of environmental responsibility in the face of climate change, the rediscovery of the charms and virtues of local communities is becoming the practical and ethical reference point for *crisis tourism*, echoing the crisis of tourism as a utopian and uchronic universe (Bourdeau 2011). After the economic crisis of 2007, slogans such as *"feel good without going far"* (Rhône-Alpes Region) or *"so close, so far"* (Isère Tourism Committee) expressed this.[3] In the case of the neo-residents interviewed in Saint-Nizier-du-Moucherotte and Engins, this phenomenon integrates both family constraints and arguments of environmental responsibility to justify the relocation of recreational practices, which voluntarily eliminates or limits the weekend long trips that characterise the usual practice of mountain sports.

Going beyond the associated-distinct systems of the Here and Elsewhere produces a dedifferentiation (Lash 1990), which rearranges the local-global, urban-rural, near-distant, tourist-non-tourist, work-leisure, everyday-vacation relationships. In the recreational sphere, this phenomenon induces significant recompositions of the geographical imagination, breaking with the unbridled mobile effervescence of the 1980s and 1990s. Against a backdrop of crises, it consecrates the return to force of what Abraham Moles (1998) has designated as the "iron law" of proxemics: a primacy of meaning is given to the close space, while distance attenuates the practice and the affective investment of the distant space. In other words, what is close always ends up counting more than what is far away. This movement of re-enchantment of geographical proximities is still partial, including insofar as it cohabits within contemporary societies with an increase in leisure travel, for example thanks to low-cost flights. It nevertheless contributes to placing the recreational sphere back on a transitional trajectory (Hopkins 2008). This perspective appears as implicit in many testimonies collected from residents of Saint-Nizier-du-Moucherotte and Engins. It makes it possible to imagine a local art of living that would not be limited to a residential and recreational hedonism but would rather be part of a voluntarist relocation project, even if the possible political impact of which is not yet documented.

What proximity does to recreational practices, and vice versa

The in-depth modification of the relationship between *dwelling* and *visiting* that results from this process is often based on the transposition of sporting practices (ice climbing, mountaineering, ski touring) that are emblematic of the high recreational sites formerly frequented by the people interviewed: Mont-Blanc massif, Gorges du Verdon, Aosta valley, Corsica, and so forth. The result is a geocultural recoding of small nearby places which echo the legitimate top spots of mountain sports: as if the Moucherotte (the summit overlooking Saint-Nizier-du-Moucherotte, altitude 1901 m.) whose different faces could be forever explored, were a substitute for Mont-Blanc.

Taking an interest in the creativity that results from this fine weave between proximity and recreational daily life allows us to identify new or unusual forms of practices that intensively invest the local field to transcend its limited adventure potential. This approach mobilises quasi-experimental recreational practices, which transfigure daily times and spaces, in the manner of a neo-situationism. Multiple re-readings of local spaces transcend their relative ordinariness and activate neglected resources, in a diversity of temporalities: weekends, (half) days, beginning and end of the day; not forgetting night-time which offers an almost inexhaustible potential for experiences of local disorientation, by modifying and amplifying the perception of places.

In the same way, we can observe the intensive use of micro-places and interstices not considered by the inventoried and marked out itineraries: exploration of paths traced by wildlife, ridges and rocky bars, gorges, dry canyons.

Paradoxically, this intensification of the use of places inscribed in "hollows" in the local territory goes hand in hand with the extensive mobilisation of techniques and materials from mountain sports. Leaving your house with skis on your feet, rope on your shoulder and an ice axe on your bag or taking your children to camp in the nearby forest, are all signs that support the dream of a mountain life imagined by former city dwellers. Even though they will be rather incongruous in view of the traditional – essentially agricultural, or hunting – uses of the place. Meteorological events (cold and frost waves, snowfall, storms, etc.) are then welcomed as opportunities to further intensify the feeling of immersion in a wilderness amplified by temporary circumstances. While having a practical dimension (compensating for the lack of time during the day), nocturnal practices then contribute to the permanent search for processes of transformation of ordinary and familiar places. Several people interviewed told us that they were actively looking for poor objective conditions to intensify their practices: skiing to the summit of Moucherotte in a snowstorm at night appears to be an experiential pinnacle that validates the meaning of the residential choice by fully inscribing it in a mountain career usually referred to great Alpine summits.

This approach is conducive to new combinations of activities: trekking-exploration, ski-canyoning, ice-climbing trekking, abseiling-mushroom picking, caving-heritage exploration. For experienced mountain sports enthusiasts, the aim is to compensate for the dispersion and relative modesty of the technical obstacles to be overcome by unbridled inventiveness. Considering the theoretical work proposed by Gilles Deleuze and Felix Guattari (1988), we are tempted to note that in these practices of proximity, the "hard lines" of the developed and marked recreational areas (marked trails, equipped climbing or canyoning sites, etc.) give way to "softer" lines (interstices, shortcuts, detours, unmarked variants) or even "escape lines": ramblings, explorations, off-piste, off-track, clandestine and ephemeral places.

While the local knowledge and attendance of the mountain practitioners from Grenoble or visiting tourists is most often limited to the most famous routes and places, the knowledge and practice of the neo-residents is much finer and sharper. It gives rise to systematic explorations of folds and nooks and crannies, which are neglected both by trail marking, by topographical guides and by traditional local uses. This intensive occupation of space aims at a form of exhaustiveness in the knowledge of the terrain, including through toponymy and naturalistic or heritage features. Although it is initially based on a very specific sporting territoriality, it is not limited to it. Thanks to the in-depth familiarity with the places acquired through recreational uses, it is also the confirmation of a sense of attachment and a "proof" of local belonging that is at stake in discussions with the oldest residents. While the latter have a functional and identity-based experience of the space that is more centred on agricultural activities – or traditional leisure practices: hunting, fishing, mushroom picking, motorised all-terrain vehicles and so forth – they also have a sense of identity.

For the new residents, the quest for legitimisation of a deep local attachment involves access to a whole world of places that are "invisible" or even "masked" for the more obvious "surface" visits of the inhabitants of Grenoble or tourists. It will be played out, for example, in the exploration and (re)discovery of heritage sites: the history of the Resistance to Nazism, which is very much alive in the Vercors; the wasteland of the Saint-Nizier-du-Moucherotte Olympic springboard. Recreational practices are therefore mobilised as a geocultural skill that go beyond the territoriality of visitors, but also that of locals. The spatial investment via nature sports of the new inhabitants we met then contrasts singularly with the classic observation of a lack of familiarity with the experience of the local space by the "rurban" inhabitants.

The commitments observed on the part of new residents in the knowledge of local heritage are often based on the transposition of professional skills such as those of a journalist, engineer or researcher. They often set themselves objectives that are at the crossroads of leisure and civic commitment, since the results of the surveys, inventories and education which are elaborated can be proposed to the Commune or local charities to foster possible projects, or can sometimes be mobilised in acts of community opposition. In addition to possible political stakes, the in-depth appropriation of local history and geography by new residents does not fail to arouse reserve and suspicions of dispossession on the part of the locals, for whom this knowledge is experienced as being part of a territorial and identity-related intimacy. Aware of these difficulties, new residents often arm themselves with patience and humility. For example, they can ostensibly show the free nature of their approach by putting together a dossier on local heritage without taking public offence at seeing it neglected by the municipality; or they seek to show the disinterested nature of their approach and the added value of their skills to the general interest by mobilising them in favour of acts of citizenship such as, for example, the cleaning of otherwise unreachable natural sites thanks to climbing techniques and equipment.

Discussion: dwelling[4] as an after-tourism figure?

After half a century of mass tourism, the boundaries between "inhabiting" and "visiting" are becoming more and more permeable. The qualities initially attributed to tourist places – landscape, heritage, leisure, conviviality – have become a standard of quality of daily life, consecrating the role of *"cultural laboratory"* (Jean Viard) played by holidays.

In this context, the notion of Amenity migration is very useful for rethinking not only the status of recreational practices, but also for the demography, economy and identity of places, to the point of constituting in some cases a possible path of post-tourist transition for destinations facing an accumulation of uncertainties about the future. In other cases, the tourism development stage no longer appears to be a necessary prerequisite in the production of residential areas with official approval. In certain regions of the Massif Central (France), Amenity migration appears as a lever for the revitalisation of rural areas without a strong tradition of tourist activity. This dynamism is directly linked to the demographic revival that many rural areas have experienced over the last 20 years thanks to a positive migratory balance. These migrations are firstly the sign of a deep change in the representations of the "countryside", which is increasingly desired by environmental concerns and the challenges of resilience in the face of crises, as the pandemic of 2020 has once again highlighted. Rural areas may then seem conducive to experimenting with figures of societal transition, providing not only available space, but also alternative and flexibility in relation to the complexity of urban problems, a representation which is of course discussed.

Based on these observations, we will not lose sight of a certain number of paradoxes: Amenity migration is largely based on national solidarity schemes (pensions, social benefits) and technologies (teleworking) which allow increased residential mobility of individuals, just as they benefit from the widespread use of cars, which pose a serious problem in a context of post-carbon transition. Similarly, the relativisation of the role of tourism in regional development goes hand in hand with the predominance of recreational values and practices in residential choices.

At the same time, Amenity migrations contribute to the cultural relativisation of "*compulsory holidays*" (Viard 2000), even if nothing prevents them from being compatible with the upkeep of tourist practices, on the scale of both places and individuals. Nevertheless, they participate in the transformation of values and recreational practices against the backdrop of crises, by creating favourable conditions for the avoidance or the rejection of tourism. This is all the more so in the face of growing security concerns about the risks of accidents, health problems, attacks or kidnappings, which revive the anxiety-provoking nature of otherness, which is being undermined by the globalisation – if even partial – of mass tourism.

This backdrop helps to shed light on the growing refocusing of recreational practices on proximity, which is taking place from the home. "*Spending one's holidays at home*" in the staycation mode (Dissart 2020) or even combining (tele)work and holidays in the workation mode (Lahaye 2020) are then forms of a process of joint mutation of tourist and residential practices, and of the relationship between the productive and recreational spheres. This relocation, discussed for a long time and highlighted by the 2020 pandemic, benefits spaces that are sought after for their recreational resources and which are conducive to a continuity – and no longer a rupture – in relation to the daily living environment, which Jean-Didier Urbain (2002) invites us to understand as a kind of non-tourism of the "*familiar elsewhere*".

In the ways of life observed in Saint-Nizier and Engins, this phenomenon manifests itself both by a relativisation of tourism and by a recreational centrality via daily practices. It remains to be examined how this apparent contradiction characterises a generalised touristification, or on the contrary a de-touristification. If both hypotheses are conceivable, it is undoubtedly because the very reference to the notion of tourism is to be questioned.

This is not to deny the contemporary globalised vitality of some of the most standardised and industrialised forms of tourism – including their promise of a hyper-individualised experience. Rather, it is to note that the imagination of what is still called "tourism" by ease, by habit, by lack of inspiration or by a desire for stability, is undergoing profound transformations. Nevertheless, we continue to refer to tourism as a form of aspiration and behaviour which tends to move away or to escape from it: "residential tourist", "useful tourism", "voluntourism", "scientific tourism", "humanitarian tourism", "creative tourism", "participatory tourism". Perhaps this inflation of "new" tourism modalities, which has the appearance of continuity, testifies above all to a real difficulty, or even a reluctance, to think about the relationship of 'free" time and spaces other than in terms of tourism.

In fact, one of the main utopia today carried by tourism seems to be that of its character of overcoming and overflowing by practices which emancipate themselves from it, implicitly or explicitly. This "Tourexit" is not limited to a post-tourist logic of residential reconversion of destinations. In the exploration of a tourist "below" and "beyond" that dissolves the traditional dialectic between "Here" and "Elsewhere", it is an after-tourism trajectory (Bourdeau 2018) that is at stake. And if Amenity migration is an emblematic indicator of this, it is not the only marker: a profusion of dissident uses of time and space that are more re-creative than recreational (Bourdeau 2020; Christin 2020) are also to be taken into account. Faced with the peak of contradictions, criticisms and crises facing tourism, it is an inversion of its dominant codes which is at stake: proximity, everyday life, cultural autonomy, frugality, recreational DIY, reduced spending, slow travel and commitment to time are thus given a meaning and positive values (Bourdeau and Berthelot 2008).

Over the last five years, both in academic and professional circles, there has been much talk of "reinventing" tourism, seeking to renew its meaning, resources and practices through a constant call for innovation. In many respects, however, it seems that the most disruptive practices seem to focus on "disinventing" it. How can we name infra-touristic or extra-touristic practices that are part of a logic of inhabiting in a chosen place? The notion of the "art of living", which is both constitutive and inherited from tourism, has hardly been the subject of conceptual development, which is why it is neglected or reluctantly examined by the social sciences. Wouldn't its contribution, which is still to be discussed, be to help shift the reflection to a transversal register, which integrates multiple dimensions of relationship to culture, space, time and social relations?

Conclusion: the Alps: residential refuge or laboratory for a new dwelling?

After more than five decades of euphoria – despite crises and criticism – the development model of the Alpine massif is facing many structural challenges, which both climate change and the health crisis are amplifying and accelerating in their own ways (Bourdeau 2020). At the very heart of the socio-economic and political system, transition issues are now being debated and re-question the most established evidence, such as the fluidity of mobility that allows visitors to access tourist destinations. This awareness accentuates the desire to *"put tourism back in its place"*, which is increasingly frequently expressed by local stakeholders faced with a feeling of loss of control and lack of resilience of the existing model.

In the mountain areas within which a diversified economy has been preserved (agriculture, crafts, services) a transition scenario is emerging which is still very uncertain, in which tourism would no longer be an end in itself, but rather the result of a set of environmental and territorial qualities, attractive firstly for year-round inhabitants, before eventually being − or remaining − attractive for visitors. It is then tempting to look at the arrival of new residents as an opportunity to rethink the future of mountain territories in terms of economic diversification, as the global and local crisis factors of tourism grow and combine. After 50 years of tourism − which for a long time did not include the question of inhabitants − has residential migration become a new myth to "save" the mountains? This is without neglecting the fact that the practices described here concern above all the most privileged fractions of the population. And of course, this requires taking into account the negative effects of residential gentrification. On this condition, from the point of view of the Alpine territories, is it not preferable to welcome inhabitants all year round rather than to go and look further and further away for tourists who are less and less loyal, at the price of low-cost air links, sold-out breaks and an overbid of under-used facilities? This is even more relevant when a health crisis durably disrupts tourist mobility.

It is obviously not so simple: the gentrified residential economy values in the short term the selective and distinctive consumption of the most attractive mountain landscapes, which accentuates the need for space and energy dedicated to housing and transport (Perlik 2011). Moreover, it competes with existing economic sectors such as agriculture and tourism without always generating social and territorial innovation significant enough to induce a change in the development model. All the more so as in the most touristy regions or those closest to the large *conurbations* (such as Graubünden, Valais, Chablais or the Zurich Oberland), there is a very high *turnover*. Amenity migrants are therefore quick to leave after having tasted the charms of the mountains for a while, but also their constraints.

How can we conceive a mountain lifestyle that is not limited to residential and recreational consumerism? Even more than new residents who are not very rooted and are volatile, what mountain regions need above all are actors and citizens ready to (self-)invest locally and sustainably. In this way, mountain areas can be more than just gentrified refuges from climatic, social and health threats. They can also act as laboratories and transition demonstrators, hosting transformative social innovations (Cognard 2006; Viazzo and Zanini 2014). The Transformont platform, led by a group of researchers and actors involved in supporting social innovation in mountain territories with the support of Labex ITTEM,[5] identifies and networks more than 270 local experiments in French Alps and Massif Central, involving a wide range of activities and economic, social and cultural sectors. It remains to be examined under what conditions this creative dynamic will be able to propose alternative solutions capable of bringing about the emergence of a new model of development, or to restructure the existing model in depth, according to the scheme proposed by Transition Studies (Grin Rotmans and Schot 2010). It is also about continuing to observe how a residential utopia contributes – with many contradictions – to the affirmation of a liveable and living Alpine mountain.

Notes

1 Source: Communauté de communes du massif du Vercors. Charte de développement du territoire.
2 Source: Parc naturel Régional du Vercors. Évaluation de la charte 2008–2018 et diagnostic actualisé du territoire.
3 It should be noted that these slogans and the geocultural recoding that accompanies them iconographically have been largely reintroduced by the 2020 pandemic.
4 We take up here the nuance proposed by Mathis Stock (2019) between "dwelling", which "signifies the overall category" and "inhabiting", which "points towards the differentiated ways individuals practice places".
5 https://labexittem.fr

Bibliography

Bachimon, Philippe, Philippe Bourdeau, Jean Corneloup and Olivier Bessy. 2014. "Du tourisme à l'après-tourisme, le tournant d'une station de moyenne montagne: St-Nizier-du-Moucherotte (Isère)." *Géoconfluences*, http://geoconfluences.ens-lyon.fr/informations-scientifiques/dossiers-thematiques/les-nouvelles-dynamiques-du-tourisme-dans-le-monde/articles-scientifiques/du-tourisme-a-l-apres-tourisme.

Benson, Michaela and Karen O'Reilly (eds.). 2009. *Lifestyle Migration. Expectations, Aspirations and Experiences.* London: Ashgate.

Bourdeau, Philippe. 2009. "Amenity Migration as an Indicator of Post-Tourism." In *Understanding and Managing Amenity-led Migration in Mountain Regions*, edited by Moss Laurence, Glorioso Romella and Krause Amy. Banff: International Amenity Migration Centre & Banff Centre, pp. 25–32.

Bourdeau, Philippe. 2013. "Visiting/Living (in) the Alps: Towards a Tourist-Residential Convergence?" In *Whose Alps Are These?*, edited by Mauro Varotto and Benedetta Castiglioni. Padova: Padova University Press, pp. 196–205.

Bourdeau, Philippe. 2016. "L'entre-deux Grenoble Vercors: laboratoire de l'habitabilité croisée ville-montagne." In *Territoires en débat. Discussing Landscape(s) in Contemporary Metropolitan Realities*, edited by Rosa De Marco and Mattiucci Cristina. Turin: Professional Dreamers, pp. 59–77.

Bourdeau, Philippe. 2020a. "Ralentir le tourisme . . . ou le dépasser?". In *Vivre slow. Enjeux et perspectives pour une transition corporelle, récréative et touristique*, edited by Florian Lebreton, Christophe Gibout and Bernard Andrieu. Lille: Presses Universitaires de Lorraine.

Bourdeau, Philippe. 2020b. "Le tourisme face à ses limites en période de crise." *Espaces, Tourisme et loisirs* 355: 56–60.

Bourdeau, Philippe and Libera Berthelot. 2008. "Tourisme et décroissance. De la critique à l'utopie?" In *Proceedings of the First International Conference on Economic De-Growth for Ecological Sustainability and Social Equity*, edited by Flipo Fabrice and Schneider François. Paris: ICE, pp. 78–86.

Bourdeau, Philippe, Jean Corneloup and Pascal Mao. 2011. "Les sports de nature comme médiateurs du pas de deux ville-montagne. Une habitabilité en devenir?" *Annales de Géographie* 4(680): 449–460, www.cairn.info/revue-annales-de-geographie-2011-4-page-449.htm.

Camenisch, Martin and Debarbieux Bernard. 2011. "Inter-Communal Migrations in Switzerland: A 'Mountain Factor'?" *Journal of Alpine Research* 99(1), http://journals.openedition.org/rga/1368.

Ceriani, Giorgia, Rémy Knafou and Stock Mathis. 2004. "Les compétences cachées du touriste." *Sciences Humaines* 154: 28–31.

Cognard, Françoise. 2006. "Le rôle des recompositions sociodémographiques dans les nouvelles dynamiques rurales: l'exemple du Diois." *Méditerranée* 107: 5–12.

Corrado, Federica. 2010. *Ri-abitare le Alpi*. Genova: Eidon Edizioni.

Corrado, Federica. 2015. "Processes of Re-Settlement in Mountain Areas." *Journal of Alpine Research* 102(3), http://journals.openedition.org/rga/2545.

Christin, Rodolphe. 2020. *La vraie vie est ici*. Montréal: Ecosociété.

David, Jean, Louis Freschi and Hervé Gumuchian. 1980. *Entre la rurbanisation et le développement touristique. St Nizier-du-Moucherotte*. Grenoble: Institut de Géographie Alpine.

Debord, Guy. 1994 [1967]. *The Society of the Spectacle*. New York: Zone Books.

Deleuze, Gilles and Felix Guattari. 1988 [1980]. *Thousand Plateaus*. New York: Continuum International Publishing.

Dissart, Jean-Christophe. 2020. "Staycation: Un phénomène parti pour rester?" *Espaces, Tourisme et loisirs* 353: 6–9.

Elmi, Marianna, Perlik, Manfred. 2014. "From tourism to multilocal residence?" *Journal of Alpine Research* 102–103, http://journals.openedition.org/rga/2608.

Guérin, Jean-Paul and Hervé Gumuchian. 1979. "Ruraux et rurbains: Réflexions sur les fondements de la ruralité aujourd'hui." *Revue de Géographie Alpine* 67(1), www.persee.fr/doc/rga_0035-1121_1979_num_67_1_2158.

Grin, John, Jan Rotmans and Johan Schot. 2010. *Transitions to Sustainable Development: New Directions in the Study of Long-Term Transformative Change*. New York: Routledge.

Hopkins, Rob. 2008. *The Transition Handbook: From Oil Dependency to Local Resilience*. Chelsea: Green Publishing.

Illous, Eva and Edgar Cabanas. 2018. *Happycratie. Comment l'industrie du bonheur a pris le contrôle de nos vies*. Paris: Premier Parallèle.

Jaakson, Reiner. 1986. "Second-Home Domestic Tourism." *Annals of Tourism Research* 13(3): 367–391.

Kaufmann, Jean-Claude. 1996. *L'entretien compréhensif*. Paris: Nathan.

Lahaye, Brice. 2020. "Le workation, de tendance de niche à norme bientôt généralisée ?" *Espaces, Tourisme et loisirs*, www.tourisme-espaces.com/doc/10563.workation-futur-tourisme-workation-tendance-niche-norme-bientot-generalisee.html.

Lajarge, Romain. 2006. "Des parcs sans jardin et des récréactifs sans touristes?" *Pour* 191: 42–46.

Laplantine, François. 2005. *Pour une anthropologie modale*. Paris: Teraèdre.

Löffler, Roland, Beismann Michael, Walder Judith and Steinicke Ernst. 2014. "New Highlanders in Traditional Out-Migration Areas in the Alps." *Journal of Alpine Research* 102(3), http://rga.revues.org/2546.

Martin, Niels, Philippe Bourdeau and Jean-François Daller. 2013. *Les migrations d'agrément: du tourisme à l'habiter.* Paris: L'Harmattan.

McWatters, Mason R. 2008. *Residential Tourism: (De)constructing Paradise.* Bristol: Channel View Publications.

Moss, Laurence. 2006. *The Amenity Migrants: Seeking and Sustaining Mountains and Their Cultures.* Wallingford: CAB International.

Moss, Laurence, Romella Glorioso and Amy Krause. 2009. *Understanding and Managing Amenity-led Migration in Mountain Regions.* Banff: International Amenity Migration Centre & Banff Centre.

Perlik, Manfred. 2006. "The Specifics of Amenity migration in the European Alps." In *The Amenity Migrants,* edited by Laurence Moss. Wallingford: CAB International, pp. 215–231.

Perlik, Manfred. 2011. "Alpine Gentrification: The Mountain Village as a Metropolitan Neighbourhood. New Inhabitants Between Landscape Adulation and Positional Good." *Journal of Alpine Research* 99–91, http://journals.openedition.org/rga/1370.

Petite, Mathieu. 2014. "Longing for the Mountains?" *Journal of Alpine Research* 102–103, http://journals.openedition.org/rga/2625.

Ray, Paul and Sherry Anderson. 2001. *The Cultural Creatives: How 50 Million People Are Changing the World.* New York: Three Rivers Press.

Richard, Frédéric, Dellier Julien and Tommasi Greta. 2014. "Migration, Environment and Rural Gentrification in the Limousin Mountains." *Journal of Alpine Research* 102–103, http://journals.openedition.org/rga/2561.

Sibony, Daniel. 1991. *Entre-deux. L'origine en partage.* Paris: Le Seuil.

Stock, Mathis. 2005. "Les sociétés à individus mobiles: vers un nouveau mode d'habiter?" *EspacesTemps.net,* www.espacestemps.net/articles/societes-individus-mobiles.

Stock, Mathis. 2019. "Inhabiting the City as Tourist. Issues for Urban and Tourism Theory." In *Tourism and Everyday Life in the Contemporary City,* edited by Thomas Frisch, Luise Stoltenberg, Natalie Stors and Christoph Sommer. London: Routledge, pp. 42–66, https://serval.unil.ch/resource/serval:BIB_4C0C454CD5B6.P001/REF.

Urbain, Jean-Didier. 2002. *Paradis verts. Désirs de campagne et passions résidentielles.* Paris: Payot.

Urry, John. 2002. *The Tourist Gaze.* London: Sage Publications.

Viard, Jean. 2000. *Court traité sur les vacances, les voyages et l'hospitalité des lieux.* La Tour-d'Aigues: L'Aube.

Viazzo, Pier Paolo and Roberta Clara Zanini. 2014. "Taking Advantage of Emptiness?" *Journal of Alpine Research* 102–103, http://journals.openedition.org/rga/2478.

12 The emergence of new "in-between" places in the context of "after-tourism" in Moroccan medina

The example of riads in the medina of Fez

Merryl Joly

Long considered as marginalised and run-down areas, inhabited essentially by poor populations, the historic centres of Moroccan cities – the medinas – have been gradually re-evaluated in the light of the social, urban, economic and political transformations attributed to the development of tourism since the 1980s. This chapter approaches questions related to "after-tourism" from the point of view of a geographical and heritage object, namely the riad, materially and symbolically reappropriated by new European residents. Etymologically defined as a dwelling built around a central patio-garden, the term "riad" has gradually taken on a broader meaning to designate today "a recent non-native creation mainly aimed at an exogenous clientele" (Madoeuf 2016, 788). New European residents have contributed to the revalorisation and attractiveness (Knafou 1991, 15) of these buildings abandoned by the local population, notably by stimulating the "cultivation of desire" (Viard 1998, 23). The acquisition of these old run-down houses with the aim of restoring and transforming them into commercial tourist accommodation manifests an "after-tourism" in the Moroccan medinas, and bears witness to the emergence of "in-between" spaces where the space-time boundaries of work and holidays form a continuum. What are the changes impelled by these new residents in the evolution of the tourism development of the riads? How are they redefining the art of living in these ordinary buildings within a context of an interculturality combining both work and leisure? The answers to these questions are structured around the emergence of new practices in the riads with regard to the concept of "after-tourism" in order to identify the forms of intercultural mingling that testify to new evolutions in the tourism development of the Moroccan medinas. The study of riads allows a better and more general understanding of how guesthouses, in all their forms, can become new hybrid space-time continuums combining work and holidays within the context of increased mobility. The tourism and residential dynamics crystallised through these riads raise issues that fall more globally within the scope of studies on small tourism businesses such as guesthouses, through which new ways of reappropriating the

DOI: 10.4324/9781003138600-15

local heritage are expressed and new forms of tourism initiated. This chapter posits that the arrival of Europeans and their taking up residence in these old houses has induced a dual process of evolution in the development of tourism in the Moroccan medinas. At the aesthetic, cultural, urban and social levels, this process leads to the redefinition of the function of the riads through an art of living expressed by the reinvention of the heritage narrative and of daily uses. At the economic and political levels, the involvement of European riad owners leads to the emergence of new dynamics engaged in the development of tourist accommodation in the medinas.

The study focuses on the case of the riads in the medina of Fez. Situated in the northeast of Morocco, Fez,[1] the country's cultural capital, has become an important pole in the geography of North-South mobility (Berriane and Idrissi-Janati 2016, 87). Following its classification as a UNESCO World Heritage Site in 1981, the medina of Fez aroused the interest of public stakeholders who relied on cultural tourism to boost its economic, social and cultural development. This process became more pronounced from the beginning of the 1990s with the arrival and investment of Europeans in search of "authenticity" and "exoticism" (Amirou 2001, 72). From a methodological perspective, this chapter is based on interviews conducted with European riad owners (particularly French owners) and artisans in the medina of Fez, as well as the use of participant observation to analyse these new practices in the riads. French riad owners dominate the tourism sector in the medina of Fez, accounting for more than 70 of the 212 foreign owners in 2017.[2] Firstly, we will show how the medina has gradually become an area prized as a place of residence by Europeans (and especially the French) with the purpose of embarking upon a new personal and professional life project. Secondly, we will discuss how these Europeans have shaped a new art of living through their taking up residence in and developing the riads, where everyday life and tourism practices are combined. Finally, we will examine how these Europeans have become players committed to the development of the tourism offer in the medina of Fez – and more generally in all the Moroccan medinas – by creating new types of tourist accommodation.

Towards the tourism development of an area in decline

Gradual awareness

From the establishment of the French Protectorate of Morocco (1912–1956), the medina of Fez constituted an area dedicated to contemplation for European tourists and a living environment exclusively reserved for the "indigenous" population. When General Lyautey was appointed the first Resident-General in Morocco in 1912, the colonial administration set up an institutional framework designed to enhance and promote the Moroccan heritage while respecting the local socio-urban context. The heritage policy implemented by the French government constructed an exotic image of the Moroccan medinas by "putting them in glass cases" (Arrif 1994, 155). The medina was considered to be "an open-air museum exhibit" devoted to observation and worship, and not as a living and evolving space (El-Ghazaly 2008, 13). In tandem with this policy, the colonial administration implemented the first tourism development plans, which aimed "to provide a place of rest for the French and for wealthy tourists. Investments [were] thus oriented towards the construction of luxury hotels in order to better respond to the demands of travellers" (Stafford 1996, 34). In Fez, the policy of distancing the medina came in response to a desire to ensure a "management of views" (Jelidi 2012, 199) for the European settlers. Among these projects, the "Tour of Fez" made it possible to conform to "pure pragmatism", this itinerary allowing quick access to all the gates of the city and providing an "urban scenography" (Jelidi 2012, 199) with the aim of offering tourists different viewpoints of the medina. These policies for the preservation and the tourism development of the medina of Fez under the Protectorate led to its degradation and progressive impoverishment up until the 1980s. Medinas throughout Morocco became areas of refuge for the populations resulting from rural exodus. This led to the departure of the urban elites for the new cities with a view to achieving a certain level of comfort, or for urban economic centres such as Casablanca.

A new phase in the heritage trajectory of the medina of Fez began with its inscription on the UNESCO World Heritage List in 1981. Several visions for the protection of the medina followed one another in an attempt to define a development strategy. Faced with the failures of the Urban Development Master Plan (*Schéma Directeur d'Aménagement Urbain*, SDAU) drawn up in 1980 by the Regional Delegation of the Ministry of Housing and Urban Development with the collaboration of UNESCO and the United Nations Development Programme (UNDP), and the Plan of 1992 drawn up by architect Michel Pinseau, new actors such as the Agency for the Development and Rehabilitation of the Medina of Fez (ADER-Fès) were created to accompany the restoration and protection programmes on site at the beginning of the 1990s. A decade later, the programme for the protection of the medina of Fez was adopted through the intervention of the World Bank, which advocated the participation of the inhabitants in the protection of the medina via a policy of combating poverty. This protection programme gradually became part of the national tourism development policies implemented from 2001 onwards. The medina was part of the Regional Tourism Development Plan (PDRT-Fès) under the Vision 2010 programme-contract,[3] the aim of which was to consolidate the restoration actions while encouraging their reuse for other purposes such as the promotion of cultural activities (Akdim and Laaouane 2010, 14). Since 2009, the medina of Fez has been integrated into the Vision 2020 programme-contract, and more precisely into the sub-programme "Patrimony and Heritage", the aim of which is to make it a "living museum city" by developing an "authentic" cultural offer. Thanks to the restoration actions undertaken for the historical monuments and the appearance of riads as a mode of tourist accommodation, the medina of Fez offers a new residential space for exogenous populations.

The arrival of the Europeans

The Moroccan medinas thus became tourist hotspots showcased by multiple public and private actors. The intervention of new actors in the "invention of tourism" (Knafou 1991, 13) for the medina of Fez played an important role in the tourism enhancement of this formerly unattractive area by bestowing new value on it. Among the private actors, Europeans were the first to restore and market new forms of tourist accommodation – the riads – for both residential and tourism purposes. Their arrival and settling in the medina of Fez can be briefly summed up in three main phases.

The first phase can be described as the discovery phase, with the first acquisitions of old houses by Europeans from the second half of the 1990s up to the early 2000s (by an Italian in 1996 and then by a French couple in 1999). This phase can essentially be explained by the combination of several factors, both political (the opening up of Morocco to Europe) and economic (policies in favour of foreign investment). The second homes owned by Europeans were gradually transformed into commercial tourist accommodation (Berriane and Nakhli 2011, 117), as were the traditional houses owned by Moroccans who left the medina. The local heritage of the medina of Fez thus became a market value, its properties being promoted through intermediaries (travel agencies, estate agencies, *samsar*[4]) and various specialised platforms (Booking.com, Airbnb, Hostelworld, etc.). The second phase, which began in 2004, saw a craze that reached its peak two years later when, out of 54 investors, 26 were of foreign origin (Escher and Petermann 2013, 112). This phase was notably encouraged by the numerous French television documentaries[5] on the Moroccan riads and their very attractive purchase prices. It changed the relationship of these Europeans to the place: the opening of a guesthouse became an end in and of itself when buying an old house and, for some, represented the starting point of a new life project. Finally, the third phase, extending from 2008 up to the present day,[6] is marked by a stagnation of the phenomenon linked largely to the saturation of the property market and to strong competition from the informal tourist accommodation sector, the latter being characterised by the promoting of riads with no operating authorisation issued by the Urban Commune of Fez or the Moroccan Ministry of Tourism. The unfavourable economic context (the crisis of 2008 and the saturation of the property market for old houses) led several owners of tourist accommodation establishments to resell their properties. Purchased by either Moroccans or Europeans, these properties were then sold in the form of ready-to-use riads with the necessary authorisations for tourism purposes. In 2017, there were some 15 such establishments for sale in the medina of Fez (Joly 2020, 60). However, far from signifying a drop in the tourism and residential attractiveness of the medina, this phenomenon remains marginal compared with the number of tourist accommodation establishments in operation. Indeed, of the more than 400 such establishments marketed on online reservation platforms, 140 are classified and recognised by the Moroccan Ministry of Tourism, while there are over 100 foreign establishments, both classified and unclassified.

The role of new European residents in the development of ordinary, everyday places

Taking a documentary approach to after-tourism allows for notably analysing "the emergence of references in terms of the art of living and of living through the diffraction of tourism in lifestyles" (Bourdeau 2018, 11). The majority of the entrepreneurs interviewed have settled permanently in the medina of Fez but have retained a second home in their country of origin. These entrepreneurs thus no longer consume like tourists, but rather demonstrate a form of tourist practice because their installation here is linked to a specific mode of "recreation", namely rest (Équipe MIT 2002, 274), materialised in the search for physical and psychological well-being and the desire to no longer be subject to a restrictive professional framework. From this perspective, these European entrepreneurs can be described as "after-tourists" because, by becoming permanent residents, they create a new hybrid space–time continuum in which work and holiday space–time boundaries merge. In this chapter, after-tourism is considered in the context of lifestyle migration because the settlement of Europeans contributes to the emergence of a new "in-between" living space. Lifestyle migration is defined as "the spatial mobility of relatively affluent individuals of all ages, moving either part-time or full-time to places that are meaningful because, for various reasons, they offer the potential of a better quality of life" (Benson and O'Reilly 2009, 8). This phenomenon has notably been highlighted in Europe (O'Reilly 2003; Benson 2011), Asia (Benson and O'Reilly 2018), Latin America (Rainer 2019, 2) and Africa (Van Laar et al. 2014). Studies on leisure migration, particularly in mountain resorts or rural areas, show the emergence of new residential places that have contributed to the touristification of these spaces (Niels et al. 2012, 13). In Morocco, studies on these new residential areas have focused on the "ryadism" phenomenon, in other words, the interest of Europeans for riads in the medinas (Wihtol de Wenden 2013, 28), but the opening of small tourist accommodation establishments such as guesthouses has also been analysed in other contexts with regard to the concept of lifestyle entrepreneurship. From this perspective, the main motivation for owners of these small establishments resides in the desire for a better quality of life and a minimum income to ensure their lifestyle (Kompulla 2004, 115–138) rather than the growth and profitability of their business (Ateljevic and Doorne 2000; Shaw and Williams 1990, 1998, 2003; Morrison and Thomas 2006). These new European residents are developing new forms of affectivity, attachment and commitment with their place of settlement that go beyond purely economic aspects and reflect a hybridisation of the functions of the living environment, both recreational and professional.

The arrival of Europeans settling in the medina of Fez is the result of a combination of personal, professional and economic motivations. Among the cases encountered, the medina of Fez is perceived as a place to reconnect with one's family roots, a place of rebirth where the search for otherness becomes a quest in and of itself, but also a "projected" place in the case of Europeans who have made the choice to invest in a second home here for their retirement. Where the Moroccan medinas are concerned, it is the riad that best symbolises these dynamics of dedifferentiation of practices. Etymologically, the riad refers to a dwelling built around a central patio-garden. In numerous tourist guides *(Le Routard, Petit Futé, Lonely Planet)*, riads are presented as architectural gems, meticulously restored and decorated, that promise tourists an immersion in Moroccan culture. The architectural style and the structure of the riads contribute to satisfy the desire for exoticism on the part of Europeans (whether the Arab-Andalusian style dating from the thirteenth to the fifteenth centuries, or the Art Deco style developed with the French Protectorate at the beginning of the twentieth century). Architecturally, the riad consists of a central courtyard or patio with up to four lounges laid out around it. There can be one or more floors, and all the houses have a terrace.

The riad represents both a tourist space intended for an international clientele through its offer of tourist accommodation, and at the same time a space of daily life where Europeans define an art of living and create an imagined "riad atmosphere" by staging the living spaces of the establishment.

The construction of an art of living in the medina

The new uses of riad spaces

By choosing to acquire a riad for both residential and tourism purposes, the owners have brought new value to this local heritage by transforming it from a hidden and hermetic space linked to intimacy and daily life into an unveiled space open to the outside.

This mix of residential and tourist practices has contributed to transform the place of the riad in the medina by bestowing on it new urban, social, cultural and symbolic functions. First of all, this private space, initially delimited by the entrance door, is made visible by certain small improvements implemented at the level of the *derb*.[7] Several of the owners interviewed have planted vegetation around the *derb* and have had surveillance cameras installed at the entrance to their riad. These measures serve to both embellish the passageway while making access both safer and more pleasing for tourists. Traditionally, the *derb* was not a place of passage and the houses had no ostentatious decor. Only the more or less well-kept doors could provide an indication on the social status of the owners. The façades were marked by just a few embrasures to let in some light and discreetly watch the street (Metalsi 2003, 74). Today, the external façades have become more attractive, which demonstrates an evolution in "the modes of appropriation of domestic heritage" (Kurzac-Souali 2010, 107). This externalisation of private spaces also manifests itself in the entrance doors to tourist accommodation establishments. The latter become immediately recognisable by their studded wooden doors and their façades, thereby changing the understanding of traditional domestic space as the place of the "hidden".

Inside the riad, the new uses of the different rooms of the house allow the owners to benefit from relaxation and rest areas while offering attractions that allow them to stand out from other establishments. During the restoration of their house, the majority of owners chose to redefine the architectural plan to create new spaces. One example is the *hammam* (wet steam bath), seen as both a differentiating attraction (there was no room dedicated to the *hammam* in traditional houses; families used to go to public *hammams* in the different districts of the medina) and an installation that meets the exoticism needs of the owners, who can take advantage of it. This new way of using the space of the riad also manifests itself in the terraces, which become living areas in their own right. Traditionally, the terrace was devolved to women. For European owners, this space constitutes one of the decisive factors when buying a riad. The terrace is used in its entirety through the installation of chairs, tables, plants and a pergola. In some cases, these small improvements are coupled with more imposing design layouts such as the construction of additional rooms to offer amenities to tourists directly on the terrace and to take in a view of the medina, for example, or to serve as storage space. The same is true for those riads offering a restaurant: the owners also enjoy the Moroccan dishes prepared by the chef (tagines, couscous, etc.).

In this "triumph of holiday values" (Viard 2006, 100), the riads are redesigned and refurbished for tourism purposes, but also with the aim of satisfying the "desire for exoticism" of their new European residents. This translates into the staging of the riad spaces to prolong this immersion within a hybrid space-time continuum.

Staging the ordinary

Beyond the atypical architecture of the old houses in the medina, the development and enhancement of the riads are reflected in the layout, redesign and decoration of their spaces. These elements participate in a tourism and cultural staging where foreigners accede to "an Oriental art of living imagined, dreamed, re-created and lived", thus demonstrating a form of "neo-Oriental perception" of the medina (Kurzac-Souali 2005, 470).

Among these elements, the obsession with *beldi* (translated as "of the country") is one of the main themes of the staging. It is manifested through the owners' attachment to the use of traditional materials and decorations, the work of the *maâlamis* (translated as "master craftsmen") and the use of rare and prized materials such as cedar wood. In the different rooms of their riads, foreign owners choose to hang kaftans on the walls, lay Berber carpets and/or display old Moroccan everyday objects (plates, containers, wall features, etc.) (Figure 12.1). The level of detail extends to the point of choosing fabrics considered as "typically Moroccan" (yellow fabric) and pictorial decorations around the mirrors and on the wooden doors. These items are coupled with the choice

Figure 12.1 An example of staging in a riad

for the owners to work with local artisans to create their own bespoke furniture and/or for their traditional know-how.

> These practices demonstrate an attachment on the part of the owners to their houses, where they build (or rebuild) Moroccan tradition, not on the basis of the past and documents relating to this past, but according to images, their taste, what the guests expect, the state of their finances at the time of conversion, their childhood memories, etc.
>
> (Istasse 2011, 40)

For the majority of the owners interviewed, taking care of the conversion and decoration of their riad is not considered as work, but rather as a stimulating activity allowing them to fully express their creativity and imagination. The staging of the ordinary in the riad provides both tourists and European owners with an immersive and "timeless" experience. Alongside Moroccan decorative features, owners choose to make the technical and logistical aspects of their riad as invisible as possible. Certain equipment and facilities (emergency exits, fire extinguishers, etc.) are concealed to reinforce the illusion. In this same perspective, the management of the tourist accommodation establishment is most often delegated to a team of Moroccan personnel, which allows the owners to free themselves as much as possible from professional constraints.

These different ways of staging the ordinary are more generally part of the re-creating of the heritage narrative of the riads that the European owners seek to enhance and exploit. This heritage narrative contributes to the definition of the art of living developed by these owners.

Re-creating the heritage narrative through the riad

Recent years have witnessed a shift in the values accorded to heritage. For tourists, "heritage can be worthwhile by the mere fact of its existence, independently of any use, whether individual or collective" (Greffe 2011, 7), which, in the context of the medina of Fez, translates into symbolic and age values. At the time of acquisition and the restoration work, these values are transformed into economic value because the choice of a tourism use is presented by the owners as a means of amortising costs while building a living space according to their tastes and sensitivities.

In the discourses of the European owners, the restoration and staging of their riads represent an integral part of their new life project. These factors are part of the "construction of the cultural biography" (Istasse 2019, 86) of old houses. The first phase of this cultural biography takes place during the restoration work when the European owners develop the specificity of their house to differentiate it from the others by revealing its "soul".

For a couple of friends from France who restored an old fondouk (caravanserai) to turn it into a luxury guesthouse, attention was paid to traditional restoration techniques. In their view, it was essential that they did not reproduce a "pastiche", but rather that they develop their property in line with its historical and cultural continuity. This approach led them to undertake significant research and reading up on the existing architectural styles in the medina and on traditional construction techniques. This was also the case of another French couple who own a youth hostel and who restored their house over a period of two years according to a strict restoration procedure. They chose to streamline the style of their riad, returning it to its initial architectural structure, removing partitions created after the fact, and preserving the original mosaic (the *zellij*).

This biographical construction continues in the highlighting of the histories attached to these houses through the concept and the name of the establishments. European owners exploit family histories to inscribe their house within a heritage continuity. For a French owner of a small four-bedroom riad, the name of her establishment was chosen in relation to the family history of the house and their taste for Gnaoua music (a ritual and initiatory style practised by the descendants of former enslaved persons from sub-Saharan Africa). Another owner of a three-bedroom riad, the former residence of the French employees of the Moroccan Minister of Finance during the Protectorate, chose a play on words *à la française* to recall the period of the French Protectorate in Morocco.

Others have opted for names in reference to the family history of the place (a French owner chose the nickname of his great-aunt in the medina), to historical places (a couple of French friends refer to the caravanserai past of their place and the links of the medina with Kairouan) and sometimes to anecdotes (a riad run by French friends makes reference to the many birds present on the site).

The art of living thus developed through the redefinition of the social, urban and cultural function of the riad, its layout, design and staging contributes to the commitment on the part of European owners in the co-production of the tourist accommodation offer in the medina.

The commitment on the part of Europeans to the tourism development of ordinary, everyday places

The involvement of European owners at the local level

The study of riads as "in-between" places bears witness to the junction between the life projects of the Europeans who have chosen to settle here permanently and their commitment to tourism development (Condevaux et al. 2016, 38). This involvement on the part of riad owners is demonstrated through their commitment within the tourism sector at the local political and cultural levels.

At the local political level, some European owners have joined the network of local tourism professionals through the Association of Riads and Guest-houses of Fez (ARMH-Fès). This association is presented as "bringing together only those establishments that are declared, classified, insured, compliant with Moroccan legislation, and implementing a quality charter".[8] This network enables European owners to position themselves economically and politically as local economic actors and to take part in discussions on the possibilities for the development of tourist accommodation in the medina (Joly 2020, 66). The ARMH has put together a directory of classified tourist accommodation establishments in the medina of Fez for use by tourists. It also organises cultural events, such as "Fès Gourmet" to discover the city's gastronomy through several partner riads and members of the association around a menu at a set price (about 25 Euros). For the medina of Fez, the ARMH seeks to develop a quality charter for tourists in order to distinguish the classified tourist accommodation establishments from the others. This charter is notably based on compliance with the labour code, obtention from the Ministry of Tourism of all the necessary authorisations for tourist accommodation establishments as well as the design, layout and decoration that must reflect "Moroccan art and tradition". The ARMH was created at the beginning of the 2000s to combat the informality in the increasingly vast tourist accommodation offer, and these economic and political networks bear witness to a form of territorial anchoring on the part of the European owners.

Several French owners who are members of networks of tourism professionals have chosen to become involved in community spaces. Represented by the Français du Monde (ADFE) association and the Union des Français de l'Etranger (UFE), these associations enable owners to establish relations with Moroccan members and to benefit from help and support in their administrative formalities. They also constitute privileged means of meeting other European owners. Activities are regularly organised between members (lunches, cultural visits, social gatherings, etc.). The majority of the French owners interviewed had chosen to join these community networks to ensure the success of their venture.

Several owners are also involved in local cultural life through associative and community spaces (Lenain and Saleilles 2012, 349). The youth hostel owner interviewed chose to host the office and activities of a local cultural and social association offering regular cultural events to tourists and to the inhabitants of the medina (concerts, conferences, dances, etc.). Other owners have built up networks of relations with local institutional partners to offer activities to tourists and inhabitants alike (including musical evenings, exhibitions and festivals). These partners are primarily composed of foreign institutions (the French Institute of Fez, the Cervantes Institute, the American Language Center and the Arabic Language Institute in Fez) and local public authorities (the Municipality of Fez and the Urban Commune of Fez). In the owners' discourse, this involvement is presented as a means of feeling useful in their district and of contributing to the impetus given to new dynamics: the showcasing of local artists, the involvement of the inhabitants in local cultural projects and the development of the local heritage through the various events.

This involvement at different levels of local life reflects a form of commitment by European riad owners in their new host environment.

New prospects for the development of the local tourist accommodation offer

This art of living thus defined by European owners within the riads is in conflict with the legal framework governing tourist accommodation establishments in Morocco. In their search for daily immersion in their riads, the owners move away from the standards of the traditional hotel sector as defined by Law no. 80-14[9] by offering a new way of presenting and managing this heritage. Riads are becoming hybrid places that cannot be reduced to a categorisation in the traditional hotel sector. Through these new forms developed in their establishments, the European owners are causing a re-examination of the place and form of tourist accommodation in the medinas.

This questioning manifests itself as soon as the establishments are acquired and restored. After obtaining the necessary work authorisations, the owners must obtain authorisation to open a tourist accommodation establishment. For the medina of Fez, this request is made to the Urban Commune of Fez. This body issues an operating authorisation that, theoretically, must be completed by an operating classification as mentioned in Law no. 80-14. Morocco introduced this classification system in 2002 in order to guarantee a certain quality of tourism services and to distinguish the different categories of tourist accommodation establishments. However, the operating classification is not accessible to many riad owners. Indeed, the tastes and sensitivities of the European owners associated with the architectural qualities of their riads can conflict with the standards imposed. Law no. 80-14 defines a guesthouse as "an establishment built in the form of an old residence, a riad, a palace, a kasbah or a villa, and located either in the medina, or along the tourist itineraries or in sites of high tourist value". To be eligible for classification, the riad must have a minimum of five rooms, all categories included. For a Category 1 riad, the rooms must have a surface area of 14 m², with a television and air conditioning. Suites must have an area of at least 25 m². For a Category 2 riad, the rooms must be no smaller than 12 m², while suites must be 20 m² and have air conditioning. For all of the European owners, these standards are seen as restrictive. The case of the youth hostel owner interviewed is evocative of the difficulties encountered. Because of his choice not to install air conditioning due to current ecological concerns and his setting up of dormitories to facilitate meetings between tourists and visiting artists in order to encourage artistic projects within his hostel, he was forced to undertake lengthy negotiations with the local authorities, thereby delaying the opening of his establishment for several months.

Other owners pointed out the impossibility of complying with the established standards due to the architectural structure of their houses (rooms that are too small, bathrooms located on the landing). The classification that establishes the standard norms is thus incompatible with the vocation of guesthouses (Kurzac-Souali 2006, 233). Faced with the growing number of riads without authorisation, the Urban Commune of Fez issued, from 2009 onwards, local opening permits in the form of "ready-to-let houses".[10] However, the decision by the Ministry of Tourism to remove the unclassified tourist accommodation establishments from Booking.com and its lack of recognition of this permit caused several owners, notably French, to form an association in 2016 to defend their interests. These collective actions are coupled with individual actions where European owners are obliged to negotiate the layout and design of their riads with the local authorities. These negotiations mainly take place during the decision to open the tourist accommodation establishment subject to the authorisation of the Regional Classification Commission, composed in part by a member of the Inspection of Historic Monuments and Sites of the Moroccan Ministry of Culture, a member of the Urban Commune and a firefighter. The main obstacles to the opening of a tourist accommodation establishment stem from the interpretation of the Moroccan style by the European owners. The majority of the owners interviewed raised the problems of the choice of paint for their riad (they did not necessarily choose green, the emblematic colour of Fez), of the design of the rooms (they refused to install standard traditional hotel equipment such as a television, telephone or air conditioning) and of the choice of decorative features subject to different interpretations.

Through the tourism development of the riads, European owners have forced the Moroccan government to rethink the law on tourist accommodation establishments. Initially, Law no. 61-00 promulgated in 2002 was intended to legislate in the face of the phenomenon of the buying up and opening of tourist accommodation establishments by Europeans and Moroccans in order to limit the informal tourist accommodation offer. To supplement this law, the new Law no. 80-14 promulgated in 2015 was defined in order to respond to the evolution in the tourist accommodation offer and to the numerous obstacles resulting from the new ways of living in riads with the impossibility for their owners to obtain opening authorisations. It came in partial response to the need to take into account riads as a "tourist accommodation establishment concept".

Conclusion

The reinvestment dynamics by Europeans in the Moroccan medinas reflect an example of places that have experienced three phases of tourism development. The first phase was characterised by distance tourism that never penetrated the space of the medina before becoming, in the second phase, an area that was prized and promoted by public and private actors following its inscription on the UNESCO World Heritage List and the raising of awareness around its tangible and intangible heritage. Finally, in the third phase, the majority of Moroccan medinas today have become residential areas for essentially European populations. In this third phase, European owners become actors involved in the evolution of the tourism development of the medinas. In the riads, the dedifferentiation of everyday and tourism practices leads to the emergence of an art of living where the space-time boundaries of work and holidays become merged. This art of living does not only manifest itself in the feeling of being on permanent holiday, but also integrates work into a new life balance. The emergence of the neologism *bleisure* (business and leisure) reflects these new dynamics (Gravari-Barbas 2017, 413) by adding a new dimension to lifestyle migration studies. In this chapter, the riad constitutes both a space for dedifferentiating living, working and recreational places, and a place for experimentation and reflection on how to engage in tourism. The originality of these "after-tourists" resides in their ability to maintain a certain distance with the host territory. Consequently, the art of living developed in the riads contributes to the definition of new perspectives for the evolution of tourist accommodation in the medinas. Nevertheless, this dedifferentiation of residential and tourism practices is also a source of tension and conflict in the medinas due to social, economic and cultural changes: the process of gentrification, the revaluation of property prices and the sometimes negative perception of the local population with regard to the acquisition of old houses by Europeans. The arrival of this new population and its involvement in the tourism development of the medinas constitutes one of the main challenges for the future prospects of the tourism sector in Morocco. The question is all the more crucial in that the sector has come to a standstill since March 2020 due to the health crisis, which is now causing the government to rethink its long-term tourism policy.

Notes

1 Specifically, the New City and the medina quarter (the New City created under the French Protectorate vs. the medina, considered an "indigenous" city).
2 Statistics of the Higher Planning Commission (*Haut Commissariat au Plan*, HCP), 2018.
3 This programme-contract lasted from 2001 to 2010 and was then replaced by Vision 2020 from 2010 to 2020. Vision 2010 had set the objectives of attracting seven million tourists and increasing hotel capacity. Vision 2020 drew on and developed these objectives by defining a regional planning policy under which each city/region was to be integrated as a tourism product.
4 This term designates an informal real estate agent working at the level of the medina and holding a set of keys for all of the properties for sale and/or for rent.
5 Examples include the television programmes *Capital* on M6 in 1998 and *Des Racines et des Ailes – Marrakech-Fès* on France 3 in 2005.
6 Study conducted by the author between 2017 and 2019.
7 Similar to a cul-de-sac. Exclusively residential space organised around a central nucleus made up of one or more houses.
8 Information available on the Association's website.
9 Law on tourist accommodation establishments and other forms of tourist accommodation, which entered into force in 2015.
10 Status granted to tourist accommodation establishments that do not comply with the standards laid down by the Moroccan Ministry of Tourism for the obtaining of an operating classification. This status has no legislative framework and can be issued only by the local authorities (Municipality).

Bibliography

Akdim, B. and M. Laaouane. 2010. "Patrimoine et développement local Fès: Priorités, acteurs et échelles d'action." *Norois* 214: 14.

Amirou, R. 2000. *Imaginaire du tourisme culturel*. Paris: Presses Universitaires de France, p. 72.

Arrif, A. 1994. "Le paradoxe de la construction du fait patrimonial en situation coloniale. Le cas du Maroc." *Revue des mondes musulmans et de la Méditerranée* 73–74: 155.

Ateljevic, I. and S. Doorne. 2000. "The Entrepreneurship of Resource-Based Theory." *Journal of Management* 27(6): 755–775.

Benson, M. 2011. *The British in Rural France: Lifestyle Migration and the Ongoing Quest for a Better Way of Life*. Manchester: Manchester University Press, pp. 103–118.

Benson, M., and K. O'Reilly. 2009. *Lifestyle Migration: Expectations, Aspirations and Experiences*. Ashgate: Farnham, p. 8.

Benson, M. and K. O'Reilly. 2018. *Lifestyle Migration and Colonial Traces in Malaysia and Panama*. London: Palgrave Macmillan, vol. VIII, p. 315, doi:10.1057/978-1-137-51158-4.

Berriane, M. and M. Idrissi-Janati. 2016. "Les résidents européens de la médina de Fès: une nouvelle forme de migration nord-sud." *Autrepart* 77(1): 87–105, https://doi.org/10.3917/autr.077.0087.

Berriane, M. and S. Nakhli. 2011. "En marge des grands chantiers touristiques mondialisés, l'émergence de territoires touristiques 'informels' et leur connexion directe avec le système monde." *Méditerranée* 116: 115–122.

Bourdeau, P. 2018. "L'après-tourisme revisité." *Via Tourism* 13, https://doi.org/10.4000/viatourism.1936.

Condevaux, A. et al. 2016. *Etat de l'art "La mise en tourisme de lieux ordinaires et la déprise d'enclaves touristiques: Quelle implication de la société civile?"* Paris: Université Paris 1, Panthéon-Sorbonne, p. 38.

Condevaux, A., G. Djament-Tran and M. Gravari-Barbas. 2016. "Avant et après le(s) tourisme(s): Trajectoires des lieux et rôles des acteurs du tourisme 'hors des sentiers battus'. Une analyse bibliographique." *Via Tourism* 9, https://doi.org/10.4000/viatourism.409.

El-Ghazaly, S. 2008. "Reclaiming Culture: The Heritage Preservation Movement in Fez." In *Chancellor's Honors Program Projects*. Morocco: University of Tennesse, p. 48.

Équipe MIT. 2002. *Tourismes, 1. Lieux communs*. Paris: Belin, coll. "Mappemonde", p. 319.

Escher, A. and S. Petermann. 2013. "Facteurs et acteurs de la *gentrification* touristique à Marrakech, Essaouira et Fès." In *Médinas immuables? Gentrification et changement dans les villes historiques marocaines (1996–2010)*, edited by E. Coslado, J. McGuinness and C. Miller. Paris: Centre Jacques Berque, pp. 101–130.

Gravari-Barbas, M. 2017. "Tourisme de marges, marges du tourisme. Lieux ordinaires et 'no-go zones' à l'épreuve du tourisme." *Bulletin de l'association de géographes français* 94–93, https://doi.org/10.4000/bagf.2097.

Greffe, X. 2011. "L'économie politique du patrimoine culturel: De la médaille au rhizome." ICOMOS 17th General Assembly, Paris, p. 7.

Istasse, M. 2011. "Circulation et rencontre du patrimoine et du tourisme dans la médina de Fès: De l'investigation de diverses formes patrimoniales." *Teoros, revue de recherche en tourisme* 2: 37–46.

Istasse, M. 2019. *Living in a World Heritage Site: Ethnography of Houses and Daily Life in the Fez Medina*. Cham, Switzerland: Springer Nature, pp. 86–218.

Jelidi, C. 2012. *Fès, la fabrication d'une ville nouvelle (1912–1956)*. Paris: ENS Editions, p.199.

Joly, M. 2020. "Du 'coup de foudre' à l'investissement: Les propriétaires français d'établissements touristiques dans la médina de Fès (Maroc)." *Annales de géographie* 732(2): 53–77, https://doi.org/10.3917/ag.732.0053.

Knafou, R. 1991. "L'invention du lieu touristique: La passation d'un contrat et le surgissement simultané d'un nouveau territoire." *Revue de Géographie Alpine* 79(4): 11–19, doi:10.3406/rga.1991.3624.

Kompulla, R. 2004. "Sucess and Growth in Rural Tourism Micro-Businesses in Finland: Financial or Life-Style Objectives?" In *Small Firms in Tourism: International Perspectives*, edited by R. Thomas. Amsterdam: Elsevier Science, pp. 115–138.

Kurzac-Souali, A. C. 2006. "Les médinas marocaines: une requalification sélective. Elites, patrimoine et mondialisation au Maroc." Thèse de troisième cycle, Université Paris-IV-Sorbonne, Paris, pp. 154–259.

Kurzac-Souali, A. C. 2005. "Ces riads qui vendent du rêve, patrimonialisation et ségrégation en medina." In *Habiter le patrimoine. Enjeux, approches, vécu, Université d'Angers*, directed by M. Gravari-Barbas. Rennes: UNESCO, Presse universitaire de Rennes, pp. 467–478.

Kurzac-Souali, A. C. 2010. "Intentions, représentations et patrimonialisation plurielle des médinas marocaines." *Hesperis-Tamuda* XLV: 89–117.

Lenain, M. A. and S. Saleilles. 2012. "Nouveaux arrivants créateurs d'activités touristiques en milieu rural et ancrage territorial." In *Les migrations d'agréement: Du tourisme à l'habiter*, edited by M. Niels, P. Bourdeau, J. F. Daller. Paris: L'Harmattan, Coll. Tourismes et sociétés, pp. 349–360.

Loi n°61-00. 2002. "Promulguée le 9 octobre 2002 portant sur le statut des établissements touristiques. Ministère du Tourisme et de l'Artisanat." 9 octobre 2002, https://www.cnt.ma/wp-content/uploads/2019/07/Loi-n%C2%B0-61-00-Establissements-Touristiques.pdf.

Loi n°80-14. 2015. "Promulguée le 4 août 2015 relative aux établissements touristiques et aux autres formes d'hébergement touristique." *Ministère du Tourisme et de l'Artisanat*, 4 août, https://autetouan.ma/web/uploads/dossier/5abcc7892e95d.pdf.

Madoeuf, A. 2016. "Voyage au pays des riads: Topiques du typique. Ambiances coïncidentes d'une expérience touristique actuelle." In *Ambiances, demain: Actes du 3ᵉ Congrès International sur les Ambiances.* Volos: Grèce, p. 788, Septembre.

Metalsi, M. 2003. *Fès, la ville essentielle.* Paris: Image du Monde, p. 74.

Morrison, A. and R. Thomas. 2006. "A Contextualisation of Entrepreneurship." *International Journal of Entrepreneurial Behaviour and Research* 12(4): 192–209.

Niels, M., P. Bourdeau and J. F. Daller (dirs.). 2012. *Les migrations d'agréement: du tourisme à l'habiter.* Paris: L'Harmattan, Coll. Tourismes et sociétés, p. 13.

O'Reilly, K. 2003. "When Is a Tourist? The Articulation of Tourism and Migration in Spain's Costa del Sol." *Tourist Studies* 3: 301–317.

Rainer, G. 2019. "Amenity/Lifestyle Migration to the Global South: Driving Forces and Socio-Spatial Implications in Latin America." *Third World Quarterly* 1–19, doi:10.1080/0 1436597.2019.1587291.

Stafford, J. 1996. *Développement et tourisme au Maroc (sous la dir.).* Montréal: L'Harmattan.

Shaw, G., and A. M. Williams. 1990. "Tourism Economic Development and the Role of Entrepreneurial Activity." In *Progress in Tourism, Recreation and Hospitality Management,* edited by C. P. Cooper. London: Bellhaven, vol. 2, pp. 67–81.

Shaw, G. and A. M. Williams. 2001. "Attributions About Entrepreneurship: A Framework and Process for Analyzing Reasons for Starting a Business." *Entrepreneurship Theory and Practice* 26(2): 5–32.

Shaw, G., and A. M. Williams. 2003. "Entrepreneurial Cultures and Small Business Enterprises in Tourism." In *Blackwells Companion to Tourism Geography*, edited by M. Hall, A. Lew and A. Williams. Oxford: Blackwell, pp. 120–131.

Viard, J. 1998. "Réinventer les vacances – La nouvelle galaxie du tourisme." *Documentation française* 23.

Viard, J. 2006. *Eloge de la Mobilité. Essai sur le capital temps libre et la valeur travail.* Paris: Editions de l'Aube, p. 100.

Van Laar, S., I. Cottyn, R. Donaldson, A. Zoomers and S. Ferreira. 2014. "'Living Apart Together,' in Franschhoek, South Africa: The Implications of Second-Home Development for Equitable and Sustainable Development." In *Contested Spatialities, Lifestyle Migration and Residential Tourism*, edited by M. Janoschka and H. Haas. London: Routledge, p. 108.

Wihtol de Wenden, C. 2013. "Migrations en Méditerranée, une nouvelle donne." *Confluences Méditerranée* 87(4): 19–30, https://doi.org/10.3917/come.087.0019.

13 Post-tourism and the Aquitaine coast

The fading concept of tourism accommodation

Myriam Casamayor

Introduction

Most of the tourist resorts on the Aquitaine coast in France (Figure 13.1) were built in the 1970s specifically for tourists. This was driven by Interministerial Task Force in Planning for the Aquitaine Coast (MIACA) through the implementation of a tourism planning scheme. With the successive increases in the number of weeks of paid holiday since 1936, the government decided to turn coastal and mountain areas into the "places to be" for holidaymakers. As such, the public policies of the time encouraged the development of a "tourism for all" that primarily materialised through the creation of a varied offer of tourism accommodation adapted to the visitors' different financial means. As a consequence, both budget and expensive stays (the holiday village and tourism residence, and the second home, respectively) emerged side by side on the tourism landscape.

Fifty years on, it is worthwhile analysing how the touristic and social functions of these facilities have evolved, and more specifically, how they have progressed regards not only the changes in tourism demand, but also the dual phenomenon of "littoralisation" and "metropolisation". Nowadays, these places also attract permanent residents because they are near to Bordeaux but have the advantage of lower property prices, and are also near to nature with the ocean, forests and lakes not far away.

This chapter is part of the general discussion in the literature on the hybridisation between tourism practices and more day-to-day practices. In particular, it raises questions on the implications of the hybridisation between tourism practices and new residential practices on the management of the real estate activities designed by MIACA. Therefore, the present chapter aims to test the hypothesis that tourism accommodation created in the 1970s is in the process of disappearing. It will also offer insight into the process whereby tourism accommodation aimed at lowest income tourists is being converted into more ordinary residential accommodation for wealthier inhabitants, or inversely, into homes for migrant families in search of a safe haven. Two case studies will illustrate these forms of hybridisation: the first is between touristic and residential

DOI: 10.4324/9781003138600-16

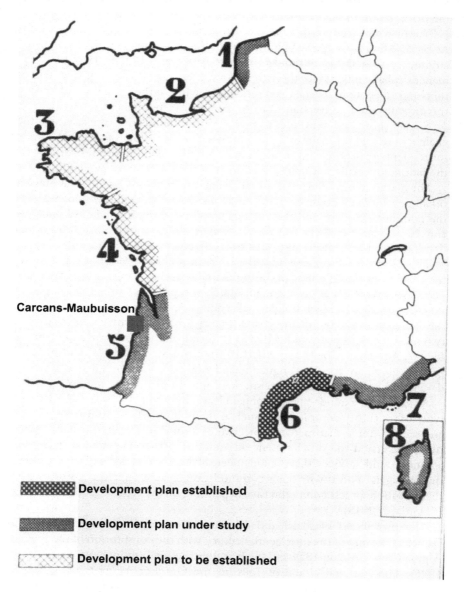

Figure 13.1 Progress of the tourism development plans in France in the 1970s

Source: *Urbanisme* n°123, p. 7

Note: The Aquitaine coast is located in southwestern France. Area 5 corresponds to the Interministerial Task Force in Planning for the Aquitaine Coast (MIACA)

function, and the second between a community-minded social function and the privatisation of public goods with wealthier people in mind.

The first case study is *Les Grands Pins* tourism residence and the second is *Le Sextant* holiday village. The former illustrates the gradual decrease in the amount of tourism accommodation in tourism residences in favour of permanent inhabitants, while the latter shows how easy it is to sell one part of tourism real estate in several main residences, while at the same time addressing the difficulty of a conversion from tourism use to permanent residential use. *Le Sextant* shows different sides to post-tourism: the relative ease at which the chalets were sold for main or second homes, the difficulties of selling the hotel for residential purposes and an additional "refuge" function for tourism accommodation, especially in the health context of the COVID-19 pandemic.

The methodology used involved gathering data from the Carcans-Maubuisson urban development archives. Semi-direct interviews were also conducted with the commune's mayor and the current property managers of *Les Grands Pins* and *Le Sextant*. Finally, a comparison was made of the original 2009 urban development plan and the new plan from 2016.

This chapter will present how the tourism accommodation created under the tourism planning policy of the Aquitaine coast has changed over the years.

In 1963 the French government launched a proactive urban development initiative to attract French holidaymakers on their way to Spain into staying on the Languedoc and Aquitaine coasts (Figure 13.1). To achieve this objective, two institutions were created: MIACA (Interministerial Task Force in Planning for the Aquitaine Coast) and MIALR (Interministerial Task Force in Tourism Development for the Languedoc and Aquitaine Coast). Their aim was to design and implement their tourism development plan at the regional level.

As part of an extended period of paid leave, their initiative was to create new types of tourism accommodation such as the holiday village, tourism residence and second home that met the objective of a tourism for all.[1] Such an objective necessitated the development of seaside resorts equipped with facilities/amenities and services that would meet all holidaymakers' expectations and their budgets. This is why the accommodation created offered a customer care that was more or less comprehensive depending on the type of accommodation (Casamayor 2019).

The first forms of social and community-oriented tourism appeared in France at the end of the nineteenth century with the constitution of the French Alpine Club (FAC) in 1874 and the first (unstructured) summer camps (Corbin 1995). The National Union of Tourism and Outdoor Associations (UNAT), that brought together actors from the social tourism sector, was created in 1920 and declared a public utility in 1929. In France, associative movements played a role in the creation of what became known as "the leisure culture" (Boyer 2007). Holiday villages are part of associative tourism that grew considerably from 1945 onwards (after the Second World War) and made tourism and holidays accessible to a greater number of people (Monforte 2006). In 1948, the Touring Club of France (TCF) designed the first campsite with tents that were already provided and pre-installed on site. Leading on from this idea, the concept of the holiday village as we know it today was developed by the VVF association and based on family values centred on leisure and sharing. It consisted of a central building of collective services (reception, catering, management and group and sports activities) surrounded by the accommodation units. The holiday village was considered to provide communal tourist facilities where different clients could share rest and leisure time, and chose from different activities tailored to their social and educational needs. VVF exists to this day and is now partly owned by the French government. It is a concept that has inspired many other holiday villages that have followed the same layout and pattern. As such, social tourism operators became increasingly involved in the regional tourism planning policy which made them key partners of the French public authorities (Urbain 2016).

Gradually, another type of accommodation developed: tourism residences. These offered more flexibility than traditional hotels, as clients stayed in apartments and therefore had more independence. For the property purchasers, this type of accommodation was the opportunity for a long-term investment from which they would receive rental income and a nine-year tax reduction. And for the region, this was a way of creating more tourism beds. This new form of accommodation increased tourism possibilities and, like holiday villages, they exist to this day (SNRT 2016).

The third form of accommodation is the second home, which appeared on the tourism landscape before 1976 but has increased exponentially since. Unlike the tourism residence or the holiday village, the term "second home" is not clearly defined in French law. The definition of second home covers a wide range of functions and housing types; the French National Institute of Statistics and Economic Studies (INSEE) defines it as "a property used for weekends, leisure activities or holidays. Furnished properties (rented or for rent) for tourism stays also come under this category" [translation author's own]. In France, a large number of second homes are old properties as 50% of them were built before 1976, and 31% between 1990 and 2015. On the other hand, the number of residences has been on the rise since 1946 and reached 3.3 million second homes in 2105, which represented 9.4% of all French real estate in 2017 (SNRT 2016). In comparison, there were only 350,000 second homes in Great Britain and 1.1 million in Germany in 1995 (Dubost et al. 1995). Second homes are also fiscally classified by the DGFiP (General Directorate of Public Finances) as "a property used for housing that is not permanently occupied, subject to basic housing tax" [translation author's own]. Both definitions do not complement each other. Second homes are considered a legal French oddity as regards their number and legal definition.

These different types of tourism accommodation were tailored to the demands of communal living (holiday villages), to the search for hotel services (tourism residences) and to clients seeking independence (second homes). The year 2021 marks the 40th anniversary of the appearance of these different forms of accommodation on the market.

Since the democratisation of tourism, the general demand has significantly changed due to new ways of working and travelling, and the increasingly easy access to information technology has increased tourist mobility as people can now go on holiday for shorter periods of time but more often, and visit and stay the night in places close to home. Tourists are also more independent: they want to organise their own holidays and be the actors of their own experience, and as such, are shunning third-party services. They look for a higher level of comfort, and more freedom in the accommodation they rent. Moreover, they want to discover a variety of different tailored activities and prefer to have extraordinary experiences (Laplante 2011).

In this context, the present chapter will address the ageing tourism properties located in seaside resorts along the Aquitaine coast, in an era of new seaside and residential practices. The aim is to study, above all, whether tourism accommodation is turning away from its original vocation of a tourism for all. It is therefore necessary to understand whether the processes at work are now undermining the original values on which the construction of these properties was based, or if the social function is being maintained. To do this, the chapter analyses an example of a tourism residence "Les Grands Pins" and an example of a holiday village "Le Sextant", both located in the seaside resort of Carcans-Maubuisson, on the Nouvelle-Aquitaine coast. The chapter concludes with the hypothesis that tourism accommodation takes on a new role during a time of crisis.

Les Grands Pins: from tourism residence to residential hybrid

The original project

Les Grands Pins is a tourism residence constructed in 1984 by Résidotel, a tourism property management company, and purchased in 2007 by the Pierre et Vacances group, the current manager. The latter manages the rental and maintenance of the apartments that are owned by individuals in a co-ownership system. The site consists of four buildings comprising 125 apartments and a main reception building. An emphyteutic lease[2] between the commune (property owner) and the manager will reach the end of its term before the end of 2026.

Difficulties with tourism rentals

The opening period of *Les Grands Pins* has decreased year on year: in 2016 it was open from 28 May to 21 September, a total of 17 compared with 20 weeks in 2013. The months of July and August were always fully booked, but outside high season the occupancy rate was low. This opening period, which has decreased over time, reflects one of the difficulties the site has faced.

Over the last ten years, the works carried out have mostly been maintenance and furniture purchases, that is small improvements and routine maintenance; the apartments under lease are serviced in the winter. There has not been any structural work since the building's construction, thus raising the question of whether the emphyteutic lease rules have been respected. As this tourism residence is built on land that the property owner does not own, all of the buildings will revert to the commune at the end of the lease. The major risk for the latter will be ending up with an old and dilapidated property.

A series of decisions by the actors involved has led to the gradual abandonment of the tourism residence

For this tourism residence, most of the owners originally purchased their apartment as a financial investment, not because they were particularly interested in the apartment itself or in Carcans-Maubuisson. This means that maintaining the entire building is rather challenging. The owner of a property can choose to terminate the lease between themselves and the manager, and if they decide to sell the property, there is no legal obligation on them or the new owner to renovate it. This can lead to a situation in which, during co-ownership meetings, owners can refuse to cover the cost of any requested structural improvements which leads to a loss in the building's value if most owners take this route. This creates a vicious circle: owners no longer maintain their properties, the residence starts to deteriorate, it becomes less attractive, and all this thus lowers the rental income (which is sometimes barely enough for the owners to cover their annual[3] property fees/charges), thus leading to a lack of tourism appeal making it harder to rent/sell the property. This creates a hybridisation between tourism and residential function when some owners turn their properties into year-round rentals.

This was the case for 26 apartments (i.e. 21% of properties) in *Les Grands Pins* in 2016. Lease cancellation is a frequent occurrence in this residence: "*We lose money every year now*".[4] This trend could gather strength as many property owners' leases are coming to the end of their term.

There are also conflicts of interest between co-owners (in and out of leasehold) in terms of either building use (e.g. the swimming pool) or works to be carried out. Difficulties involved in covering the ever-growing costs can result in the residence manager's hasty departure, leaving most of the tourism accommodation abandoned.

On the other hand, as landowner, the commune is also responsible for this degradation. The suggestion by the mayor to renew the emphyteutic lease (interview with the mayor in 2017), so as not to be responsible for the maintenance, does not address the property owners' difficulties of renting out the apartments. This passive response suggests that the commune supports the residentialisation of these properties, while recognising that a number of tourist beds will be lost. Indeed, if the management of the residence reverts to the commune, there would be steep costs involved in the development of the property.

Today, it is easy to see the limitations of what were once considered advantages of an emphyteutic lease. Because the land is public, the property manager has no interest in investing money in the renovation of a property that does not belong to them.

Consequently, it can be concluded that a tourism residence is a type of accommodation that works as long as it is properly maintained and the managers have tailored it to the current tourism demand. On the other hand, two elements may be problematic: first, a tourism residence does not work on its own. It is dependent on the region's strengths and weaknesses. Second, because of the way it operates, there is no guarantee that the accommodation units will remain under management and therefore remain marketable accommodation. A growing number of owners prefer to leave the traditional structure of a tourism residence either because they no longer wish to be part of such a system (indicating a desire for independence), or because they are no longer satisfied with their contract with the property managers. In both cases, the properties leave this commercial system and become second homes. Figure 13.2 shows a brief outline of this growing trend.

A comparison of the urbanism plans between 2009 and 2016 shows that there has been a change in policy direction towards a residentialisation of this

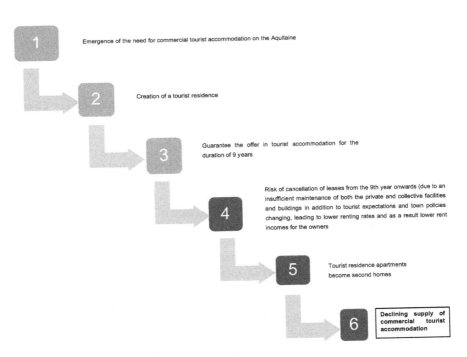

Figure 13.2 The process of decline in the supply of commercial tourist accommodation

tourism accommodation, not only in the case of *Les Grands Pins* but also in other places. For example, the UTc zone, which was once exclusively a tourism zone (only the construction of hotel resorts and tourism residences authorised) is currently a hybrid zone in which private residences can also be built. And the UZb zone is no longer the only zone authorising the construction of suburban housing allowing for the change from tourism to residential function, or the creation of new homes.

Les Grands Pins tourism residence is the perfect example of the gradual hybridisation from a touristic to a residential function, whereas for the case of *Le Sextant* holiday village, although there was a distinct change in function, another form of hybridisation in terms of values was in action.

Le Sextant: a holiday village with a new social purpose

The transition from a social-oriented tourism accommodation to a more upmarket accommodation

This holiday village originally consisted of a main residence with 53 rooms, a restaurant, recreation rooms, and 25 chalets (Figure 13.3). Residence guests had access to the catering area, whereas the chalets were independent, self-catered units.

Figure 13.3 Le Sextant holiday village

Source: Gironde Habitat and Myriam Casamayor, 2015

Figure 13.3 Continued

The *Le Sextant* programme, designed in 1978, is based on a 60-year emphyteutic lease between Gironde Habitat (owner of the property complex) and the commune (landowner). It was first owned by Locage, a social tourism-oriented association, who filed for bankruptcy in 1989. Under the new management of the Maeva group, the site then changed from a social function to a midrange product. In 2004, the property no longer matched the company's move into the higher end of the national tourism market so Maeva returned the site to Gironde Habitat. The chalets were always rented out easily, however, the hotel's full board offer did not attract enough tourists to achieve a satisfactory occupancy rate.

From holiday village management to a reclaiming of residentiality

Gironde Habitat offered weekly stays at *Le Sextant* but these did not meet tourists' new ways of travelling. In a context where individuals seek tailor-made travel and holiday experiences, the characteristics of this form of leisure and activities is no longer suitable, causing the communal aspect of holiday villages to lose its visitor appeal.

With no new buyers lined up in 2004, and after they had purchased the whole landholdings from the commune, Gironde Habitat decided to put the chalets on the market as individual units. This meant that the local authority of Carcans-Maubuisson would no longer have the onerous responsibility of managing tourism accommodation that would not work when the lease expired. Besides, the local authority's focus in this regard had shifted from maintaining the number of tourism beds in this area to prioritising residential development. A comparison of the urbanism plans shows the change in land use: zones that were up until then only allocated for tourism accommodation became wider in scope and also included residential use.

Le Sextant is a good example of how the core function of a holiday village can be adapted from a commodity into a non-market good with a purely residential function. The phenomena of metropolisation and residentialisation, linked to the proximity of Bordeaux, explain the conversion of this tourism accommodation into main homes. Nevertheless, the site has kept its original architectural form, no extensions have been added to the chalets and the new constructions are perfectly integrated with their surroundings.

On the other hand, no decisions have been taken about the future of the hotel; the current manager, Mr Lanneluc, who is in charge of the sale of the hotel for the social lessor Gironde Habitat, said that he had been in contact with potential buyers. However, this kind of property is not exceptional along the Aquitaine coast, and this makes it particularly difficult to sell. States Mr Lanneluc: *"I was contacted by people who wanted to buy the hotel, but they informed me on the day of their visit that they had three or four other viewings in the same area"*. Taking into account the hotel sector in this area, *Le Sextant* is a complicated sale, and if a buyer cannot be found, as is the case for the other previous properties, the site could deteriorate and become a derelict wasteland.

Hybridisation of the original social function of the holiday village

Finally, at the end of 2016 after the hotel had been closed for nearly a decade, it was converted into a migrant reception centre. At the time, one social assistant hired by the charity Emmaüs provided support for the five migrant families who were already on site, with more families due to arrive in 2017.

The department prefect visited the site to ensure that everything was in place and that the living conditions complied with the applicable standards. This visit shows the importance of this reception and the hybridisation between the very different functions of touristic (tourists who typically came to Carcans-Maubuisson) and social (migrants). *"These families have reluctantly left their country, they have left behind everything to flee from war and persecution. They are people who have been traumatised and they are still frightened. Their stories are painful, often they have had to watch family members die"*, explained the social assistant Cécile. She added: *"These families want to remain in France and hope to eventually find peace here, their children ask to go to school every morning"*.

In this case study, the tourists' desire for the shore is replaced with the migrants' desire to find peace in France. This hybridisation between the touristic and residential function, however, is characterised by maintaining the holiday villages' original social character and by a tourism criterion, that is movement from an everyday place towards a place outside the daily routine or in the realm of the unknown. All this suggests that there has been a clear departure from tourism in this seaside resort as regards people's motivations to go there.

Conclusion

Over the last 50 years, the tourism accommodation created at the time of the democratisation of tourism for all in the seaside resorts of France's Aquitaine coast have all undergone changes to their original function. These changes have given rise to the emergence of a new blend of places that were once exclusively used for tourism activities.

Through the two case studies – the tourism residence *Les Grands Pins* and the holiday village *Le Sextant* – in this chapter, it can be seen that two forms of hybridisation are in action.

The first concerns the change from tourism to residential function, which is the result of several concurrent factors such as changes in the expectations of holidaymakers who are now in search of a more independent form of tourism, one that is more tailored to their expectations and is more original. This is also the result of ageing infrastructures whose costly maintenance and renovation over the last 20 years are no longer sufficiently covered by the property owners or managers. In addition, the development of a tourism accessible to all, that was once encouraged through funding from CAF (Family Allowance Office) and Région Nouvelle-Aquitaine, is no longer a priority, and this will gradually lead to the residentialisation of tourism sites. Naturally, the reception of tourists is still relevant today in the Aquitaine seaside resorts, but the shift towards a residentialisation of tourism properties is a growing phenomenon. As coastal communes are selling their public land to private actors, over time, the homeowners from a higher income social group have gradually moved into these areas. This functional hybridisation, even if it does not reflect a sudden departure from tourism, raises the question of whether the financial help provided by the government through MIACA in the 1970s promoted the gradual privatisation of the coastline.

The second form of hybridisation observed covers the development of the social function of this tourism accommodation. The first form shows the gradual disappearance of social-oriented holiday villages designed for the least well-off members of society, whereas the second refers to the persistence of the social function that appears to be self-perpetuating as part of a function other than tourism and in times of economic crisis. The case of *Le Sextant* shows that the tourism function completely disappeared when the accommodation was converted into main homes and the hotel a migrant reception centre. The decision taken by the prefect to mobilise this emergency accommodation, located in the middle of a commune that is a seaside resort and one hour from Bordeaux, reflects a new type of motivation, or rather compulsion, behind people's desire to stay in coastal areas. It goes without saying that exile and holiday experiences are polar opposites, but there are some similarities in the two situations: both a break that forms between a tiring daily life and the search for an elsewhere, in a restful and rejuvenating place giving people the strength to face the world afterwards. This also calls into question the actual definition of seaside resort ("*station balnéaire*") in French. The etymology of the word "station", from the Latin *statio* meaning a stage, a pause that one makes on one's journey, a place where one stops (Boyer 2000), questions the new ways in which seaside resorts are being used, and how long these will last, and people's motivations for visiting these places.

The context of crises, whether they be sanitary, ecological, economic or social, raises the question whether their increased frequency in the future will, for this tourism residence constructed in the 1970s, ultimately contribute to the change from touristic to refuge function.

At first sight, the impacts of the 2020 sanitary crisis caused by the COVID-19 pandemic call for further research. Some people were able to go and stay in their second homes during this crisis, even though their main motivation was not holiday oriented. Contrary to the foundations of social tourism for a coastal access to all, during the national lockdowns, it became clear that seaside access and activities became the reserve of the privileged few with second homes as tourism activities were prohibited for others. It can be hypothesised that a new refuge function is emerging that goes beyond the existing touristic and residential functions. These new hybrid places offer shelter from the outside world, and the opportunity for rest and rejuvenation in coastal areas. This will open new avenues of research on the hybridisation between tourism and (residential and social) shelter.

Notes

1 The concept of "tourisme social" in French.
2 An emphyteutic lease consists of the lessor granting the lessee, for a duration of between 18 and 99 years, an immoveable real right which relates only to buildings. The land remains the property of the lessor. At the end of the lease the lessor becomes the owner of the buildings constructed or renovated on the land.
3 The rent is calculated as a percentage of turnover.
4 Ms Gagzéry, Pierre et Vacances manager, interviewed by Laurie Egiziano and Myriam Casamayor in April 2016.

Bibliography

Ascher, François. 2005. *La société hypermoderne: Ces événements nous dépassent, feignons d'en être les organisateurs*. La Tour-d'Aigues: Editions de L'aube.
Boyer. Marc. 2000. *Histoire de l'invention du tourisme XVIe–XIXe siècle: origine et développement du tourisme dans le Sud-Est de la France*. Paris: Éditions de l'Aube.
Boyer, Marc. 2007. *Le tourisme de masse*. Paris: L'Harmattan.
Casamayor, Myriam. 2019. *La planification du littoral aquitain. L'héritage de la MIACA à l'épreuve du temps*. Bordeaux: Université Bordeaux Montaigne.
Corbin, Alain. 1995. *L'avènement des loisirs. 1850–1960*. Paris: Aubier.
Dubost, Françoise et al. 1995. "Les résidences secondaires, nouvelles orientations." Rapport final à la DATAR (convention d'étude n°93–42), par le groupe de prospective sur l'avenir, p. 340.
Knafou, Rémy, Bruston Mireille, Deprest Florence, Duhamel Philippe, Gay Jean-Christophe and Sacareau Isabelle. 1997. "Une approche géographique du tourisme." *Espace géographique* 26(3): 193–204, https://doi.org/10.3406/spgeo.1997.1071.
Laplante, Marc. 2011. *L'expérience touristique contemporaine: Fondements sociaux et culturels*. Québec: Presse de l'Université du Québec.
Monforte, Isabelle. 2006. "La fréquentation des centres de vacances depuis 1954: Contre quelques idées reçues." *Recherches et Prévisions* 86: 90–97, https://doi.org/10.3406/caf.2006.2257.
Syndicat national des résidences de tourisme. 2016. "Dossier de presse." https://www.snrt.fr/wp-content/uploads/2019/12/Dossier-de-presse-septembre-2019.pdf.
Urbain, Jean-Didier. 2016. "Aller à la plage, aller à la mer. Pratiques balnéaires du XVIIIe siècle à nos jours." In *Tous à la plage*, edited by Bernard Toulier. Paris: Cité de l'architecture et du patrimoine et Lienart éditions, pp. 23–46.

Press journal

Sud-Ouest. 2016. *Julien Lestage avec Pierre Vallade, Les migrants accueillis à Carcans dans la sérénité*. Paris: La commune revendique son droit à la solidarité, 22 octobre.

14 The changing role of tourism-oriented theme parks as everyday entertainment venues during COVID-19

Salvador Anton Clavé, Joan Borràs Nogués, Jonathan Ayebakuro Orama and Maria Trinitat Rovira Soto

With a global economic size bigger than several countries' annual gross domestic product, the theme park industry has experienced a great disruption during 2020 because of the COVID-19 pandemic (Masters 2020). Theme parks are commercially operated entertainment facilities based on fictional characters and themes that offer amusement attractions ranging from mechanical rides to immersive cinematic experiences to an enormous number of visitors each year. Important measures related to the fight against the coronavirus such as social distancing requirements, capacity constraints, health-oriented operational adjustments, the closing of facilities during periods of the year and travel and mobilities restrictions have challenged the industry as a whole (IAAPA 2020a). International and national air travel regulations have directly affected theme parks with tourism audiences.

Related to the effects of the transformed context created by the travel and mobility restrictions, the main goal of this chapter is to explore the changing role of tourism-oriented theme parks during the pandemic as everyday entertainment venues for people living nearby. This could be attributed both to the efforts of theme parks to attract the domestic market in response to limitations or inconveniences to travel during the majority of 2020 and to the changing decisions made by people when choosing, for entertainment activities, local day trips rather than longer travels (Sivan 2020).

Despite the millions of people who visit theme parks annually, the theme park industry is indeed an under-researched topic and, therefore, available studies and regular data about characteristics and spatial behaviour of visitors are scarce. In fact, in deep demand analysis are usually made in-company and little is known, in general, about mobility patterns of theme park visitors. This is an issue when trying to decipher actual changes as those related to the attraction of domestic and closer markets in tourism-oriented theme parks. Hence, because data are scarce and opportunities for field work have been limited due to the pandemic, the empirical final analysis for this chapter focuses on the analysis of the characteristics and vacation trends of visitors to one specific European

DOI: 10.4324/9781003138600-17

tourism-oriented theme park, PortAventura, using social media information gathered from Twitter. First, characteristics of Twitter users who uploaded a post from PortAventura between July and October of both 2019 and 2020 (which is the period when the park was opened in 2020) are analysed. Second, an exploratory spatial data analysis using Global Moran's I of the geolocation of Twitter post of PortAventura visitors during seven days before and after their visit to the park is applied.

This chapter runs as follows: the first section gives a basic background on the global theme park industry. The second section identifies the main challenges that the pandemic originated in the operation and attendance to the theme parks from existing literature and reports. The third section presents and discusses the PortAventura case analysing changes between 2019 and 2020. Finally, the fourth section provides conclusions regarding the changing role of tourism-oriented theme parks as everyday entertainment venues.

Tourism, entertainment and theme parks development

Theme parks and themed out-of-home attractions are common components of the contemporary dynamics of commercialisation and spectacularisation of most aspects of the everyday life as well as its increasing "McDonaldization" (Ritzer 1993, 1999). These processes occur in a broad context of transformation of the role of leisure characterised by the increase of hedonistic attitudes (Schmid 2009 7). As a consequence, the theme park industry has been continuously growing during recent decades and while in 2000 the estimated number of total visitors to theme parks in the world was 545 million, in 2018 the estimated attendance increased to 1,121.6 million (ERA 2003; IAAPA 2019). According to the last five-year period before COVID-19 (2013–2018) with existing comparable estimated data available, the total spend on theme and amusement parks worldwide evolved from 35,784 million USD in 2013 to 58,637 million USD in 2018 (IAAPA 2019). Spending data included admission fees and, if applicable, food, souvenirs and other related purchases made at the parks.

Even though there is a lack in the definition and classification of theme park facilities resulting in ontological, epistemological and methodological shortcomings (Leask 2008) and misunderstandings (Anton Clavé 2022), there is a consensus among specialists that several types of theme parks exist. Wanhill (2008) distinguished between destination parks, regional parks, traditional parks and water parks. Based on size but especially on their different ability to attract tourism demand, Anton Clavé (2007) differentiated among destination parks, regional parks, urban parks and niche parks. Similarly, Younger (2016) stated that from a business model standpoint, theme parks operate at a variety of scales, each one with its own market size. According to him, these scales are transient, local, regional and global. Finally, the Park Database (2020) differentiates between mega theme parks, superregional and regional parks, indoor theme parks and water parks.

Destination, global or mega-parks are tourism-oriented theme parks catering to visitors at the international level. Developed mostly by The Walt Disney Company and Universal Studios, these parks cost over 1 billion USD and represent high-end resorts and entertainment complexes that include a range of branded attractions, hotels, shopping, restaurants, night life, sports, as well as conference and tourism facilities, all driven by intellectual property. Designed to draw and entertain visitors over multiple days, they were not meant to be part of everyday life, but to supply extraordinary experiences that can be remembered for a lifetime (The Park Database 2020).

Regional parks (including the superregional category listed by The Park Database 2020) are mid-sized entertainment facilities but the largest in their market area. They may or may not have globally renowned branding like Legoland or Six Flags. Depending on their characteristics, size, location, resort integration and themes, they attract significant tourist flows (as is the case with Europa-Park and De Efteling, for example), and in some cases they are located at popular tourist destinations (like Parc Astérix near Paris). They cost several hundreds of millions in US dollars and in most cases have diversified their amusement core activities with hotels and complementary leisure options within or next to the site where they are located in order to attract tourists. This is the case for the park selected for the market change analysis performed in this chapter, PortAventura, a theme park located in an entertainment complex, PortAventura World, at a tourism destination, the central Costa Daurada of Catalonia, along with other entertainment, accommodation and tourism facilities that, as reported in the third section of this chapter, cater to domestic and international markets.

Finally, there are theme parks oriented mostly towards urban and metropolitan markets. This broad category includes out-of-home theme entertainment attractions such as traditional parks, urban parks, local amusement parks, water parks, indoor parks and niche-themed parks which represent, in fact, the majority of existing parks. Interestingly, they do not give rise to significant tourist flow as is the case with popular urban and metropolitan ride parks.

The COVID-19 impact on the theme parks industry

Due to the unprecedented situation originated by the COVID-19 pandemic, the worldwide growing demand and supply of theme parks has been abruptly stopped. It was already well known that the tourism, leisure and hospitality industry was extremely sensitive to epidemic situations (such as SARS in 2002–2003, as the most recent significant episode before COVID-19). Nevertheless, until COVID-19, effects such as the reduction of attendance to entertainment facilities, a lower occupancy in the hotels, restaurants and other recreational and amusement centres and the decrease in revenue and benefits for firms and destinations were shortly recovered.

However, as stated by Lee and Chen (2020), it is quite clear that COVID-19's influence on the travel, tourism and leisure industry is going to have devastating effects, which cannot be comparable to any previous health crises. Hence, global and regional companies within the theme park industry are trying to manage massive losses in the short term, while it is uneasy to predict impacts over the medium and longer term on demand attraction, facilities operation, and experience design.

Due to reactions from governments, public organisations and private businesses to fight the pandemic, the 2020 situation resulted in almost zero tourism, hospitality and entertainment activity during some periods of the year in most of the regions of the world and in a reduced and transformed level of activity during the rest of the year. In parallel, as most people feel COVID-19 as a probable life risk, the pandemic, together with the above-mentioned travel restrictions and constraints, has altered travelling lifestyles around the world, leading to the emergence of new patterns of behaviour. This includes a shift to home-based and close-to-home-based activities, the proliferation of online offers and uses, a growing need for connectivity, an accentuated inequality in the access to recreational practices, transformed operational practices in the leisure industry, an increased demand for psychological support and enhanced acts of helping hands and voluntarism (Sivan 2020). Complementarily, job losses and shut-down businesses have undermined the well-being of part of the population, announcing a potential new economic crisis derived from COVID-19. Regarding the specific dynamics of the theme park industry, this may result in a lower capacity to spend time and money.

Indeed, following Niewiadomski (2020), to stop the pandemic, many national, regional and local authorities have resorted to various measures that have changed the world in a way that would have been entirely unthought of just a few months ago. From the perspective of destination and purposefully tourism-oriented theme parks, five issues have heavily disrupted both the demand side and the supply side of the business, originating a heavy negative impact, such as travel restrictions; facility closures; capacity constraints; social conduct regulations, including social distancing mandates; and new operational procedures related to the cleaning and sanitisation of facilities. Additionally, social perceptions might have changed, inducing new mental distance between the "ordinary" and the "extraordinary".

As data have evidenced that less human mobility is associated with lower COVID-19 cases and deaths (Yilmazkuday 2020), in 2020 international travel was largely suspended, domestic travel was severely restricted and quarantine measures in many countries and regions were enforced for travellers. Therefore, disrupting the regular transportation system, COVID-19 has reduced the possibility that tourists, who are a fundamental part of the demand of tourism-oriented theme parks, travel during periods in which they have been opened. Moreover, regarding the air transport system, not only have many flights been canceled, resulting in the entire system reducing its activity globally (Saadat et al. 2020), but also even the desire to travel has dropped, at least during the first period of the pandemic (Gallego and Font 2020). This is likely due to health security being a key issue for travellers making their travel decisions

(Lee and Chen 2020) and to a new travel context where feelings (at least in the short- and mid- term) about what is "home" and "away" are mostly based on new considerations related to place health conditions and COVID-19 spread probabilities. In this context, visitors might restrain themselves from travelling "away" when health conditions are not completely perceived as safe as they are at "home". All in all, for the theme park and entertainment industry, and especially for theme parks with a significant portion of customers arriving to them as tourists, travel restrictions are critical. This situation has also been reinforced by the appeal of governments to the population to avoid unnecessary tourism, face-to-face meetings and social events.

A second of the above-mentioned issues that have disrupted the theme park business is the direct (occasioned by the absence of demand or by the rule of law) closure of entertainment facilities and theme parks during some periods of the year. Obviously, together with the travel limitation regulations, closing facilities or even temporary suspension of theme park operations have severe economic consequences for the companies (and, of course, for the whole economy). This has resulted in forcing furlough of employees and executives, and also in revenue losses. Mitigation efforts deployed by theme parks – such as eliminating seasonal labor, salary and wage reductions, renegotiating credits, deferring or eliminating projects or developing incentives to maintain monthly membership commitments – have been not sufficient to counteract the adverse impact COVID-19 has had and may continue to have on theme parks revenues.

Capacity constraints derived from social conduct regulations have also had a great impact on theme parks when they have been opened. In this vein, for instance, Gabe (2020) has examined the impacts of COVID-19 related to capacity constraints on attendance at Disney's Magic Kingdom theme park. Results suggest that limiting the number of guests to less than about 60% of the park capacity has large impacts on annual attendance and, more important, on revenue. For example, a scenario of 50% capacity, which means about 50,000 daily visitors, would constrain attendance in 274 out of 365 days of the year, and would result in an estimated annual attendance of 10.6% lower than the average annual attendance between 2014 and 2018. Other social conduct measures also have particular severe impacts on theme parks because, as stated by Gabe (2020, 1), "such businesses commonly welcome large numbers of people congregated in very close physical proximity" and, thus, one of the main perceived benefits when enjoying a theme park is restricted.

Related to this, to gain the confidence of the audience, theme parks are not only following governments' health instructions (CDC 2020) to protect staff, guests and communities, but also deploying new operational schemes, which have been designed by the own industry (IAAPA 2020b). Those measures include, among many others, hand washing stations, replacement of materials and systems, the frequent sanitising of surfaces, the use of face coverings by employees and visitors and the above-mentioned limitations related to the number of guests. All this represents additional costs to companies. In the case of The Walt Disney Company, for example, it has been estimated that it may total approximately 1 billion USD in fiscal year 2021 accounting only for its parks, experiences and products segment (The Walt Disney Company 2020).

In addition to policy and business issues, there is the question of changes in social perceptions. As reported by Gössling et al. (2020), sentiment surveys made across China, Italy, Spain, the United Kingdom and the United States by McKinsey and Company (2020) suggest that consumer optimism varies between countries and that consumers regain confidence when the recovery process evolves. Nevertheless, in the case of theme parks, it should be not forgotten that masks, temperature checking at the gates and limited contact with others reminds visitors that they are not in the "extraordinary" environment that was supposed to be a theme park as a fantasy world (Sylt 2020). This might restrain potential visitors from travelling mid and long distances to visit a theme park, especially when the situation has not been normalised.

Even though particular processes can be identified and effects may vary depending on the regional context, initial available data confirm the disruptive impact of COVID-19 in the economic and financial performance of theme parks. This was foreseen from the beginning of the pandemic when, in April 2020, the IAAPA (International Association of Amusement Parks and Attractions) launched surveys in the Asia Pacific, North America, and Latin America regions asking attractions, manufacturer and supplier companies about the effects of reactions to the situation created by COVID-19 (IAAPA 2020a). At that time, most companies across all three regions were expecting a loss between 31% and 90% for the full 2020 year, with loss of operating income, operating expenses and cash flow as the main issues. Staff adjustments and delayed investment projects were the primary strategies of the responding companies for dealing with the COVID-19 impact. Of course, the extent to which the pandemic will finally impact theme parks' economic performance is still highly uncertain and could not be predicted at the end of 2020. Additional mid-term impacts would be caused by the continuous negative effect of the pandemic on customers' economies and financial markets and on the cessation of business activities.

Available data at the end of 2020 indicate that both destination and tourism-oriented theme parks and other regional and metropolitan theme parks have suffered massive losses. This is the case, for instance of the major worldwide destination theme parks firm, The Walt Disney Company, but also of the world's largest regional theme park company and largest water park operator in the United States, Six Flags. In the case of Disney, the impact from COVID-19 for the quarter ending on 3 October 2020, and with the fiscal year beginning on 29 September 2019, was approximately 2.4 billion USD and 6.9 billion USD respectively in operating income at Disney's Parks, Experiences and Products segment (The Walt Disney Company 2020). This is a decrease of 61% for the quarter and of 37% for the entire fiscal year. Segment operating results decreased 2.5 billion USD to a loss of 1.1 billion USD only during the last quarter with available data. This loss is the result of the closures and reduced operating capacities as, since the second quarter of the fiscal year, Walt Disney parks and resorts were closed or operating at significantly reduced capacity and cruise ship sailings, which are also included in the Parks, Experiences and Products segment, have been suspended. All of the reopened parks and resorts operated at significantly reduced capacities during the last 2020 quarter (The Walt Disney Company 2020).

Six Flags Entertainment Corporation also reported a massive decline in revenue and earnings for the third quarter and first nine months of 2020 as compared with 2019 (Six Flags Entertainment Corporation 2020). Due to COVID-19, Six Flags suspended operations on 13 March 2020. Reopening started in the second quarter even though nine of the company's 26 parks remained closed during the third quarter and, as indicated in the case of Disney, parks that opened during the period were subject to attendance limitations. According to the company reports, comparisons to prior years exclude attendance from Six Flags Discovery Kingdom and Six Flags Great America, as these parks have modified operations with minimal attendance in 2020.

To summarise, only during the third quarter of 2020, the attendance to Six Flags parks counted as 2.6 million guests, a decline of 11.4 million guests from the third quarter of 2019 representing 19% of prior year total attendance, and approximately 35% of attendance at the parks that were open, relative to the comparable prior year period. Total revenue was 126 million USD, a decline of 495 million USD from the third quarter of 2019, and net loss for this quarter was 116 million USD, a decline of 296 million USD from the third quarter of 2019. According to the company's own report, the decrease in revenue was primarily the result of the decrease in attendance, but it was minimally offset by improved guest spending per capita primarily due to recurring monthly membership revenue from members who retained their memberships following the initial 12-month commitment period. An increase in the mix of single-day guests who tend to spend more on a per visit basis also contributed to the improvement (Six Flags Entertainment Corporation 2020).

Tourism-oriented theme parks market transformation during COVID-19: the case of PortAventura

A specific issue to explore in analysing the effects of COVID-19 on theme park performance is market transformation due to the new mobilities regime associated with the pandemic. This is significant in the short term because of the current travel restrictions. Additionally, it might be a potential mid- and long-term driver of changes if the observed decision-making transformation persists due to an increasing perception that tourism-oriented theme parks could also play roles as entertainment venues in everyday life. To what extent this may result in future trends is rather uncertain.

To try to explore changes in demand attraction in tourism-oriented theme parks between 2019 and 2020, a case study focused in the PortAventura theme park has been conducted. Notably, with 3.75 million visitors in 2019, PortAventura was the sixth most visited theme park in Europe according to the ranking elaborated by TEA/AECOM (2020) only after Disneyland Paris (9.74 million), Europa-Park (5.75 million), De Efteling (5.26 million), Walt Disney Studios Park (5.25 million) and Tivoli Gardens (4.58 million). The turnover in 2018 was 230 million Euros. Interestingly, PortAventura hosts one of the top three highest roller coasters in Europe (Shambala, 76 m high), the first being Red Force, located in Ferrari Land (112 m) which is the second theme park gate at the PortAventura World entertainment complex. The two rides are also among the top five roller coasters ranked by speed in Europe (180 km/h Red Force and 134 km/h Shambala) together with another PortAventura ride, Furious Baco (135 km/h).

Even though PortAventura is a park located south of Barcelona with an important residential market area in Catalonia, it also has a strategic tourism orientation and location. Indeed, PortAventura caters to tourists from the coastal region where it is located (the Costa Daurada) and tourists specifically motivated by the park mainly from Spain and from the most significant European markets. In fact, the park opened its gates in 1995 with the support of the local and regional public administration with the goal of improving the local tourism product (Anton Clavé 1997). Currently, it is part of an entertainment complex that includes under the PortAventura World ownership, two theme parks (PortAventura and Ferrari Land), one water park (Costa Caribe), one five-star hotel and five four-star hotels, as well as a conference centre, three golf courses and a beach club within the same planning area but under different ownership. In total, 55% of customers of the PortAventura World hotels were from abroad in 2019.

Because of the pandemic, during 2020 PortAventura began operations on 8 July and closed its doors on 16 October. The capacity of the park was initially restricted to 30%, and daily opening time was reduced. The water park did not open, nor did some of the hotels. All social contact regulations, including social distancing, were deployed, and park officials reported an investment of four million Euros to adapt the facilities to conform to the required health conditions (Europa Press 2020). As a result, PortAventura has seen a massive decline in visitors, and it is expected that it would suffer significant economic losses for the year 2020. In this sense, it might be informative that, according to data reported by the Costa Daurada Observatory, the coastal tourist area where PortAventura is located experienced for the nine first months of 2020 (including the peak summer season) a 68.97% decline in the number of tourist arrivals to regulated accommodation, which was 4,443,834 in 2019; a 71.14% decline in the number of nights in regulated accommodation, which was 17,854,254 in 2019; and a significant change in the mix of markets: international markets decreased 63.93%, while the Spanish market grew 66.55% from 2019 to 2020. Thus, decreasing the total number of tourists and transformed markets were two main features of the destination during the first year of the COVID-19 impact.

In the absence of other available data an analysis of Twitter social media activity related to PortAventura during the years 2019 and 2020 was performed to analyse market changes specifically related to this theme park during the time it was open in 2020 (mostly the third quarter of the year). Like other social media sources, Twitter has the capacity to contribute to tourism spatial analysis

(Mariani et al. 2018), particularly because it provides geolocated social media data that can be used as a valuable proxy for spatial behaviour and mobility patterns at different scales (Mirzaalian and Halpenny 2019). There are, however, drawbacks that arise when using geolocated social media data, the most important being user penetration, reliability of the obtained information and characteristics identification (Hecht et al. 2011). Still, these data make it possible to reach the objective of the proposed analysis.

For the current analysis, all the tweets made from the PortAventura theme park according to geolocalisation during the period from 8 July to 16 October of 2019 and 2020 were selected and analysed (859 tweets in 2019 and 233 in 2020). A fundamental issue was to identify the home location of people tweeting from PortAventura (either locals or tourists), in order to analyse their spatial behaviour during tourism activities. To this end a key procedure was to classify tweets depending on whether or not they were made during a tourist activity. In this chapter, a post made by a tourist is defined as one that is sent from a location other than the user's established home location. The home location of a user is where the user is not a tourist. These locations are established by making a count of the number of days a user tweets from a location. If the count exceeds 20 days, the user is no longer a tourist and the user location provided by the user in his or her profile is the home location. The pseudocode for this process is shown in Table 14.1.

Table 14.1 Pseudocode designed to identify tourist- and home-based tweets

---

Get tweets from database (T)
/ *'Twitter location of residence' is residence information provided by the Twitter user converted to geolocation using the Open Street Map API/*
Get user id (U) and Twitter location of residence (L).}
Set
//**Update the location of residence of each user to include other frequented locations**
for users in U **do:**
  Initialise an empty list of location of residence for user
Add Twitter location of residence
Get tweets of user from Twitter
Group tweets by their tweet location
if the count of days with tweets in a tweet location exceeds threshold **then:**
Add tweet location
end if
  // **Start classification**
  for tweet in **do:**
if tweet location is in **then:**
  Set tweet as *not tourist*
  else
Set tweet as *tourist*
  end if
end for
end for

Source: Authors

Table 14.2 summarises differences in profiles in terms of origin and behaviour of the Twitter users who uploaded posts from PortAventura in both 2019 and 2020. Taking into account the necessary precautions when analysing results (as Twitter users are not a representative sample of real demand at the park), they show first a relevant decrease in number of users (477 in 2019; 149 in 2020). Additionally, regarding changes in the market share, the proportion of Spanish users grew in 2020 (70.8% vs. 49.3% in the previous year), and England (which accounted for 7.5% of tweets in 2019 and 3.4% in 2020) disappeared from among the top three user regions of origin. Table 14.2 also highlights that the top three regions of origin of Twitter users in 2020 represent 57.5% of the total with a more than remarkable increase in the case of Catalonia (44.8% in 2020 compared with 26.2% in 2019). This is relevant as to the role of the park as a space for everyday entertainment. It is also worth noting, in the same sense, the increase in visits per user that occurred in 2020 compared with 2019 (18.1% of park attendees visited the park only one time in 2020 vs. 35.4% in 2020). This may indicate a pattern of everyday use of the park by Twitter users residing in nearby areas.

To obtain more detailed results regarding the role of PortAventura as an entertainment venue in the everyday lives of people living nearby during the pandemic, this study investigated the travel behaviour of Catalan users who tweeted from the park in both 2019 and 2020. To do so, the timeline of Twitter users was analysed in order to identify what other places they had visited the days before and after they visited PortAventura. Figure 14.1 displays the destinations from where Catalan visitors (the population living nearby the theme park) to the park tweeted during the seven days before and after their visit to the park in 2019 and 2020. Additionally, an exploratory spatial data analysis (ESDA) of the distribution of places from where users tweeted was performed.

ESDA is concerned with how spatial distributions tend to show a spatial order (spatial autocorrelation) (Fischer and Getis 2009). When there is a tendency for high-value and low-value spatial clusters to form, spatial autocorrelation is positive. When high values tend to be surrounded by low values, and vice versa, spatial autocorrelation is negative. Finally, random patterns indicate the absence of spatial autocorrelation. For this analysis, the Global Moran's I statistic is applied. It measures the degree of spatial autocorrelation of a set of geolocalised data and determines the sign of this autocorrelation. This statistic evaluates whether a spatial pattern tends to be clustered, dispersed or random. The obtained z-score and p-value indicate whether or not the null hypothesis can be rejected. The null hypothesis states that the observed spatial distribution is randomly distributed across the study area. When there is statistical significance and the null hypothesis can be rejected, a positive Moran's I index value indicates a tendency towards clustering, while a negative index indicates tendency towards dispersion. In this case, Euclidean distances between tweets were measured, and an inverse distance squared relationship among tweets was defined in order to prioritise the closest neighbours.

Table 14.2 Profile of users tweeting from PortAventura during the period 8 July to 16 October (2019 and 2020)

		2019		2020	
Origin [country] (%)					
	Spain	49.3	Spain	70.8	
	United Kingdom	8.8	United Kingdom	3.5	
	France	5.3	France	3.5	
Top three country origins (%)	63.9		77.3		
Origin [region] (%)					
	Catalonia	26.2	Catalonia	44.8	
	England	7.5	Madrid	6.3	
	Madrid	5.2	Valencia	6.3	
Top three region origins (%)	38.6		57.5		
Origin [city] (%)					
	Barcelona	*13.9*	*Barcelona*	*20.1*	
	Madrid	**2.8**	**Madrid**	**4.9**	
	Moscow	**2.1**	**Valencia**	**4.2**	
	Tarragona	1.6	**London**	**2.8**	
	Zaragoza	**1.4**	Tarragona	2.8	
Top five city origins (%)	21.8		34.8		
Top local area cities	1.6		2.8		
Other top Catalonian cities	*13.9*		*20.1*		
Other top Spanish cities	**4.2**		**9.1**		
Other top European cities	**2.1**		**2.8**		
Number of visits (%)					
1 day	35.4		18.8		
2–3 days	26.9		28.1		
4–5 days	7.3		12.5		
6–20 days	19.5		25.0		
>20 days	11.0		15.6		
Total users (N)	477		149		
Total tweets (N)	859		233		

Source: Authors

The results summarised in Table 14.3 indicate that there is a slight change from 2019 to 2020 towards a lower clustering of tweets made seven days before and after the visit to the park by Catalans – the visitors living closest to the theme park – tweeting from other Catalonian destinations. This is not observed with the same intensity in the case of tweets made by Catalans from other European and Spanish destinations. Hence, it might be understood that travel restrictions and changes in spatial travel behaviour due to COVID-19 restrictions

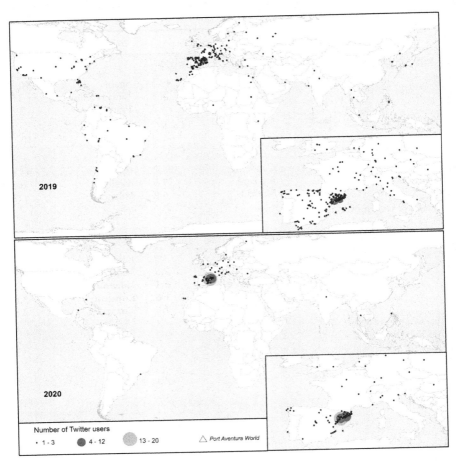

Figure 14.1 Places from where Catalan people in PortAventura tweeted during the seven days before and after their visit to the park

Source: Authors

transformed the travel decision-making of Catalans visiting PortAventura in 2020. More precisely, compared with 2019, Catalan visitors in 2020 tweeting from PortAventura exhibited a less clustered pattern of visits to other places in Catalonia during the seven days before and after their visit to the park. This might be interpreted in the sense that the park would not be visited if the contextual conditions were different and travel to alternative destinations was possible. Therefore, the data indicate that not only has the profile of visitors to the park changed, but also the tourist spatial behaviour of nearby people visiting the park is different under COVID-19 restrictions. In this case, the park has

Table 14.3 Spatial autocorrelation of tweets made by Catalan visitors from PortAventura during the seven days before and after their visit to the park (Global Moran's I statistics)

	p-value	z-score	Moran's I	Pattern	Number of tweets
Tweeting from other **European** destinations: **2019**	0.000019	4.271418	0.550398	Highly clustered★	88
Tweeting from other **European** destinations: **2020**	0.009283	2.601449	0.412761	Highly clustered★	63
Tweeting from other **Spanish** destinations: **2019**	0.000256	3.656647	0.473490	Highly clustered★	76
Tweeting from other **Spanish** destinations: **2020**	0.025249	2.237578	0.352395	Clustered★★	55
Tweeting from other **Catalonian** destinations: **2019**	0.010879	2.546564	0.335480	Clustered★★	51
Tweeting from other **Catalonian** destinations: **2020**	0.069885	1.812654	0.277594	Low clustering★★★	43

★ There is a less than 1% likelihood that this clustered pattern could be the result of random chance.
★★ There is a less than 5% likelihood that this clustered pattern could be the result of random chance.
★★★ There is a less than 10% likelihood that this clustered pattern could be the result of random chance.
Source: Authors

been able to provide new alternatives to Catalan visitors and to attract people to the area where it is located. Interestingly, in spite of the observed change, the resulting spatial pattern is still clustered. This might also indicate that tweeting from the park has been part of a non-random pattern of tweeting from other places and attractions among the Catalan population. This might indicate that a visit to the park in 2020 was integrated with complex decision-making among Catalan people, involving visiting other Catalan tourist attractions and places during the seven days before and after their PortAventura visit.

Conclusions

Travel and mobility restrictions together with new social distancing require-ments, capacity constraints and specific operational adjustments in rides and attractions have completely disrupted the business model of the tourism-oriented theme park industry, including destination parks, during the time they have had during 2020 to be open and operating. Obviously, the closing of theme parks has been a principal factor impacting the financial situations of operating firms. In the context of this transformed environment, this chapter introduced the impacts of COVID-19 on the theme parks' industry performance during 2020 using mostly documentary data and company reports, and it evaluated market changes and trends in the case of a tourism-oriented theme park, PortAventura, using social media data from Twitter. The goal has been to show how the downsized mobility regime and the long- and medium-haul travel restrictions have transformed the theme park experience from an extraordinary event to an everyday leisure practice perhaps linked to a new near-home travel trend. To what extent this type of practice will remain when the COVID-19 pandemic is over is unpredictable. Nevertheless, understanding it might be useful in terms of partially increasing tourism-oriented theme parks' resilience.

Although results are limited, sources are scarce, data from social media have limitations and the impact of COVID-19 has created an entirely new scenario, the designed tool has provided new evidence with which to better understand the implications of such a critical event and, thus, to anticipate and build better tools to handle the consequences. Regarding the potential role of a tourism-oriented theme park as an entertainment venue in the everyday lives of people living nearby, following Hannam and Zuev (2020), results suggest that attractions and destinations can provide an experience for visitors living nearby as if they were tourists in their own homes. In this sense, because they might become alternatives to other attractions, tourism-oriented theme parks may develop new attractive approaches that, grounded in the idea of "staycation" (Germann Molz 2009), welcome residents to a new tourism experience in their own place (the area where the park is located). In so doing, a new process might be integrated into ordinary travel decision-making that includes not only going "abroad", but also visiting "home" and going places near the site where the theme park is located.

References

Anton Clavé, Salvador. 1997. "The Port Aventura Theme Park and the Restructuring of Coastal Tourist Areas in Catalonia." *European Urban and Regional Studies* 4(3): 257–262, https://doi.org/10.1177/096977649700400305.

Anton Clavé, Salvador. 2007. *The Global Theme Park Industry*. Wallingford and Cambridge: CABI.

Anton Clavé, Salvador. 2022. "Industry: Global Trends, Players, and Networks in the Theme Park Industry." In *Key Concepts in Theme Park Studies: Understanding Tourism and Leisure Spaces*, edited by Salvador Anton Clavé, Filippo Carlà-Uhink and Florian Freitag. Cham: Springer, forthcoming.

CDC. 2020. *COVID-19 Considerations for Traveling Amusement Parks and Carnivals*. Centers for Disease Control and Prevention. www.cdc.gov/coronavirus/2019-ncov/community/parks-rec/amusement-park-carnival.html. Retrieved 15 December 2020.

ERA. 2002. *Big Fun 2003*. Los Angeles: Economics Research Associates.

Europa Press. 2020. "PortAventura alcanzó la cifra "récord" de 5,2 millones de visitas en 2019." www.europapress.es/catalunya/noticia-portaventura-world-alcanzo-cifra-record-52-millones-visitas-2019-20200702131646.html. Retrieved 1 November 2020.

Fischer, Manfred M. and Arthur Getis (eds.). 2009. *Handbook of Applied Spatial Analysis: Software Tools, Methods and Applications*. Cham: Springer.

Gabe, Todd. 2020. "Impacts of COVID-Related Capacity Constraints on Theme Park Attendance: Evidence from Magic Kingdom Wait Times." *Applied Economics Letters*, https://doi.org/10.1080/13504851.2020.1804047.

Gallego, Inmaculada and Xavier Font. 2020. "Changes in Air Passenger Demand as a Result of the COVID-19 Crisis: Using Big Data to Inform Tourism Policy." *Journal of Sustainable Tourism*, https://doi.org/10.1080/09669582.2020.1773476.

Germann Molz, Jennie. 2009. "Representing Pace in Tourism Mobilities: Staycations, Slow Travel and the Amazing Race." *Journal of Tourism and Cultural Change* 7(4): 270–286, https://doi.org/10.1080/14766820903464242.

Gössling, Stefan, Daniel Scott and C. Michael Hall. 2020. "Pandemics, Tourism and Global Change: A Rapid Assessment of COVID-19." *Journal of Sustainable Tourism*, https://doi.org/10.1080/09669582.2020.1758708.

Hannam, Kevin and Dennis Zuev. 2020. "Revisiting the Local in Macau Under COVID-19." *Atlas Review* 2: 19–22.

Hecht, Brent, Lichan Hong, Bongwon Suh and Ed H. Chi. 2011. "Tweets from Justin Bieber's Heart: The Dynamics of the Location Field in User Profiles." Proceedings of the SIGCHI Conference on Human Factors in Computing Systems, Vancouver, pp. 237–246, https://doi.org/10.1145/1978942.1978976.

IAAPA. 2019. *IAAPA Global Theme and Amusement Park Outlook 2019–2023*. Orlando: International Attractions and Amusement Parks Association.

IAAPA. 2020a. *IAAPA Member Survey on the effect of COVID-19*. Orlando: International Attractions and Amusement Parks Association. www.iaapa.org/research-resources/research/iaapa-member-survey-effect-covid-19. Retrieved 28 November 2020.

IAAPA. 2020b. *IAAPA Reopening guidance: Global Attractions Industry*. Orlando: International Attractions and Amusement Parks Association. www.iaapa.org/reopening-guidance-considerations-attractions-industry. Retrieved 24 October 2020.

Leask, Anna. 2008. "The Nature and Role of Visitor Attractions." In *Managing Visitor Attractions*, edited by Alan Fyall, Brian Garrod, Anna Leask and Stephen Wanhill. Oxford: Butterworth-Heinemann, pp. 3–15.

Lee, Chien-Chiang and Mei-Ping Chen. 2020. "The Impact of COVID-19 on the Travel and Leisure Industry Returns: Some International Evidence." *Tourism Economics*, https://doi.org/10.1177/1354816620971981.

Mariani, Marcello, Rodolfo Baggio, Matthias Fuchs and Wolfram Höpken. 2018. "Business Intelligence and Big Data in Hospitality and Tourism: A Systematic Literature Review." *International Journal of Contemporary Hospitality Management* 30(12): 3514–3554, https://doi.org/10.1108/IJCHM-07-2017-0461.

Masters, Brooke. 2020. "Covid Sends Rollercoasters on a Big Plunge." *Financial Times*, 7 October. www.ft.com/content/b7e4f300-9a50-4cd1-9bcc-1856e16cf2df. Retrieved 24 December 2020.

McKinsey and Company. 2020. "Global Surveys of Consumer Sentiment During the Coronavirus Crisis." www.mckinsey.com/business-functions/marketing-and-sales/our-insights/global-surveys-of-consumer-sentiment-during-the-coronavirus-crisis. Retrieved 20 October 2020.

Mirzaalian, Farshid and Elizabeth Halpenny. 2019. "Social Media Analytics in Hospitality and Tourism: A Systematic Literature Review and Future Trends." *Journal of Hospitality and Tourism Technology* 10(4): 764–790, https://doi.org/10.1108/JHTT-08-2018-0078.

Niewiadomski, Piotr. 2020. "COVID-19: From Temporary Deglobalisation to a Re-Discovery of Tourism?" *Tourism Geographies* 22(3): 651–656, https://doi.org/10.1080/14 616688.2020.1757749.

The Park Database. 2020. "The Business of Theme Parks (Part I): How Much Money Do They Make?" www.theparkdb.com/blog/the-business-of-theme-parks-part-i-how-much-money-do-they-make/. Retrieved 28 January 2020.

Ritzer, George. 1993. *The McDonaldization of Society*. Thousand Oaks: Pine Forge Press.

Ritzer, George. 1999. *Enchanting a Disenchanted World: Revolutionizing the Means of Consumption*. Thousand Oaks: Pine Forge Press.

Saadat, Saeida, Deepak Rawtani and Chaudhery Mustansar Hussain. 2020. "Environmental Perspective of COVID-19." *Science of the Total Environment* 728, https://doi.org/10.1016/j. scitotenv.2020.138870.

Schmid, Heiko. 2009. *Economy of Fascination: Dubai and Las Vegas as Themed Urban Landscapes*. Berlin: Gebrüder Borntraeger.

Sivan, Atara. 2020. "Reflection on Leisure During COVID-19." *World Leisure Journal* 62(4): 296–299, https://doi.org/10.1080/16078055.2020.1825260.

Six Flags Entertainment Corporation. 2020. "Quarterly Report for the Quarterly Period Ended 30 September." https://otp.tools.investis.com/clients/us/sixflags1/SEC/sec-outline.aspx?FilingId=14464597&Cik=0000701374&PaperOnly=0&HasOriginal=1. Retrieved 28 December 2020.

Sylt, Christian. 2020. "The Financial Formula for Reopening Theme Parks." *Forbes*, 2 May. www.forbes.com/sites/csylt/2020/05/02/the-financial-formula-for-reopening-theme-parks/?sh=f8fca584cd8f. Retrieved 28 June 2020.

TEA/AECOM. 2020. *Theme Index and Museum Index 2019: The Global Attractions Attendance Report*. Burbank: Themed Entertainment Association.

The Walt Disney Company. 2020. "The Walt Disney Company Reports: Fourth Quarter and Full Year Earnings for Fiscal 2020." https://thewaltdisneycompany.com/the-walt-disney-company-reports-fourth-quarter-and-full-year-earnings-for-fiscal-2020/. Retrieved 28 December 2020.

Wanhill, Stephen. 2008. "Economic Aspects of Developing Theme Parks." In *Managing Visitor Attractions*, edited by Alan Fyall, Brian Garrod, Anna Leask and Stephen Wanhill. Oxford: Butterworth-Heinemann, pp. 59–79.

Yilmazkuday, Hakan. 2020. "Stay-At-Home Works to Fight Against COVID-19: International Evidence from Google Mobility Data." *Journal of Human Behavior in the Social Environment*, https://doi.org/10.1080/10911359.2020.1845903.

Younger, David. 2016. *Theme Park Design and the Art of Themed Entertainment*. London: Inklingwood.

Acknowledgements

This research was financially supported by the Spanish Ministry of Science, Innovation and Universities [POLITUR/CSO2017–82156-R], the AEI/FEDER, UE, the Department of Research and Universities of the Catalan Government [GRATET-2017SGR22] and the Catalan Agency for Business Competitiveness through the funding grant ACCIÓ-Eurecat.

Figure 14.1 was created using ArcGIS® software by Esri. ArcGIS® and Arc-Map™ are the intellectual property of Esri and are used herein under licence.

15 Tourist wastelands

A "cold" time opening up possibilities of territorial redefinition

Philippe Bachimon

Introduction

Tourism wastelands are frequent components of the touristic landscape. This chapter will document them on the most frequented French Polynesian islands, specifically, Tahiti, Huahine, Moorea and Bora Bora. Firstly, tourism wastelands will be categorised by their degree of abandonment and the length of time they have been in existence. Secondly, we will explain the mechanisms that lead to the creation of a stock of tourism wasteland, which in the present-day COVID-19 situation continues to expand.

Even though in a humid environment, tropical vegetation re-growth occurs quite quickly, any attentive observer would notice that tourism wastelands block public access to important parts of the islands. This results in inaccessibility to the seaside and in social impacts which transcend the tourism sector. Both public opinion and scientists agree that this is linked to land possession issues, as in Melanesia for example, where land is linked to customary laws. This chapter, without minimising the land possession aspect, will go further into the analysis and will examine the impact of wastelands on tourists, on investors who sometimes covet them and on the locals who live next to them or are squatting in them.

The spread of tourism wastelands

A tourism wasteland is a space seized, ultimately, by tourist activity, totally or partially abandoned for a short or long period of time, without substantial demolition of the built infrastructures and without formal reconversion to new economic activity (Soja 1996; Chaline 1999). It ranges from limited abandonment to seasonal, multi-annual or even permanent desertion. The size and duration of the wastelands' desertion can be used as an indicator of the economic and structural difficulties of adaptation of the tourist facilities. The most important wastelands, in terms of duration and size, will therefore be considered as indicators of low reactivity or even as a failure to adapt. However, they are also a sign of local reappropriation of the land, both literally and figuratively. In a way, a state of ambivalence (Vannier 2003; Clément 2004), or a third space (Soja 1996).

DOI: 10.4324/9781003138600-18

Table 15.1 includes only the tourist accommodation without scheduled reopening dates, except for three (in boldfaced).

Tourist wastelands in the four main touristic islands

The island of Tahiti is where the tourist wastelands first appeared, and where they often last the longest. Together with the abandoned site of *Matavai Hotel (Holiday Inn)* in Tipaerui neighbourhood, located to the east of Papeete, the main town, *Bel Air Hotel* in Punaauia municipality was until 2014 the oldest tourism wasteland in French Polynesia. Due to its state of ruin, the *Bel Air Hotel*, built by the beach between the *Maeva Beach Sofitel* (closed in 2012) and *Beachcomber Hotels* (two of the three biggest hotels on the island), was considered an eyesore. In downtown Papeete, *Prince Hinoï* (1984–2007) located on Vaiete Square, is also abandoned. And so is the mythical *Royal Papeete* built in 1930 and closed in 2009, facing the ferry-boat dock. There are plans to build a parking lot in its place. Ten km further east, there is the *Tahaara Hotel (Hyatt Regency Tahiti)*, a beautiful construction located on a rocky spur overlooking the sea and surrounded by eight hectares of landscaped garden. Closed in 1998, it is now deteriorating (with a leaking ceiling) while the *Beach Club* has also been closed since 2009.

There are other, less spectacular examples, related to once prized tourist attractions which are close to becoming wastelands. In Papearii, the Botanical Garden and the Gauguin Museum[1] are a mere shadow of their former selves. The garden is partly abandoned: the wooden pontoon enabling the access to the *mape* (chestnut) forest is dangerous, invaded by termites, and the orchid greenhouse is destroyed. Only the lawns continue to be taken care of. The stray dogs attack scandals in 2009 and 2018, that ended by killing one of the two Galapagos giant tortoises housed at the Botanical Garden, indicates that security service was no longer provided, and even less since the site has been closed in 2013. A site renovation project was adopted in 2019 for work that should begin in 2021.

Huahine, another island of the Society Islands, is a site where the phenomenon of tourism wasteland has been most visible during the past decades. Out of six hotels active in the late 1990s, only the *Te Tiare Beach Resort* (opened in 1999 and renovated in 2003) is still operating. The five others have all closed down, even though at the airport, tourists can still locate them on a big rosewood *(miro)* sculpted map of the island. *Bellevue Hotel* (linked to PEC – Pacific Experimentation Center) and especially the Bali Hai (1973–1998/2001) in the port of Fare (where tourist activity never really recovered after the violent cyclones in 1983) are among the oldest wastelands. The *Hana Iti* and the *Huahine Beach Club*, in Parea, closed in 1998 after the passage of a violent tropical depression. The *Sofitel Heiva* in Maeva closed in 2005. The story of the *Hana Iti Hotel* deserves to be mentioned. This original and luxurious hotel, built by the co-founder of Microsoft, Paul Allen, was the symbol of successful integration into the natural habitat. The wasteland resulted in a revealing exhibition of illegitimate appropriations. First of all, the looting of utensils (especially sanitary ones), the theft of installations (frames, doors, roofs, etc.) leaves only concrete slabs rotting in the ambient humidity of the undergrowth. The property was bought by the Polynesian government and for a while was occupied by the PIG.[2] At present, only the *mutoi* (local policeman), who is still paid by the Polynesian government, lives there. To increase his income, the "guard" plays the role of a *Robinson*. Thus, he offers tourist services: visits of the *Hana Iti* wreckage, preparation of the *maa'a tahiti* (typical cooking) with Tahitian oven and fruit picking. He also makes and sells flower and shell necklaces and drives off mosquitoes and *nonos*[3] from the beach to welcome boat passengers coming from Bora Bora to discover this heavenly environment. Moreover, the guard owns the adjoining land where the access track to the *Hana Iti* wreckage is located, and hence bans automobile circulation. As a result, the area has become a quite well-preserved isolate.

At Moorea, the *Club Med Resort* (1963–2005), the *Moorea Village* (also called *Fare Gendron*) and the *Cook's Bay Hotel*, all historic French Polynesian hotels and resorts, have been closed, and now, with the pandemic, the definitive closure of the *Intercontinental* in 2020, the most important resort on the island. All facilities closed without being demolished; looting is thus common on these wastelands, and a fire broke out in *Club Med*, destroying parts of it. Indisputably this reality has a high impact on the landscape of Moorea, the most touristic island of French Polynesia. These impressive-in-size tourism wastelands are located on the "seaward side" ring-road. Their considerable size in the tourist zone became the main obstacle in maintaining tourism activity. Here, too, reappropriation operates. Owners squat bungalows left on their piece of land and cruise passengers come alongside the pontoon of *Cook's Bay Hotel* where a Tahitian dance show and a tourist market are held. This hotel wasteland, according to the systematic census we conducted between 2009 and 2018, leads to further abandonment. Thus, about 20% of the additional businesses outside of accommodation (catering, pearl and souvenir sales) were closed. Some "almost wastelands", like the *Tiki Village* in Haapiti (Moorea island), were damaged and partly squatted by their service providers. They were even visited as such, in a kind of hyper-realistic presentation, offering an inversed vision of the traditional decor usually shown to visitors.

The island of Bora Bora is the third most popular tourist destination in French Polynesia, after Tahiti and Moorea. It is the one that receives the high-income international tourists (often as a honeymoon destination) in luxury hotels, thus multiplying the pontoons of *fare* ("traditional" bungalows) constructed on the lagoon. On the highest part of the island, one by one, hotels closed, while some never opened after being built (e.g. the *Hyatt Hotel*). Thus, legendary hotels such as *Bora Bora* (closed in 2010 after 40 years of activity) or the *Club Med* (closed in 2007) ceased to exist. But even on islets (*motu* in Tahitian language), where upscale resorts were recently built (*Sofitel, St-Regis, Four Seasons*), some are already closed. This is the case for the Lagoon resort, closed since 2010. Paradoxically, Bora Bora is the island that has benefited the most from the tax exemption to ensure the rise in quality of its hotel park, and this without taking into account the existing ones. In the end, this island is in itself a series of abandonments, especially towards the emblematic Matira Point where there are only two hotels and a few bungalows rented to residents. Only six guesthouses remain open, and they work more with the clientele of long-stay employees than with affinity tourism.

Polymorphism of the "stock"

The preceding inventory reveals the great vulnerability of French Polynesia to tourism wastelands. When this phenomenon appears – sometimes insidiously – and lasts, it reflects and amplifies the high instability of a tourist system extremely scattered with small size components. Hence the importance of accurately measuring the tourist wasteland's magnitude and identifying its various forms. As the tourist wasteland is paradoxically the most stable state of being of the tourism sector.

To assess the phenomenon of accommodation abandonment, it is necessary to first consider it as an "inactive stock", which grows with every new hotel closure. On the other hand, openings (of hotels or other leisure activities) rarely take advantage of the land and property resources represented by this "inactive stock", as new establishments are often constructed on new locations rather than reusing the old ones (Table 15.1). Thus, the particularity of French Polynesia seems to lie in its very weak aptitude to revitalise wastelands, as we will see ahead, especially if it consists in maintaining the tourist or leisure activity in these sites. This may seem paradoxical in view of the often-exceptional locations of the concerned wastelands.

The following graphic model (Figure 15.1) gives us a representation of processes in action. The "inactive stock" is strongly fuelled by hotel closures, whereas it is insignificantly influenced by the few reopenings. As a result, there are increases around what we must call its core (Table 15.1), that is to say the oldest wastelands *(Bel Air, Holiday Inn, Hyatt)* which tend to become static in their decay as they age. However, because the closure date is vague – partial activity, reopenings followed by closures, all this is quite confusing even for the best archivists. Thus, the signage of a hotel can remain for decades after the establishment has been completely closed.[4] If the core of the "inactive stock" seems well consolidated, its peripheries are blurred. If we go back to the *Novotel Hotel* example in Bora Bora, at the beginning of 2011, it was presumably still open. However, the few clients who have spent their holidays there reported its decay on the internet: the hotel's signage disappeared, and the site was occupied by the staff and their relatives *(fetii* in Tahitian), becoming a shadow of its former self, before it finally closed in 2013. This little known "inactive stock" consists of a spatially discontinuous group, presenting only some important concentration in Haapiti district on the Moorea Island and in the city of Papeete on Tahiti Island. Fallen in denial for commercial "reasons"[5] in its transitional stage, the inactive stock is *de facto* disparate (resorts, villages, pension

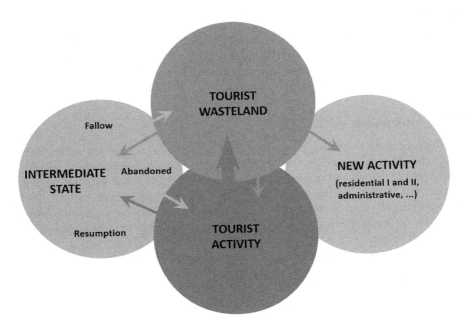

Figure 15.1 Tourist wasteland

hotels, small hotel businesses, restaurants, curios), making it hardly identifiable as such. Yet it is the lack of awareness of the whole phenomenon that we will examine.

We shall describe the dynamics of the wasteland which always start with insidious micro-evolutions that can lead to the sterilisation of sites for years – the most ancient wastelands actually disappear in "secondary" forests.

The first visible aspects of abandonment come after a significant drop in maintenance (the weekly mowing of the lawns is no longer being done, the surface of the buildings is chipping, the *fare*'s *niau* roofs (palm thatch) are leaking, piles of plants rot under old tires and mosquitoes are nesting in pools of standing water, etc.). Within a few months, the first "irreparable" deteriorations of the building start to appear. The leaking roofs are, at best, "waterproof" sheeted, and the invasion of wild and luxuriant plants starts (such as the shrubby and thorny Sensitives and Lantanas plants, which can grow up to 1 m high, or the woody plants like Guavas, Falcatas and Miconias).[6] The impenetrable jumble evolves into a dense forest and the air gets even more humid. Ambient humidity accelerates the processes. In particular, it undermines the enclosure of the plots by the rusting of the fences and the rotting of the posts. The beach is recolonised by the *Purau*[7] and gets infected with *nonos*. And when the beach is artificial, it is eroded by heavy swells and storms.

Table 15.1 Example of Net stock of tourism wastelands in French Polynesia

Name	Closing date	Island	Upcoming changes	Name	Closing date	Island	Upcoming changes
Bel air	1980	Tahiti	Demolition 2014	Club Med Anau	2004	Moorea	wasteland
Holiday Inn	1988	Tahiti	studios	Fare Nana'o	2004	Tahiti	wasteland
Hyatt	1990	Bora Bora	wasteland	Moorea Village	2005	Moorea	wasteland
Club Med Nunue	1991	Bora Bora	wasteland	Prince Hinoi	2007	Tahiti	wasteland
Cook's Bay	1993	Moorea	restoration project since 2019	Hilton	2008	Tahiti	closed
Hana Iti	1994	Huahine	wasteland	Hotel Bora Bora	2008	Bora Bora	Royal Bora 2017
Tetiaroa	1998	Tahiti	**Brando 2014**	Club Med Anau	2009	Bora Bora	closed
Bali Hai	1998	Huahine	wasteland	Bellevue	2009	Huahine	closed
Huahine Beach Club	1998	Huahine	**new hotel**	Bora Bora Lagoon Resort	2010	Bora	closed
Tahaara (Hyatt)	1998	Tahiti	wasteland	Relais de la Maroto	2010	Tahiti	restaurant park 2017
Huahine Village	2000	Huahine	**Maitai Lapita**	Maeva Beach	2012	Tahiti	closed
Shogun	2000	Tahiti	wasteland	Sofitel	2012	Bora Bora	closed
Royal Papeete	2000	Tahiti	wasteland	Meridien Ia Ora Beach Resort	2020	Bora Bora	closed
Matavai	2003	Tahiti	apartment-hotel	Intercontinental	2020	Moorea	closed
Sofitel Heiva	2003	Huahine	new hotel project				

Note: This table includes only the tourist accommodation without scheduled reopening dates, except for three (in boldfaced)

As a result, irregular activities can appear in this re-naturalised deserted area, ranging from short-cuts that go to the beach, to the reappropriations by squatters, to numerous activities (culture of *Paka* [cannabis], rave parties, depredation of ruins). The large lobby of the *Club* in Moorea was used as a skateboard track while the one of *Hana Iti* housed a PIG base. This stage of depredation being characterised by incivilities (graffiti, illicit trade, fires) and trespassing, some owners employ a security guard or sell what can be sold (bungalows to be disassembled, bathrooms, ornamental plants).[8] From 2005 to 2007 it was possible to buy the wooden frameworks of the *Club's* bungalows. This is still possible for those of the *Fare Gendron* or the *Bora Bora Hotel*. At the end of this stage only the concrete stabs of bungalows' septic holes are still visible, reflecting the existence at one point of tourism infrastructure, scattered in a dark and inextricable undergrowth.

The spillover effect of the tourist wasteland on the social, economic and cultural environment eventually completes the process of neglect. Near *Club Med*, the first and liveliest commercial centre on the Moorea Island was built: there were ten restaurants, medical offices, service providers (car rental, gas) and tourist shops (pearl sales, *curios* souvenir shops). Twelve years after the resort's closure, the commercial centre is still active, although more than half of the shops are closed. It is worth remembering that *Club Med* was the biggest employer on Moorea Island, with about 170 employees, without counting indirect beneficiaries (fisher purveyors, farmers, etc.). All lost either their job or an important part of their incomes and some of them had to leave the island and abandon their houses.

To this "fatal" spiral we should add elements of resumption which are perturbing and complexifying the phenomenon. French Polynesia hotels are characterised by their enclosure, by a fence which bans access to the site from the mountain side while the seaside remains largely open to the beach so that it can be easily reached by hotel customers. After closing their site, in order to preserve their installations, hotels extended their enclosure also on the seaside. This often takes place while a series of short-lived reopening projects are launched on the site. The "recycling" process occurs in this fluctuating setting as these barriers are seldom impenetrable. It may result in dismantled, stored and resold equipment (e.g. sanitary appliances and fare from the Bora Bora hotel) until there is nothing left. It may also result, for some owners, in clearing of brushwood to keep the place tidy. On weekends, other owners would squat in patched-up bungalows with no running water or electricity connections. They would then set up rainwater tanks and generators. This leads to a landscape of glades (manicured lawns around bungalows in a rather good state) encircled by undergrowth and forests.

These mechanisms of reappropriation, which *in situ* are considered "legal" as they are the result of the actions of "owners" and their families, are not made without typical abuses. Thus, if the residence becomes permanent, while in a touristic area, the main encroachment noticed is towards the sea. We observed that on the *Club Med's* wasteland, the "pushing the fence towards the beach" attitude had become widespread. An owner who had been able to gain 12 m over the supposedly public beach told us he did that because he considered that his propriety "extends up to the coconut trees". However, the annexed back-shore was an embankment, sheltered by a *Patu* (groyne). Through this example we can identify an important function of the wasteland. Away from prying eyes, illegal activities lead to "faits accomplis", "facts" that someone hopes to make indisputable as the memory of a former reality fades away.

The abandonment that leads to re-naturalisation and then to uncertain reap-propriations, sometimes resulting in new wastelands, is spreading. It is a phe-nomenon that can be analysed both as an indicator of a serious crisis of the tourism activity, unable to survive in the most beautiful natural sites, and as a catalyst of this crisis. Thus, the wasteland can be analysed through a territorial diagnosis (Dérioz 2008).

Questioning a tourism-based economy

If we compare the "inactive" stock (the tourist wasteland) and the "active" stock of establishments still in activity, we find that the former with 1,500 closed units (beds taken out of the market), compared with 3,000 opened units for the latter, has considerable weight. Indeed, the "inactive" stock is well sup-ported by closures that regularly affect the "active" stock. The average time of staying open has come down to 15 years, whereas we know that investments in tourism are made based on a 20-year return on investment calculation. On the other hand, the average length of closure has risen to nine years. French Polynesia tourist wastelands can no longer be linked to an adjustment variable, that is to say a short period of time passing between two successive activities in the same place. In the medium and the long term, the wasteland's expansion shows that it is not considered to be a land reserve nor a real estate opportunity. Actually, it is just the opposite. The tourist wasteland seems to stop any plans of new tourism investments. This latter specificity must be explained, as tour-ism wastelands have become a lasting and renewable phenomenon in French Polynesia. Although this is based on the specific problems of wastelands, as are the squats on the land by their owners, the illegal occupation in the name of the customary law of the first occupant . . . and sometimes even by the guardian appointed by the owners to avoid this last avatar. Nevertheless, we must remember that in French Polynesia, tourism investors do exist – as the numerous projects put forward indicate – and the financial sources, boosted by tax exemption, are there too. Therefore, the observed blocking mechanism deserves to be particularly well deciphered.

Let us go back to the *Club Med* example, on Moorea Island. The resort was set up in 1963 in the Haapiti Village (Northern Moorea) on 37 hectares of land bordered by a beach of 300 m in length facing a *motu*. There are about 30 bungalows built with local materials (pandanus roofs and coconut tree trunk foundations). In the 1970s the number of bungalows doubled. Unlike other companies, especially in Huahine Island, the *Club Med Resort* did use the climatic disaster argument to close the site. In 1983, after the passage of cyclone Veena, the *Club* rebuilt its bungalows to anticyclonic standards, and in 1987, after the passage of a strong swell that damaged a part of the lobby, a *Patu* (stone wave breaker) was placed as protection. From 1866 to 1918, Ferdinand Pater was the property's legal owner. After his death, the property was owned jointly. In 1978, this enabled *Club Med* to sign a 33-year but conditionally permanent lease (falling due in 2011) that could be renewed once. For the 29 owners of the property (in the 2000s), the extension of the lease is more problematic than the issue of getting out of the joint *possession* agreement.

Club Med's closure in Moorea is generally explained as the result of family conflict which would have occurred between the owners during the renewal of the lease. In 2002, the *Club* offered Pater's heirs a chance to renew the lease ten years before its expiry as the resort intended to make major renovations (about five billion CFP Francs, the equivalent of 40 million Euros).[9] During negotiations *Club Med* offered to increase the rent from 72 to 660 CFP Francs (from one to five Euros) per square meter. In addition, it also offered fringe benefits like giving hiring priority to the owners' family members for positions such as waiters, bartenders or service agents. Thus, the owner of a 5,000 m² property (this is the mean size of land ownership in Moorea) would have an annual rent increase from 360,000 to more than three million CFP Francs (from 2,800 to 24,000 Euros). Some families refused this offer, saying that they wanted their land back for their personal leisure use – the only way the land can be used in a touristic zone. This decision concerned families living in Tahiti and looking for a weekend destination. This attitude led to a break between, on the one hand, the low-income owners for whom the land rent is a major part of their revenues, and on the other hand, the high-income owners, public servants living in Papeete, for whom the lease increase is at most an income supplement that cannot completely justify a long-term immobilisation of their property. The argument of the Polynesian government's priority to maintain and develop tourism activities was for the latter a minor or unsubstantiated claim.

Club Med stopped negotiating in 2003, arguing that a higher rent would have a negative impact on the business profitability. After 40 years of activity, the Moorea resort closed in 2005, becoming the largest tourism wasteland in French Polynesia. However, it is not a "complete" wasteland as other sites described earlier, being still partly used by the owners themselves (20% *fare* out of 70). For lack of any official strictly legal plan, the owners made a *de facto* division. This very common practice of "legal or claimed owners squatting on the property"[10] takes precedence over the site's "tourist vocation". Consequently, the squat comes down to a substitution of the international tourism-oriented purpose with a more and more permanent residential occupation, even though there is neither running water nor electricity on the site. Despite this precariousness, opposition to any resumption is increasing as time passes by.

In the public sphere, tourism wasteland is a taboo subject. The bigger the tourist wasteland gets, the more invisible it becomes (the neighbourhood ignores it, and tourists take it for a natural setting). Memory of the site fades away, and shut-down hotels can become difficult to spot. That is the case for the *Hyatt Hotel* on Bora Bora Island (never really completed). The neighbours themselves forgot about the hotel's existence. Yet they live in *fare* identical to those of the *Hyatt's* (are they using them for themselves and thus deny their existence?). Occasional informants (sometimes the security guards) make up apocryphal contradictory stories, rendering the wasteland invisible. This "out of sight" state is quite at the opposite of the exposure that characterises wastelands in their beginnings, when their recovery projects flourish and make the headlines in the local press, even though these projects have no reason to succeed and are perhaps simply a *Freudian slip*. This buzz punctuated *Club Med's* long-agonising story. It actually started with putting the *Club Med* project forward, in case the lease was renewed. The project consisted of building a five-star village with 220 rooms and 30 bungalows on the water. The opening was intended for the end of 2003, and the investment would have been about 50 million Euros (15 million Euros in reality, after tax exemption).

As the project of the new *Club Med* failed, other projects emerged, about four or five, among which the *Daleo* was the most mediatised. The *Daleo* was a Fulton Group's project (2007–2009) aiming to replace the existing one with a brand new resort, more luxurious but with fewer bungalows (about 60 rooms in the same building) and without any *fare*, except a restaurant.[11] *Daleo* offered either an annual lease of 1,200 FCP Francs (10 Euros) per square meter or to buy the property for 25,000 FCP Francs (200 Euros) per square meter, the equivalent of about 3.8 billion FCP Francs (30 million Euros) investment. It also offered to pay *Club Med's* remaining lease, about 45 million FCP Francs (360,000 Euros). An overwhelming majority of owners agreed on the lease conditions. However, five owners refused the offer, saying that they want their land back, about one hectare out of a total of 15. Since the *Daleo* project was abandoned, the number of new project suggestions decreased in the midst of an unfavourable economic context (stagnation of visitor numbers after the 2008 economic crisis).

Beyond appearances, there is no consensus on tourism

If we highlight the lack of a vision of common interest by the owners refusing new tourist projects and we associate this attitude with the chronic political instability, which means that ministers change repeatedly and thus avoid making coercive decisions, then a new factor must be incorporated into the analysis. One should take into account that tourism is far from being perceived as a blessing, a windfall without perverse side effects, by a large part of the population. Some landowners are no longer country people making their living out of the land rent, but city dwellers (public servants) looking for leisure activities. A property with a good location, by the beach, can hold a high consumerist value, and thus be much more important for personal use, than from a land income perspective. Tax exemption also changed attitudes. Investment is made at the level of one-third of a project's real value. Therefore, the project's "partners" (landowners, banks, hotel chains) became greedier. *A priori*, the investor loses important expected capital gains and has to cut down on profit margin by reallocating the benefit from its low risk-taking, and that, from the earliest stages of the contract negotiations (Reboud et al. 2007). This is the adverse effect of the policy, and it destabilises the whole tourism sector. Consequently, the tenure status of land devoted to tourism is less important than the gap between the investor's short-term tax advantage (recovery of the investment five years after the project's implementation) and the long-term lease (the owner will get back his or her property in about 50 years).

Is tourism in French Polynesia an end in itself? No debates were held at a local level on whether French Polynesia wants tourism development or not, except perhaps on the Maupiti island, where a referendum on the opening of a new hotel was held in 2005. The inhabitants voted against the local government's decision to accept this project. The main reason was that the new establishment, of grand scale, would be competing with the existing local pension hotels. The lack of consideration of the local opinion is reminiscent of the archipelago's past as a French colony. No referendum was made either for the decision to build the PEC or for the current status of the community in French Polynesia between autonomy and independence. However, the most astonishing thing to note is, through quantitative and qualitative data, how insignificant the locals' contribution to the development of the tourism sector in French Polynesia is.

Tourism is presented as a way of obtaining economic freedom, a wealth coming from the outside, a benefit that has to be appropriated according to the cargo cult practices, in Micronesian societies (Worsley 1957). In practice, things are quite different because as international tourism arrivals increase at the global level, they decreased in French Polynesia, starting in 2000. One of the most interlocking aspects of this reality is the patronage and nepotism behaviours that characterise tourism activity in the archipelago. Thus, regardless of the political context, the tax exemption decision – the main tool for public assistance – has had the exact opposite to the expected effect: it slowed down tourism activity rather than developing it. Under the four presidencies of Gaston Flosse (1991–2014) and the current presidency of Edouard Fritch (2014–present), policies favoured large-scale international chain hotel projects (*Wane, Hilton, Accor, Sheraton*) to the detriment of smaller local initiatives and the restoration of existing establishments (Reboud et al. 2007). In compensation, under the seven separatist presidencies of Oscar Temaru (2004–2013), financial aid was mainly directed to local pension hotels (paying for labelling process, buying *fare*, solar panels and windmills at cost prices or sometimes even getting them for free). In some cases, the owners opened their establishments for tourists for only short periods of time or even worse, they never opened them at all. During the "good times" of tourist activity in the archipelago, the two types of accommodation coexisted peacefully, the pension hotels targeting the locals and the luxury chain hotels targeting the international tourists. However, when tourist arrivals lowered, both looked for solutions to avoid bankruptcy. The chain hotels lowered their prices (especially on Moorea Island, very close to Papeete), targeting high-income local tourists. The pension hotels used the same strategy and were communicating their offers in "National Tourism Fairs", with the support of Air Tahiti, the public airline company that monopolises transportation to and from the Society Islands (Du Prel 2003). This resulted in considerable tension between the two types of accommodation and a weakened profitability of the whole. Pension hotels may have seemed more resistant than chain hotels in this kind of strategy (fewer employees, lower fixed costs) provided that the family-owned business is professionalised. But this is not always the case, and discouragement (the famous *fiu*) pushes owners to slow down the activity (minimum maintenance of the accommodation, restricted opening times, carelessness). This ends in a partial abandonment of small structures, temporary or permanent. It then becomes understandable how the tourist wasteland phenomenon is spreading, from the resort to the pension hotel, and affecting the whole sub-contractual end of tourist services.

A conflict will definitely emerge from the contradiction between the official public discourse – unanimously in favour of tourism development – and the private discourse – accompanied by a practice closer to *fetii*'s (relatives) and some voters' expectations. If not, perhaps this ignoring the increasing tourism wasteland will drag on, especially when the "rational" speech is held in French and the "cultural" one, in *reo maohi* (Saura 2008, 2020). In the end, bilingualism could help in the perpetuation of the conflict between the local and the global, with tourism wasteland being its recurrent spatial expression. It is worth noting that the few reopenings that occurred were due to second homes projects. We mentioned the *Huahine Beach Club*, closed in 1998 and replaced by newly built houses in Parea. While the *Bali Hai* in Moorea, the *Manava* and the *Radisson* in Tahiti were converted into apartment hotels. Finally, most of today's projects that do not succeed (or have not yet!) are in the field of housing for seniors. As if second home projects are receiving a broader approval than tourism projects.

Conclusion: tourist wastelands' just apparent paradoxes

Tourism wastelands are far from being apprehended locally in all their extent and even less in their diversity. While the wasteland is visible, no retrospective or introspective analysis is made. Moreover, the tourism wasteland is not called by its name, as Polynesians talk about "abandoned places", and that happens only when a reopening project is considered. The wasteland is visible when the time comes to consider a new project, often not carried out or not feasible, like an umpteenth remake of the cargo cult (Worsley 1957), while all indicators (impact on landscapes and leisure activities, echo on the peripheral tourism activity) show how widespread and concrete its consequences are. This is often explained by joint ownership of the land, "the French Polynesia scourge". Numerous resorts (*Club Med, Bel Air, Méridien*, etc.) appear to be its victims. However, this detail is simply a way of confirming bad management strategies, as hotels not facing land joint ownership problems are also closed (*Cook, Tahaara, Hana Iti*, etc.).

The growth of tourist wasteland is mainly filled by "squatting" landowners. It results in unsightly, precarious housing conditions and, most importantly, it is synonymous with obstruction (numerous lawsuits but few evictions). Local populations reject economic development based on inbound tourism. This attitude can be an unspoken consensus between, on the one side, those who copy the tourism model for their own use, and on the other side, those for whom land has a symbolic value. The Polynesian government, in the last ten years, has become aware of the question of access to the sea for all, posed by both the establishment of resorts on the water and the privatisation of hotel wastelands. This is how it changed the largest wasteland, that of *Maeva Beach* and *Bel Air* in Punaauia, into a large seafront park, open to the public since 2017.

Conversely, territorial policies, where the economic or political independence objective is based on tourism development, could be an illusion, especially in the context of increasing climatic and pandemic uncertainties. Analysing territorial policies and their outcomes, we can see that they are rather more restrictive than expansionist. Therefore, by favouring "enclosed" tourism (golf, resorts, cruising holidays) (Cazes 1984) to family and friends' tourism for example (much more open to the outside world of tourism), the territorial policies accentuate the marginalisation of tourists, causing their rejection. This is all the more "true" since no serious quantitative study was undertaken on tourism development (Gay 2009). Indeed, for a territory to live solely from tourism as a monopoly activity, it should welcome about five to ten tourists per year per inhabitant. This means that French Polynesia should welcome each year about two million tourists instead of the actual 150,000 to 200,000 visitors per year. However, who in French Polynesia would want to see two million tourists arriving each year? Tourism companies, of course, but they are almost never consulted when it comes to political decisions.

Ultimately, tourism wastelands could become the subject of cultural tourism, like the *marae*, ancient polytheist temples, or like the nineteenth-century old colonial coconut plantations abandoned in the 1920s, where the main tourist infrastructure has now been built (Bachimon 1998). Taking preservation measures is possible and the tourism wasteland could become a Polynesian heritage site, a testimony of the main economic activity in the second half of the twentieth century. Thus, tourism wastelands would be part of the tourism "identity" and heritage (McKay 2008). In the *Varai Park*, located on the *Maeva* and *Bel Air* wastelands, a sign was put up this year recalling the site's tourist vocation. This is a first in Polynesia (Figure 15.2). Tourist wastelands could then be introduced, as a preventive measure, in identified and truly protected tourist zones, in order to avoid the urban sprawl that results from squatting on the land resources dedicated to tourism activities and makes any reopening project, let alone their conservation, impossible.

Figure 15.2 Signs in Varai Park (Tahiti) recalling the site's tourist history

Source: Anthony Tchekemian

Acknowledgements

The author warmly thanks Professor Nelson Graburn who edited this text with great care and expertise.

Notes

1 The Botanical Garden was created in 1919 by Harrison Smith. Inaugurated in 1965, the Gauguin Museum is an initiative of the Singer Polignac Foundation. The museum opened 60 years after the painter's death in the Marquesas Islands (1905) and is situated in the park of the Botanical Garden (Staszak 2006).
2 PIG: *Polynesian Intervention Group*. Gaston Flosses's praetorian guard (1995–2004).
3 The *nono* is a midge *(Culicoides)* known by the sunbathers for its painful stings.
4 We mentioned the imposing map at the Huahine airport indicating non-existent accommodation. In Tahiti too, we can still find indications for the *Bel Air Hotel* even though it had been closed for 30 years and it is now destroyed. In fact, some of these indications are in a roundabout that was built several years after the hotel's closure. In its oral naming, the site (that has become touristic) lasts longer than its function.
5 The *Tiki Village* case on Moorea Island is symptomatic. Still open, it is likely to work as an adrift boat, taking on water. Saved from liquidation in 2013, nevertheless it is

presented as one of the best accommodations on the island and many tourists are actually satisfied with its services. This has a logical explanation. The *Tiki Village* is a unique concept, a mix of history, customs and local products . . . in a sort of genuine atmosphere that tourists can find only in this place, in an allegorical environment – made out of stucco – around a dinner-show.

6 More precisely, this invasive vegetation is made of shrubby and thorny plants like the Sensitive *(Mimosa pudica)* and the Lantana *(Lantana camara)* and trees like the Chinese Guava also called Tava tinito *(Psidium cattleyanum)*, Miconia or Pa'ahonu *(Miconia calvescens)*, Falcata *(Molucca albizia)* and the African tulip tree *(Spathodea campanulata)*.

7 The Purau *(Hibiscus tiliaceus)* is a tree that transforms the area where it is growing in a mangrove-like environment.

8 Some resorts, like the *Hana Iti*, in Huahine, were systematically depleted (roof structure, hinnies, sanitary appliances) even though they were guarded.

9 Pater legatees are divided into seven families sharing the land's ownership. The seven families are the Maioas, the Bonnets, the Tessiers, the Salmons, the Estalls, the Paoas and the Paters.

10 Actually there are three possible situations: occupancy for leisure purpose, in an area where no main residence is permitted; occupancy in the name of an aboriginal right refuted by the legal owners; unofficial shared occupancy of a jointly held property. There is also another situation, more complicated, when the property is occupied by a paid or unpaid keeper, having no legal rights on the property's ownership (Bambridge and Neuffer 2002; Bambridge et al. 2007).

11 This detail is quite interesting. The argument is ecological (protecting the lagoon) even though in reality, no *fare* would be built because of neighbourhood disputes (the neighbours didn't want any *fare* in front of their properties).

Bibliography

Bachimon, Philippe. 1998. "From Eden to Tourist Paradise Tahiti and the Geography of Paradisiac Spaces." In *The French-Speaking Pacific: Population, Environment and Development Issues*, edited by Christian Jost. Australia: Boombana (coll. work), pp. 205–220.

Bachimon, Philippe. 2004a. "Un paradis touristique sous le soleil de Satan." In *François Mitterrand et les territoires français du Pacifique 1981–1988 Mutations, drames et recompositions. Enjeux internationaux et franco-français*, edited by Jean-Marc Regnault. Paris: Librairie de l'Asie Culturelle, pp. 177–186.

Bachimon, Philippe. 2004b. "L'image de Tahiti véhiculée par les artistes anglophones et francophones à l'époque coloniale." *The Journal of Pacific Studies* 27(1): 23–37.

Bachimon, Philippe. 2012. "Tourist Brownfields in French Polynesia – Revealing a Destination Crisis and a Form of Resistance to International Tourism." *Via* 1, http://journals.openedition.org/viatourism/1318.

Bambridge, Tamatoa and Philippe Neuffer. 2002. "Pluralisme culturel et juridique: le foncier en Polynésie française." In *La France et les Outre-Mers. L'enjeu multiculturel*, edited by Tamatoa Bambridge, Jean-Pierre Doumenge, Bruno Ollivier, Jacky Simonin and Dominique Wolton. Paris: CNRS Éditions, Hermès, vol. 32–33, pp. 307–315.

Bambridge, Tamatoa, Paul Ottino, Bernard Rigo and Edgar Tetahiotupa. 2007. "Appropriation du littoral à Tahiti et à Nuku-Hiva (Marquises)." In *Risques et Nature. Sociétés et Développement*. Papeete: Publication des Assises de la Recherche française dans le Pacifique.

Cazes, Georges. 1984. "Tourisme enclavé, tourisme intégré: Le grand débat de l'aménagement touristique dans les pays en développement." In *Cahiers du Tourisme*. Aix-en-Provence: CHET.

Chaline, Claude. 1999. *La régénération urbaine*. Paris: PUF.

Clément, Gilles. 2004. *Manifeste du Tiers paysage*. Paris: Sujet/objet.

Dérioz, Pierre. 2008. "L'approche paysagère: un outil polyvalent au service de l'approche opérationnelle et interdisciplinaire des problématiques environnementales." In *Interdisciplinarité et gestion environnementale: Partage d'expériences autour de la psychologie environnementale*. Nîmes: ARPEnv.

Du Prel, Alex W. 2003. "Paroles et actes." *Tahiti Pacifique Magazine* 143.

Gay, Jean-Christophe. 2009. *Les cocotiers de la France*. Paris: Belin.

McKay, Ginger. 2008. "The Effects of Nuclear Testing in French Polynesia." *Annual Review of Undergraduate Research, College of Charleston* 7: 109–116.

Pearce, Douglas G. 1980. "Tourism in the South Pacific: The Contribution of Research to Development and Planning." UNESCO Tourism Workshop. Rarotonga, 10–13 June.

Poirine, Bernard. 1994. *Tahiti: la fin du paradis*. Paris: l'Harmattan.

Reboud, Valérie, Christian Montet and Jean-Pierre Laffargue. 2007. "Analyse des effets du dispositif de défiscalisation local en Polynésie Française. Un premier essai sur le secteur hôtelier". *Mémoire de Paris* 1.

Saura, Bruno. 2008. *Tahiti Mā'ohi: culture, identité, religion et nationalisme en Polynésie française*. Pirae (Tahiti): Au Vent des Iles.

Saura, Bruno. 2020. *Un poisson nommé Tahiti. Mythes et pouvoirs aux temps anciens polynésiens*. Pirae (Tahiti): Au Vent des Iles.

Soja, Edward William. 1996. *Thirdspace. Journeys to Los Angeles and Other Real and imagined places*. Cambridge, MA: Blackwell.

Staszak, Jean-François. 2006. *Gauguin voyageur, du Pérou aux îles Marquises*. Paris: Solar-Géo.

Vannier, Martin. 2003. "Le périurbain à l'heure du crapaud buffle: tiers espace de la nature, nature du tiers espace." *Revue de Géographie Alpine* 91–94: 79–89.

Worsley, Peter. 1957. *The Trumpet Shall Sound: A Study of "Cargo Cults" in Melanesia*. London: MacGibbon & Kee.

Conclusion

Aurélie Condevaux, Maria Gravari-Barbas and Sandra Guinand

The premise for this volume was a radical re-evaluation of tourism, defined and experienced until recently in terms of clearly circumscribed places and temporalities, in order to examine the in-between situations in which everyday and "non-everyday" activities and spaces for leisure and work are becoming hybridised. The aim was to highlight "before" and "after" tourism both in "ordinary" places and practices (re)invented for viewing and tourism consumption, and in enclaves and tourism locations whose specialist functions have been subverted.

The publication project and most of the contributions pre-date the health, economic and social crisis associated with COVID-19. Although this volume was planned before the crisis and independently of it, this major event has nonetheless impinged on it. Almost all the authors mention it, even if it is peripheral to their main theme. Furthermore, current events reframe the issues addressed in the book. Now more than ever, the "end" and the "afters" in tourism are becoming a critical social issue.

The literature on changes in tourism associated with COVID-19 clearly emphasises its unprecedented nature, particularly in terms of its global scope and interconnected impacts (Sigala 2020), and the fact that for the first time ever, every country in the world is subject to travel restrictions (Clivaz and Loloum 2020). As is highlighted by Sigala (2020, 312), "*unforeseen trajectories instead of historical trends are expected and the predictive power of 'old' explanatory models may not work*". In this volume, we have adopted a slightly different approach and examine how trends emerging during the crisis are, in some cases, an extension of existing dynamics.

Does the crisis associated with the COVID-19 epidemic prompt us to think differently about issues around "before" and "after" tourism? Or should we, on the contrary, view current aspects as a continuation of the trends described in this volume? Should we interpret changes in some of the case studies presented as indicative of the shape of new developments in tourism?

We will examine these issues in relation to the literature on tourism crises and the COVID-19 crisis, and contributions in this volume.

DOI: 10.4324/9781003138600-19

Crises in tourism and the COVID-19 crisis

Despite extensive media coverage of the impact of the COVID-19 epidemic on tourism, with the hotel and catering industry and transport sectors being the hardest hit, little has been said about the crises regularly faced by these sectors in the past. Yet, despite the unprecedented scale of the 2020 crisis, there are elements in the literature of tourism crises and the thinking presented in this volume on the cyclical transformations of destinations which allow us to reflect on the "after" scenario for the current crisis and what it means for tourism. The long-term nature of research makes it possible to situate current changes in a wider context and to adopt a more detached position than the media, which is focusing on the idea of a break with the past and a radical opposition between "before" and "after".

According to the World Tourism Organization,

> *A crisis is an undesired, extraordinary, often unexpected and timely limited process with ambivalent development possibilities. It demands immediate decisions and counter measures in order to influence the further development again positively for the organization (destination) and to limit the negative consequences as much as possible.*

(UNWTO 2012, 18)

This definition encompasses political and/or religious events as well as "natural causes" (severe climate events and epidemics). The opposition between natural and social causes is the focus of intense debate as natural catastrophes are often exacerbated or even created by human activities. Tsunamis (Coate et al. 2006; Calgaro and Lloyd 2008; Cohen 2008; Ichinosawa 2006; Robinson and Jarvie 2008; Rittichainuwat 2008, 2011; Smith and Henderson 2008; Ghaderi and Henderson 2013), and the 2014 tsunami in particular, terror attacks (Floyd et al. 2003; Ghaderi et al. 2012; Robinson and Jarvie 2008), and political events such as the Arab Spring are well documented in tourism literature. Some of these events have led to a sudden shutdown of tourism, generally limited to either one or just a small number of destinations.

Epidemics and their effects on tourism are also the focus of study. During the foot-and-mouth disease epidemic in the United Kingdom in 2001, no human infections were confirmed, but the fear of infection effectively dried up tourism to the United Kingdom for most of the year, putting tens of thousands of people out of work and necessitating a huge promotional campaign by the United Kingdom to restore the country's image as a destination (UNWTO 2012). The SARS (severe acute respiratory syndrome) epidemic between November 2002 and July 2003 had a major impact on travel to and within Asia and airlines and hotels suffered significant losses. Life did not return to normal until mid-2004 (UNWTO 2012). Lastly, the H1N1 flu pandemic in 2009 had a major impact on tourism, which was exacerbated in this instance by human transmission. The economic cost of the virus to Mexico alone was more than 3 billion Euros (approx. 3.6 million USD), half of it in the travel and tourism sector. According to the UNWTO, a return to 2009 pre-pandemic levels of activity was achieved in spring 2010.

In these different situations, the shutdown of tourism activities was temporary. It would appear to be rare for "crises", whatever their origins, to cause an irreversible exit from tourism. "Tourism wastelands" affect small, infra-local hotels and facilities rather than entire areas such as the Catskills in the United States in 1824 (Brown 1998), and the hotel wastelands in French Polynesia described by Bachimon in this volume. The term "resort ruins" (Rostock and Zadniček 1992) was coined to describe these burnouts. They refer to situations in which the cost of reconstruction exceeded the benefits for developers and so venues were quite simply abandoned, as was the case in the West Indies after cyclones Luis (in 1995) and Lenny, in 1999 (Magnan 2008). In many other instances, severe events led to a sudden shutdown, but activities were able to resume. Taking the example of terror attacks, Liu and Pratt (2017) examined the connection between the Global Terrorism Index (GTI) and international tourist arrivals in 95 destinations between 1995 and 2012. The GTI is based on four factors: the total number of terrorist incidents in a year, the death toll from terrorism in a year, the total number of people injured due to terrorism in a year and the approximate level of damage to property in this time frame. They showed that the impact of terrorism was significant in the short term in 25 of the 95 destinations. Conversely, tourism demand is not very sensitive to the GTI in the long term. Just nine of the 95 destinations showed any significant link between international arrivals and a high GTI. Notable exceptions include Nepal, Colombia and Thailand.

This relative "lack of sensitivity" of international arrivals to crises in the long term can, however, conceal more fundamental changes. Tourism to North Africa and the Near East, for example, experienced a sudden shutdown in 2011 during the Arab Spring uprisings. While for obvious reasons activity has not resumed in some destinations such as Syria and Libya, others in contrast had returned by 2018 to international arrival levels comparable with the pre-crisis period. At the same time, the tourist profile changed, with a significantly higher number of tourists from the Maghreb alongside European tourists. Tourism studies are particularly interested in the strategies which must be implemented to tackle these crises, notably from a communications perspective (Avraham 2015; Masetti 2013).

Our interest lies less in studying restart strategies implemented than in the nature of the recovery; is the post-crisis picture similar to the pre-crisis situation? What changes and developments have occurred?

Some authors point out that if we look beyond their traumatic impacts, post-disaster tourism crises in areas where rapid reconstruction has occurred can have benefits for tourism. This is the case for the Nitmiluk Katherine Gorge in Australia, where there was an opportunity to rebuild and improve ageing infrastructure and to make the local population aware of the importance of tourism (Faulkner and Vikulov 2001). Similarly, in Thailand after the 2003 tsunami, the crisis provided an opportunity to rebuild in a better way. The Royal Government of Thailand and various NGOs, with assistance from the UNDP, launched the Building Back Better programme (Coate et al. 2006). The aim of the scheme was to extend rebuilding from the purely physical sphere to social welfare systems, livelihoods, environmental regeneration and preparedness programmes for similar events. This programme acknowledged that reconstruction had cultural and social components.

What picture is emerging in the case of COVID-19? Will we use the crisis as an opportunity to move to an "after" mass tourism scenario, or to return to normal? This question runs through many recent reflections and publications, however, Clivaz and Loloum (2020) underline that it is difficult to see into the future. Instead, we can examine whether or not trends and changes already observed in the pre-crisis period are still continuing in the current crisis.

Trends updated in this volume

The contributions in this volume offer a variety of insights into and perspectives on the trends which existed before the crisis.

Several chapters analyse whether or not new ways of organising tourism reassess tourism space and practices which are usually considered to be quite separate from the everyday. Some authors, such as Girard and Schéou, examine the new hospitality models recently developed on digital platforms, and highlight how these expand rather than challenge the tourism ethos. They emphasise that enhancing the ordinary is an intrinsic element of the tourism imaginary and that these opportunities to meet local residents and free accommodation options consolidate the main tourism routes.

Other contributions place greater emphasis on the subversive aspect of new forms of tourism intermediation. Drawing on the ethnography of city tours organised by Paris residents, Loisy examines whether these activities can create "authenticity" without a staged framework. She concludes that these tours, which are highly personalised and focus on very mundane places and amenities (schools, children's playgrounds, supermarkets), challenge MacCannell's theory that the search for authenticity is always an illusion. However, the hybridisation of places encounters obstacles, as access to life "backstage" is constantly under threat.

Contributions from Bourdeau and Joly offer a fresh insight into "lifestyle migration" and the challenges it poses to existing categories in tourism studies. In the medina of Fez in Morocco or the Isère Alps, these mobilities create hybrid spaces where the ordinary and the extraordinary converge on a daily basis. In the first instance, riads in Morocco are becoming home to new foreign residents and hospitality venues exploiting the allure of the exotic for their guests. In sports activity spaces in the Isère, secondary peaks are developing into areas for trying one's hand at "extraordinary" physical challenges. The concept of "in-between places", which is associated with hybridity, promotes the development of new practices around the use of time, where an activity usually associated purely with holidays takes place in the morning, evening or even at night. Lastly, in these instances, hybridity also refers to the practices of people such as entrepreneurs in the medina in Fez who consider that certain aspects of their businesses – especially those relating to decoration – are not "work" but creative activities. For Bourdeau, these trends reflect a "disruption" in tourism which could actually prompt us to question the relevance of the term "tourism".

Other contributions in the volume, such as chapters authored by Bachimon, and by Freytag, Korff and Winsky, invite us to examine these dynamics from a diachronic rather than a synchronic perspective. They distance themselves from Butler's Tourism Area Life Cycle and explore the tourism dynamic as a process of co-construction involving tourism professionals, visitors and local residents. According to this approach, human stakeholders and their practices, as well as non-human agents such as materialities and representations, interact and build a co-constructed network. This transcends a purely "before" and "after" approach and demonstrates instead how forms of tourism appear and disappear. The most recent developments in their Black Forest case study area are attributable notably to global warming and the COVID-19 crisis.

Bachimon's thinking also addresses the destination scale – focusing on French Polynesia, and the Society Islands in particular – from a diachronic perspective, but taking changes in accommodation structures more specifically as his starting point. French Polynesia is characterised by a significant number of hotel wasteland sites due, as the author explains, to a multitude of factors including a combination of lifestyle changes among landowners, land tenure, changes in tourist demand (in decline for several years) and taxation. The author describes new uses for this wasteland and the many forms of reappropriation which occur. He points out that the COVID-19 crisis has accentuated this phenomenon.

Lastly, the contribution by Anton Clavé, Borràs Nogués, Ayebakuro Orama and Trinitat Rovira Soto also addresses the issue of "before" and "after" tourism from a temporal perspective (albeit a more restricted one) by comparing footfall at the PortAventura theme park in Catalonia in 2019 and 2020. This chapter analyses social media to show clear changes in footfall models for the theme park based on the geographic origins of visitors and the crisis caused by the COVID-19 epidemic. As might be expected, footfall in 2020 was much lower for international tourism and conversely much higher for inhabitants of Catalonia. This raises the question of whether these changes and local tourism will continue after the crisis and how this will impact facilities and jobs.

With the exception of this chapter, none of the contributions in the volume focus exclusively on the effects of the COVID-19 epidemic on tourism. However, on the basis of these inputs and international guidelines provided by the UNWTO and, at the other end of the spectrum, the cumulative practices of stakeholders since the start of the crisis, we can identify elements which continue to exist in the present.

Aspects of continuity and revival

Destination management organisations' response to the current crisis was developed under extreme pressure in most countries and seems to consist predominantly of economic and legislative measures to save tourism businesses. To date, we are not aware of any "holistic" restart plans for destinations or any real thinking about transforming activities in the sector. In France, for example, the Tourism Restart Plan (Plan relance tourisme) aims to provide economic support to stakeholders experiencing hardship. Atout France, a national body promoting France as a destination, launched the #CetÉtéJeVisiteLa-France campaign "*to reassure holidaymakers about the hygiene protocols implemented by stakeholders in the sector. It also aims to inform people about the options available and to provide inspiration by suggesting new destinations and themes for 'off the beaten track' trips*".[1]

On a global scale, in spring 2020 the UNWTO launched guidelines to restart tourism (UNWTO 2020a) developed by a Tourism Crisis Committee comprising the UNWTO, representatives of member states, the International Civil Aviation Organization, the International Maritime Organization, the World Bank, the International Labour Organization and representatives from the private sector. Based on a drop in international tourist arrivals of between 60% and 80% in 2020, the organisation advocates measures aimed principally at restarting international travel in the current situation through initiatives to protect travellers from risk of infection and by offering products adapted to circumstances, temporarily at least (a virtual element to events in the business sector, targeted products for certain customer sectors, etc.). The last of the seven priorities listed is to see "*Innovation and Sustainability as the new normal*". However, there is little evidence that this recommendation is being translated into practical action, and it currently barely features in the recommendations to "*approach recovery as an opportunity to jump start the sector towards a new model of sustainable production and consumption*" (UNWTO 2020b).

Though there may be few obvious signs of innovation so far on the part of tourism stakeholders, tourist practices by contrast are displaying trends which suggest what post-COVID-19 tourism might look like. In many respects, these trends reflect continuity with the pre-COVID-19 period rather than a break.

In several countries, at the start of or prior to lockdown, there was significant mobility as people travelled to spend lockdown in locations other than their normal place of residence – notably holiday resorts, but also rental accommodation and family properties (a phenomenon documented in France by one of our contributors, Loisy n.d.). Not only did these locations become even more hybrid (a place to live, work, study, etc.), but spending several months living in these places prompted many people to reflect on their lifestyle and created an appetite in certain cases for increased remote working, sometimes involving plans to move to places which had previously been resorts or holiday locations.

The hybrid nature of the places mentioned in this volume may be accentuated post-crisis.

The summer of 2020 was characterised in northern hemisphere countries by holidaying close to home or in neighbouring countries. Despite a strategy focusing essentially on a return to a pre-crisis situation, as mentioned earlier, the UNWTO plan lists as one of its objectives to *"promote proximity and domestic tourism in the short-term by enhancing the local value chain (e.g. local producers)"*, and also to *"implement marketing campaigns to communicate corporate values and support to local providers and workers"* (p. 18). Domestic travel and short trips are advocated *"in the short term"*. National tourism promotion bodies offered similar advice, with campaigns encouraging people to (re)discover domestic destinations (cf. the aforementioned Atout France campaign). Staycations did not emerge in 2020. The term was a major feature of campaigns in previous years, partly in response to the identification of changes in practices (tourists taking more frequent short breaks), and due to environmental concerns. The term had already been leveraged for several years by political stakeholders in their destination strategies (in France, for example, several regional destinations are promoting this aspect: Lyon Tourisme et Congrès; Picardie, 2010–2015 development plan; PACA 2012–2016 development plan, etc.). It is clear that there were precedents for the "enforced" staycations in the summer of 2020 in the northern hemisphere and in the summer of 2020–2021 in the southern hemisphere and that these form part of a process of changes and plans favoured by certain stakeholders.

Another development linked to the current crisis is the use of digital technology to allow people to "travel" from the comfort of home. Leading the way are private stakeholders who have transferred some of their activities which usually take place in physical locations online. These include the expansion of online services by Airbnb, and professionals enhancing their offer to preserve their visibility and business (e.g. the hospitality operator Selina is offering live streaming of concerts). Also of note are cultural and heritage sites, some of which have offered, or attempted to offer, online activities to explore collections or monuments, in particular through the use of video (MoMA), and often with tools such as the Google Arts app. These trends are not new. They are part of the growing footprint of the platform economy and "surveillance capitalism" which was already active prior to the crisis (Sigala 2020). In this case, the crisis has highlighted the poor job security associated with platforms:

> COVID-19 has worsened the already difficult situation (e.g. high labour flexibility at the expense of low salaries, lack of job security, insurance and other benefits) faced by an increasing number of tourism micro-entrepreneurs (e.g. food delivery people, "Uber taxi drivers", "Airbnb hoteliers") (Sigala and Dolnicar 2017).
>
> (Sigala 2020, 320)

Some of these trends will certainly become permanent. In the immediate post-lockdown period in destinations which reopened for some domestic and international tourists, online experiences continued. Furthermore, given their expansion before the crisis, as demonstrated in several chapters in this volume, it is likely that new ways of thinking the relationship between holiday places and workplaces will increase and that the hybridisation of these places will become more marked. However, we can also expect to see a "catch-up" dynamic. The replacement of long-distance travel by travel closer to home will depend on support in the form of incentive measures based on more than just immediate economic issues.

Contributions to this volume which take a long-term view (Bachimon, Freytag et al.) show that the impact of COVID-19 on a destination scale is ultimately just one of several disrupting factors. It is certainly not out of step with existing trends linked either to an awareness of climate change (Freytag et al.) or a to multitude of other factors including fiscal policy, and the pursuit of recreational activities close to home (Bachimon).

Diversification of the range of products marketed by some professionals is also likely to continue, notably with a view to greater resilience in the event of future crises.

Although many people appeared to anticipate that the crisis would offer potential for change in the sector (Sigala 2020), this transformation is unlikely to occur. Observers note a return to "business as usual" in several contexts, such as in Switzerland where " analysis of thinking carried out and measures taken to date in relation to the COVID-19 crisis clearly suggest that the aim is to return as soon as possible to the pre-crisis situation" (Clivaz and Loloum 2020), despite hopes of a restart in the form of a green deal. However, we need to recall that "business as usual" is no longer twentieth century mass tourism and that significant measures have been implemented in recent years. Furthermore, it is essential to remain aware of the risk of a consolidation of the dynamics already in place before the crisis, which were factors driving an increase in inequalities and lack of security in the tourism sector. In conclusion, the COVID-19 crisis emphasises how important it is not to think "before" and "after" tourism in terms of disruption and opposition, but to consider these transformations from a long-term perspective, taking economic, environmental and societal changes into account.

Note

1 www.atout-france.fr/actualites/une-campagne-de-communication-federatrice-pour-rassurer-et-inspirer-les-francais-cet-ete

References

Avraham, Eli. 2015. "Destination Image Repair During Crisis: Attracting Tourism During the Arab Spring Uprisings." *Tourism Management* 47: 224–232.

Brown, Phil. 1998. *Catskill Culture: A Moutain Rat's Memories of the Great Jewish Resort Area.* Philadelphia, PA: Temple University Press.

Calgaro, Emma and Kate Lloyd. 2008. "Sun, Sea, Sand and Tsunami: Examining Disaster Vulnerability in the Tourism Community of KhaoLak, Thailand." *Singapore Journal of Tropical Geography* 29(3): 288–306.

Clivaz Christophe and Tristan Loloum. 2020. "Réponses politiques au Covid-19. En Suisse, pas de transition écologique en perspective." *Espaces* 355: https://www.tourisme-espaces.com/doc/10503.reponses-politiques-covid-suisse-pas-transition-ecologique-perspective.html.

Coate, Bronwyn, John Handmer and Wei Choong. 2006. "Taking Care of People and Communities: Rebuilding Livelihoods Through NGOs and the Informal Economy in Southern Thailand." *Disaster Prevention and Management* 15(1): 135–145.

Cohen, Eric. 2008. "The Tsunami Waves and the Paradisiac Cycle: The Changing Image of the Andaman Coastal Region of Thailand." *Tourism Analysis* 14(3): 221–232.

Faulkner, Bill and Svetlana Vikulov. 2001. "Katherine, Washed Out One Day, Back on Track the Next: A Post-Mortem of a Tourism Disaster." *Tourism Management* 22: 331–344.

Floyd, Myron F., Heather Gibson, Lori Pennington-Gray and Brijesh Thapa. 2003. "The Effect of Risk Perceptions on Intentions to Tourist in the Aftermath of September 11, 2001." *Journal of Tourist and Tourism Marketing* 15(2–3): 19–38.

Ghaderi, Zahed and Joan C. Henderson. 2013. "Japanese Tsunami Debris and the Threat to Sustainable Tourism in the Hawaiian Islands." *Tourism Management Perspective* 8: 98–105.

Ghaderi, Zahed, Ahmad P. M. Som and Joan C. Henderson. 2012. "Tourism Crises and Island Destinations: Experiences in Penang, Malaysia." *Tourism Management Perspectives* 2(3): 79–84.

Henderson, Joan C. 2005. "Responding to Natural Disasters: Managing a Hotel in the Aftermath of the Indian Ocean Tsunami." *Tourism and Hospitality Research* 6(1): 89–96.

Ichinosawa, Jumpei. 2006. "Reputation Disaster in Phuket: The Secondary Impact of the Tsunami on Inbound Tourism." *Disaster Prevention and Management* 15(1): 111–123.

Liu, Anyu and Stephen Pratt. 2017. "Tourism's Vulnerability and Resilience to Terrorism." *Tourism Management* 60: 404–417.

Loisy, M. n.d. https://medium.com/@MarineLoh/ethnographie-confin%C3%A9e-dun-exode-r%C3%A9sidentiel-chronique-d-une-cohabitation-en-p%C3%A9riode-de-crise-f37308a2fd76.

Magnan, Alexandre. 2008. "Subir . . . sans réagir? Reflexions soulevées par la persistance des friches touristiques littorales de l'île de Saint-Martin (Petites Antilles)." In *Le littoral: subir, dire, agir. Actes du colloque international pluridisciplinaire organisé par l'Ifresi (Lille, 16_18 janvier)*, www.ifresi.univ-lille1.fr/littoral2008.html.

Masetti, Oliver. 2013. "Two Years of Arab Springs: Where Are We Now? What's Next?" *Current Issues: Emerging Markets*, www.dbresearch.com/PROD/DBR_INTERNET_EN-PROD/PROD0000000000300328/Two+years+of+Arab+Spring%3A+Where+are+we+now%3F+What%E2%80%99s.pdf.

Rittichainuwat, Ngamsom. 2008. "Responding to Disaster: Thai and Scandinavian Tourists' Motivation to Visit Phuket. Thailand." *Journal of Travel Research* 46(4): 422–432.

Rittichainuwat, Ngamsom. 2011. "Ghosts: A Travel Barrier to Tourism Recovery." *Annals of Tourism Research* 38(2): 437–459.

Robinson, Lynn and Jim K. Jarvie. 2008. "Post-Disaster Community Tourism Recovery: The Tsunami and Arugam Bay, Sri Lanka." *Disasters* 32(4): 631–645, ftp://ftp.shef.ac.uk/pub/uni/academic/A-C/ar1mb/RobinsonJarvie_PostDisastercommunityTourismRecoveryVolume32Issue4.pdf.

Rostock, Jürgen and Franz Zadnicek. 1992. *Paradies/Ruinen -Das KdF-Seebad der Zwanzigtausend auf Rüge*, Berlin: Christoph Links Verlag.

Sigala, Marianna. 2020. "Tourism and COVID-19: Impacts and Implications for Advancing and Resetting Industry and Research." *Journal of Business Research* 117(C): 312–321.

Sigala, Mariana and Sara Dolnicar. 2017. Entrepreneurship Opportunities, in S. Dolnicar, *Peer-to-Peer. Accommodation Networks: Pushing the boundaries,* pp. 77–86. Oxford: Goodfellow Publishers Ltd.

Smith, Russell A. and Joan C. Henderson. 2008. "Integrated Beach Resorts, Informal Tourism Commerce and the 2004 Tsunami: Laguna Phuket in Thailand." *International Journal of Tourism Research* 10(3): 271–282.

UNWTO . 2012. *Toolbox for Crisis Communications in Tourism: Checklist and Best Practices,* Madrid: OMT.

UNWTO . 2020a. "Global Guidelines to Restart Tourism." https://webunwto.s3.eu-west-1.amazonaws.com/s3fs-public/2020-05/UNWTO-Global-Guidelines-to-Restart-Tourism.pdf.

UNWTO . 2020b. *Supporting jobs and economies through travel and tourism. A Call for Action to Mitigate the Socio-Economic Impact of COVID-19 and Accelerate Recovery*, Madrid: OMT. https://www.e-unwto.org/doi/pdf/10.18111/9789284421633.

Index

Page numbers followed by 'n' indicate a note on the corresponding page.

Printed in the United States
by Baker & Taylor Publisher Services